WORK AND THE
WELFARE STATE

Public Management and Change Series
Beryl A. Radin, *Series Editor*

WORK AND THE WELFARE STATE

Street-Level Organizations and Workfare Politics

EVELYN Z. BRODKIN
and
GREGORY MARSTON
Editors

GEORGETOWN UNIVERSITY PRESS
WASHINGTON, DC

Library of Congress Cataloging-in-Publication Data

Work and the welfare state : street-level organizations and workfare politics / Evelyn Z. Brodkin and Gregory Marston, editors.
    pages cm.— (Public management and change series)
    Includes bibliographical references and index.
    ISBN 978-1-62616-000-2 (pbk. : alk. paper)
    1. Social policy.   2. Welfare state.   3. Welfare recipients—Employment.
I. Brodkin, Evelyn Z.   II. Marston, Gregory.
HN18.W67   2013
361.6—dc23
                                                                    2013000036

This book is printed on acid-free paper meeting the requirements of the American National Standard for Permanence in Paper for Printed Library Materials.

15 14 13   9 8 7 6 5 4 3 2   First printing

Printed in the United States of America

CONTENTS

PREFACE

EVELYN Z. BRODKIN AND GREGORY MARSTON

This book emerged out of the collective sense of an international group of scholars that the full workfare story has yet to be told. We share the belief that this is an important story, because of workfare's profound implications for how we organize our societies and economies. In conducting our own research, we had come to deeply appreciate the work of other scholars in this field. But we often found striking discontinuities between our experiences examining workfare on the ground and research conducted at a more abstract level.

In addition, we suspected that there was more than met the eye to the governance and management reforms we saw accompanying workfare's advance in countries around the globe. These reforms appeared to be shaping workfare policy and politics in significant, but largely unseen ways. In our research, we saw indications that they might be intensifying workfare's harsh, regulatory features and eroding its potentially enabling ones. Surely, this merited deeper investigation.

We decided that it was time to open the street-level practices of workfare to direct, systematic examination and to investigate how governance and managerial reforms are shaping the organization and production of workfare policies in different national settings. It is these concerns that animate this book. Adopting an approach that puts street-level organizations at the forefront of analysis, we examine these policies, not just on the page, but in practice, drilling down to the street-level to make visible the complex ways in which they operate on the ground. We also explore commonalities and contrasts between US-style workfare and European-style activation policies, investigating how they actually work and what that means for the unemployed, poor, and disadvantaged who are subject to workfare rules or who turn for help to activation programs. Ultimately, we see workfare as part of a broad and conflicted political project pushing back the boundaries of the welfare state and asserting the primacy of work and the market. In this book, we explore this conflicted project and the street-level organizations in which it is taking shape.

This book was a collaborative effort, one that most clearly involved the authors who are credited by name in the text. As editors, we are grateful, not only for the chapters they contributed, but also for their engagement at various stages in the development of this book. We also wish to acknowledge the contributions of others who were essential to this effort, but whose names do not appear in chapter credits.

First and foremost, we express our appreciation to the many unnamed workfare participants, agency staff, community advocates, and officials who were generous with their access and insights. We hope that our work gives fair expression to their perspectives and experiences.

We also are indebted to Els Sol and Flemming Larsen, who collaborated with Brodkin to bring the RESQ international research network to the University of Chicago for a 2009 symposium, on "Welfare States in Transition." The ideas that inform this book began to develop in conversations at RESQ meetings, culminating in the Chicago symposium and companion workshop at which we launched this book project. We also thank the University of Chicago, School of Social Service Administration, and the Danish Social Science Research Council for providing financial support for the symposium and workshop. In addition, we are grateful to Matthias Knuth and Martin Brussig for hosting a book authors' workshop at the University of Duisburg-Essen.

We have benefited immeasurably from exchanges among this book's authors and other colleagues who either were part of the Chicago symposium or who provided advice as we developed the manuscript. We would like to express our appreciation to Kelvin Baadsgaard, Jean-Claude Barbier, Joel Handler, Yeheskel Hasenfeld, Henning Jørgensen, Norma Kriger, Iben Nørup, Omar McRoberts, Jennifer Mosley, William Sites, Els Sol, and Ludo Struyven. We also have benefited from anonymous reviewers, who offered probing and thoughtful comments.

Graduate students at the University of Chicago made important contributions to this project, intellectually and editorially. We are grateful for support from Nathan Dunlap, Florian Sichling, Matthew Spitzmueller, and Lindsey Whitlock. Jessica Darrow deserves special mention, as she took time from her own street-level dissertation research to assist in the preparation of this book. She was part of this effort from start to finish, making the analysis sharper and keeping authors (and editors) on track.

We thank Beryl Radin, editor of this book series, and Donald Jacobs, our editor at Georgetown University Press, for their invaluable support and intellectual guidance. We also appreciate support from the press's editorial and marketing teams and the DJØF team in Denmark, especially Wilfried Roloff. We also wish to acknowledge Letta Wren Page for her superior editorial assistance with the manuscript and Keith Madderom at the University of Chicago for his generous administrative support.

We would be remiss, indeed, to conclude without having publicly acknowledged our friends and families for their patience and unflagging support throughout this project.

PART I

Introduction

1

Work and the Welfare State

EVELYN Z. BRODKIN

The policies of workfare and labor market activation occupy contested terrain, where the structuring institutions of the market and the welfare state meet. That gives these policies strategic significance, positioning them to play a role in reshaping the boundaries between work and the welfare state. Over the past few decades, these policies, and the workfare project they comprise, have developed global reach. They are now deeply embedded in the architecture of public policy from North America to Australia and throughout Western Europe. Yet, despite considerable study of the varied policies of workfare and activation, there is little clarity—let alone consensus—about what this project is, what it does, and, especially, how it works.

Part of the confusion and dissensus, no doubt, derives from the complicated nature of this project, which has advanced in different countries under a bewildering array of policy labels, among them welfare-to-work, labor market activation, and *revenu minimum d'insertion*. In addition, these policies incorporate an assortment of features, some of which offer training and work supports to the unemployed. But other features attach conditions to income benefits, for example, requiring that individuals satisfy specified job-seeking tasks, accept any job offered to them, or, in some cases, engage in unpaid work assignments. These requirements essentially revise the terms under which the unemployed and disadvantaged may obtain income benefits that were previously based primarily on need, legal right (e.g., compensation to unemployed workers), or family status (e.g, welfare benefits for families with children). The complexity and variety of workfare-style policies has complicated scholarly efforts to understand them and surely calls into question simplistic popular slogans suggesting that these policies offer a "hand up" rather than a "handout." What they actually do is precisely what is at issue.

Here we take a closer—and deeper—look at the unfolding workfare project. We believe that neither existing policy studies nor fulsome political rhetoric have

3

adequately captured the complex realities unfolding on the ground. In order to more fully understand this project, we contend that it is necessary to move beyond analysis of how policies have advanced on the page and to turn attention to how they have advanced in practice.

In this book we focus on the street-level organizations (SLOs) whose practices, effectively, constitute workfare in everyday organizational life.[1] What SLOs do under the rubric of policy is more often assumed than interrogated in policy studies. This may be, in part, because these practices are difficult to examine, largely operating beyond the metrics of administrative data and outcomes measurement. However, the significance of these practices is evident; decades of implementation and organizational research make clear that what you see in terms of formal policy may not be what you get.

That said, we are interested in more than the well-rehearsed details of workfare's implementation. We offer a theoretically grounded approach that recognizes the complex and multidimensional role SLOs play in the policy process, one in which they not only implement policy, but also transform it. These processes of transformation—and their consequences—are not easily visible, making them difficult to assess and also to contest. As we will discuss, this has critical implications, not only for policy, but also for welfare state politics, in which visibility and the potential for political feedback are closely linked.

This book takes up the challenge of investigating and making visible the processes of policy transformation. In order to do this, we closely examine the ways in which SLOs have shaped the workfare project and, thus, the experiences of unemployed and disadvantaged individuals who find themselves subject to workfare rules or who seek labor market support through workfare services. We conceptualize an approach to analysis that sees SLOs as more than mere implementation functionaries, but also as mediators of both policy and politics. This approach, elaborated in chapter 2, builds on the fundamental insights of street-level theory regarding the relevance of practice, recognizing the pivotal, if underappreciated, role that SLOs play in shaping policy (Lipsky 1980a, 1980b). Our approach also extends street-level theory to examine the role of SLOs in the politics of welfare state change and retrenchment. Studies in this book investigate how SLOs shape workfare policy through their practices, and, more broadly, how these practices are redrawing the boundaries between work and the welfare state.

In a departure from research that focuses on *street-level bureaucracies,* the large public organizations that once dominated the landscape of policy delivery, we present a framework that takes account of the varieties of *street-level organizations*—the public, private, and hybrid agencies —now engaged in policy delivery around the world and increasingly operating under the influence of new governance and managerial regimes. We pay close attention to the emerging regimes of managerial control that have accompanied the advance of the workfare project. We examine how they have evolved across countries, where similar managerial strategies have been introduced even as policy approaches differed.

These regimes of managerial control have more than technical interest. We see them as providing a hidden track for shaping the workfare project by indirectly and (largely) invisibly influencing the street-level production of workfare. Analyses in this volume probe beyond the implicit political neutrality of management and governance strategies to investigate whether, in practice, they have tended to intensify workfare's harsh, regulatory features and erode its potentially enabling ones. Interrogating these managerial and governance regimes is a central concern of this book.

In short, we put SLOs at the center of study in order to examine the interaction between policy, politics, and management and to assess its consequences. We recognize that this is a different way to approach the global workfare project, a departure from more commonly used analytic strategies. However, we believe that this approach enables us to address gaps in existing research and bring a fresh perspective to familiar debates.

Our book has three principal objectives. First, it aims to bring the literature on SLOs into conversation with literature on the politics of the welfare state in order to illuminate the pivotal role of organizations and management in welfare state transformation. These literatures tend to be treated as discrete areas of research and theory. But we see them as deeply connected and elaborate the connections in setting out the analytical framework for this volume. Studies in this book contribute theoretically to conceptualizing why SLOs matter to policy and politics and empirically to demonstrating how they matter.

Second, we aim to shed new light on old arguments about workfare by moving beyond the policies of workfare to examine the practices of workfare. As noted, we draw attention to the strategic role that governance and management reforms have come to play in workfare's development in very different national and political contexts. In contrast to studies that focus either on formal policies or on governance arrangements, we examine the interaction between the two and how they play out at the street level, revealing ordinarily unseen dimensions of organizational practice that are shaping the workfare project.

Third, we bring a comparative perspective to analysis. Contributors from the United States, Europe, and Australia shed light on how the workfare project has evolved since its emerging features were first explored more than a decade ago (Peck 2001; Lødemel and Trickey 2001). But the nationally based studies in this volume offer more than a progress report on the global workfare project and recent policy developments; their deeper purpose is to interrogate what kind of project this is. Individual studies are grounded in specific national and organizational context, providing for close examination of developments by country and laying the basis for comparison across six countries: the United States, United Kingdom, Denmark, Germany, the Netherlands, and Australia.

This chapter briefly introduces the issues we address in this book and explains how our approach relates to other studies of workfare policy and welfare state politics. It concludes with a short guide for readers on the structure of the volume.

The Workfare Project

We refer here to the workfare project, which may best be understood as a composite of policies and practices through which countries have promoted participation in the paid labor market and reductions in income assistance to those outside the labor market. Workfare, as a policy requiring individuals to work off their benefits, began in the United States in the 1970s. But the term has since come to encompass a variety of initiatives, ranging from active labor market policies in Europe to job-seeker programs in the United Kingdom to welfare-to-work in the United States.

Although there is a common thrust to these policies across countries, they are neither consistent in their design nor fully coherent in their approach. As discussed in chapter 4, national policies vary in important respects, and they also have evolved over time, in ways both visible and obscure. In some countries, policies have more perceptibly hard edges. For example, workfare in the United States was part of a legislative overhaul of welfare law that incorporated manifestly regulatory features, among them a "no work, no welfare" approach to income assistance and a five-year lifetime limit on welfare benefits for families of nonworkers. But these regulatory features were combined with federal funding enabling state governments to develop welfare-to-work programs and offer work supports such as child care and transportation. These mixed features of US policy have made "welfare reform"[2] something of a Rorschach test for observers, who see the subsequent shedding of welfare rolls (which were cut nearly in half in fifteen years) either as a success story in reducing "benefits dependency" or as the apotheosis of punitive social regulation and increased immiseration (as deep poverty rose nearly 20 percent over that period).[3]

In contrast, active labor market policies, promoted under the auspices of the European Employment Strategy (EES), generally have been associated with an emphasis on labor market supports and a tempered approach to the regulatory side of workfare. A hallmark of activation policies has been the provision of education and training aimed at remaking the labor force to meet changing market demands. Reductions in social assistance (the program of cash assistance for those outside the labor market) have tended to occur less directly and more often at the margins. Yet efforts to reduce benefits for the unemployed are part of most European workfare programs, albeit less determinedly so than in the United States.

Despite significant differences in emphasis, workfare-style policies around the globe share a familiar programmatic tool kit, channeling participants through processes of "assessment," "job search," "work preparation," and "work experience" (a term sometimes used for mandatory, unpaid work assignments). In this sense, there is considerable programmatic alignment among the policies of workfare. Yet exactly what takes place under these program labels is far from clear. As studies in this book show, there is great variation in how these features are translated into practice and what that means for how workfare really works.

The Analytic Challenge: Moving Beyond Policy to Practice

Under these circumstances, it may not be entirely surprising that there are wide differences in how the workfare project is understood. Some analysts see it as emerging out of a political consensus and providing an effective strategy for reducing reliance on welfare and increasing well-being through work (Gueron 1987; Haskins 2002; Mead 2001). Others see this project as deeply regulatory, even punitive, exercises in "regulating the poor" (Piven and Cloward 1971; Piven 2008; Wacquant 2010) that do little to alleviate the economic insecurity of those at the margins of the economy (Handler and Babcock 2006; Peck 2001). In part, these opposed views derive from fundamental theoretical and analytical differences—differences that outcomes studies have not resolved. But, to an extent that has yet to be fully considered, these opposed views also derive from different assumptions about what workfare actually does.

Consider that workfare policies may promote or enable work by creating opportunities for human-capital building. They also may provide supports that make work in the paid labor market more feasible and rewarding. But at the same time, these policies may function to enforce work by restricting income support from the state, limiting or eliminating benefits that provide an alternative to income acquired through the market. In this second sense, workfare may be understood as commodifying (Esping-Andersen 1990), valuing individuals based on their monetized contributions to the market economy, not their contributions to the family, community, society, or polity.

The challenge for those seeking to understand the workfare project begins with its underlying ambiguities and inconsistencies. Efforts to assess this project by examining formal policy provisions have been confounded by the difficulties of making nominal distinctions among its manifestly "enabling," "regulatory," or "social investment" features. As Giuliano Bonoli and David Natali observe in their review of activation policies, "it is clear that it is difficult, conceptually, to draw a line between the measures described . . . as 'enabling activation' and those that are considered part of social investment" (2011, 6). We agree. And this is not the only difficulty. Assessments that review formal policy features or evaluate policy by using benchmarks or other selected outcomes measures essentially assume rather than investigate what policies actually do and how they work. This is problematic when formal policy provisions are ambiguous or inconsistent and policy production depends on the discretionary practices of SLOs.

As a general matter, neither policy-focused nor state-centered research offers systematic strategies for understanding the practices of workfare and examining their implications. In this sense, the practices, which essentially constitute workfare on the ground, have been relegated to what we refer to as the *missing middle*. They may be noticed and casually remarked upon, but not systematically examined. To understand the problem of the missing middle, it is useful to take a brief look at some major lines of research. This is not intended as a comprehensive literature review, but to indicate where we see an analytic gap and why it matters.

First, there is a large and robust policy-focused literature assessing workfare-style policies, from which we have benefited and which informs our analyses in many respects. However, this literature sheds little light on the practices of workfare that are the focus of our inquiry. Although this literature is highly varied and cannot be simply characterized, as a general matter, policy-focused studies tend to use policy and programmatic labels as if they indicate what policy does without directly investigating what goes on under the rubric of these labels. This is problematic, in part, because it fails to take account of the highly discretionary character of policy delivery, which allows SLOs to put their imprint on policy-as-produced. In addition, policy-focused studies, generally, render invisible the complex and conflicted dimensions of the workfare project that impart political significance to workfare practices. Whether workfare operates on the ground in ways that emphasize its supportive or its regulatory features cannot be discerned from studies that ask only if policy does what it "should" (e.g., using selective metrics such as caseload reduction or earnings), but do not make visible how these metrics were achieved or reveal what else workfare practices may have produced.

A second line of research we draw on involves comparative, state-focused studies that place the workfare project in broader perspective. Without attempting to summarize a vast and complex literature, we simply note that a central contribution of these studies is that they provide a framework for considering where different countries set their boundaries between work, the market, and the welfare state. One significant approach has been to create nominal categories of welfare states and assess key factors that distinguish among them. Gøsta

Esping-Andersen's (1990) influential *Three Worlds of Welfare Capitalism* differentiated among welfare states according to the degree to which their policies decommodified individuals (i.e., recognized them as citizens and not only as units of market labor). Based largely on differences in specific types of social spending and formal policy elements, he constructed a typology of three ideal types of welfare states: social democratic (e.g., Denmark, Sweden), corporatist-statist (e.g., Germany, France, Italy), and liberal (e.g., the United States, Canada, Australia).

This approach has generated considerable attention and discussion, beyond what is possible to take up here. Suffice it to say that the regime typology raises important questions about alternative paths to workfare. This book is informed by Esping-Andersen's perspective, offering case examples from each regime type. But, we find that the varied policies of workfare and activation do not fit neatly into a categorical approach built around the construct of commodification. As discussed, formal policies tend to combine supportive, enabling, and regulatory elements, producing many variants of workfare and activation. More problematic, neither formal policy features nor expenditures reveal how these policies operate in practice. We believe that by examining workfare practices directly, we can investigate the processes through which variations develop and interrogate how commodification may (or may not) be produced on the ground.

Another significant approach to welfare state research focuses on outcomes. Robert Goodin and colleagues have argued that the "three worlds" model is, at best, incomplete (Goodin et al. 1999). They contend that an analysis based largely on government expenditures and formal policy elements offers too partial a picture, because it does not reveal what welfare states really *do*. As a corrective, the authors offer what one might call an outcomes view, examining socioeconomic statistics that show how people fare under different welfare state regimes and assessing these outcomes according to an explicitly moral evaluative standard. Indeed, this view offers an important vantage point from which to consider differences in economic and social well-being under alternative welfare state arrangements. Still, as the authors themselves recognize, it is difficult to make clear causal links between specific sets of policy arrangements and social outcomes.

Our inquiry is indebted to and informed by the work of these and other scholars. But we also recognize the limitations of other approaches, particularly the problem of the missing middle. Put simply: one approach emphasizes inputs, another outcomes. Yet neither interrogates the processes that occur between them. What goes on in the name of policy—that is, how the policies of the welfare state operate on the ground—remains unknown. In this sense, both policy-focused and state-centered research reflect a kind of deus ex machina view of welfare states and their policies. It is a view in which the processes through which policies are realized and reach their subjects—and the forms in which they reach them—remain hidden.

This is partially addressed in research adopting what might be regarded as a hybrid approach. In *Workfare States*, Jamie Peck examined the emergence of workfare in three countries, analyzing formal policies but also bringing workfare practices into the picture. His insightful study builds on the welfare state typology, tracing the emergence of workfare in three liberal states: the United States, the United Kingdom, and Canada. It provides a picture of the early stages of this global project. We regard Peck's work as particularly relevant to this volume because it emphasizes the importance of investigating "different forms and mutations of workfare in a range of settings" (2001, 7). We, too, are interested in these mutations and believe it is important to extend analysis over both time and place. The workfare project has evolved considerably since Peck's groundbreaking study, extending well beyond the geographic boundaries of the liberal states he examined more than a decade ago, and, potentially, forming new mutations in the course of its evolution.

In this book we turn to contemporary workfare, examining its evolution since the time of these earlier studies. We build on prior research, but drill deeper into its operational core, focusing on the SLOs through which workfare has taken shape. Our analysis is based on the fundamental premise that, in studying the policies of workfare, one cannot assume a simple correspondence between what policies say and what they do. As Esping-Andersen has advised, "identifying broad policy objectives with no regard for their practical political relevance and implementation within diverse European welfare models would easily end up as a sterile academic exercise" (2002, 25). We share that view.

Fortunately, implementation issues have received more attention in recent years. There is now a rich literature that has begun to identify discontinuities between what the provisions of workfare seem to promise and what they actually provide.[4] Studies show, for example, that street-level discretion allows for informal sorting and "creaming," resulting in different training opportunities for more or less employable activation participants (De Graaf and Sirovátka 2011; Kildal 2001),[5] and that individual activation plans mean more on paper than in practice (Forslung, Froberg, and Lindqvist 2004).[6] These findings are consistent with other research demonstrating that one cannot simply assume what the interactions that constitute casework actually provide to workfare participants (Meyers, Glaser, and MacDonald 1998; Riccucci 2005; Van der Aa 2009).[7]

From our vantage point, implementation studies are valuable, not primarily because they document the usual litany of practical difficulties and gaps, but because, cumulatively, they demonstrate that the policies of workfare cannot adequately be understood by examining formal policy provisions, programmatic spending, or even benchmarks typically used in standard evaluations (e.g., number of counseling sessions, placements into training programs or jobs, etc.). Our reading of this literature leads us to ask how well we really know what goes on under the rubric of the workfare project and how it operates in street-level practice.

Investigating the Global Workfare Project: An Organizational Approach

In this book we offer a distinctive perspective from which to understand the global workfare project, adopting an approach that puts SLOs at the center of analysis. This approach recognizes that SLOs effectively create policy through their practices, often in ways that are far from transparent. Beyond that, it recognizes that SLOs function as strategic locations for initiating changes in the boundaries of the welfare state. In this role, SLOs have become not only the manufacturers of reform, but also the targets of governance and managerial reforms. These reforms are significant to the extent that they change the arrangements under which workfare practices evolve and indirectly influence the practices themselves.

If the formal policies of workfare and activation constitute the first track of the global workfare project, a second track has developed, less visibly but no less importantly. This second track is constituted by strategies of managerial and governance reform. In many countries, the move toward workfare and activation has been accompanied by new managerial strategies, among them devolution, privatization, contracting, and performance measurement. These strategies are now deeply embedded in the arrangements through which policy is delivered in the United States, and they are becoming much more familiar in European countries, as well. They have been widely adopted, even in countries that traditionally relied on "old public management" strategies of hierarchy and control and on large state bureaucracies for the delivery of social policy. Where public bureaucracies continue to play a dominant role, they, too, have become the targets of managerial reform.

Studies in this book show that managerial and workfare reforms have become closely intertwined, a development largely unexplored in policy- and state-focused studies. As Rik van Berkel advises in chapter 6, it is important to recognize a new welfare state project of "triple activation," which reaches beyond the unemployed individuals who are policy's official subjects, to the organizations which are policy's implementers, and down to the street-level staff who are policy's putative producers. A central concern of this book is to examine these new managerial regimes and trace their effects on the street-level production of workfare.

Although reform's second track, thus far, has received relatively little attention in the policy and welfare state literatures, inquiry into new management and governance strategies has been central to a developing, critical management literature (see, e.g., Considine 2000, 2005; Hupe and Hill 2007; Larsen and Van Berkel 2009b; Moynihan and Herd 2010; Radin 2006; Rosenbloom and McCurdy 2006; Rothstein 1996; Sol and Westerveld 2005; Van Slyke 2003). In addition, an emerging European literature has begun to examine governance reforms in the context of the EES, a matter explored further in this book. Studies in this volume bring the insights of these literatures to bear in investigating the workfare project; they also extend their reach. In contrast to governance and management studies that operate at a higher institutional level, our interest is in tracking emerging regimes of managerial control down to the street level.

Chapters in this book closely examine these developments in varied national settings. Through highly textured, deeply contextualized analyses, they expose commonalities and variations in the ways the policies and practices of workfare have developed, and they explore the political implications of these developments. Together, these studies offer a distinctive picture of the workfare project. Instead of a steady march toward a uniform global workfare project, they reveal a dynamic process of change marked by variation and contestation. Analyses in this book also uncover surprising and unanticipated commonalities in workfare's management and practices that might otherwise escape notice. As we will discuss in greater detail, we find that, even in very different national contexts, managerial strategies are bearing down hard on street-level practices, often in ways that emphasize workfare's regulatory features. This is a striking and, for us, troubling discovery.

On the Origins of This Book

This book originated in discussions at an international symposium titled "Welfare States in Transition" at the University of Chicago in 2009. The symposium provided a forum in which scholars from the United States, Europe, and Australia could share research on the interplay between the policies of workfare and activation and the projects of governance and managerial reform. It was here that our common perspective came into focus, producing the collaboration that resulted in this book. However, we did not arrive at this shared approach quickly; it evolved over the course exchanges that began two years earlier, in Aalborg, Denmark, with informal conversations among a smaller group of social and labor market policy researchers.

Initially, we lacked a common framework or vocabulary; the policies of work-fare seemed almost too distinct for comparison. US-style workfare, with its rigid work requirements and time-limited welfare support, seemed quite unlike Euro-pean activation policies, which emphasized investment in building the human capital of workers and in securing them against unemployment risks in a precari-ous labor market. For US participants (including this editor), it was evident that the United States was regarded as an outlier in terms of European social and labor market policies, making the possibilities for a common research agenda hard to see. However, over years of exchange, we began to realize that formal policy and institutional differences—significant as they were then and still are today—might be eclipsed by an emerging movement of governance and man-agement reform that was, before our eyes, changing the practices of workfare and activation across many countries.

Even so, this book's comparative, organizational approach did not come eas-ily. We were acutely aware that the demands of comparative analysis could lead to studies that operated at a relatively superficial level, focusing on readily com-parable features (such as formal policy elements, expenditures, or the common quantitative indicators that are available in large-scale administrative and survey databases). But these approaches simply don't allow for the kinds of fine-grained analyses that the street-level perspective requires. This is why we chose to build this book around the work of international policy and organizational scholars with deep localized knowledge and a common analytic vocabulary developed through extended exchange.

A Short Reader's Guide

As discussed, in this book we take analysis beyond the policies of workfare to investigate the practices of workfare and how they are changing the boundaries between work and the welfare state. Adopting a perspective that puts SLOs at its center, we move down through successive layers of the workfare project. We begin with overarching issues of policy and politics, move to the governance and management strategies that have formed workfare's second track, and then drill down to the practices of workfare in everyday organizational life. We also exam-ine the administrative-justice arrangements for appeal and redress that are used to keep street-level practices in check.

We have organized this book according to key analytic concerns rather than providing a country-by-country tour of the workfare map.[8] The sections are arranged to take up key elements of our framework, with studies from both the United States and European countries (and, in one instance, Australia) in each part. Readers may find general background on US and European policies in chapter 4, while individual chapters in parts III through V offer a more detailed examination of developments in specific countries.

The book is divided into six parts. Part I includes this overview and, in chapter 2, a discussion of the book's framework, which brings a street-level perspective to the study of welfare state policies and politics.

Part II provides the context for the empirical studies that follow, discussing what is at stake in changing the boundaries between work and the welfare state. In chapter 3, Michael Lipsky provides historical perspective on the politics of the US welfare state. He explores the path to the development of social welfare policies, including welfare reform and workfare, and suggests how two contrasting narratives have shaped these developments. In chapter 4, Flemming Larsen and I discuss the policies of workfare in the United States and Europe, how they traverse the boundaries between work and the welfare state, and why that matters. Susan Lambert and Julia Henly, in chapter 5, examine the organization of private-sector jobs and how they structure the real world of lower-wage work. Their inside view of the types of jobs that supposedly await graduates of workfare programs is a key organizational part of the policy story that is too rarely explored.

Part III traces the emergence of the managerial/workfare project and examines how governance and managerial strategies have been deployed in workfare's advance. In chapter 6, Rik Van Berkel examines the interplay between policy, politics, and governance in the development of Dutch activation reforms. He proposes, as mentioned earlier, that workfare be understood as a project of triple activation reaching to the SLOs that, effectively, create policy on the ground. Flemming Larsen, in chapter 7, probes the strategic role of managerial and governance reforms in changing directions in Danish activation policy. He argues that manifestly nonpolitical management reforms were used to advance a political project aimed at intensifying the regulatory features of activation policy. In chapter 8, Joe Soss, Richard Fording, and Sanford Schram and take up questions about the relationship between managerial strategies and the practices of workfare in the United States. They closely examine how contracted agencies in Florida and the street-level staff within them adapted to performance-driven contract management, advancing, in the process, a decidedly disciplinary approach to welfare-to-work.

Part IV investigates the street-level practices of workfare, analyzing not only how they shape policy, but also how they reshape social and political relations. Chapters in this section direct attention to the role of SLOs in mediating policy and in mediating the sociopolitical status of marginalized populations, focusing specifically on race, ethnicity, and disability. In chapter 9, I interrogate everyday organizational life in a US welfare agency in order to see how the street-level practices of workfare may effectively enable, commodify, or regulate the subjects of workfare. This organizational ethnography examines how processes of commodification and inclusion work on the ground. Celeste Watkins-Hayes, in chapter 10, investigates how race and ethnicity are mediated in US welfare offices. She reveals a racial dimension to workfare practices that is far more complex than it appears from other perspectives. In chapter 11, Martin Brussig and Matthias Knuth consider the ways in which German job centers mediate the sociopolitical status of migrants. They show that processes manifestly aimed at assuring equitable treatment effectively reinforce inequality by denying relevant differences in the characteristics and needs of migrant populations. And in chapter 12, Gregory Marston considers disability as a sociopolitical category and examines how that status is mediated in the Australian job centers that apply workfare policy to the disabled.

Part V directs attention to administrative justice and how SLOs mediate opportunities for voice and redress by the subjects of workfare policy. Michael Adler, in chapter 13, examines the organizational structures and processes through which individuals subject to workfare rules in the United Kingdom may attempt to seek redress. And in chapter 14, Vicki Lens takes up related questions in the context of US welfare bureaucracies. She reveals how systems for adjudicating complaints not only structure but also limit the possibilities for articulating grievances and reforming street-level practice.

The book concludes with a discussion in part VI of what the study of SLOs brings to research on the policies and politics of workfare, specifically, and the welfare state, more broadly. In chapter 15, I also highlight key findings from the studies in this book and reflect on their implications for the future of the global workfare project.

Notes

1. As discussed further on this chapter and more fully in chapter 2, SLOs include both public bureaucracies and private nonprofit and for-profit organizations that directly deliver policies and services to individuals.

2. "Welfare reform" is placed in quotation marks to indicate that it is being used in its colloquial sense, referring to the package of legislation enacted by the US Congress in 1996. But the term "reform" also may connote "improvement" or "progress," perhaps one of the reasons it is a much-used political convention. However, in this book, it is the actual character of reform that is the subject of inquiry.

3. In addition, the term "dependency" is in quotation marks to denote its rhetorical use as a political label, rather than to ascribe a psychological or social status to individuals who receive welfare benefits.

Finally, "Deep poverty" refers to the economic status of individuals and households whose incomes are below 50 percent of a poverty-level income. In 2011, a poverty-level income for a US family of four with two children was $22,811.

4. It is not possible, or perhaps even useful, to provide an exhaustive list of studies that identify various implementation difficulties. For a selection of interesting examples from Europe and the United States, see De Graaf and Sirovátka (2011); Forslung, Froberg, and Lindqvist (2004); Kildal (2001); Lødemel and Trickey (2001); Lurie (2006); Meyers, Glaser, and MacDonald (1998); Riccucci (2005); and Van der Aa (2009).

5. In a comprehensive review of activation programs in Sweden, Norway, and Denmark, Kildal (2001) found repeated evidence that creaming was taking place in the selection of candidates for training that could lead to jobs and that the most marginalized and vulnerable participants were shunted into the unpaid assignments that were least likely to result in positive employment outcomes. In another multinational programmatic review, De Graaf and Sirovátka (2011) make remarkably similar observations. For example, in Germany they report that "private providers adopted the strategy of risk minimization and inclined to the positive pre-selection of well-equipped clients" (12). They see evidence of creaming and selection bias as a "prevailing trend" in multiple European activation programs (14).

6. In their review of the Swedish "activity guarantee," Forslung, Froberg, and Lindqvist (2004, 15) note that, despite policies requiring an individual "action plan" to guide the development of each activation participant, "three-fifths of the participants did not even know that they had an individual action plan."

7. For example, in Sweden, despite requirements for "intensive" individual counseling and interchange, "almost half of the participants met with their personal counselor less than once a month" (Forslung, Froberg, and Lindqvist 2004, 15).

8. For readers interested in developments in specific welfare state regime types, chapters in this book provide examples from each: Australia, the United Kingdom, and the United States as liberal regimes; Germany as a corporatist regime; and Denmark and the Netherlands as social democratic regimes. However, readers should bear in mind that regime analysis is not the focus of our book, and the selection of specific countries is not intended to test regime theory, but only to include examples from across categories. In addition, we recognize that the precise fit of specific countries into regime types has been a matter of debate, and scholars may place them differently. The Netherlands, for example, is variously regarded as "social democratic" or "corporatist," and even at times as a hybrid (Oorschot 2006). What is relevant for this book is that we offer examples from across regime types, even if one might categorize them differently. For additional discussion of regime typologies, see Goodin (2001) and Cook and Beckley (2001).

2

Street-Level Organizations and the Welfare State

EVELYN Z. BRODKIN

Welfare states are dynamic, continually adapting to changes in political, social, and economic conditions. Transformations occur, in part, through formal policymaking; however, policies and the processes that lead to legislative enactment or defeat are only part of the political story. Welfare state adaptations also take shape less visibly through the activities of street-level organizations (SLOs), the public bureaucracies and private agencies that do the day-to-day work of the welfare state.

Welfare state studies frequently reference SLOs as policy implementers, whose activities are, at best, problematic. But they tend to see these organizations merely as functionaries of the state. This one-dimensional view, while important, is limited in its analytic vision by its focus on what SLOs should do, a view implicitly based on hierarchical notions of political authority that regards SLOs as state agents. But SLOs do more than their prescribed role suggests. They also function as institutional locations in which political projects of change and welfare state transformation are advanced, contested, and, at times, realized, although rarely in overtly political terms. This calls for an expanded understanding of SLOs that reaches beyond a single functional dimension.

In this chapter I will show how two-dimensional and three-dimensional perspectives extend analysis of SLOs to systematically investigate what else they do beyond their instrumental role as executors of legislative and executive dictates. A two-dimensional view regards SLOs as de facto mediators of policy, locations in which both policy's terms and the distribution of benefits and services are (re)negotiated. A three-dimensional view extends analysis one step further, regarding SLOs not only as mediators of policy, but as de facto mediators of the politics and processes of welfare state transformation. As mediators, SLOs are not overtly political, but advance political change indirectly, whether as a

17

by-product of governance and management initiatives or through patterns of informal practices that develop in specific contexts. A three-dimensional perspective raises questions about how SLOs structure not only policy possibilities, but also possibilities for making claims on the state, asserting rights, and pursuing redress. It also raises questions about how SLOs themselves become targets of managerial reform and how these reforms may become strategic instruments for advancing contested policy projects under the political radar.

To date, SLOs have not occupied a prominent place in welfare state research. Perhaps this is because the one-dimensional view of SLOs gives them limited utility in explaining political dynamics. A second reason may be that, despite wide attention to SLOs in other areas of study, their broader relevance to welfare state research has not been clearly conceptualized. The central aim of this chapter is to bring SLOs into the conversation by elaborating a conceptual framework that shows how they matter. As I will explain, welfare states should be understood as partly constituted by the SLOs that do the work of the state (for better or worse). Structurally situated between the state and individuals, they are locations in which people, policies, and politics interact. This positions SLOs to function as mediators of both policy and politics.

This multidimensional view of SLOs moves beyond analysis of the large, central bureaucracies and executive agencies that have received considerable attention in political-institutional research in order to reach deeper into the operational core of the welfare state. A political-*organizational* view puts SLOs at the center of analysis, offering a different perspective on how welfare states work. It links the micropolitics of SLOs to the macropolitics of the welfare state: it's a way of seeing big by looking small. The political-organizational approach also raises critical questions about how SLOs transform policy, structure political conflict, and become strategic targets themselves for political projects of managerial reform.[1] To be clear, this approach does not reject other perspectives; in fact, it is indebted to and seeks to contribute to them by opening to examination some of the otherwise hidden organizational spaces where welfare state politics—and policymaking—take place.

SLOs as Analytic Subjects

This chapter considers three different ways of understanding the relationship between SLOs and the welfare state. By SLOs, I mean those agencies and governmental departments that directly deliver policy to people. A subset of these organizations are the widely familiar street-level bureaucracies (SLBs), which came to occupy analytic importance through the seminal work of Michael

Lipsky (1980b). He provided an insightful treatment of the large public bureaucracies that, at one time, were the main providers of human services and social policies. Lipsky's approach generated a rich empirical literature aimed at understanding the practices of government agencies operating at the front lines of policy delivery. SLBs can be distinguished from other public bureaucracies by their role in direct provision and by the availability of discretion at the front lines of organizational practice. In SLB research, the main challenge is to understand how discretion is exercised in public agencies and what that means for the production of policy on the ground.

The study of SLOs builds on this line of inquiry, but takes account of the new organizational environment in which policy delivery occurs today. In the United States and many other countries, the policy world has changed; large public bureaucracies are not the only, nor necessarily the most significant, locations in which the work of the welfare state takes place. Policy may be delivered through a variety of organizational forms—among them, public bureaucracies, nongovernmental organizations, for-profit firms, and mixed public-private arrangements. In addition, there have been significant developments in management and governance that are transforming the conditions under which policy delivery occurs. In many countries, strategies associated with new public management (NPM)—among them devolution, contracting, and performance management—have reshaped the conditions of street-level work. The study of SLOs brings attention to this new world of street-level work and what it means for both policy and politics. It also raises questions about the strategic use of management to advance contested policy projects of welfare state transformation.

This chapter sets out three conceptual approaches to the study of SLOs, beginning with a brief review contrasting one- and two-dimensional perspectives. It then outlines the elements of a three-dimensional view, drawing on chapters in this volume as well as other research to illustrate how SLOs matter to the study of welfare state change and transformation.

SLOs as Agents of the State: A One-Dimensional View

SLOs have both practical and political importance to the welfare state. They have obvious practical importance in that both the content and quality of policy as delivered depends on what SLOs do and how they do it. That is, the realization of policy objectives depends, most proximately, on what happens every day in schools, hospitals, social service organizations, police departments, child-protection agencies, and so forth. From a normative perspective, these organizations are agents of the state, charged with faithfully carrying out policies determined by legislative and executive authorities.

Of course, enacting policy doesn't make it so. As Graham Allison (1971) famously observed, only 10 percent of the work of policymaking has been achieved when legislation is enacted. The remaining 90 percent occurs in the course of implementation, a process fraught with hazards. This hard fact of policy life received powerful analytic expression in the 1970s with the emergence of implementation as a field of study, in part a response to political developments that had substantially enlarged the US government's social welfare role. In their iconic book *Implementation*, Pressman and Wildavsky (1973) puzzled over how the great ambitions of policy projects like the War on Poverty and the Great Society could end up in fizzled dreams and disappointment.[2] As colorfully expressed in the book's subtitle, they sought to understand "how great expectations in Washington are dashed in Oakland." They referred to themselves as "sympathetic observers who seek to build morals on a foundation of ruined hopes"—perhaps more than a bit of hyperbole. But their portrayal of "dashed expectations" and "ruined hopes" resonates rather strikingly with the political narrative, described in this volume by Michael Lipsky (chap. 3), that questions government's administrative and political capacity to address social problems. In the United States, Lipsky suggests, this "antigovernment" narrative has contributed to undermining support for government as an instrument for advancing social welfare.

Implementation research brought much-needed attention to the so-called black box in which the processes of converting policy into action take place. However, studies documenting implementation's complexities and uncertainties tended to share a common interest: explaining implementation failure. They focused on the gap between apparent legislative intentions and the actions of implementing organizations. This approach was consistent with a view of SLOs as agents of the state, responsible for policy's execution. It contributed to an emphasis on deviance—the purposeful or inadvertent sabotage of policy dictates.[3] This deviance perspective has continued beyond the early implementation literature and can be seen in contemporary welfare state research that, if it mentions SLOs at all, does so only tangentially and as impediments to the realization of policy.

To be sure, there is no shortage of empirical examples of bureaucratic misdeeds and misdirection. However, the agents-of-the-state approach, with its emphasis on deviance, is analytically problematic. Because it begins from a premise that what matters is the fealty of "agents" to "the state," it offers a truncated view of SLOs and what they do under the rubric of policy. Of course, they *are* agents of the state that play a key role in policy implementation. But that is not all they are. Under certain conditions, they should be understood as performing functions beyond those that are prescribed. It is these latent functions that make SLOs a matter of more than passing interest to the analysis of welfare state politics and the dynamics of policy change.

SLOs as Mediators of Policy: A Two-Dimensional View

A new approach began to take shape in the 1980s, one that moved beyond a one-dimensional view of SLOs as agents and, instead, offered a two-dimensional view of SLOs that also recognized them as translators of law. This view is associated with Lipsky's (1980b) theory of street-level bureaucracy, which saw SLBs as de facto mediators of policy. From a two-dimensional perspective, the interesting question was not whether there were gaps between intent and practice or whether organizations were faithful or subversive. Rather, the analytic challenge was to understand how policy was made on the ground, focusing on how organizational practices shaped both the content and the distribution of public benefits and services. Lipsky's (1980a) advice to "stand the study of public policy on its head" helped to inspire a shift from policy-centered to organization-centered research.

A two-dimensional view addresses a critical flaw of the SLOs-as-agents approach: the assumption that formal policy can or should be treated as definitive. The agency approach more or less requires the analyst to treat formal policy as definitive: how else could deviance be observed? Seemingly straightforward, this assumption is problematic for two reasons. First, policymaking often takes place in a political context that makes compromise, obfuscation, and internal inconsistency strategically useful in securing legislative agreement. Second, in some areas of policy (especially, but not only, policy involving human services), implementation either requires or allows discretion, infusing formal policy with considerable operational uncertainty. A two-dimensional perspective flips the script and treats policy as an indeterminate construct (at least partially so). It examines what SLOs do in order to see how policy is constructed on the ground. Although this is a somewhat uncomfortable posture from a normative perspective, it fits comfortably with perspectives on the politics of policymaking that examine sources of indeterminacy.

Generally, the political conditions that produce policy indeterminacy have been well studied. In his classic critique of American policymaking, Lowi (1979) contended that legislative bargaining, logrolling, and deal making tended to produce policies that were less than authoritative, rife with ambiguities and internal contradictions. He suggested that policymaking in practice was far removed from the normative vision of a process marked by reasoned resolution of conflicting views and interests. Studies of legislative politics have indicated that the strategic challenges of coalition building tend to lead to policies that blur irreconcilable differences, favor abstraction over clarity, and combine contradictory objectives rather than resolve them (Arnold 1990; Nelson 1984; Pierson 1994; Price 1978).

A reasonable inference is that the more contentious the issue and the more competitive the opposing interests, the more likely that compromise and obfuscation will be strategically useful in avoiding gridlock or defeat.[4] In this context, it is, perhaps, unsurprising that many politicians favor the aphorism (adapted from Voltaire) that one should not let "the best be the enemy of the good." If "the best" involves the search for consensus and clarity of purpose, "the good" allows for fudging over differences in order to facilitate agreement.

Although the political conditions that produce policy indeterminacy will vary in different periods and countries, this problem is hardly unique to the United States. For example, so-called framework laws, common in the Scandinavian states, explicitly eschew policy details in favor of broader principles and goals. There may be more than one rationale for this approach, but it nonetheless serves to defer some difficult policy choices to the implementation process. Paul Pierson (1994) offered important insights into this type of practice in his comparative study of welfare state retrenchment. He found that policymakers purposely designed policy to obscure potentially unpopular choices. His analysis of the politics of social welfare retrenchment highlighted the strategic utility of designing policies in ways that could limit transparency, visibility, and traceability of potentially negative policy consequences.

Jean-Claude Barbier has reflected on the functions of policy indeterminacy in the politics of European welfare states. In his studies of work activation and other policies advanced by the European Union under the rubric of "flexicurity," Barbier highlights the strategic use of nominal policy terms. He regards them as a "political *référentiel*" or cognitive frame (Barbier 2007), deriving political utility, in part, from elevating "fuzzy generalities" while masking "divergent realities" (Barbier 2005, 65). In the case of activation, (explicit) policy seems to blur the lines between regulatory and enabling elements (see discussion in chaps. 1 and 4).

Policy indeterminacy is compounded by the discretionary character of many tasks of policy delivery. The practices that come to constitute education, health care, public security, and social welfare policy require the exercise of discretion on the part of those who do the day-to-day work of policy delivery. In some respects, their discretion may be regarded as authorized. Policies both allow and depend on the judgments of teachers, police, social workers, and other professionals to make them work. However, discretion also derives from the character of street-level work, in which practitioners find unauthorized spaces in which they use discretion to manage the often daunting demands of the workplace. From an agents-of-the-state perspective, the question is whether frontline practitioners do what policy tells them they should. But from a street-level approach, the questions are: What do these practitioners do to manage their work lives, and what does that mean for policy as constituted through their informal practices?

A two-dimensional view of SLOs recognizes that frontline workers are neither agents who simply do what they are told nor fully autonomous actors who simply do what they want. Rather, they do what they *can* under organizational conditions that shape the range of possibilities in critical ways (Brodkin 1997, 24). It is partially through adaptive responses to their organizational environment that they indirectly construct policy on the ground. A rich empirical literature demonstrates how SLOs effectively shape policy through their practices, directing attention to factors influencing discretion and their consequences for policy as produced. This literature is far too large and diverse to reference here beyond a small number of examples.[5] However, street-level studies provide illustrations of how SLOs effectively mediate policy, examining how these processes work in diverse policy areas (among them criminal justice, social assistance, welfare-to-work, child protection, and education) and varied organizational settings (among them public bureaucracies, nonprofits, and for-profit firms) (Lin 2002; Dias and Maynard-Moody 2007; Miller 1983; Morgen 2001; Smith and Donovan 2003; Price 2003; McCleary 1978; Hasenfeld 2000). These studies show that when street-level adaptations are systematic, they can result in rationing, sorting, selectivity, and other common practices that occur beneath the radar of most oversight (Lipsky 1980b).

In short, a two-dimensional view sees SLOs as more than state agents and identifies matters of interest beyond deviance from officially sanctioned behaviors and outcomes. It recognizes that formal policy is necessary to authorize action and provide resources to enable it, but insufficient to fully determine what will happen in its name. Ambiguity in explicit policy coupled with opportunities for the exercise of discretion in the processes of policy delivery create conditions under which it is analytically appropriate to regard SLOs as de facto policymakers, shaping policy content and the distribution of benefits and services through their actions. Their indirect policymaking function imparts obvious political significance to SLOs, a matter that moves from the background to the foreground in a three-dimensional approach.

SLOs as Mediators of Politics: A Three-Dimensional View

From a two-dimensional perspective, the primary matter of interest is how SLOs mediate policy through their practices. A three-dimensional view considers how the structural location of SLOs positions them as mediators not only of policy, but also of politics. The three-dimensional perspective directs attention to SLOs as sites of policy conflict, wherein politically contested policy projects may be advanced indirectly through administrative means, including through managerial reforms that alter the arrangements and conditions of street-level policy work.[6] In this sense, SLOs matter because they affect what Theda Skocpol (1992) calls "policy possibilities."

This perspective also directs attention to how SLOs mediate politics by structuring the possibilities for advancing claims on the state, asserting rights, and pursuing redress. In this sense, they may be understood as sites within which individuals indirectly negotiate sociopolitical status. This raises questions about how SLOs may effectively mediate status differences associated with race, ethnicity, nationality, and gender. As may be apparent, this is a rather complex matter that cannot be fully elaborated in this space. However, it is possible to set out key elements of the three-dimensional view and suggest how it contributes to understanding welfare state dynamics and processes of transformation.

SLOs, "Obfuscation," and the Politics of Managerial Reform

The work of SLOs should be understood as deeply political in part because their practices determine "who gets what, when, and how"—the essence of politics according to Harold Lasswell's (1936) classic definition. But this is a different form of policymaking from that which occurs through legislative or other authorized channels: it is difficult to observe and has consequences that are difficult to assess and trace. Because its visibility is limited, it follows that it is a form of policymaking that reduces the potential for overt conflict. As E. E. Schattschneider (1960) famously explained, politics is the "mobilization of bias." How can mobilization occur when policy is made in ways that are largely unseen and where its implications are obscured?

Paul Pierson (1994) takes up this point in his comparative examination of welfare state retrenchment. He emphasizes what he calls the "centrality of obfuscation strategies," contending that "if policymakers are attempting to pursue unpopular courses of action, they will do their best to camouflage their activities" (Pierson 1994, 48). Pierson's study of obfuscation strategies focuses on legislated policies, examining how they may be designed to hide or blur social welfare cuts.[7] This research offers important insights into the politics of welfare state transformation, but it stops at the organization's edge. Bringing SLOs into the picture takes analysis one step further. It directs attention to how retrenchment—and other potentially politically charged projects—may be obscured by initiating change indirectly through SLOs. In short, it examines how political projects may be advanced indirectly by altering the arrangements for and practices of policy delivery. This can be an effective strategy to the extent that changing the conditions of street-level work substantively changes what SLOs produce as policy, while limiting the visibility of the processes of policy transformation. From this perspective, strategies of managerial and governance reform assume considerable political interest.

Yet, efforts to reorganize and reform the organizational architecture of policy delivery often advance under the rubric of making things work better, offering to improve efficiency, accountability, or coordination. These are widely desirable objectives, nonpolitical in appearance and, at times, arguably in purpose. However, a growing critical literature demonstrates that these managerial projects may, intentionally or inadvertently, reallocate political power and provide a back door to advancing politically contested policy ideas (Considine 2005, 2000; Moynihan and Herd 2010; Radin 2006; Rothstein 1996). A case in point involves EU efforts to reform the public employment services (PES).[8] The European Union has promoted PES reforms in pursuit of what some analysts refer to as "modernization" (Taylor-Gooby, Kananen, and Larsen 2004, 478). In contrast, these reforms are seen by others as strategies to limit the political and administrative influence of organized labor and its so-called social partners. They do this by circumscribing or outright eliminating the organizations through which labor and its partners once actively participated in making labor market policy and in overseeing the administration of employment and activation services.[9]

As Flemming Larsen (chap. 7) explains: "There is more to governance reforms, especially the abolition of the PES, than simply improving service delivery. In Denmark and other northern European countries, governance reforms also have been used in ways that undermine corporatist political structures. . . . The PES . . . enabled employers' and labor organizations to have a major influence on both policymaking and administration. . . . [The PES] also provided a mechanism for consensus building around expansion of welfare state activities. . . . This role has come under increasing pressure, in part through governance reforms."

However, reorganization, while of limited interest to the general public, is not entirely without visibility. Consequently, it is more likely than other types of governance and managerial reform to encounter resistance, at least from those whose interests are most visibly harmed. Certainly, efforts to restructure or abolish the PES have not gone unnoticed or uncontested by those most obviously affected, notably labor parties and organizations representing public workers. In contrast, other types of managerial reform (among them, devolution, contracting, and performance measurement) present a more technical face, with potential political implications more difficult to discern. Their implications derive not only from how they reallocate influence over formal policymaking and supervision, but also, less transparently, from the ways in which they alter the conditions of policy delivery and, through that, what is produced as policy.

From a street-level perspective, managerial reforms may be understood as a form of politics by indirection. They change where discretion in policy delivery is exercised (e.g., whether implementing organizations are public, nonprofit, or for-profit and whether they are federal, state, or municipal) and under what organizational conditions it is exercised (e.g., through various contract incentives, fiscal arrangements, performance monitoring, and so forth). To rephrase Harold Lasswell's classic formulation: managerial reform is political because it changes who does what and how.

It is neither feasible nor necessary to fully discuss types of strategies here; many of them are closely examined in individual chapters of this book. However, a brief discussion of performance measurement, arguably one of the more ubiquitous strategies, helps to illustrate the political utility of managerial reforms that alter the conditions of street-level work.

Performance measurement appears to bring accountability to organizations by monitoring and then rewarding or sanctioning key aspects of what organizations do. There is surely managerial value to using performance metrics and oversight to track specified (and especially measurable) aspects of organizational practice. But, as many scholars have observed, identifying what aspects of performance matter and determining how to measure them is both technically difficult and politically problematic (Considine 2005; Heckman, Heinrich, and Smith 1997; Lawton, McKevitt, and Millar 2000; Wichowsky and Moynihan 2008; Radin 2006). It requires the selection of which policy features will be monitored and which ignored. It also means reducing complex policy objectives to relatively simplistic, at times even reductionist, elements.

Performance measurement alters the production of policy by biasing the exercise of discretion in systematic, if often circuitous, ways. Essentially, it changes the implicit calculus by which street-level practitioners adjust to the conditions of work (Brodkin 2011a).[10] In the most basic sense, such measurement creates incentives to pay attention to what is measured and to be less attentive to what is not measured. This is the so-called displacement effect. In the case of US welfare-to-work policy, performance measures created incentives to place welfare recipients in jobs. But because the measurement scheme, by and large, did not distinguish jobs providing security and prospects of upward mobility from insecure, dead-end McJobs, caseworkers required to meet quotas had an incentive to press individuals into those jobs most readily available. And, as Lambert and Henly (chap. 5) explain, "bad jobs" were the most available—that is, lower-wage jobs characterized by high-turnover, unstable work hours, and insecurity.

Commenting on the perils of performance measurement as an accountability strategy, McGuire (2004, 276) has astutely observed, "There is a place for measurement in performance reporting, but there is more to quality than what can be counted. . . . The conceptual richness of the qualities of public services does not translate easily into standardized measures, scales, or indices. Quantitative measures cannot adequately capture the duty of care and equity qualities that are integral to professional public services." Viewed as a political strategy, performance measurement may be understood as an instrument for selectively determining what aspects of policy will matter, but in manifestly nonpolitical terms.

For example, studies show that performance schema may be used in ways that effectively stack the deck for advancing a certain conception of welfare reform or work activation in street-level practice. In the US case, the performance that matters was largely defined in terms of reduced welfare caseloads and increased work effort. What escaped scrutiny was how measured aspects of performance were achieved. Did agencies achieve performance benchmarks for increasing work effort by advancing economic opportunities for poor adults or by channeling them into insecure or dead-end jobs? Did they reduce caseloads by reducing poverty, thus making cash assistance unnecessary, or by making benefits more difficult to obtain, regardless of need? Clearly, performance measurement may be used in ways that indirectly privilege one set of policy purposes (in this instance, caseload reduction and increased work effort) over others, like improved economic prospects or family well-being.

Paradoxically, performance measurement gives the appearance of advancing accountability while, in an important sense, doing the opposite. Or perhaps it is more accurate to say that it advances, at best, an incomplete version of accountability. And the ways in which it is incomplete can have crucial political implications, limiting policy feedback to selectively measured outcomes and generating virtually untraceable policy biases in organizational practice.

In short, there is more to performance measurement and other so-called governance reforms than meets the eye. Beyond their manifest uses, they also have strategic utility in advancing politically contested changes in the welfare state through indirect means that limit visibility, traceability, and feedback. These are precisely the characteristics that Pierson (1994) regards as key to the politics of retrenchment.

As this discussion suggests, SLOs mediate politics in part by providing channels through which contested political projects can be advanced indirectly using administrative, rather than overtly political, means. In many countries, SLOs have become targets of managerial reform, raising questions about how these reforms restructure who does what and how. Although managerial strategies are largely incremental, that does not necessarily mean they are inconsequential (Lindblom 1979). These strategies may be used to smuggle in small changes that, in the aggregate, advance broader political projects, including alterations in the boundaries between work and the welfare state that are of central interest in this book.

SLOs and the Politics of Voice, Rights, and Redress

A second way SLOs mediate politics is by providing channels for making claims on the state, asserting rights, and seeking redress. It is within SLOs that individuals seek to exercise voice—to express their interests and concerns and have those expressions recognized in some way. As discussed, SLOs occupy a critical structural position that places them at the intersection of the state, its policies, and individuals. This structural position makes SLOs the most proximate institutions of the welfare state for those seeking benefits or services. For disadvantaged and marginalized populations, in particular, SLOs arguably are more directly accessible and more directly relevant than explicitly political institutions, such as legislatures, parties, or organized interest groups.[11] This requires expanding analysis of the welfare state beyond these large-scale institutions and bringing SLOs into the picture. Moving from a political-institutional to a political-organizational perspective directs attention to how SLOs structure the processes through which individuals assert voice, negotiate sociopolitical status, and seek group recognition.[12] These structuring processes are often as subtle as their implications are broad.

Consider that a fundamental principle of democracy is political equality. As democratic theorists from Dahl (1956) to Bartels (2006) have argued, political equality requires more than equality of one's vote. In his classic formulation of democracy, Dahl emphasizes the importance of voice and responsiveness. He proposes as a basic principle that "all active and legitimate voices" must be able to "make themselves heard" in the process of political decision making (1956, 137). But what do voice and responsiveness require? Critics of contemporary US electoral politics have argued that equality of vote is insufficient to assure responsiveness under conditions of economic and social inequality (Bartels 2006; Gilens 2005). Focusing on the gap between voters' policy preferences and legislators' voting records, they have found a disturbing skew. As Gilens (2005, 778) succinctly puts it: "When Americans with different income levels differ in their policy preferences, actual policy outcomes strongly reflect the preferences of the most affluent but bear virtually no relationship to the preferences of poor or middle-income Americans. The vast discrepancy I find in government responsiveness to citizens with different incomes stands in stark contrast to the ideal of political equality that Americans hold dear. Although perfect political equality is an unrealistic goal, representational biases of this magnitude call into question the very democratic character of our society."

What if one looks beyond legislative policymaking? What are the opportunities for voice and responsiveness in the administrative core of the welfare state—in the SLOs where individual and state directly interact and where the individual stakes for achieving responsiveness tend to be both personal and high?

Although it is not the manifest function of SLOs to provide avenues for voice, it often is their task to respond to claims of need. Street-level studies provide insights into the interactions between citizens and state, revealing how, under certain conditions, SLOs may develop tendencies that work at cross-purposes to recognizing and responding to individual claims of need and expression of interests. These studies suggest that responsiveness is most at risk when frontline staff have inadequate resources (including time, knowledge, and access to useful services), performance measurement focuses on selective benchmarks (excluding indicators that might be reasonably associated with responsiveness), and individuals asserting claims are from marginalized and disadvantaged sectors of society (Brussig and Knuth, chap. 11 in this volume; Brodkin 1997 and chap. 9 in this volume; Handler and Hollingsworth 1971; Hasenfeld 2000; Herd and Lightman 2005; Marston, chap. 12 in this volume; McCleary 1978; Miller 1983; Morgen 2001; Smith and Donovan 2003; Soss 2000; Soss, Fording, and Schram, chap. 8 in this volume; Watkins-Hayes, chap. 10 in this volume).

Under these conditions, street-level practitioners may go to great lengths to discourage voice, claims making, and the assertion of rights, avoiding—even suppressing—efforts by individuals to discuss their needs and life circumstances. Studies in a variety of settings (see above) have shown how street-level practitioners can discourage and delegitimate claims for help, assertions of rights, and expressions of voice. Some of the case examples Celeste Watkins-Hayes recounts (chap. 10) illustrate how efforts by individuals to have their needs and interests acknowledged may be discouraged by SLOs. She relates a claimant's description of his experience after being interviewed by a food-stamp caseworker: "I'm here and I'm not feeling like he's doing the best for me. . . . There was some resentment, but it wasn't spoken, you know what I mean, but there was definitely some tension. He wouldn't look me in the face and talk to me . . . just focusing on the papers and the computer. So nothing he had said outright, it was just the feel."

In his study of housing benefits in France, Pierre Edouard Weill (2011) recounts the frustration of a saleswoman from a perfume shop who sought to express her housing needs and sense of deservingness in her encounter with a local administrative agency. She felt the officials wanted only to focus on documents and rules, resisting her efforts to voice her concerns and to express her view of social justice. Instead, she vented her frustration to a researcher, saying: "It's impossible to live in Paris with my daughter. . . . I work, I pay taxes, and I'm forced to live in a 12 meter maids-room with the toilet on the landing because there is nothing correct [that meets policy requirements] under 800 euros per months in Paris and my wages are not three times more than the rent!"

SLOs not only structure opportunities for expression; in a more practical sense, they also structure possibilities for claims making and realizing rights. Their practices can either facilitate or hinder efforts to navigate claims-making processes. The ability to advance claims on the state through SLOs depends, among other things, on the accessibility of offices (location, hours), the volume and complexity of claiming tasks (e.g., in providing documentation, arranging appointments, or attending meetings), and the degree to which street-level practitioners are likely to lighten the burden or add to it. For example, an empirical study of welfare claiming in the United States found that "to the extent that organizational practices—both formally prescribed and informally created—are complicated, confusing, or cumbersome, they can add hidden costs to claiming, in some cases raising costs beyond the capacity of individuals to 'pay'" (Brodkin and Majmundar 2010, 1). When these practices are systematic, they produce what Majmundar and I have called "administrative exclusion."

In addition to structuring opportunities for voice and claims making, SLOs also shape the possibilities for realizing rights and pursuing redress. In her study of administrative appeals, Vicki Lens (chap. 14) finds that the discretionary behavior of judicial hearing examiners affected possibilities for individuals to be heard when trying to voice their grievances. One common practice was for judges to discount claimants' efforts to explain their experiences dealing with street-level staff. She notes a tendency, among some judges, to blame claimants for their difficulties, ascribing roadblocks to inadequacies on the part of claimants, rather than contemplating that agency practices also may be at fault.

By closely examining the hearing process, Lens discovers an interesting paradox with subtle but significant implications for voice and redress. She finds that settlements offered by officials to correct agency errors prior to a hearing had the effect of keeping systematic agency misdeeds off the judicial table. She concludes, "Matters at the crux of . . . disputes, such as the appropriateness of assignments or the availability of supports or resources to address obstacles to work were . . . never addressed. Nor were the consequences of the agency's actions, including the deprivations and hardships created by the threat or reality of discontinuance of benefits. . . . Appellants' individual and immediate needs were sanitized, transformed into disputes over paperwork and process rather than substance and need." In short, the processes of redress can be structured in ways that circumscribe voice and leave systemic problems unarticulated and unchallenged.

Michael Adler (chap. 13) suggests that managerial reform could make redress even more problematic. In reforming administration of British New Deal programs for the unemployed, Adler finds that independent adjudicators were eliminated and responsibility for adjudication of claimants' grievances was transferred to agency managers. His research suggests that agency efficiency was

achieved by circumscribing external review of agency practices, in effect, allowing the agency to police itself. Adler concludes that these managerial reforms
make it "extremely difficult for anyone who is required to take part in the New
Deal programs to challenge any sanctions that are imposed on them or complain
about the advice and help they are given."

In a variety of ways not yet fully understood, SLOs also play a part in mediating status claims associated with gender, race, ethnicity, and nationality. Studies
in this book are at the forefront of an emerging literature exploring the role of
SLOs as sites in which sociopolitical status is indirectly negotiated. For example,
Watkins-Hayes (chap. 10) examines how racial identity complicates the relationship between caseworkers and their clients. She finds that either party can,
at times, deploy race strategically—clients, to win a sympathetic hearing from
racemates, and caseworkers, to present a sympathetic face to clients. However,
she also discovers, contrary to the expectations of representative bureaucracy
theory, that minority caseworkers may avoid race, effectively providing less of a
voice to racemates. Watkins-Hayes suggests that racial responsiveness depends
on organizational factors, with more highly bureaucratized organizations "likely
to undermine racial representation by generating strong boundaries in
bureaucrat-client interactions, even between racemates. In addition, representation is less likely to occur in organizations where minority employees feel compelled to act to protect their hard-won access to employment."

SLOs mediate sociopolitical status in other ways, as well. Martin Brussig
and Matthias Knuth (chap. 11) suggest that German agencies administering
activation policy have effectively discriminated against migrant groups, not purposefully, but, somewhat ironically, as a consequence of organizational practices
that emphasize equal treatment. Procedural equality essentially displaces substantive equality when agencies fail to create the resources or incentives to
respond to difference. In this sense, Brussig and Knuth argue that activation
agencies indirectly reinforce inequality among migrant groups, underscoring
rather than mitigating their marginalized status in German society. Their study
provides insights into how migrants' efforts to have their differences heard are
structured by street-level practices. Similarly, in his study of French family welfare agencies, Vincent Dubois has observed that "family benefit offices are particularly sensitive places where tensions between 'born and bred French' and
'foreigners' occur" (Dubois 2010, 4).

In addition to race and ethnicity, gender has been a particular point of conflict in policies of welfare-to-work and activation, in no small measure because
these policies raise questions about women's social role and the importance of
caretaking in the home relative to work in the paid labor market. But, as in
other areas, these questions are not fully resolved by formal policy. Individual
cases present complicated sets of issues through which these questions may

effectively be renegotiated at the street level. Brussig and Knuth (chap. 11) provide examples as they discuss the dilemmas caseworkers face in applying activation rules to women from migrant Turkish Muslim households. They describe what may be seen as a tripartite negotiation among husbands, wives, and caseworkers over whether women should be "forced" into the labor market or "liberated" from male-dominated households.

Significantly, the street-level practices of workfare and labor market activation are deeply infused with issues relevant to women's status as homemakers, mothers, and workers (Handler and Hasenfeld 1991; Levine 2013; Morgen 2001). Anna Korteweg's (2006) comparative study of two job-preparation workshops, one in the United States and one in the Netherlands, offers insights into how gender and citizenship are informally constructed through street-level practices. Despite nominally similar formal policy arrangements, she found that contextual differences produced quite dissimilar practices. In the United States, informal practices advanced a woman-as-worker model of citizenship, while in the Netherlands they produced what Korteweg calls a "feminized mother/worker/citizen" model. As these studies illustrate, a three-dimensional approach to analysis provides a window into the ways SLOs structure claiming, voice, the assertion of rights, and the pursuit of redress—in the process, also mediating sociopolitical status.

Reconceptualizing SLOs: Doing the Work of the Welfare State

This chapter conceptualizes SLOs as critical sites for welfare state politics and transformation. It offers a vantage point from which to examine how SLOs shape the boundaries of the possible for advancing contested policy projects and for negotiating rights and sociopolitical status. This perspective does not require ascribing purposeful political intent to street-level practitioners (nor does it rule out purposeful behavior). The political significance of SLOs derives largely from their indirect effects, that is, from how they mediate policy and politics through their practices. In this sense, the practical is political.

For the most part, research on SLOs and research on the welfare state have progressed along two different but parallel tracks. Certainly, research adopting a political-institutional approach has contributed to understanding the politics of the welfare state by revealing the importance of structuring institutions (among them, electoral systems, legislatures, interest groups, formal policy arrangements, and so forth). But it has yet to reach into the functional heart of the state where SLOs do not only policy work, but also, indirectly, political work.

In this book we adopt a multidimensional view of SLOs that recognizes them as mediators of both policy and politics and as locations for conflict over the character and scope of the welfare state. Studies in this book probe beyond explicit policy elements in order to examine the practices of workfare and activation. In the process, they illuminate the otherwise-hidden spaces where the politics and dynamics of welfare state transformation take shape.

Notes

1. Here and throughout the book I use the word "reform" without implying that the changes it embodies are either negative or positive. In fact, it is the effects (broadly understood) that, I argue, should be the object of study. As noted in chapter 1, this is different from the common usage that equates reform with improvement or progress. The connotative properties of this term, arguably, make it more politically attractive than terms such as "change" or "alteration."

2. Although Pressman and Wildavsky, among others, focus on implementation "failure," other types of policy studies highlight the achievements and successes of US antipoverty initiatives. For an insightful review, see Page and Simmons (2000).

3. For one influential approach to assessing deviance in organizations, see Brehm and Gates (1999).

4. Arnold (1990, 271) highlights the political utility of designing policies to limit their traceability: "When a causal chain is short and simple, citizens are more likely to know which policy instrument will produce the appropriate effects and are better able to monitor the performance of their representatives. When a causal chain is long and complex, or when a problem in society stems from multiple causes, citizens may be incapable of doing the appropriate policy analysis and political analysis."

5. For a fuller discussion of the literature inspired by the street-level bureaucracy approach, see Brodkin (2012).

6. See, e.g., Brodkin (1997, 1986).

7. Pierson also notes the strategic value of policy designs that effectively create a lengthy "causal chain." He observes that "the more stages and uncertainties that lie between a policy's enactment and its perceived result, the less likely it is to provoke a popular response. Policymakers have a significant degree of control over this. They may choose interventions that create causal chains of varying lengths" (Pierson 1994, 46). This is an important insight, but does not go far enough. Causal chains and "traceability" are not only a matter of policy design, but are also, as I will discuss, determined by arrangements for policy delivery and, more specifically, by what SLOs do and how they do it.

8. See n. 1 on my use of the term "reform" as a synonym for change.

9. "Social partners" is a term generally used by European policymakers to refer to collaborative arrangements between labor and employer groups.

10. According to this metric, $C = f(R:D, i)$, where C is the calculus of choice, R is resources, D is demands, and i is incentives. As I have elaborated elsewhere: "The analytic task is to probe the logic through which street-level practitioners use their discretion to adjust informal practices to conditions of work, including work demands, resources, and incentives.

In the development of informal street-level patterns of practice, it is theorized that street-level practitioners will respond to an individual calculus of costs and benefits that derive from the ratio of resource availability to demand burden (R:D) as moderated by incentives. According to this calculus, one can assume that street-level practitioners will select action A over B when A is less costly and more rewarding. It also follows that management strategies that change the informal calculus of costs and benefits will result in different patterns of discretionary choice" (Brodkin 2011a, i259).

11. As Lipsky (1980b, 4) explains, "in a sense street-level bureaucrats implicitly mediate aspects of the constitutional relationship of citizens to the state. In short, they hold the keys to a dimension of citizenship."

12. I build here on Theda Skocpol's (1992) important insights on the relationship between institutional structures and the politics of the welfare state, which led to a turn to institutionalism in welfare state studies. This has been a highly generative approach. But SLOs largely have remained outside of its range of vision. To adapt Skocpol's (1985) well-known turn of phrase, I am arguing that it's time to "bring SLOs in" to institutional studies of the welfare state.

PART II

What's at Issue

Politics, Policies, and Jobs

3

The American Welfare State

Two Narratives

Michael Lipsky

The stories societies tell about themselves powerfully shape their choices and their subsequent actions. They affect how people understand their relationship to one another. They guide the futures people can imagine. They suggest the links between past events and current and future developments. They remind us of what we want and how we may achieve our objectives. Narrative is fundamental to social development. We evolved as story-telling beings, and our stories are critical to making sense of what we are doing. Without organizing narratives we are in a sea of random observations.

Moreover, people sort out new information and connect it to their underlying values according to the preexisting narratives that structure public discourse. Since government is a critical character in narratives of the state, it is signally important whether the persona of government registers as capable and supportive of the common good, or whether it registers as unreliable and incompatible with common concerns. What people think of government is an assessment not simply of its performance and stature but also of its character as portrayed in extended narratives presented and available over time.

This chapter examines two key narratives that have helped shape the political discourse of contemporary social welfare politics in the United States. It offers a broad view of this discourse, suggesting how the narratives influenced or failed to influence the political context that led to changes in welfare policy and management that are of central interest to this volume. It examines this discourse in historical perspective, reviewing key stages in the development of the American welfare state and highlighting trends and moments of change.

My point of departure is the turn to the right in American politics, with its rejection of government as an instrument of constructive problem solving. This shift was orchestrated in part by a set of interlocking institutions deliberately put in place by conservative intellectuals and activists and well funded by like-minded sponsors. This development is well understood. The intriguing questions that have not been adequately addressed are why liberal counterweight institutions did not develop during the critical decades, and why supporters of welfare state policies acquiesced in the negative views of government.[1]

One answer I want to suggest is that liberals failed to respond to the conservative challenge because they were involved in a parallel but different discourse. Engaged in "perfecting the welfare state," they took for granted that progress on welfare state policies could proceed in only one direction. They ignored the possibility that the premises of the welfare state could be called into question.

I will not argue that if counterweight liberal institutions had been in place, the conservative perspective would have been neutralized. This is unlikely, and in any event cannot be known. Moreover, the welfare state is in retreat more widely, and surely this trend would have been reflected in the United States. as well (Gilbert 2002). However, it now seems undeniable that the terms of welfare state debates in the United States are strongly influenced by an antigovernment perspective that has grown up relatively uncontested. As a result, advocacy of robust social policies is much more difficult than it might have been if conservative perspectives had been more consistently challenged.

Narrative and the Welfare State

Robert Reich has argued that there are foundational American stories through which Americans organize their opinions about public affairs. The conservative perspective is consistent with the American story of the "triumphant individual," the paragon of hard work and self-reliance who is capable of succeeding on his or her own terms. The social welfare perspective fits the story of the "benevolent community," a narrative that draws on such mythic developments as communal barn raising and organizing of schools in frontier settlements (Reich 1987).

At the community level these stories have a basic equivalence. The American character recognizes both the triumphant individual and the benevolent community as stand-ins for many particular scripts. However, at the national level, the story of the benevolent community only resonates if one is able to see government as the equivalent of community and the forum for popular will. The demonization of government, if allowed to dominate the discourse, degrades the benevolent community as a cultural resource for action because the community, at the national level, has no equivalence. Liberals regularly try to evoke the logic of the benevolent community by referencing the GI Bill, extension of electrification to rural areas, and public works from railroads to the internet. These references are powerful only if the public face of government is seen as constructive and working toward the common good.

In principle, there were always two strands to the welfare state narrative. One strand is the story of those policies and institutions that shape systems of support for people who cannot support themselves. This strand of the welfare state narrative concerns, among other things, who should be protected under the umbrella of social provision, what sorts of support should be offered, and at what level. A second strand of the welfare state narrative is the story of the state: how nationhood has been constructed over time, and how people relate to each other through the mediating polity. This strand typically receives much less attention in discussions of social welfare policy. It concerns, among other things, the following questions:

- the purposes of the state and priorities among those purposes;
- who is included in the polity;
- which choices would be best for the nation.

In short, we may say there is a narrative of the *welfare* state, with an emphasis on the first word in the phrase, and there is a narrative of the welfare *state*, with an emphasis on the second word. In this chapter I argue that supporters of social welfare policies in the United States focused on the former, and neglected the latter, ultimately to their regret.

It is tempting to see these competing perspectives as mostly responsive to economic and developmental conditions. And it is surely the case that the viability of social programs is related to national prosperity and apparent affordability. While this is undoubtedly true to an extent, it is misleading to understand the vigor of welfare state policy advocacy exclusively in such terms because social and economic trends are often ambiguous, and in any event there are always trade-offs to be made among policy choices. To take a recent example, some observers concerned about budget deficits believe programs should be cut, while others, who think economic stimulus is imperative during a period of very high unemployment, insist that budget cuts are premature.

In the development of the American welfare state, material context surely influenced public discourse at different times. For example, the long-term reduction of defense spending after World War II, as Eugene Steurle has explained, allowed lawmakers to shift funds to other purposes without raising taxes. Inflation also pushed taxpayers into higher brackets, thereby increasing revenues without requiring congressional action. In addition, some benefit programs were structured in ways that initially produced relatively high revenues but required low initial payouts (Steurle 1996).

This era of easy finance gradually ended during the 1960s, leading to more restricted capacity for strong social-policy initiatives in the 1970s. It was during these years that conservative rhetoric shifted from an emphasis on traditional values, such as freedom from excessive government control, to a focus on economic issues and state capacity (Smith 2007, 103).

But even if material conditions influence policy choices, the nature of those conditions emerges only through a socially constructed process. The facts don't translate directly into public understanding; rather, facts are filtered through a guiding narrative. To borrow an observation from framing theory, "If the facts don't fit the frame, people will reject the facts."[2] Facts that don't fit the controlling narrative are likely to be disregarded, while facts that do fit the controlling narrative are easily assimilated and contribute to the superstructure of society's guiding ideas.

In thinking about guiding narratives, it will be good to keep in mind that, though they may seem to be naturally produced by society, in fact, society's stories are shaped and exploited by commercial and politically oriented interests to aid their objectives, particularly in the age of media omnipresence. The origins of dominant ideas may be difficult to trace, but we may be certain that social forces are directing their production off camera. They influence how often a story is repeated, the consistency of the message, choices of messenger, and how various messages are woven together in the larger narrative.

Narratives are increasingly driven by entrepreneurs who seek to influence developments by shaping what people understand to be the underlying values and historical experiences of the polity. In this sense, the pop historian writes the future. A stable and powerful policy narrative draws both on perspectives endemic in the society and on those derived from pundits and intellectuals who exercise influence by affecting people's wants and their understanding of the way the world works.[3]

Before going further, I should acknowledge that there is surely more art than science in describing the content and origin of narratives that drive large policy developments. Also, it is prudent to be wary of seeing too much coherence in the narratives whose character we hypothesize. Stories tend to be retrofitted, in the sense that coherence emerges as people reflect on developments and try to explain their relationship to one another. As incidents accumulate, people begin to see through the lines and connect them to each other. Later, the accomplishments and precedents of the past appear as guides to future action (so that the events truly, not just notionally, relate to one another).[4]

The Conservative Narrative

There has always been a strain of American political thought that is suspicious of government, and rightly so. American government has promoted the interests of the powerful at the expense of the powerless, engaged in episodes of extreme cruelty, and tolerated unjust private behavior. Public policy decisions such as when to go to war or whether to restrict private use of public lands engender great loyalty in some, but disapproval among others. The ascendant conservative movement has drawn on antigovernment sentiment in putting in place a narrative that directly challenges the notion that a primary task of government is to protect vulnerable populations and insure their full integration into society.

The conservative movement has many strands, but this discussion focuses on two of its major propositions. The first is that a society in which markets are as free as possible from interference produces better outcomes than a society whose resources are organized and deployed through nonmarket mechanisms. The second is that the widest prosperity will result if people, as much as possible, are left to their own resources. The apparent indifference of conservatives to inequality and their tolerance for policies that appear to serve rich over poor follow from these propositions.

In this view, many of the instruments of modern government are inimical to a good society. Government agencies are inherently incapable of acting effectively, they are presumptively wasteful and inefficient because they operate in environments that lack market discipline, and other means of accountability do not work. Smaller government is better government. Whenever possible, government functions should be transferred to private entities, where they are likely to be performed more effectively and at lower cost. In this view, taxes should be low because they constrain personal freedom and reduce resources better deployed by individuals and businesses.

Since government is inimical to markets in the conservative worldview, government is the focus of attack along two related lines. One highlights the negative consequences of government actions. The other seeks to reduce resources for government programs, too often creating the self-fulfilling prophecy that public programs do not work.

The conservative perspective could hardly be more at odds with a welfare state perspective. While a welfare state perspective recognizes the importance of mutual aid and pooling of resources for the common good, the conservative perspective shifts risk to the individual and increases individual responsibility for well-being. A compassionate public policy, in the conservative view, might subsidize people who cannot afford to purchase health insurance or pension security. But it would not interfere with the governance of existing health care institutions.

In what sense is the conservative frame of reference a narrative? The conservative framework offers a narrative in that it strings together observations about society to explain how the world works, the individual's place in it, and the likely consequences of taking certain actions. The conservative worldview reserves a special place for the individual as the central character in the story. Given any set of facts, through a conservative lens, the individual can see what the consequences will be for her and the nation.

As has been well told in many places (Blumenthal 1986; Rich 2005; Smith 2007), the conservative worldview has been successfully promoted at state and national levels by an infrastructure of foundations, think tanks, journals and other media outlets, scholarly assemblies, judicial seminars, campus-leader and candidate-recruitment campaigns, legislative forums, and other institutional developments deliberately constructed to move a political agenda. In alliance with business interests for part of the agenda and social conservatives for another part, these organizations have come to play key roles in debates over social policy.

The Liberal Narrative

In principle, there is a liberal model of how the world works, though it is rather complex. In the liberal view, public actions pave the way for economic success for individuals and businesses and for the nation. Government actions create the legal and regulatory frameworks on which markets depend and invest in infrastructure and human capital. In the liberal model, markets thrive and prosperity ensues when government makes strategic choices in the public interest and balances the needs of commercial enterprises with the requirements of a prosperous, healthy, and economically secure populace.

In the liberal worldview, the state gives rise to the economy, making efforts to insure prosperity, while creating laws and policies that protect people who cannot protect themselves and that moderate the negative consequences of unfettered market forces. In contrast to a conservative perspective, the liberal view promotes nonideological thinking because the need to strike a balance requires the weighing of contending values and interventions.[5]

But this account of the role of government in a mixed economy is not the story that welfare state activists were telling over the years. Perhaps supporters of the welfare state took for granted that the United States was making advances in social welfare policies and would continue to prosper, making resources for social programs available. In any event, they did not concern themselves with the purposes of the state.[6] They neither created institutions to articulate directly a liberal perspective on the state, nor did they incorporate a rationale for the state in the course of other discussions. Instead, a different set of considerations animated supporters of social welfare policies. This was the task of perfecting the welfare state.

The Welfare State Narrative

It is not surprising that American supporters of the welfare state tended to take the role of government for granted. After all, for several decades the American people had been expanding the social compact. The United States famously "discovered" poverty in the early 1960s through the writings of Michael Harrington (1962), Dwight McDonald, Harry Caudill (1963), and others, and enacted various laws to reduce poverty through the administrations of Presidents Kennedy, Johnson, and Nixon.[7] In addition, the conflicts and accommodations of the 1960s began to redress the status of African Americans and remove economic, social, and political barriers to their participation in American life. Subsequent broadening of the social compact embraced the equal status of women, and later of gays and lesbians.

During this period, the American state expanded not only in social provision but also in regulatory mandates (Pierson 2007), building a new legal infrastructure in areas such as environmentalism and consumer protection. Liberals may well have thought they were also expanding welfare state concerns to a broader spectrum of social justice issues (Berry 1999).

In subsequent decades, social protection and support extended to more narrowly defined groups. Sometimes this aid was provided through entitlements, as in the case of the education of children with special needs.[8] More often it was extended through special grant programs operating through state and local governments and nonprofit service organizations. In recent decades, victims of domestic violence, schoolchildren requiring remediation in English as their second language, and people living with HIV/AIDS have been acknowledged as newly deserving recipients of public benefits in the United States.[9]

Much has been made of the infrastructure erected by conservatives to promote their agenda. Welfare state advocates also had an infrastructure of sorts in the government agencies created to implement and administer new social welfare policies. In 1964, the federal Office of Economic Opportunity was created to manage programs for the poor, such as Head Start and Legal Services, and to administer funding of the community-action program aimed at reducing poverty at the local level. In the early 1960s, the federal agency most concerned with the circumstances of low-income Americans was the federal Housing and Home Finance Agency (HHFA), which helped fund low-income housing. In 1965, HHFA was absorbed and its concerns greatly amplified with the creation of the massive Department of Housing and Urban Development, in some respects an advocacy institution within government to support low-income housing programs.

Other federal departments, including Health, Education and Welfare (later Health and Human Services) and the Department of Education, provided bases for advocacy and research on social welfare issues. The creation of these government agencies provided institutional capacity, albeit within government, to support research and advocacy to advance welfare state concerns. Thus, social welfare advocates may have felt little pressure to create philosophically compatible institutions outside government.[10]

Suddenly there was money to study poverty and social programs. The 1960s witnessed the flowering of graduate schools of public policy and investment in systematic public policy research. The University of Wisconsin's Institute for Research on Poverty in 1966 received federal funds to study poverty from a variety of perspectives and blazed a trail with its study of the work effects of a hypothetical negative income tax. In addition to policy schools, researchers at private consulting organizations such as Abt Associates, and nonprofit research centers such as Mathematica and Manpower Development Research Corporation, worked on antipoverty policy design and program evaluation. The RAND Corporation and other research contractors added human services research to their portfolios. The annual meetings of the Association for Public Policy Analysis and Management, where the agenda regularly featured the latest research on poverty, became rolling seminars on critical program-design issues.[11]

Beyond periodic efforts to deepen welfare state commitments through legislation, there was much work to be done to set the stage for reform. One constant theme was the need to develop a more complex understanding of what it meant to be poor in America. The social policy infrastructure of researchers, government officials, and foundation staff members also began to examine the effects of a changing job market and sought to develop policies to better integrate work and family life.[12] Researchers criticized the much-maligned official poverty standard and showed its inadequacy for describing the resources of people in need (Citro and Michael 1995).[13] They challenged the child support system that failed to help fathers earn enough money to be able to pay child support or bring them closer to their children.[14]

Researchers also promoted asset-development policies. The emerging realization that African Americans trailed whites, not only in income but even more dramatically in ownership of personal assets, gave rise to activities focusing on asset building among low-income people, including expanding mortgage eligibility, creating educational and children's savings accounts, encouraging microfinance programs, and others (Sherradan 1991; Oliver and Shapiro 1997).[15]

These activities floated on a narrative that took for granted that the country was on a path to respond to the needs of low-income people. Liberal social-policy advocates were concerned with tactical questions of how to take advantage of opportunities to realize incrementally the full expression of the welfare state. There was no apparent discussion of the purposes of the welfare state, nor was there conversation on the role of government.

An Evolving US Welfare State

Since the 1930s the story of the American welfare state has been one of consistent progress, sometimes suspended, but then picking up again. This progress has been punctuated by episodes of hardship occasioned by financial crises and fluctuations in the business cycle. It also reveals one particularly grievous reversal of social progress—the collapse of African Americans' legal and social status following a period of progress after the Civil War of the nineteenth century.[16] However, with the possible exception of welfare reform in the 1990s (soon to be discussed), there are no comparable reversals in social welfare policy.[17]

This narrative of welfare state development occurred in four overlapping stages.

Stage 1. For much of the post–World War II period, the American welfare state was widely described as "exceptional" because the country lagged in adopting key elements of social provision and expenditures for existing social protections tended to be low relative to the Organization for Economic Co-operation and Development (OECD) countries with which the United States is typically compared. Particularly notable were the failure of the United States to offer universal health care and the lack of robust support for unemployed workers. The view that the United States was extraordinarily backward as a welfare state was later partially reassessed, but nonetheless it constituted part of the narrative (Howard 2003).

Stage 2. Notwithstanding its reputation as a laggard, the American welfare state did progress, particularly with the creation in 1965 of Medicare, a national health insurance program for the elderly, and Medicaid, a joint federal-state health insurance program for the poor and the disabled. In addition, the American welfare state expanded through various income-transfer policies. The Food Stamp program gradually transformed from a cumbersome experimental effort in 1964 to a substantial contributor to the household income of low-income people by the 2000s. The program, now called the Supplemental Nutrition Assistance Program (SNAP), expanded support beyond the very poor to include lower-income households, including some without children. This partly mitigated the collapse of state-level general assistance programs that in earlier periods had offered some support to individuals without children. More recently, the Earned Income Tax Credit (EITC) has become a powerful antipoverty program. The credit, which is restricted to working people who file tax returns, raised 6.5 million people out of poverty in 2009 and has become an essential instrument of welfare state coverage.[18]

These developments are consistent with an intentional strategy by policy advocates to build the American welfare state piece by piece. Political scientist Lawrence Jacobs writes that health reformers, recognizing failures to establish national health insurance under Presidents Roosevelt and Truman, opted for "an incremental strategy that would take a series of gradual steps over time to extend health insurance to all Americans" (Jacobs 2007, 77).[19] Incremental progress in American legislation is hardly confined to the social welfare arena. Many of the most substantial government achievements of the post–World War II era were accomplished through incremental changes (Light 2002).[20]

Stage 3. In recent decades American social welfare advocates became more comfortable with the US version of the welfare state. They came to understand that it could be seen as a public-private hybrid. In this view, when contributions of employers were taken into account, the American welfare state seemed more competitive with European counterparts, particularly in health care and pensions (Hacker 2002; Howard 2003).

This part of the story became more problematic toward the end of the last decade, when employers massively changed their pension systems from defined-benefit to defined-contribution plans requiring substantial contributions from employees. They also began to transfer substantially higher health insurance costs to workers or dropped coverage entirely (Hacker 2006). These developments, arguably, were instrumental in paving the way for business support for health care reform in the Obama era.

Stage 4. During the Clinton and two Bush administrations, welfare state policy expansion was the product of pragmatic compromises in which liberals sought common ground with conservatives. The EITC combined liberal support for income assistance to working families with conservative support for a program that reduced federal revenues and helped only workers and not welfare recipients.[21] Another compromise extended health insurance coverage to poor children whose family incomes were too high for Medicaid eligibility, but made it subject to annual appropriation rather than guaranteed as a federal entitlement.[22]

These and other pragmatic compromises produced some substantive victories. But as political scientist Ira Katznelson has pointed out, pragmatism provides a weak philosophical base on which to build a politics that can sustain a long-term social policy agenda. Pragmatism in pursuit of policy victories takes government for granted; it does not reinforce or embrace an understanding of the purposes of government that can be drawn on for future expansions (Katznelson 1996, 39).

These stages of American welfare state development constitute a narrative of steady progress. They also reflect what appears to be a shared belief among many liberals in a systematic, if not scientific, approach to policy reform.

Narratives and the Welfare Reform Debate

Paradoxically, a sign that liberals were perfecting the welfare state may be found in accounts of the most significant setback to welfare state progress in the postwar years: the transformation of the country's core welfare program—Aid to Families with Dependent Children (AFDC)—in 1996. As examined in detail in this book (chaps. 1, 4, 8, and 9), "welfare reform" constituted an important legislative vehicle for advancing changes between work and the welfare state.

For decades, while AFDC was defended as necessary to deliver assistance to children in poor families, in truth very few liked the program. Liberals criticized its paternalistic and sometimes racist administration and recognized that its focus on dependent children created barriers to assisting poor people who had no children or whose children had become adults. In the late 1960s, AFDC became the focus of a concerted and, for a time, influential welfare rights movement designed to demonstrate the inadequacy of the cumbersome AFDC structure. At the same time, conservatives maintained that AFDC discouraged self-reliance and was rife with cheats and shirkers.

In the 1980s, echoing criticisms now heard in many countries that such programs discourage work and unwisely undermine personal responsibility, American welfare policy turned toward an emphasis on job seeking and placement. While some welfare policy specialists resisted this orientation, others strived to design policies that gave work-oriented reforms the best chances of succeeding. The Family Support Act (1988) mandated that states implement welfare-to-work programs and provided states with resources to provide job counseling and work placement. The Greater Avenues for Independence (GAIN) program in California received a great deal of attention at the time as researchers strived to discover whether and to what extent welfare recipients' incomes would increase and welfare uptake would decline as a result of the new program and resources.[23] Acting under waivers granted by the federal government, states began experimenting with welfare-to-work models, including, notably, Massachusetts in the 1980s, with its Employment and Training (ET) program, and Wisconsin in the 1990s, with Wisconsin Works.

During his 1992 campaign for the presidency, Bill Clinton pledged to "end welfare as we know it."[24] Liberals took him to mean that he would seek to replace AFDC with a plan that followed the outlines traced by Harvard professor David Ellwood, who was advising his campaign. In his book *Poor Support*, Ellwood (1988) suggested that the nation could begin to make a dent in widespread poverty and craft an alternative to AFDC by supplementing earned income with refundable tax credits, strengthening the child support system, providing child care subsidies for working mothers, and guaranteeing medical care. When President Clinton took office in 1993 his administration initially appeared to be pursuing a constructive welfare reform path, bringing Ellwood into the government and implicitly endorsing his approach to welfare reform.

Stymied by Republican opposition, however, the president settled for the approach ultimately written into law in 1996—an end to welfare as an entitlement, a five-year eligibility limit, and more rigorous work requirements. Clinton indeed ended "welfare as we know it," breaking the social compact by revoking the promise that the state would support children of indigent parents. Many liberals strongly opposed this development, and their opposition has proven to be justified.[25] America's poor families are now much poorer than they were. States have been cutting back their block-grant spending on welfare to fund other priorities during the recession, and the percentage of poorly educated single mothers in poverty has not improved (Schott and Pavetti 2010).

Some observers, however, have processed these developments in a way that seems to sustain the theme of welfare state progress. In mainstream political discourse, welfare reform came to be defined as progress because the new law was said to take welfare off the table, where it no longer could serve as a lightning rod for criticism of the welfare state and a Democratic Party widely viewed as supporting programs for low-income people.

In addition, support for the principle that welfare recipients should actively seek work was not particularly controversial. As discussed elsewhere in this volume, many welfare systems around the world now require recipients of public benefits to seek and accept employment, even if it will not make them economically better off. The acceptability of such policies to a liberal, however, depends upon whether good jobs appropriate to an individual's skill levels are available and accessible, and whether individuals have affordable, accessible options to meet their responsibilities as parents or caregivers.

Welfare administration, however, had virtually no defenders during this critical period. The debate might have presented an occasion to draw attention to the role of government in protecting people who cannot protect themselves. It might have been a time to challenge the country to be more responsive to the problems of poverty among the substantially larger group of poor people who would never use welfare. Yet, for the most part, the discussion took place entirely within the confines of debates about individual responsibility and how to manage a population now required to work in order to receive assistance.

Continuing Efforts to Perfect the Welfare State

Welfare reform represented a defeat for social welfare advocates who sought to increase the state's capacity to help low-income people become fully incorporated into the economy. Health care reform under Presidents Truman and Clinton had failed as well, as did President Nixon's efforts to introduce a negative income tax that would have replaced welfare with a system of salary supplementation for working families. While to policy insiders defeats may be momentous, these experiences soon become part of the landscape. They are folded into a new understanding of progress, but it is one in which lessons about setbacks or the heroic struggles for progress are lost.

By the late 1980s, American social reformers seemed to believe and behave as if their task was to complete the welfare state. During this period, for example, the Ford Foundation, the country's largest foundation at the time, engaged in a multiyear effort to conceptualize and advance, once and for all, an American welfare system that would provide comprehensive support for people in need. The foundation projected a series of programs that would help people cradle to grave, paid for by taxing Social Security benefits as regular income beyond existing limits.[26]

The theme of perfecting the welfare state is persistent. In 2009, a year into the Great Recession, amid enormous cutbacks in state spending and growing concern about funding all aspects of government, two antipoverty researchers from the highly respected Urban Institute continued the search for a better welfare state with the publication of *Repairing the U.S. Social Safety Net* (Burt and Nightingale 2009).

Postwelfare Reform: The Liberal Narrative and the Role of Government

By the 1990s, the influence of the conservative campaign to call into question the capacity and role of government could not be ignored. What were liberals doing to counteract or respond to the extraordinary growth of the conservative apparatus? Essentially, they defended policy elements of the welfare state that they had succeeded in putting in place. They supported research to sharpen program effectiveness. They absorbed some lines of conservative social-policy philosophy in rethinking long-established approaches to social problems, not only with regard to workfare and welfare reform, but also in other areas of social policy. For example, liberals also conceded that housing for poor people might be delivered more effectively through vouchers than through traditional public housing projects.

At the same time, they joined the conservative chorus in denigrating government—conceding the criticisms and choosing not to defend government. They defended specific policies, but program-by-program defense and advocacy, however necessary and desirable, does not engage the much more profound conservative challenge to the premises of the welfare state architecture.

For the most part, conservative attacks on government for waste and inefficiency went unanswered, even by public figures whose sentiments might have been supposed to align with strong government action.[27] Elected officials lauded their own accomplishments, to be sure, but almost never drew attention to government's essential role. Public officials' shortsightedness in failing to draw positive attention to the role of the public sector was all the more significant because communications media treat as news any government failure, but do not fit government successes into their conventions for newsworthiness. To oversimplify, while conservative politicians were advocating for smaller government on principle, liberal politicians were advocating for programs but not for the role of government as such. This advocacy failure occurred even when politicians were applauding undeniable government successes such as Social Security protections and cleaner air and water (Lipsky et al. 2005, 6).

In the 1980s and 1990s, liberal public officials adopted the view that hostility to government might be mitigated if government were smaller and citizens' experiences more pleasant. President Clinton famously embraced the conservative critique when he declared that "the era of big government is over."[28] He more or less did the same when, in advocating health care reform based upon managed competition, he sought to enhance reform's prospects by conceding the incapacity of government and holding up the virtue of private markets (Jacobs 2007, 91).

Vice President Gore's well-publicized campaign to "reinvent" government, while somewhat successful on its own terms (Stone 2003; Kettl 1998), also had contradictory elements. In urging that government treat people as "customers," the campaign implicitly conceded that citizens are typically treated poorly. Reinventing government also came across to the public as a series of anecdotes about bureaucratic failures. For a political leader to say that something needs to be fixed, to paraphrase political scientist Murray Edelman, is to communicate that there is a big problem the public needs to worry about (Edelman 1964).

During this period there were many signs that supporters of the welfare state thought that they could maximize their gains by trimming advocacy, avoiding divisive politics, and searching for common ground with ideological opponents. On the national scene, President Clinton and the centrist Domestic Leadership Council sought to pursue a "third way" through policy proposals that were neither right nor left, hoping they might gain acceptance in the highly partisan environment (Marshall and Schram 1993). Welfare reform in 1996 was perhaps the most evident example of this strategy.

However, comparable developments were occurring below the radar of national politics. The Aspen Institute, for example, for many years brought together prominent people from the two sides of the political spectrum to facilitate a meeting of the minds on social welfare issues. The theory of Aspen's Domestic Strategy Group, funded by various centrist foundations, was that if ideological opponents could get to know one another, trust could be built and positive outcomes would result. In this same period, foundations also funded bipartisan congressional gatherings on the theory that informal socializing might result in greater bipartisan cooperation.[29]

In a survey conducted in 2004, a research team at Demos, a New York think tank, asked officers at centrist American foundations, presumptively sources of support for robust social welfare policies, about their grants in support of the public sector. The inquiry revealed a variety of ways in which foundations underwrote public policies, but little engagement with the much larger problem I have been discussing—eroding support for government.[30] Only one foundation initiative appeared to promote an understanding of the role of government or draw attention to its accomplishments—an annual awards program at Harvard University highlighting the achievements of American governments.[31]

Reframing the Discourse: In Support of an American Welfare State

In its component parts, the American welfare state enjoys broad popular support, as opinion polls regularly indicate. Despite occasional hysteria in the media, Americans should be fairly confident that the core programs will remain mostly intact, although health insurance programs (post-"Obamacare") and Social Security likely will require some adjustment. But debates on the future of the welfare state are troubling. When liberals defend the programs or challenge conservative proposals to radically restructure them, they do so on the basis of self-interest. In debates on the future of Social Security, seniors are assured that their entitlements will not be affected. In discussions of health care reform, citizens are assured that "you can keep the coverage you have," reinforcing the view that everyone is in it for themselves. Missing are the regular reminders that deep support for these programs requires a belief that the welfare of all citizens is the hallmark of a good society.

Supporters of expansive welfare state policies have not entirely neglected appeals to collective interest. President Clinton cast the conflict over Medicare in 1995–96, for example, as a "debate . . . about two very different futures . . . :

whether we will continue . . . to go forward under our motto, . . . out of many, one; . . . or whether we will become a more divided, winner-take-all society."[32] Similarly, in the face of massive antigovernment sentiment, President Obama drew on the theme of collective responsibility when he insisted that individualism and personal responsibility must be balanced by a notion of common fate. In discussing fiscal issues in April 2011, he stated:

> There has always been a . . . belief that we are all connected; and that there are some things we can only do together, as a nation. . . . Part of this American belief . . . expresses itself in a conviction that each one of us deserves some basic measure of security. We recognize that no matter how responsibly we live our lives, hard times or bad luck, a crippling illness or a layoff, may strike any one of us. "There but for the grace of God go I," we say to ourselves.

He continued:

> And so we contribute to programs like Medicare and Social Security, which guarantee us health care and a measure of basic income after a lifetime of hard work; unemployment insurance, which protects us against unexpected job loss; and Medicaid, which provides care for millions of seniors in nursing homes, poor children, and those with disabilities. We are a better country because of these commitments. I'll go further—we would not be a great country without those commitments.[33]

President Obama's remarks are exceptional. Such sentiments are more taken for granted than regularly articulated. They are not part of the drumbeat of common concerns that shape the American frame of reference on a day-to-day basis.

It might be argued that the current debates are about the details of social welfare programs, not whether such programs should exist. But details are the heart of social welfare policy reform, as students of social policy regularly remind us. In my view, supporters of robust social welfare policies would be well served by framing discussions of the mechanics of programs in the broader context of the fundamental purposes of government. Reminded of those fundamental purposes, debates on program details can be much more successful and compromise easier to negotiate on favorable terms.

It is commonly understood that the key to a successful communications strategy is to continually repeat messages and themes. The conservative critique of the welfare state has been promoted successfully in this way. As the United States at long last confronts the sustainability of its welfare state armature, the habits of mind developed over decades will continue to slant the public discourse away from a belief in government capacity and recognition that the public sector should play a vigorous role when critical issues arise. This calls for the development of a new narrative.

Writing over twenty years ago, political scientist Steven Kelman (1988, 52) observed that to overcome the "thundering force of self-interest" people look to government as one of the forums through which they can display their concern for others. This is one of the frames for government, where the public sector is seen as the arena in which societies redeem themselves with acts of compassion and enlightened self-interest. It is much harder to mobilize for the greater good if the instrument for enacting and implementing policies to assist people in need is debased.

Notes

This essay is a revised version of the 2011 Richard M. Titmuss Memorial Lecture, presented at the Hebrew University in Jerusalem in June 2011.

1. "Conservative" and "liberal" in this essay refer to broad perspectives on the relationship of political institutions and economic systems, as detailed in the following sections. People who broadly subscribe to these views are called conservatives and liberals.

2. Meg Bostrom, "When the Facts Don't Fit the Frame," FrameWorks Institute, 2005, accessed January 11, 2012, www.frameworksinstitute.org/assets/files/eZines/facts_don%27t _fit_the_frame.pdf.

3. Classic treatments of the exercise of power through affecting the preferences of mass publics include Mills (1956); Edelman (1964); Lukes (1974).

4. Paul Pierson (1993) makes a similar point.

5. This is not to say that there are no liberal ideologues; some liberals are uncompromisingly committed to pieces of the liberal policy agenda. My point is that the need to balance contending interests inherently drives liberals toward compromise and negotiation.

6. They also took for granted that the proportion of workers to dependents would continue to support a generous old-age pension system (Samuelson, December 5, 2011).

7. See Dwight McDonald, "Our Invisible Poor," *New Yorker*, January 19, 1963.

8. Starting with the federal Education for All Handicapped Children Act (1975).

9. This paragraph draws on Lipsky (2008, 140).

10. Writing about the civil rights movement, John Skrentny (2002) makes parallel observations—the creation of agencies devoted to protecting civil rights in the 1960s contributed to the decline of mass mobilization and the ascendance of a professionalized civil rights leadership. One indication that these agencies represented a structure supportive of a liberal policy agenda is the efforts of opponents of the welfare state to curb the role of these agencies when Republicans controlled the presidency (1981–92 and 2001–8).

11. For an account of trends in poverty research, see O'Connor (2001).

12. For a summary of developments in this area see the Sloan Work and Family Research Network, accessed December 20, 2011 (renamed Work and Family Researchers Network), https://workfamily.sas.upenn.edu/.

13. On the sufficiency of the official poverty standard to meet basic needs, see Martha Holstein, "Economic Security across Generations: Background, Analysis, and Policy Recommendations," 2008, on the Wider Opportunities for Women website, accessed January 15, 2012, www.wowonline.org/resources/publications/index.asp.

14. Irwin Garfinkel, "Bringing Fathers Back In: The Child Support Assurance Strategy," *American Prospect*, March 21, 1992.

15. See also "Policy Agenda: Financial Assets and Income," Corporation for Enterprise Development, accessed January 11, 2012, http://cfed.org/policy/policy_agenda/financial _assets_and_income/.

16. Another might be immigration restrictions in the 1920s.

17. To be sure, policies toward Native Americans varied over time, but until very recently the policies remained grievous even if they changed (Henson et al. 2008, 1–14).

18. Nicholas Johnson and Erica Williams, *A Hand Up: How State Earned Income Tax Credits Help Working Families Escape Poverty in 2011*, accessed April 18, 2011, www.fns.usda .gov/snap/rules/Legislation/about.htm.

19. As late as the 1990s, health reformers were still acting on the assumption that expanded coverage could still be achieved by expanding Medicare incrementally (Jacobs 2007, 90–91).

20. The Food Stamp program illustrates this well, with substantial expansions and adjustments in 1977, 1985, 1987, and 1993. See "A Short History of SNAP," US Department of Agriculture, accessed December 26, 2011, www.fns.usda.gov/snap/rules/Legislation/ about.htm.

21. Johnson and Williams, *A Hand Up*.

22. Funding the Special Children's Health Initiative Program (SCHIP) in 1997 through appropriations rather than an entitlement represented a compromise with fiscal realities, but congressional opponents still thought that the program was virtually an entitlement, since states would have difficulty cutting health care for children.

23. The potential of the program in California was the subject of scrupulous study by the Manpower Development Research Corporation (Riccio, Friedlander, and Freedman 1994).

24. William Jefferson Clinton, State of the Union address, January 23, 1996, http:// clinton4.nara.gov/WH/New/other/sotu.html.

25. Welfare caseloads declined by two-thirds from their peak in 1994, but the decline is not attributable to recipients obtaining jobs through the new Temporary Assistance for Needy Families program. See Elizabeth Lower-Basch, "Cash Assistance since Welfare Reform," TANF Policy Brief, CLASP website, updated January 21, 2011, www.clasp.org/admin/site/ publications/files/CashAssistance.pdf. Another result of welfare reform's block-grant funding structure was that the American welfare system no longer provided countercyclical funding to states in hard times. For a critique of welfare reform, see Peter Edelman, "The Worst Thing Bill Clinton Has Done," *Atlantic Monthly*, March 1997. Also see chaps. 8 and 9 in this volume.

26. The initiative would draw on a solidarity that was presumed to exist in society. According to the project's report, "social welfare is properly the concern of all Americans, not just because all may benefit from improving it but because it is the right thing to do. The moral integrity of our society depends in no small measure upon our ability to unite behind this belief" (Ford Foundation 1989, 9).

27. A notable exception was the work of Robert Kuttner (1996).

28. "The Era of Big Government Is Over," CNN transcript of President Clinton's radio address, January 27, 1996, www.cnn.com/US/9601/budget/01-27/clinton_radio/.

29. Also in the 1990s, new policy organizations sought traction (and funding) by promising postpartisan approaches to policy. The New America Foundation fits this description. It

was founded on the belief that voters had become disenchanted by the dogmatic two-party system and that a new perspective might unite an electorate alienated from the extremes (Halstead and Lind 2001).

30. Examples of engagement with government mentioned by foundation officials included funding commissions to appraise the crisis in public service recruitment and making public policies more accessible to citizens through analyses of the quality of child welfare programs and of federal and state government expenditures (Lipsky et al. 2005).

31. See "Innovations in American Government Awards Program," Ash Center for Democratic Governance and Innovation, Harvard Kennedy School, accessed December 27, 2011, www.innovations.harvard.edu/award_landing.html. As a program officer at the Ford Foundation from 1991 to 2003, I was responsible for grant making in support of the Harvard awards program.

32. Greg Sargent, "Lessons from the Clinton Era," *Washington Post*, April 12, 2011.

33. "Remarks by the President on Fiscal Policy," April 13, 2011, White House, Office of the Press Secretary, www.whitehouse.gov/the-press-office/2011/04/13/remarks-president-fiscal-policy.

4

The Policies of Workfare

At the Boundaries between Work and the Welfare State

Evelyn Z. Brodkin and Flemming Larsen

In recent decades, policies of workfare and activation have been redrawing the relationship between work and the welfare state. These policies may be understood as part of a broader project through which states are promoting the primacy of work and limiting the provision of welfare. This project is now widespread, incorporated into the social and labor market policy arrangements of developed countries around the globe.

However, what looks, at first glance, like a growing project of global workfare is not a clear march toward a common mission. An evolving policy construct, workfare has moved beyond its early meaning as a policy requiring US welfare recipients to work off their benefits in unpaid assignments. Worldwide, it now operates in a variety of ways and under many different labels, among them welfare reform, welfare-to-work, work first, active labor market policy (ALMP), activation, and insertion *(revenu minimum d'insertion)*. Further, the path toward this plurality of workfare policies has been uneven, varied, and politically contested. Even the very nomenclature is problematic, potentially obscuring more than it reveals. As Jean-Claude Barbier (2010) has suggested, workfare may best be understood as a "political *référentiel*," a label that suggests a policy direction, but is not definitive in practice.[1]

Still, the workfare project is more than a discrete assortment of policies. It also is part of a broader political project that is evolving in ways that are far from simple to explain or easy to discern. In this chapter we provide an analytic map of this project, explaining what's at stake in adjusting the boundaries between work and the welfare state and how workfare matters. We also present a general guide to the varied policies of workfare, highlighting different historical paths through which they have developed in the United States and parts of Europe. The issues raised here set the stage for the in-depth analyses of workfare policies and practices in the chapters to follow.

On the Boundaries between Work and the Welfare State

It seems fair to say that two of the major structuring institutions of modern life in the developed world are work, as constructed through the market, and welfare, as constructed through the politics of the welfare state.[2] Workfare matters because of its role in determining where the boundaries between work and the welfare state are placed. The policies and practices of workfare involve politically difficult choices—among them, who deserves to be excused from work, the value of unpaid care work, and the role of the state in providing alternatives to market-derived income. The workfare project also plays a part in defining the state's role in protecting and supporting workers. The policies and practices of workfare set the terms for what constitutes acceptable work (i.e., the kinds of work the unemployed can be required to perform), what value should be placed on work relative to other possible values (e.g., values favoring work-family balance, job satisfaction, or economic security), and what kinds of supports workers should receive. In these and other ways, workfare performs a boundary-setting function.

Although neither markets nor welfare states exist in a pure form in the real world, each of these institutions structures society—and the place of work and workers within it—in distinctive ways. In principle, markets organize work by the hidden hand of supply and demand, and individuals derive their market value from their labor. For most individuals, the market value derived from work is critical to well-being: paid work is a necessity, at least for those without great inherited wealth or other nonmarket sources of income. The importance of work in the pre–welfare state era was vividly depicted by British historian R. H. Tawney, who wrote about the desperate plight of unemployed men in the sixteenth century. He famously observed that, although men were subject to physical punishment if they left their towns in search of work, "the whip has no terrors for the man who must look for work or starve" (Tawney 1912, 272).

Unlike the market, democratic institutions, ideally, are organized around principles of political equality, with equal value accorded to each individual's vote. In democratic states, however imperfect, citizens have opportunities to use the authority of the state to further social goals. These may include the protection of the general social welfare, or, in the case of Scandinavian welfare states, the advancement of social solidarity (Esping-Andersen 1990; Furniss and Tilton 1977).[3] Despite the sometimes peculiar political rhetoric found in the United States, most advanced welfare states are not socialist in the sense that production is collectively owned.[4] Rather, they are market-based democracies that use public policies to buffer certain market effects regarded as socially or politically undesirable. Particularly relevant to this book are the ways that welfare states respond to the economic insecurity and disadvantage that derive, at least in part, from market arrangements. Even relatively well-functioning economies experience cycles that result in unemployment; they also experience structural changes that displace sectors of the labor market. At times, as in the post-2007 recessionary period, economic disruptions may be severe and prolonged.

Welfare-promoting policies, including the social and labor market policies that are of interest here, can be used both to mitigate market harms and to improve market functioning. These policies are too highly varied and complex to be exhaustively detailed here, but two general categories should be noted. One includes policies that provide cash or in-kind benefits that function (at least in part) to protect individuals who, for economic or other reasons, find themselves disadvantaged by the market economy and vulnerable to deprivation.[5] The second type supports the development and maintenance of the workforce, either through human-capital building or work supports.

The first category includes programs of cash assistance, some of which are universal, provided through a family allowance or minimum-income scheme. Others are targeted, as in the case of public welfare, social assistance, family benefits to individuals outside the labor market, or pensions for the disabled and elderly. In addition, income schemes may be configured in what is sometimes referred to as a "two-tiered approach." In the first tier, social insurance programs (e.g., unemployment benefits and workers' pensions) are available to individuals with a substantial work history or occupational membership. Policies in the second tier (e.g., welfare and social assistance) provide benefits for those without a significant work history or occupational ties. Although they vary in important ways, as a general matter, welfare policies that provide cash assistance affect the boundaries between work and the welfare state by relieving selected groups from the market's demands, however temporary or partial the relief may be.[6]

Beyond cash assistance, services or in-kind benefits can help meet basic human needs such as health care, housing, and food. These supports, which may be targeted or universal, are particularly important to those most disadvantaged by labor-market or social structures. Depending on how all of these varieties of welfare policies are arranged, they may reduce the market imperative to work at any price, an effect Gøsta Esping-Andersen (1990) calls "decommodification."

But the policies of welfare do more than provide direct support, decommodifying labor by offering an alternative to market-based income. A second category of policies supports the development and maintenance of the labor force. These policies underwrite the well-being of the workforce by partially mitigating some of the limitations of a labor market that includes lower-paid, irregular, or insecure jobs. They may provide earnings supplements and targeted subsidies (e.g., for child care, housing, food, or health care) that effectively top up income for those disadvantaged by their market position. Other policies support workers in improving their market status through, for example, education and training that build human capital or help in job placement and matching.[7]

One way to think about this second type of policies is to say that they enable individuals to participate in the labor market on more favorable terms than the market alone would allow. These enabling policies do not fit neatly into a commodification/decommodification dichotomy. They do not provide an alternative to the market, but they hold the potential to improve the welfare of individuals either by compensating for some of the disadvantages caused by market arrangements or by supporting individuals' efforts to improve their competitive market position.

The policies of workfare occupy the intersection of these different responses to market-generated inequalities, disruptions, and disadvantages. They complicate easy categorization because they essentially combine regulatory, compensatory, and enabling features. It is how they combine them and, most importantly, how these elements operate in practice that effectively determines the boundaries between work and the welfare state in specific contexts. Positioned between state and market, then, workfare policies raise politically difficult questions about who deserves state support, who should be excused from work, and what kinds of work make a social contribution. More broadly, workfare raises questions, if only implicitly, about what constitutes fairness in the distribution of both welfare and work, what role the state should take in assuring jobs for those who want them, and what distinguishes work from exploitation. These critical questions traverse contested boundaries, making the workfare project politically fraught.

On the Policies of Workfare in Europe and the United States

Although the policies of workfare may be understood as part of a broad global project, they have not evolved along a single path nor adopted a uniform approach. In Europe, workfare (or "activation," as it is generally known) developed from labor market policies aimed at building and sustaining the well-being of an active workforce. Over time, many European countries have introduced ALMP into their national programs of social (or income) assistance. In effect, they have modified activation policies not only to advance the employment prospects of the unemployed, but also to impose new requirements (or "conditions") on those receiving support. What was once almost entirely an enabling strategy now, in some countries, also includes regulatory elements.

In contrast, in the United States, workfare was originally conceived as a largely regulatory strategy directed at recipients of cash welfare. It was first introduced in California, where adults receiving family cash-assistance benefits could be required to perform unpaid work duties. Over time, workfare has broadened nationally into a mix of supportive and regulatory provisions under the revised nomenclature "welfare-to-work," a term that's arguably more evocative than informative.

From a comparative perspective, we can see that the global policies of workfare have developed differently, but feature notable points of intersection.[8] To be sure, the policies of workfare and activation draw on the same programmatic toolbox for variously promoting and enforcing work (e.g., individual assessments, personal contracts, training, education, work assignments, sanctions for noncompliance with work rules, and so forth). However, in general, European policies have tended to emphasize programmatic features aimed at building human capital and supporting worker flexibility.[9] Among other things, this has meant providing opportunities for the unemployed to obtain extended and upper-level educational preparation or training. Activation schemes also have supported "flexibility" (i.e., movement in and out of jobs) by underwriting periods of unemployment and retraining. Even with recent reductions in duration, unemployment benefits in European countries may extend from six months to five years (with an average of about two years in continental Europe). In the United States, benefits vary by state and range from ten to twenty-two months. (During the Great Recession, the federal government temporarily gave funds to states with high rates of unemployment, enabling them to extend the duration of benefits. But that federal supplement was set to expire by the end of 2013. Without federal funds for extended benefits, the duration of state unemployment benefits ranges from 19 to 26 weeks.)

Recognizing that "history matters" (Pierson 2005; Skocpol 1992), we next consider countries' different paths toward the global workfare project, beginning with the development of European activation policies and then turning to welfare-to-work in the United States. This brief, and necessarily selective, review of workfare's evolution provides context for the developments to be explored more closely in the subsequent sections of this book.

ALMP and the European Path to Workfare

European activation policies (or ALMPs) vary in their specific features, but they reflect a common policy framework advanced under the auspices of the European Employment Strategy (EES). This approach had its origins in Scandinavian labor market policies, as we will discuss, paying particular attention to the contemporary Danish "flexicurity" model. Over time, activation-type policies have been adapted and reconfigured into a variety of country-specific policies. The current details of these many varieties of activation may be found elsewhere.[10] In this chapter we provide a comparative account of the global workfare project that focuses on its historical paths, underlying premises, and patterns of development.

Although the origins of activation, or ALMP, are difficult to precisely pinpoint, they can be traced to the 1940s, in postwar Sweden. Sweden introduced labor market policies designed to address the challenges of economic growth. The Swedish approach aimed to support a flexible labor market, while also promoting social cohesion, as exemplified by "solidaristic" union wages (Kildal 2001, 2). According to Rudolf Meidner, who played a formative role in the development of these policies,

> active labour market policy measures have the task of alleviating or rather eliminating the negative consequences of the solidaristic wage policy. Mobility-promoting allowance and retraining courses are appropriate methods to smooth the transition of redundant labour into more productive parts of the economy. The wage policy of solidarity, which is the very core of union ideology, depends in reality on the government's willingness to clear away employment problems caused by the solidaristic wages policy. This dependency illustrates well the close link between government and union efforts to reach the common goals: *full employment and equality.* (Meidner 1997, 92; emphasis added)

The approach Meidner describes is reflected in contemporary policies associated with Denmark's so-called flexicurity state—arguably, the apotheosis of the ALMP approach. The flexicurity ideal comprises "a set of policy and institutional arrangements through which Denmark balances its dual commitments to social protection and growing the economy" (Larsen, chap. 7 in this volume). It facilitates labor market flexibility in part by underwriting some of the risks that this flexibility presents to individual security and well-being. Among other things, policies help workers adjust to changing labor market needs by supporting them as they move in and out of jobs and as they build the human capital new types of jobs require. This stands in contrast to inflexible labor markets that achieve economic security for workers by guaranteeing job tenure, standardizing job arrangements, and limiting job mobility. This latter approach is associated with the kinds of labor market rigidities and limited opportunities for labor market entry that have plagued many southern European countries, which have experienced devastating rates of youth unemployment in the current economic contraction.

Of course, Denmark represents only one of many varieties of ALMP. Despite EU efforts to advance a common approach to labor-market and social welfare issues, national arrangements vary widely in the degree to which they facilitate social investment, make social benefits conditional on work, or even determine which parts of the population should be subject to ALMP's provisions. Efforts to make sense of the varieties of ALMP have produced many different conceptual schemas, typologies, and categories.[11] But the researchers applying them are among the first to recognize their limitations. As Leschke (2011, 162) observes in her comparative review, "the complexity of the policy design makes it very difficult to create comparative indicators that capture the policies in a comprehensive and accurate way and allow comparisons between countries."

There is variation, not only in policy elements, but also in the direction of the broader activation project, a project that is only loosely constructed and continually under reconstruction. There is an emerging sense that ALMP is very much a work in progress, arguably moving away from what Meidner initially envisioned. These developments, and what they mean for the changing faces of activation, are not well understood or easily observed. In reviewing developments occurring under the auspices of the EES, Leschke comments on a sense that changes are developing outside the view of available data on policy provisions, government spending, or targeted benchmarks. These developments, she suggests, involve a stronger focus "on employment growth and much less on more qualitative aims such as job quality or social cohesion" (Leschke 2011, 162).

Indeed, chapters in this volume indicate that there may be some erosion on the security side of the flexicurity bargain. This can be seen, even in Denmark, where there have been reductions in the duration of unemployment benefits, the introduction of conditionality in social assistance, and, of special interest for this book, a subtle shift from a human-capital-building to a more regulatory approach to activation. The regulatory approach is associated with work-first strategies that require the unemployed to accept the first job offered, regardless of its qualities. Work first is, essentially, a directive approach that assumes work is desirable on its face, regardless of whether the most readily available jobs offer reasonable prospects for economic security or rewarding forms of social engagement. However, as a practical matter, there is growing evidence that some of these assumptions regarding the rewards of work may be unwarranted, especially for certain populations targeted by activation policies (Loeb and Corcoran 2001; Looney and Manoli 2012).

The introduction of conditions and work-first approaches, not only in Denmark but also in other parts of Europe, indicates pressure on the various European activation models and, in some countries, emerging tendencies toward more of a US-style workfare approach. However, these tendencies—and conflicts over their direction—cannot be adequately discerned by looking only at formal policies, categories, or benchmarks. That is why it is necessary to dig deeper. The empirical studies in this book probe further, investigating activation and workfare practices and how governance and management reforms are shaping their evolution in different national contexts and under different institutional arrangements.

Welfare Reform and the US Path to Workfare

In the United States, the path to workfare began not with efforts to reform labor market policies, but with a long and contentious battle to reform welfare, the income assistance program for poor families with children. Welfare originated in 1932 as part of the national response to the Great Depression. It began as a very modest program through which the federal government reimbursed states for part of the cost of income supplements they offered to poor families in order to support their children. As welfare expanded to include income support for parents and as it grew in numbers (with welfare caseloads tripling and costs soaring in the late 1960s to early 1970s), political attacks on welfare and its recipients intensified (Katz 2001; Piven and Cloward 1971). Work requirements were among a variety of initiatives adopted to reduce costs and caseloads. Like work first, they asserted the primacy of work, whether as a means of rising out of poverty or, simply, as a moral or civic gesture (Brodkin 2009; Handler and Hasenfeld 1991; Katz 2001).

Workfare first drew national attention in the 1970s, when California governor Ronald Reagan (later President Reagan) promoted it as part of his state's welfare policy. Initially, it referred specifically to a programmatic initiative called "community work experience" (CWEP). CWEP required selected recipients of income assistance to work off their benefits in unpaid work assignments. Over time, additional states introduced variants of CWEP and other workfare initiatives into their administration of AFDC, a joint federal-state program providing modest cash support to families with children.[12] However, despite the nominal expansion of workfare, only a small minority of beneficiaries were subject to the strict "work for your welfare" requirements. In fact, through the 1980s and into the mid-1990s, the dominant trend was to modify the workfare approach and introduce activation-style features under the broad rubric of welfare-to-work. The result was a blurring of workfare's precise meaning, as it came to include both work-promoting and work-enforcing activities.

Regardless of terminology, "work for your welfare" requirements and subsequent policies that required work registration or engagement in work activities had relatively little bite, largely because of uneven enforcement. They also showed little value as an antipoverty strategy, in part because they brought relatively meager financial resources to human-capital development and uncertain quality to work-promoting services (Handler and Hasenfeld 1991; Brodkin and

Kaufman 2000). Despite their dubious record, between 1980 and 1996, workfare initiatives increasingly assumed prominence in American welfare policy-making, culminating in the enactment of the TANF program in 1996. TANF was the product of extended and highly contentious battles over what is commonly referred to as welfare reform (Weaver 2000). Among its important governance features, TANF replaced an open-ended federal guarantee to reimburse states for part of their welfare expenditures with a fixed block-grant allotment. It also gave states increased discretion to set eligibility for welfare benefits.[13]

In terms of its policy features, TANF struck a new balance between welfare and work. On the one hand, it incorporated more activation-like provisions. Under the rubric of welfare-to-work, states received federal funds enabling them to provide a variety of services, including education, training, job placement, and supportive services (e.g., child care and transportation supplements).[14] On the other hand, TANF allowed states to institute much tougher work requirements and sanctions, and extend them to lone mothers with young children and infants. In addition, TANF's most visible (and most debated) provision capped federal benefit payments at a cumulative lifetime maximum of sixty months.[15] Since its enactment, TANF has been revised to further limit opportunities for education and training and to allow states to require individuals to participate in work activities even before income benefits are granted.

TANF presented a substantially harder workfare edge than most European activation schemes. However, there is more to TANF than these policy features alone indicate. TANF also introduced new governance and managerial strategies—devolution to states, contracting for services, and performance benchmarks tied to caseload reductions and increases in work activities. These strategies, discussed more fully in chapters 8 and 9, created substantial space for state-level governments to shape their own approaches to workfare. They also, effectively, redesigned the spaces within which SLOs have shaped workfare through their practices, changing the boundaries between work and welfare in the process.

Changing Boundaries

In this chapter we have sought to make the case that the workfare project matters because it traverses (and impacts) the boundaries between work and the welfare state. Changes in these boundaries have profound implications for individuals who are disadvantaged by market arrangements and confronted with increasing risks in an economic landscape that demands worker flexibility, produces job instability, and makes job-related benefits more difficult to secure. As the workfare project reconfigures the welfare state's boundaries and its capacity to buffer risks inherent in contemporary market economies, this project has critical importance for those who find themselves at the precarious margins of the labor market or outside it altogether.

As discussed, neither US-style workfare nor European-style activation are clear-cut policy schemas, so simple statements about the workfare project and what it does are highly problematic. Efforts to understand the policies of workfare as part of a broad global project defy simple comparison of formal policy features. That is why we seek, in this book, to shed new light on workfare by looking beyond its policies to closely examine its practices. The stakes are high. If workfare practices develop in ways that support workers and enable them to advance in the labor market without significantly diminishing welfare protections, then the boundaries may shift little, if at all. However, if the practices of workfare develop in ways that effectively privilege work at the cost of increased vulnerability and hardship, then this project can be seen as one that pushed back the boundaries of the welfare state.

Notes

This chapter is adapted from Brodkin and Larsen (2013). © 2013 by the Policy Studies Organization. Text used by permission.

1. Barbier (2010, 2) also argues that, despite substantial political differences among nations, their activation policies should be understood as "types of a wider reform of social protection across the developed world."

2. We use the term "welfare" to refer to the variety of social welfare policies that provide income, in-kind benefits, and services. These policies are discussed in the second part of this chapter.

3. Esping-Andersen (1990, 21) has argued that "the welfare state cannot be understood just in terms of the rights it grants. We must also take into account how state activities are interlocked with the market's and the family's role in social provision." This is a helpful specification in terms of the argument of this book. Indeed, part of what makes the policies of workfare politically problematic is that they operate at the intersection of market, the family, and the state.

4. For a review of polling data that shed light on how "socialism" is understood by the American public and used in political rhetoric, see Mark Trumball, "Is America Becoming a 'Socialist' State? 40 Percent Say Yes," *Christian Science Monitor*, July 13, 2012.

5. To say that the policies of welfare function to assist individuals disadvantaged by the market is not to say that they necessarily do this well or that this is all they do. These policies also may have regulatory and social control functions.

6. Piven and Cloward (1971) further complicate this picture in arguing that the provision of assistance itself has a regulatory function, especially when it is stingy and degrading. In this sense, even the granting of assistance may serve as a cautionary tale meant to persuade workers to pursue work at almost any cost.

7. In many parts of Europe, these types of policies are regarded as labor-market rather than social policies, in part because they are manifestly intended to improve labor market

functioning. Means-tested policies that support lower-income workers are generally regarded as part of social policy in the United States. In any event, these distinctions have begun to erode under the activation regime, in which social benefits and labor-market interventions are now linked.

8. This discussion highlights alternative paths to workfare without entering the ongoing debate over convergence and divergence between different models of workfare policy. Rather than create typologies of workfare policy and compare their features, this book seeks to move beyond formal policies and typologies in order to investigate the practices of workfare and how they have developed in diverse contexts.

9. As noted, there is considerable variation across Europe. For example, analysts have pointed to fairly significant policy differences between the countries of northern and southern Europe. See, e.g., Clasen and Clegg (2006).

10. See, e.g., Carcillo and Grubb (2006); Clasen and Clegg (2006); Kildal (2001); Leschke (2011).

11. For some interesting examples, see Bonoli and Natali (2011); Carcillo and Grubb (2006); Kildal (2001); Lødemel and Trickey (2001); Vis (2007).

12. In the United States, states determine the amount of benefits they pay to families. The benefit levels vary from state to state, but in no case are they high enough to raise a family out of poverty. Under Temporary Assistance for Needy Families (TANF), the program that replaced AFDC, state benefit levels for a family of four in 2011 ranged from $170 per month in Mississippi to $758 per month in New York State. Benefits provided no more than half of a poverty-level income in any state, and less than 30 percent of a poverty-level income in the majority of states.

13. Among TANF's key features are that it ended the federal guarantee of income support and placed a lifetime five-year limit on assistance; it imposed work requirements as a condition for receiving assistance; it required adults to participate in workfare activities within no more than two years of receiving assistance, but permitted states to set tougher standards; and it capped federal expenditures within a $16 billion block grant, but it also gave states increased discretion in using federal funds. TANF was linked to companion legislation that provided $2.3 billion to help subsidize child care for working mothers and $3 billion in a two-year block grant for workfare programs. For what is arguably the definitive account of the legislative battle over TANF, see Weaver (2000). For additional views on the political conflicts that resulted in TANF, see Brodkin (2003a); Katz (2001); see also Peter Edelman, "The Worst Thing Bill Clinton Has Done," *Atlantic Monthly*, March 1997; David Ellwood, "Welfare Reform as I Knew It: When Bad Things Happen to Good Policies," *American Prospect*, May-June 1996, 22–29; Frances Fox Piven, "Was Welfare Reform Worthwhile?" *American Prospect*, July-August 1996, 14–15.

14. In the United States, child care is a private responsibility, although families paying for child care may receive a tax credit that defrays a small part of their expenses.

15. States could choose to use their own funds to extend benefits for a portion of their welfare caseloads.

5

Double Jeopardy

The Misfit between Welfare-to-Work Requirements and Job Realities

Susan Lambert and Julia Henly

If a work-based welfare state is to improve low-income families' economic security, it must be based on a realistic appraisal of jobs in today's labor market. In particular, it must be clear that the policies of workfare and welfare-to-work can ensure that low-income families can access needed supports and, in the longer term, avoid poverty. But policymakers may be expecting too much from jobs lodged at the lower end of the labor market. Although many individuals participating in welfare-to-work initiatives have moved off public assistance and into the workforce, the types of jobs available to them are of poor quality and recipients finding work often remain in or near poverty (Friedlander and Burtless 1995; Hendra et al. 2010; Scott et al. 2004).

A synthesis of results from state welfare leaver studies conducted during the first five years following welfare reform in the United States indicates that the average wages of leavers were low ($7 to $8 an hour). Average family incomes continued to hover around the poverty line, and the majority did not receive employer-sponsored health insurance or other benefits (Acs and Loprest 2001). Although researchers and policymakers may differ in their interpretation of the various successes and failures of welfare reform, research amassed since welfare reform was enacted in 1996 leaves little doubt that most recipients leaving welfare for employment fare poorly in the labor market.

However, there are surprisingly few studies of welfare-to-work initiatives that incorporate the workplace as a central object of study. As a result, limited attention has been paid to how firm policies and practices may contribute to the poor labor market outcomes of welfare-to-work participants or, importantly, whether the expectations built into welfare rules and eligibility requirements make sense

69

given the realities of work in low-level jobs. To deepen understanding of why leaving welfare for work is not always, or even often, a route to economic security, we focus on the work side of the welfare-to-work equation. Brodkin (2011b, i199) argues that "research that puts street-level organizations first aims at the opaque spaces between formal policies and outcomes, in part by making visible the organizational mechanisms that link (or de-link) them."

In this chapter we treat the firm as a street-level organization (SLO) of a sort, suggesting that firms operate as policy intermediaries. They are organizations that not only influence the relationship between policy intentions and policy outcomes but also produce additional outcomes of their own, both welcome and not. To make this case, we draw from studies of the low-wage workplace that elucidate everyday firm practices and show how they shape employment experiences for low-level workers. We pay particular attention to conditions of work that can render the work-hour requirements built into so many workfare-type policies unrealistic.

A basic assumption undergirding work-hour requirements is that workers can decide how many hours they will work. Failing to meet work-hour requirements may be viewed as a matter of participants' preference for limited hours or as an outcome of personal barriers to fuller employment. To address the first case, policies can include financial incentives for additional work effort, as is evidenced by work disregards in TANF or the EITC. To address the second case, work-support policies such as child care subsidies, job training, or mental health counseling are designed to reduce so-called barriers to employment.

We contend that neither of these approaches recognizes a fundamental reality of today's workplaces, both in the United States and elsewhere. Employment is becoming increasingly precarious, a global phenomenon driven by the declining power of labor, the globalization of markets, industrial shifts, and technological change (Kalleberg 2009, 2011). Even prior to the recent economic downturn, substantial proportions of US workers reported that they would prefer to work additional hours for additional income. In addition, rates of involuntary part-time employment have been increasing both in the United States and in Europe (Mason and Salverda 2009; Galtier 1999; Lambert, Haley-Lock, and Henly 2012).[1]

Regardless of the growing precariousness of employment, the United States is making eligibility for many social programs—unemployment insurance, food stamps, child care subsidies, and housing vouchers—contingent on the number of hours worked. Even an unpaid parental leave through the Family and Medical Leave Act (FMLA) is only available to workers who have been with their current employer for a full year and have logged a minimum of 1,250 hours (24 hours per week) during the year.

Although work-hour requirements are generally lower than familiar defini-tions of full-time employment in the United States (commonly 35 or more hours per week), they may still defy job realities. In the case of the US welfare-to-work program, TANF, federal legislation conditions eligibility on working a minimum of 30 hours each week, if the recipient is a single mother with children age 6 or older, or a minimum of 35 hours each week in households with two parents. Even with the lesser 24-hour-a-week requirement, only 62 percent of all US workers were eligible for leave under FMLA in 2000 (Cantor et al. 2001). Notably, approximately one-half of the participants in New Hope—an innovative program that provided work supports to low-income workers living in Milwaukee, Wisconsin—did not meet the program's 30-hour-a-week work requirement during the program's operation (1994–98) (Duncan, Huston, and Weisner 2007).

In this chapter we adopt an organizational approach to assess low-income workers' prospects for meeting the work-hour requirements codified in welfare-to-work legislation and for earning an adequate income. We draw on evidence from our own and others' research on low-level jobs. We look at how corporate policies intended to control outlays for labor fuel a set of frontline manager practices that limit both the number of hours available to hourly workers as well as workers' ability to control when and how much they work. We identify a mismatch between work-hour requirements and job realities as well as a set of policy conundrums that arise from it. We discuss how this mismatch places low-income workers at risk of double jeopardy: having public benefits reduced or terminated at the same time that earnings plummet. Our chapter concludes by considering what an organizational focus on firm practices reveals about terms of inclusion at the lower end of the labor market. It also suggests how the welfare state can intervene in ways that reduce, rather than heighten, low-income families' exposure to the risks of the market.

Cost-Containment Policies

Firms operating in the United States use the discretion afforded them under the law to curtail outlays for labor in low-level jobs through policies that limit not only wage rates and benefits but also the number of hours available to assign to employees. In doing so, corporate policies constrain employee work effort and the ability of workers to earn an adequate living and to meet the work-hour requirements codified in welfare legislation.

Business models that give priority to the containment of costs rather than the quality of goods or services as the route to profitability have expanded in the United States, particularly over the last thirty years (Kalleberg 2011; Lambert

2008). This transformation might not be so troubling if firms did a decent job of assessing the real cost of labor. But as management scholar Jeffrey Pfeffer (1998) has observed, not only do firms tend to ignore opportunity costs (e.g., customers who leave stores out of frustration), they also tend to confuse labor rates (total outlays for wages and benefits) with labor costs (outlays divided by productivity). As a result, curtailing outlays for labor (i.e., labor rates) becomes a goal in and of itself, with little attention given to the relationship between input (labor) and output (products, service)—that is, to labor costs.

US law provides few restrictions on the kinds of cost-containment strategies employers pursue (Lambert, Haley-Lock, and Henly 2012). The United States has no federal laws requiring employers to pay employees, either part-time or full-time, for a minimum number of hours. Similarly, no laws require employers to offer employees benefits such as health insurance, and only a handful of states or municipalities require employers to provide paid time off for illness (Maloney and Schumer 2010). Although employers must pay a minimum hourly wage, federal law does not require adjustments for increases in the cost of living. The 2009 minimum wage remained 17 percent lower than in 1968 when adjusted for inflation (Filion 2009).

The low levels of unionization in the United States offer few countervailing pressures on wages, hours, or benefits. For example, in 2010, just 8.3 percent of employees in the accommodation industry were represented by unions, 5.3 percent in retail, and 1.3 percent in food services. These industries had some of the highest rates of job growth (US Bureau of Labor Statistics 2011). A significantly higher proportion of adults in the United States have low earnings as compared to their counterparts in Western industrialized nations where a greater proportion of workers are covered by unions and labor wields markedly more power (Mason and Salverda 2009).

Firms operating in the United States have enormous discretion when it comes to structuring the employment relationship (Osterman and Shulman 2011). Because labor rates in hourly jobs are primarily a function of benefits, hourly wages, and hours worked, employers seeking profit through cost-containment strategies strive to restrict all three. In many firms, benefits are a matter of corporate human resource policy and are defined in terms of job classification (salaried vs. hourly, regular vs. temporary) and job status (part-time vs. full-time). For example, health insurance and paid time off may be available to salaried workers alone. Or hourly workers may be covered only if they hold full-time status. Such stratified human resource (HR) systems allow firms to curtail outlays for labor in low-level jobs while extending the compensation of professional and managerial staff beyond their salary.

Wage rates in hourly jobs also are a matter of corporate policy. Corporations establish pay bands that limit variation in hourly wages within the same job classification. For example, a pay band for sales associates might specify that associates be paid $7.25 to $8.50 an hour. Corporate policies also provide guidelines for raises, which in lower-level jobs tend to be based more often on seniority than performance. Workers who top out of a job's pay band are able to increase their wages only by moving into a different job with a higher pay range. Because corporate policies establish benefit packages, pay bands, and raises, frontline managers—and individual workers—can exert little, if any, control over these components of compensation.

In some respects, policymakers seem to recognize that benefits and hourly wages are set by firms rather than by individual supervisors or individual workers. Notably, eligibility for public assistance is not conditioned on participants securing a particular wage rate or certain benefits. To the contrary, public programs such as the EITC are designed to supplement the low wages characteristic of jobs at the bottom of the labor market. In the case of Medicaid, policy may offer health insurance benefits if they are not provided by one's employer. However, in other ways, policymakers implicitly treat work hours as though they were under the control of individual workers rather than corporations. This is reflected in policies that require a minimum number of work hours to establish eligibility for benefits. Yet because hours are a key component of outlays for labor, corporate policies restrict their availability.

In Lambert's (2008) comparative study of hourly jobs across several industries, she found that corporate policy restricted work hours by holding frontline managers accountable for "staying within hours." In retail firms, for example, managers responsible for scheduling hourly workers are held accountable for maintaining a particular ratio between demand for goods or services and the number of hours worked by their staff (see also Carré and Tilly 2008). The total number of hours to divide among their staff is typically based on projected sales derived from recent retail trends and last year's sales numbers (Lambert and Henly 2012). Similar accountability structures are found in food services for airlines, where shifts are booked depending on the mix of domestic and international flights; in hotels, where hours depend on room census; in financial services, where workers are scheduled according to projections of payments to process; and in restaurants, where managers monitor food sales and flow of customers (Haley-Lock and Ewert 2011).

Because managers are held accountable for staying within hours at an aggregate level—for their department, store, restaurant, or hotel—and variation in hourly wage rates is minimal, how many hours a particular individual works is of less consequence to satisfying accountability requirements than the number of hours the staff works in total. In other words, frontline managers are limited in the total number of hours available to their staff. But, as we discuss below, they often have considerable discretion in how they allocate those hours among individual employees.

Cost-Containment Practices

Work schedules are commonly created by managers on-site at a particular work-place; for example, a particular store, department, hospital, hotel, or restaurant. The fact that schedules are created and implemented locally provides the opportunity for slippage between corporate policies that establish the maximum number of hours frontline managers are supposed to assign their staff and what hours they actually give their workers. In other words, street-level actions by managers may diverge from policy expectations if frontline managers do not feel particularly constrained by the requirement to stay within hours.

Our survey of store managers in one national retail apparel firm suggests that accountability pressures to stay within hours are quite high and are seldom challenged by managers (Lambert and Henly 2012). Although managers reported that maximum hour limits interfered with their ability to meet business objectives, fewer than one-third reported going beyond the hour limits assigned to their store more than a few times a year.[2] The importance of managing within hour limits based on variations in consumer demand found here is consistent with other research examining management practices, for example, in electronic retailers and grocery stores (Carré and Tilly 2008), call centers (Batt, Holman, and Holtgrewe 2009), hotels (Hilton and Lambert 2012), and restaurants (Haley-Lock and Ewert 2011).

Drawing on our research on low-level jobs and firms, we discuss a set of practices that frontline managers use in their quest to navigate the often-competing demands of staying within hours and fulfilling productivity goals. Although there are many troubling practices found at the bottom of today's corporations, our focus here is on those practices that play a particularly important role in shaping workers' access to hours of work per se. This is directly relevant to understanding recipients' efforts to meet the minimum hour requirements imposed by TANF and other public benefit programs.

Keeping Head Counts High

One strategy managers pursue is to keep head count—the number of workers on the payroll—high. This gives them a pool of workers whose hours can expand or contract depending on business needs and who can be slotted to work short shifts during peak business times. For example, when asked about their staffing strategy, the majority (67 percent) of store managers in our study of a national apparel retailer chose the statement "I like to keep my sales associate staff on the large side so that I have several associates I can tap to work when needed" (Lambert and Henly 2012). Only a third (33 percent) chose the statement "I like to keep my sales associate staff on the small side to help ensure that workers get hours."

Managers' preference for a small rather than large staffing strategy has important implications for the number of hours individual employees receive. Because managers are responsible for staying within the allocated hours, no matter how many workers on their payroll, the more workers on the payroll, the fewer hours available, on average, for each. Because most hiring occurs during seasons when demand is strong, and because demand, not head count, determines allocated hours, waning demand may result in more employees than there are hours.

The practice of keeping workers on the payroll who are assigned very few (in our retail study, as low as four) or literally no hours per week is euphemistically referred to as "workloading." Using these informal layoffs enables managers to maintain a ready pool of workers to draw on when consumer demand increases. All 22 workplaces included in Lambert's (2008) study of low-level jobs in the Chicago area—in retail, hospitality, transportation, and financial services—reported informal layoffs of at least some workers during the prior year, a time period before the current economic downturn. The firms in that study based hour reductions on employee seniority. Employees experiencing dramatic reductions in hours are placed in the position of having to decide whether it is to their advantage to look for a new job that will provide them with more hours and earnings in the near term or to hold on to their job despite limited hours. By staying on, they may hope to accumulate enough seniority to avoid a reduction in work hours in the longer term.

Last-Minute Work Schedules

Managers employ varied scheduling practices to meet productivity targets while staying within allotted hours. One practice found in several industries is to post schedules with limited advance notice. In Lambert's (2008) study of Chicago workplaces, all but one hotel posted schedules the Thursday or Friday before the workweek that began on Sunday. Similarly, all but one retail firm posted schedules the Wednesday or Thursday before the workweek that started on Sunday. In our survey of store managers in a national apparel retailer (Lambert and Henly 2012), the majority (64 percent) reported that they typically posted a single week's schedule at a time, usually on the Tuesday or Wednesday before the workweek that began on Sunday. Posting schedules with limited advance notice makes it possible for managers to easily incorporate any changes, especially declines, in consumer demand into their employees' schedules, lessening the risk that they may inadvertently exceed corporate guidelines.

Once schedules are posted, managers also change them to accommodate demand fluctuations or other last-minute scheduling needs. The practice of adding or subtracting hours from the posted schedule a day or two in advance is rampant in many lower-level jobs (Carré and Tilly 2008; Haley-Lock and Ewert 2011; Hilton and Lambert 2012). Real-time adjustments—sending workers home or calling them in to work as demand changes during the day—are commonplace as well. These scheduling practices mean that workers' hours may vary from week to week; thus, both their schedules and their incomes are largely unpredictable (Carré and Tilly 2008; Henly and Lambert 2005; Lambert, Haley-Lock, and Henly 2012).

Preferring Employees with "Open Availability"

Varying work hours to fit demand, making last-minute changes to work schedules, and reducing work hours during seasons of low demand are made all the easier if one hires and maintains a workforce that can accommodate fluctuating hours. One strategy frontline managers employ to meet hour targets is to give preference to workers with "open availability"; that is, employees who can work varying and unpredictable work hours. HR staff in the workplaces we studied acknowledged that they gave priority to applicants who could work varying shifts. Our research suggest not only that workers with open availability are more likely to be hired, but also that they are scheduled for a greater number of hours (Lambert, Henly, and Hedberg 2011).

Workers whose availability is limited by family and other personal responsibilities are at heightened risk of low work hours and, in turn, of not meeting the hour requirements defined in public policy. For part-time workers, this is likely to be a matter of being scheduled for far fewer than the 30 hours required by TANF legislation. According to corporate records for a thirty-seven-week study period in 2008, work hours for part-time employees in a set of twenty-one retail stores in Chicago averaged 12.75 hours per week (11.18 hours, median), varying on average by 7 hours from week to week. Part-time associates who restricted their availability worked significantly fewer hours than those who did not, controlling for not only workplace and personal characteristics but also their preferences for additional hours of work (Lambert, Henly, and Hedberg 2011).

Summary

The manager practices we have highlighted call into question the basic assumptions that low-income workers can control the number of hours they work and that they can work more hours if they prefer. Rather, our discussion reveals how corporate policies and practices constrain the number of hours available to work-ers in low-level, hourly jobs. Firm policies restrict the number of hours managers have available to allocate among their staff. In turn, restricted hours, coupled with managers' penchant for keeping head count high, make it unlikely that there will be enough hours for everyone on staff. Managers' preference for work-ers with wide availability means that workers who have significant nonwork responsibilities, or limited resources to fulfill them, are particularly disadvan-taged when it comes to garnering hours of work.

The Mismatch between Job Realities and Welfare-to-Work Programs

How can the "firm as policy intermediary" lens that we have applied in this chapter help us understand the relationship between policy expectations and outcomes? As we discuss below, the twin policy objectives of quick labor force attachment and substantial labor force participation (a minimum of thirty hours per week) operate as incentives for short job searches and hasty job departures, neither of which is likely to benefit low-wage workers' economic outcomes in the long run.

First, with a policy objective of quick labor force attachment driving welfare-to-work logic, recipients' prospects are shaped almost exclusively by job avail-ability. Yet, as Lane (2000, 190) points out, "high-turnover firms are more likely to have job openings than low-turnover firms." She explains that nearly half of turnover is found in retail (which has a 26.75 percent quarterly turnover rate) and business services (21.83 percent quarterly turnover rate), industries with disproportionate shares of disadvantaged workers and welfare leavers (see Presser and Cox 1997; Lawson and King 1997). Lambert's (2008) study of low-level jobs in Chicago also reveals high rates of turnover in jobs with few hiring requirements; half of these low-level jobs had an annual turnover rate exceeding 50 percent and a third had a rate over 80 percent. The highest annual turnover rates in Lambert's study were in the transportation industry, among package handlers, where the average length of time in the job was at longest sixteen weeks for one employer, and only five to six weeks for another. According to HR staff in these firms, they were "always hiring" for package-handling jobs, which they explained was due in large part to high turnover in that job rather than business expansion. Similarly, local banks studied as part of this project reported using hiring centers with the acknowledged purpose of quickly replac-ing workers in jobs with high turnover. Holzer (1996) draws similar conclusions from a study of employers in Detroit, Los Angeles, Atlanta, and Boston, observ-ing that "the fairly high gross hire rates mostly reflect turnover rather than net employment growth" (44).

High-turnover jobs may be especially prone to cost-containment practices that limit the availability of work hours (Appelbaum, Bernhardt, and Murnane 2003; Bernhardt et al. 2008; Carré and Tilly 2008). For example, one of the firms studied in Chicago (Lambert 2008) actively recruited workers from local welfare offices, even though recruiters acknowledged that if hired, clients could expect to work ten to fifteen hours a week, less than the number needed to meet the minimum weekly work hours required by TANF at that time. The industries where welfare recipients disproportionately find employment, such as retail trade and business services, are also those that disproportionately hire part-time workers and have especially high turnover rates (Lawson and King 1997; Lane and Stevens 1997; Presser and Cox 1997). A focus on quick labor force attachment would seem to encourage the placement of welfare recipients into particularly unstable and poor-quality jobs.

Second, the policy objective of ensuring substantial labor force participation on the part of welfare recipients by requiring minimum weekly work hours also butts up against firms' cost-containment practices that cause hours to be scarce. This mismatch between what is available in the labor market and what is expected by policy would seem to create an incentive for workers to leave jobs that do not reliably deliver sufficient hours to meet program requirements. Although all workers are likely motivated to leave jobs when incurring unwanted hour reductions regardless of whether or not they are receiving public assistance, work-hour requirements provide an additional incentive for doing so. Low and reduced work hours may contribute to the high turnover rates observed in several studies of welfare recipients.

At the point of hire, it may be difficult for job seekers to accurately estimate whether a job will consistently provide sufficient work hours to meet program eligibility rules. Even in jobs in which vacancies are driven by high rates of turnover, employers are most likely to (re)fill positions at times when consumer demand is strong and the need for labor great (Holzer 1996; Holzer and LaLonde 2000). Under these conditions, even newly hired workers are likely to get enough hours—at first. When business needs change, however, or managers add more staff to increase their flexibility, the newly hired may be the first to have their hours reduced. Workers may accept a job believing that it meets the minimum hour requirements of a public assistance program. But if they find that hours decline during lower-demand periods, they may be motivated to (again) seek employment in another, or additional, job.

There is more to learn about the extent to which welfare-to-work recipients leave jobs because they cannot meet the hour requirements of programs. Research is also needed that sheds light on the role caseworker practices may play in shaping recipients' decisions of whether or not to seek new employment. The interaction between fluctuating work arrangements and welfare sanctions raises additional questions about how caseworkers deal with these circumstances. Zatz (2006b) notes that definitions of "work activities" under TANF may include more than time in paid employment. This opens the possibility that some caseworkers may count hours differently when recipients incur hour reductions. In addition, studies show that caseworkers exercise considerable discretion in applying sanctions for ostensible violations of work rules (see chaps. 8, 9, and 14 in this volume). This raises the question of when they may choose to classify work-hour reductions as noncompliance with work rules and, thus, an occasion for sanction (Meyers et al. 2006).

Job changes that result in a better job in the long term would be a positive sign of labor market advancement. But Bernhardt et al. (2001) document the "growing stickiness of low-wage careers," in which workers cycle from one poorly paid job to another, never making significant headway in the labor market. To the extent that welfare-to-work rules encourage recipients to make job changes that are only temporarily better—that is, that provide more hours for the time being while labor is in higher demand—these programs may be contributing to this stickiness of low-wage careers. Moreover, such job changes may be counterproductive in jobs where seniority brings advantages to workers.

Despite incentives to leave jobs with scarce and fluctuating hours, there are several benefits to tenure in a low-level job. First, in the United States, new workers must usually survive a waiting period, ranging from ninety days to a year, before becoming eligible to use employer-sponsored benefits such as health insurance, vacation days, or sick time, when those benefits are available at all (Lambert and Waxman 2005). Second, employers often set work schedules with seniority in mind, resulting in seasoned workers having greater input over when and how many hours they work. And, when hours are scarce, seniority may shield workers from severe hour reductions. Third, when full-time positions become available, many employers, especially in service industries such as retail and hospitality, hire full-time workers from those on their existing part-time staff who have demonstrated the work skills and schedule availability required for the position.[3] Thus, frequent job switching—even when it is motivated by an expectation of improved hours or better work prospects—nevertheless results in workers starting over at the bottom of the seniority ranking with each job change. In some jobs, seniority may bring few rewards, and workers may not lose much by forfeiting it. In other jobs, however, seniority may pay off in terms of hours, advancement, and benefits. These workers may be better off weathering hour reductions and other challenging conditions of work rather than gambling that a new job will provide greater rewards. Whether staying or moving is optimal in a given circumstance, the immediate incentives of welfare-to-work programs operate to encourage job switching when hours are insufficient or variable.

Focusing as we have on cost-containment practices that result in scarce and variable hours, our primary concern has been the difficulty low-level workers face in meeting policy expectations around minimum work hours. But in cases when minimum hour requirements are met (either by securing one good job or by working multiple jobs), low-income individuals may face a different challenge that also thwarts policy objectives. In particular, earnings increases that come with expanded work hours expose workers receiving public benefits to extremely high implicit marginal tax rates, sometimes over 100 percent (Romich 2006). Acs et al. (1998) estimate that due to high marginal tax rates, increasing minimum-wage work effort by 75 percent (from part- to full-time) results in an average 20 percent increase in household income. Romich (2006) demonstrates that the complexity and sheer opaqueness of program and tax rules around earnings increases, especially for individuals on multiple public assistance programs, makes it almost impossible for low-income individuals to make decisions that optimize the mix of work and public supports.

Given convoluted program and tax rules, combined with limited employee control over work hours, it is not surprising that low-income workers are found to be unresponsive to implicit marginal tax rates, contrary to what economic theory would predict (Meyer 2002; Keane and Moffitt 1998; Gruber and Saez 2002). Adding further to this difficult calculus, earnings increases may be short-lived, given the precariousness of work schedules, as we have discussed. Thus, workers who earn their way off programs may soon requalify for the very same programs from which they were recently terminated. Program entry, exit, and reentry are seldom seamless, though, involving additional caseworker visits and waiting periods before benefits are reinstated (Romich 2006). Moreover, the time limits on TANF benefits eventually preclude reentry altogether.

Given pressures to find a job quickly that appears to deliver enough work hours to meet eligibility requirements, welfare recipients have limited employment options. Moreover, the incentives structured into welfare-to-work programs likely propel them to seek different employment when they experience work-hour reductions, even in jobs in which seniority is a gateway to greater earnings and stability.

Discussion and Conclusion

The organizational approach we have adopted in this chapter views firms as policy intermediaries that influence the relationship between policy intentions and policy outcomes. This perspective draws attention to everyday firm practices that shape job conditions on the ground, producing insights into the fit between workplace realities and policy goals and requirements. The cost-containment policies and practices that we have highlighted here, and that are prevalent in low-level jobs today, suggest a substantial gap between policy provisions and job conditions. This may, at least in part, help explain the poor economic gains of welfare recipients observed since the enactment of the 1996 changes to welfare legislation (Acs and Loprest 2001; Blank 2002).

A work-first approach coupled with minimum work-hour requirements has been a hallmark of US welfare-to-work programs since the 1996 reforms. In the short term, focusing recipients' attention on quick labor force attachment and minimum hour requirements may effectively increase employment. This was especially likely in the tight labor market of the late 1990s, when job openings were relatively plentiful. Indeed, employment rates of welfare recipients did increase during this time (Blank 2002). However, an approach to welfare-to-work that emphasizes work first and minimum hour requirements may be untenable even in the short run during recessionary times when both job openings and hours are scarce. Perhaps more importantly, the changing nature of employment at the low end of the labor market suggests that even in relatively good economic times, available jobs are increasingly "bad jobs," subject to the cost-containment practices discussed above that expose low-income individuals to significant market risk (Kalleberg 2011).

The growing precariousness of employment amplifies calls for the state to play a more active role in protecting individuals and families from the risks of the market, or at least in mitigating their negative effects. Welfare-to-work policy, as currently implemented, does little to protect low-income families from the risks of the market and in some circumstances may even add to them. Quick work attachment increases the risk of being placed in a job with fluctuating hours and high turnover. Work-hour requirements provide an incentive to sacrifice seniority for what may be a short-lived boost in the number of hours worked.

Most ironic is how minimum work-hour requirements exacerbate the negative effects of unstable jobs on workers and their families. Instability in hours and employment provides opportunities for sanctioning families off of welfare, a prospect made more likely in welfare agencies operating under incentives favoring caseload reductions (see chap. 9). Rather than supplementing income that has been lost in the private sector, welfare-to-work policy may exacerbate a family's income loss by effectively placing recipients in double jeopardy—losing income support at a time when earned income has declined.

Welfare state scholars such as Esping-Andersen (2006, 163) have observed that welfare states vary in the extent to which social rights are conditioned on contributions to the market or whether it is possible to "maintain a livelihood without reliance on the market." The probability that public policy reduces individuals' dependence on the market relies in part on the terms by which workers are incorporated into the labor market. At the upper end of the labor market, workers such as managers and professionals may be referred to as "talent," or at least "resources," whose labor is viewed as an asset in which to invest. However, workers at the lower end of the labor market are regarded almost exclusively as a cost to be contained, and "workers" become "hours." Unlike in professional jobs, such as law or consulting, where hours are a source of revenue, in low-level jobs, hours are an expense. The practices employers use to contain outlays for labor provide a sobering view of what the US welfare state is up against should the government choose to take seriously the charge of improving terms of inclusion at the lower end of the labor market.

What avenues would be available if policy were to take seriously both the realities of low-level jobs and the goal of protecting workers from the vicissitudes of the low-wage labor market? One possibility would be to redesign welfare/workfare policy to improve its fit with job realities and its ability to mitigate the negative effects of poor job conditions on individuals and families. For example, policymakers might revise minimum work-hour requirements downward to reflect current labor market realities. This would help ensure that workers are not penalized for employer practices over which they have little control, and could help stabilize families' incomes. Simply establishing longer accounting periods for eligibility-redetermination processes would allow for fluctuations in hours and earnings—upward and downward—and help smooth variations in income that result from employer staffing and scheduling practices in hourly jobs (also see Duncan, Huston, and Weisner [2007] for a discussion of this point).

In addition, providing supplemental wages during periods of reduced work hours could give low-income workers the time and the choice to find a higher-quality job. Although we do not advocate that incentives be restructured to keep people in their current job regardless of its quality, seniority can effectively transform some poor jobs into better ones by lowering the risk of reduced hours and allowing workers to access available employee benefits. We agree with Hendra et al. (2010) that "programs designed to affect employment retention and advancement among those already working should be very deliberate about how job change and job loss are addressed." Part of this deliberation should include a recognition that returns to seniority vary by job and employer and that workforce development programs are on shaky ground when they universally promote job retention over job mobility, or vice versa.

The other direction for policy would be to intervene to improve terms of inclusion in the labor market directly, by encouraging or requiring employers to improve the quality of lower-level jobs, with regard to both wages and work hours. Requiring employers to schedule and pay employees for a minimum number of hours each week increases the fixed costs of hiring a worker, thereby countering pressures to keep head count high (Lambert, Haley-Lock, and Henly 2012). Some union contracts with hotels and grocery chains in Chicago require that employers schedule all union workers for a minimum number of hours, commonly sixteen to twenty-four hours per week. Seven states as well as a range of collective bargaining agreements incorporate "reporting pay" or "minimum daily pay" provisions that require employers to pay workers for a minimum number of hours for shifts when they report to work. But by and large, employers in the United States today face few formal constraints on the terms of employment of their lowest-level workers.

The challenges created by work-based social benefits in a time of declining job quality are not limited to the United States. Although the United States may be leading the race to the bottom among Western industrialized countries when it comes to the quality of jobs, other countries may not lag far behind. For example, in 2010, 7.3 million Germans held what are termed "mini jobs," up 27 percent since 2003.[4] As reduced-hour jobs have expanded in Germany, Denmark, and France, so have these countries' rates of involuntary part-time employment (Mason and Salverda 2009).[5] As we see it, the misfit between broader labor market trends and the move to work-based social benefits is likely to expose families around the globe to greater economic risk and insecurity.

Notes

1. See also Dagmar Breitenbach and Gerhard Schneibel, "Germany's Part-time Jobs System Is Thriving despite Fierce Criticism," *Deutsche Welle*, April 27, 2011, www.dw-world.de/dw/article/0,,15032531,00.html.

2. Fully 83 percent of the store managers surveyed in our research (Lambert and Henly 2012) in a national apparel retailer reported that staying within the hour limits set by the corporation was "very important" in scheduling their store, whereas only 32 percent said that employees' preferences for work hours and days were "very important" and 60 percent said that having the right mix of skills was "very important." Managers reported that the hour-limits directive interfered with meeting sales goals either weekly (22.4 percent) or a few times a month (19.8 percent), providing good customer service (28.4 percent, weekly; 20.7 percent, a few times a month), and giving sales associates sufficient hours (27 percent, weekly; 22.6 percent, a few times a month), and said that it got in the way of following other company directives such as maintaining minimum staffing levels (27.6 percent, weekly; 16.4 percent, a few times a month). Still, two-thirds (69.3 percent) reported rarely exceeding hour limits (14.9 percent, never; 20.1 percent, once or twice; 34.3 percent, a few times).

3. However, in retail, few workers may have the chance to move into full-time positions regardless of their seniority and work performance, because of a decline in the proportion of frontline jobs that are full-time. Carré and Tilly (2008) suggest that the greatest increase in part-time jobs in retail was in the 1970s and 1980s and that part-time employment is no longer growing rapidly in the retail sector, at least in certain segments. Still, they report that close to half of the typical workforce in a full-sized grocery or electronics store is part-time,

and others (e.g., Jordan 2011; Lambert and Henly 2010) find much higher proportions of part-time jobs in other segments of the sector.

4. Breitenbach and Schneibel, "Germany's Part-time Jobs System."

5. In 2009, 10.9 percent (4.2 million) of German workers reported that they would like to work more hours for more pay (Statistisches Bundesamt 2010).

PART III

Governance and Management

Workfare's "Second Track"

6

Triple Activation

Introducing Welfare-to-Work into Dutch Social Assistance

RIK VAN BERKEL

This chapter argues that the introduction of welfare-to-work reforms in welfare states—"activation,' as it is usually called in Europe—in practice involves a process of "triple activation." This means activating beneficiaries of social assistance, the organizations that administer benefit payments and activation services, and frontline staff in these organizations.[1] Through the processes of triple activation, welfare states redefine the rights, obligations, and responsibilities of the unemployed, transform the core business of public welfare and employment agencies, and reshape the practices of frontline workers. Beginning in the mid-1990s, the Dutch government initiated a series of reforms designed to transform social assistance from a program of income support to one emphasizing labor market participation. In this chapter I analyze this transformation to a policy regime of work activation from a triple-activation perspective.

This perspective directs attention to three key dimensions of the reform process. The first is formal policy reform. Legislative provisions are usually the focus of study in European policy research, which primarily examines social policies at the national level. This becomes problematic when reforms involve decentralization and devolution to subunits of government. Under these circumstances, policy decisions involve complex configurations of national, regional, and local actors. Thus, one must be careful about treating social policies simply as national policies (Van Berkel, De Graaf, and Sirovátka 2011).

Governance is a second dimension of the reform process. Here the analytical focus is on the principles that structure interactions between levels of government and reach down to the street-level organizations (SLOs) that implement policy (Kooiman and Bavinck 2005). Governance reforms may involve decentralization and devolution and the introduction of new public management (NPM) strategies, such as quasi markets for service provision (Considine 2001), contracting (Sol and Westerveld 2005; Bredgaard and Larsen 2007), and performance measurement (see chaps. 1, 2, 6, 8, and 9 in this volume). (In addition, reforms may involve consolidation or integration of implementing agencies [Van Berkel, De Graaf, and Sirovátka 2011].)

A third dimension of reform involves the organization of activation policy in street-level work. It examines the organizations and direct service staff that are, in effect, the actual "agents of the welfare state" (Jewell 2007). It is through the interactions between staff and beneficiaries that the practices of SLOs ultimately come to embody the modern objectives of the activating welfare state (see chaps. 1 and 2 in this volume and also Brodkin 2007; Meyers, Glaser, and MacDonald 1998; Lurie 2006). In Europe, there is limited research into the organizational dimensions of reform.[2] This chapter, like others in this volume, seeks to address this research gap, in this case using the concept of triple activation to examine Dutch activation reforms.

In this chapter I elaborate on a theme introduced by Michael Lipsky; namely, that SLBs "hold the keys to a dimension of citizenship" (Lipsky 1980b, 4). I argue that this becomes increasingly important with the introduction of activation policies that give a more significant role to frontline workers as de facto policymakers. Activation policies may affect street-level work in different ways. First, reforms that primarily involve relatively straightforward changes in income-transfer rules—for example, by altering eligibility or by reducing benefits—are likely to require relatively minor changes in street-level work. Second, more significant changes are at stake when activation policies require caseworkers to scrutinize, monitor, and evaluate the behavior of benefit recipients and to make moral judgments concerning their "deservingness" (Hasenfeld 2000; also see chaps. 11 and 12 in this volume). Third, the nature of frontline work depends on specific features of policy and governance. For example, when activation programs are uniform, standardized, and targeted at clearly defined groups, casework may be more administrative in nature than when the emphasis is on individualized assessments and tailor-made service provision (Jewell 2007; Brodkin 2009). Governance reforms may significantly impact street-level work when they increase discretion, relocate it to private providers through contracting, or alter the conditions of work through performance measurement (Larsen and Van Berkel 2009b). To speak simply of "activation policy" without recognizing its organizational dimensions may obscure these important structural variations and their implications for how activation takes shape in practice.

This chapter presents a study of triple activation in the case of Dutch social assistance reforms. It begins by briefly discussing key features of the national social policy reforms. Next, it discusses governance reforms ostensibly introduced to provide more effective and efficient implementation of activation policy. This is followed by an examination of changes in the organization of local welfare agencies—the public agencies responsible for the administration of social assistance benefits and activation. It analyzes how these agencies adjusted to the new policy and governance contexts. The next section discusses evidence from my research in Dutch welfare agencies, focusing on changes in frontline work. I conclude with a discussion of triple activation and the future prospects for Dutch activation reforms.

National Social Policy Reforms: Activating Dutch Social Assistance Recipients

In the two-tier Dutch income protection system for the unemployed, individuals qualify for unemployment insurance based on their work history. Those not eligible for unemployment insurance may receive social assistance. Social assistance is a national safety-net program, administered by municipalities, that provides a means-tested benefit to eligible households.[3] Generally, individuals receive social assistance if they have exhausted their entitlement to unemployment insurance or lack sufficient work history to qualify for it. In 2011, approximately 312,000 households received social assistance. Social assistance is not time limited, and the average recipiency extends for five years. Until recently, the national government fully funded social assistance, which contrasts with other European countries that require financial contributions from subunits of government. However, as will be discussed, Dutch funding arrangements have changed in recent years to shift some of the financial burden to municipalities.

The early 1980s marked an important turning point in the reform of Dutch social assistance. Economic recession, coupled with reforms of other social security arrangements, produced sharply increased numbers of social assistance recipients (see table 6.1).

It is in this context that the first activation reforms were introduced, largely targeting unemployed young people. Although the term "activation" was not

Table 6.1.   Social assistance recipients of working age in the Netherlands, 1980–2011 (thousands)

Year	1980	1984	1988	1992	1996	2000	2004	2008	2011
Number	217	543	467	480	481	335	339	259	312

Source: Data from UWV 2007, http://statline.cbs.nl.

used until later, social assistance provisions began to include activities and services promoting labor market participation. As local welfare agencies began to process increasing numbers of social assistance claims, the traditional social-work character of these agencies came under pressure. Casework had been based on the philosophy that people receiving social assistance needed not only income support but also social support in dealing with problems involving housing, children, debts, and social isolation, among others. This began to change, and casework increasingly focused on administrative functions involving eligibility and payments. This transformation in the traditional character of casework was legitimated ideologically as expressing a more "businesslike" approach toward social assistance recipients (Terpstra and Havinga 2001). In general, it implied a stricter focus on "people processing" technologies and a decreasing importance of "people changing" technologies (Meyers, Glaser, and MacDonald 1998). Eventually, this resulted in a shift in the profile of caseworkers. Instead of trained social workers, local welfare agencies turned to staff with an administrative educational background.

The past two decades may be regarded as the era of the activating Dutch welfare state. Two new social assistance acts were introduced in 1996 and in 2004, as well as several other measures mandating activation for social assistance recipients (Van Berkel 2006).[4] Although Dutch activation reforms had a mix of policy and governance elements, their central thrust was to strengthen work obligations and enforcement and to provide activation services. This presented a new challenge for frontline work in municipal welfare agencies.

Work requirements had long existed on the books, but welfare agencies had been relatively lax in enforcing them. In the wake of activation reforms, these agencies found themselves responsible for implementing policy provisions that ramped up enforcement of work requirements. For example, policy no longer required that a job fit the definition of "suitable work"; that is, a job consistent with an individual's qualifications and experience. Instead, it changed to obligate social assistance recipients to accept any job offer made to them, so long as it fit the definition of "generally accepted" work. (When asked what kind of work is not considered generally acceptable, policymakers usually mention one example only: prostitution.) In addition, ever-larger proportions of social assistance recipients were made subject to activation requirements, including the older unemployed, single parents with young children, and individuals regarded as "hard to employ."[5]

Significantly, changes in social assistance policy were accompanied by governance reforms. Most notably, activation was transformed from a nationally regulated program with standardized services to a decentralized and deregulated array of locally run programs. In a sense, there is no longer a "national" activation program. In addition, procedures and tools for profiling social assistance

recipients in order to sort them into activation service categories were deregulated and decentralized (RWI 2009). Municipalities became responsible for creating procedures and tools for assessing an individual's employability and labor
market difficulties. They no longer were required to use standardized national
instruments.

Governance Reforms: Activating Local Welfare Agencies

As in other countries (including those discussed in this book), Dutch activation
reforms have been accompanied by significant governance reforms. These
reforms, promulgated by the national government, were aimed at changing what
had traditionally been a bureaucratic and hierarchical mode of governance. Over
time, reform introduced elements of NPM, including contracting and performance measurement, strategies that some have characterized as relying on an
"incentive paradigm" (Van der Veen and Trommel 1999). However, the governance reforms introduced during the 1990s and 2000s were not consistently
implemented. Van Gestel, De Beer, and Van der Meer (2009) have characterized Dutch governance reforms as a "reform swamp" with no clear plan and
rapid shifts in strategy—often to correct the disappointing results of prior
reforms. As a brief history of these reform efforts show, Dutch reforms have not
constituted a straightforward shift from one dominant mode of governance to
another. Rather, they have been beset by trial and error, feedback and correction,
and inconsistency.

In the early 2000s, the national government started to make performance
agreements with municipalities and their local welfare agencies. These agreements set performance targets for the numbers of recipients participating in
activation and for job placement.[6] Farther-reaching governance reforms initiated
in 2002 required privatization of activation services. Municipalities were
required to assume the role of service purchaser and private agencies to assume
the role of service provider (Struyven and Steurs 2005; Van Berkel and Van der
Aa 2005). With public welfare agencies and employment agencies obliged to
outsource most activation services, service provision was almost fully privatized.
Implementation was contracted to private, for-profit companies, and the public
employment services (PES) were largely deprived of a role in service provision.
These dramatic changes required rapid development of a service market. They
also made the Dutch case exceptional in the European context.

Subsequently, the Social Assistance Act of 2004 made additional changes.
The 2004 act constitutes what is commonly called a "framework" act, because it
regulates the rights and obligations of the unemployed in general terms but

leaves decision making on the nature of activation and the organization of ser-vices to local authorities. Generally, this act set in motion a threefold decentral-ization process. First, a significant deregulation and devolution of policy authority took place. The act gave municipalities and their local welfare agencies considerable room to decide on the content of activation services. Second, soon after the act was introduced, municipalities were allowed more discretion in how services should be provided, retracting the previous requirement for local authorities to outsource activation services to private providers. Third, the act decentralized financial responsibilities. It shifted from a system of open-ended national financing of social assistance benefits to a block-grant arrangement.[7]

The block grant was designed to create incentives for municipalities to invest in measures that would reduce social assistance payments. If municipalities spent less on social assistance payments than the block grant provided, they could use the surplus funds in any way they liked. However, if the budget was insufficient to fund social assistance payments, municipalities would have to cover the defi-cit. These elements of the decentralization process were closely linked. The increased financial responsibilities of the municipalities were coupled with increasing municipal autonomy in policymaking and the organization of services.

Local Policy Changes and the
Organization of Service Provision

Activation reforms were justified by policymakers, in part, as a strategy for encouraging local welfare agencies to reduce individual reliance on social assis-tance. One econometric study concluded that in the period 2004–6, the new financing system reduced the number of social assistance recipients by 4 percent or 13,300 individuals (Kok, Groot, and Güler 2007). The researchers expected reductions from 2003 caseload levels of about 14 percent by 2010, from both lowering entries and increasing exits. In fact, by the end of 2010, the number of social assistance recipients of working age was 9 percent lower than it had been in 2003. As table 6.1 shows, caseloads in the 2000s remained below the peak reached in the 1980s. However, after the economic and financial crises that began in 2008, there was evidence of a new, but relatively modest, increase.

Looking beyond caseload-reduction statistics, what did increased municipal control over social assistance mean for the practices of activation? Arguably, municipal control could lead to increasing diversity in policy and practice, or it could lead to convergence. That is, decentralized policy choices could reflect local circumstances and preferences, contributing to diversity. Alternatively, municipal control could lead to convergence in policy and practices, given that all municipalities were confronted with incentives to reduce social assistance in order to keep their budgets under control. These fiscal incentives may encourage municipalities to adopt a common set of so-called best practices (sometimes defined on the basis of more or less robust and valid research data and other times simply based on common sense).

Monitor studies conducted on behalf of the association of directors of local welfare agencies provide some insights into these questions. Available data from these studies present a mixed picture. They indicate that by 2008, about half of all municipalities kept social assistance expenditures within budget caps. However, the other half faced deficits in their social assistance budgets. This picture was more or less unchanged from 2004 (Divosa 2007, 2009). It is difficult to know how to interpret these data. They could suggest either municipal resistance to reducing social assistance or an inability to contain municipal caseloads.

In 2008, the national government announced retrenchments in spending for activation services (which were funded in the so-called participation budget), with the prospect for further cuts in the context of a worsening economic climate. In the face of these cutbacks, 71 percent of municipalities indicated that they expected to pay less attention to the activation of hard-to-employ social assistance recipients, those often regarded as the most vulnerable recipients (Divosa 2008).[8] This would be consistent with a strategy of "creaming," as it would enable municipalities to manage increasing social assistance expenses by focusing their efforts on those considered relatively easy to place into jobs and, thus, remove from social assistance caseloads. As will be discussed, evidence suggests that this may have occurred.

In terms of the content of local activation programs and services, there is some evidence of increasing diversification in service provision. This can be interpreted as reflecting an emphasis on individualized services, recognizing the heterogeneity of needs of social assistance recipients. However, other evidence is contradictory. Although activation services for the hard to employ have become more diversified, the objectives of activation appear to have become more standardized, increasingly focused on work first rather than human capital development or social care. There also is some evidence that local welfare agencies have upgraded their assessment of the labor market participation capacities of more vulnerable clients, classifying them as "job ready" without notable changes in their education, training, or experience (Divosa 2007, 2008).

How this evaluation of clients' employability should be explained is not clear. One could argue, for example, that given the financial risks associated with block-grant financing, services that do not directly lead to work and/or departure from social assistance may not be considered efficient and effective. This type of financing creates incentives to give priority, at least in the short run, to the financial bottom line—that is, to making more use of work first as a way to reduce social assistance expenses.

Evidence from the monitor studies suggests homogenization rather than diversification in the activation experience of new social assistance claimants. These studies indicate that some 88 percent of municipalities had implemented work-first projects in 2008 (Divosa 2009).[9] This has important implications for new claimants, who are immediately placed in work activities as a condition for receiving income support. This strategy potentially reduces pressures on municipal social assistance budgets in two ways. First, municipalities can pay for work-first participants using their participation budget rather than their social assistance budget. Second, work-first requirements may dissuade people from claiming social assistance in the first place (Sol et al. 2007). If individuals prefer to avoid work first, perhaps they will make more effort to find a job.

Significant changes also occurred in the organization of service provision. When the requirement to outsource services was rescinded in 2004, there was a partial return to municipal provision. Services were partially demarketized, as more were provided in-house (Hefetz and Warner 2004). And they were partially deprivatized, with less contracting out to private providers, due both to more in-house provision and to contracting with other public agencies for services (Plantinga, de Ridder, and Cora 2011). In 2005, 56 percent of activation funds went to private providers (Divosa 2006). In 2008, private providers received only 22 percent (RWI 2009).

As these data suggest, the strategic choices of local welfare agencies for organizing services changed over time, in part, in response to changes in national policy. Initially, agencies tended to refer clients to external providers almost exclusively. Apart from the selection of service provider, agencies and their frontline workers were largely uninvolved in the activation process. This delegated to private providers considerable autonomy in deciding what activation would look like. Of course, the fact that outsourcing was obligatory played a key role in this strategy, but so did other considerations (De Koning 2009; Van Berkel and Van der Aa 2005). Local welfare agencies had little experience with activation services. Before activation, caseworkers were trained to apply social assistance rules and regulations in order to determine eligibility; they were not trained to intervene in people's motivation and behavior or to serve as labor market intermediaries. Referring clients to private providers relieved the urgency for changing frontline practices.

However, welfare agencies soon discovered that this strategy had disadvantages as well. When services were outsourced, municipal welfare agencies had little control over what private providers were doing. This became an increasingly important issue when contracted providers produced disappointing results. Evaluations indicated that job placements were low, services were standardized rather than individualized, and services for the most difficult to employ were poorly developed and implemented (De Koning 2009; Divosa 2005). This was troubling given the potential financial risks to municipalities. With national financing of social assistance capped by block grants, a failure to reduce social assistance rolls placed municipalities at risk of having to pay for any deficits themselves.

When municipalities were freed from an obligation to outsource, they attempted to strengthen their control over activation services. In-house service production increased, and the use of external providers changed. Local welfare agencies started to purchase more diverse services and to purchase services in different ways, including more modular approaches.[10]

Local welfare agencies also began to monitor client status more closely. This seems to have had the consequence of increasing bureaucratization for external providers, obliging them to meet specified deadlines and to deliver regular progress reports to the agencies. These consequences were revealed in a study of contracting documents in twenty municipalities (Corra and Plantinga 2009). This study indicated a strong emphasis on process-related requirements, rather than on outcomes, and suggested efforts to increase local agency control over activation processes. In a sense, the first period of outsourcing of activation services can be characterized as exporting discretion to private providers (Brodkin 2007). In the second period, discretion was partially reimported to local welfare agencies as they sought to assert more control over contracted service provision.

Reforming Frontline Work in Local Welfare Agencies

What did these reforms mean for frontline work? Unfortunately, there are limited data to show how street-level practices have adjusted to changing policy and governance. Monitor studies provide some general indicators at the municipal level, but do not give much insight into casework practices. The discussion to follow reviews the monitor studies and then turns to data from my own research (with two colleagues) in four local welfare agencies. For this project, eighty-three group and individual interviews were conducted with caseworkers, managers, and senior administrators or aldermen. Data collection took place in 2006 and 2007 (Van Berkel 2009; Van Berkel, Van der Aa, and Van Gestel 2010).

One of the issues raised by the introduction of activation concerned the division of work and the function of frontline workers in welfare agencies (Scrivener and Walter 2001; Hill 2006). As there is no national regulation concerning the organization of work in Dutch welfare agencies, the picture is diverse. About half of Dutch welfare agencies have integrated income provision and activation tasks into one frontline work function. The other half have separated the tasks (Divosa 2007).

Monitor studies show considerable variation in individual caseloads. For workers combining activation and income tasks, the average caseload was 60 in 2006. The average caseload of specialized workers varied between 91, for those responsible for work reintegration, and 130, for those responsible for "care." Care workers provide social and labor market services for the most difficult-to-employ social assistance recipients (Divosa 2007). The relatively high caseload for care workers could be interpreted as reflecting the low priority given to the most difficult to employ. Alternatively, it may reflect that more services for this group are outsourced, which was clearly the case in one of the local welfare agencies in our study. Caseloads also vary considerably among municipalities. Caseworkers have an average caseload of 167 in municipalities with more than 60,000 inhabitants, but only 52 in municipalities with 40,000–60,000 inhabitants (Divosa 2007).

Without sufficient contextual information, the data from monitor studies are difficult to interpret. Nevertheless, they suggest that one cannot assume caseloads will be lower for workers with the most difficult task—that is, for those working with the most disadvantaged client groups.

With local welfare agencies assuming a more direct service role, it is important to consider managerial strategies affecting caseworkers' functions, discretion, qualifications, and skills. The management of local welfare agencies might adopt one of the following models: a bureaucratic and hierarchical approach, professionalization, or performance-based management (see, e.g., Hasenfeld 1983; Mintzberg 1983). Each has different implications for discretion and how it is exercised.

In the four welfare agencies in our study, we found a mix of managerial strategies rather than a straightforward shift from one dominant strategy to another. Although the bureaucratic and hierarchical approach has become less dominant, it has not been abolished entirely. However, both professional and performance-based approaches have become more important. Welfare office staff we interviewed in the four agencies explicitly indicated that rules, regulations, and hierarchy had become less important and suggested that more professionalization of frontline work is needed.[11] Managers said they wanted frontline workers to have more of a role in activation processes, including client profiling, program content, service organization, and client monitoring. Most frontline workers we interviewed supported this view; but not all did. Some indicated that they would be more comfortable in a bureaucratic and standardized work environment.

All four agencies in our study introduced reforms moving toward a more professional model and increased caseworker discretion. They moved away from the previous hierarchical model of decision making in which caseworkers prepared a recommendation for superiors on a plan of action for their clients. Caseworkers now have more decision-making responsibility.[12] As part of this shift, the traditional practice of referring difficult cases to officials higher in the hierarchy changed. Caseworkers are now expected to engage with each other in a process of consultation and discussion using a professional problem-solving approach. Some agencies have introduced "quality officials" to support the professionalization process and act as consultants and have added some staff training and education.

In general, our interviews suggest that a process of professionalization is taking shape. In contrast to the administrative character of frontline work in the 1990s, with its strong emphasis on accurate and timely administration of social assistance, current management discourse and practices tend to emphasize the professional nature of activation work. This shift is consistent with the view that activation casework requires professional skills, capacities, and competencies. Whether caseworkers really have these skills, capacities, and competencies is another issue. Our observation was that many do not. Although functions changed, many traditional caseworkers are still in place.

These steps toward professionalization, although significant, do not tell the whole story. Another significant change has involved the introduction of new managerial strategies using performance measurement. Although performance indicators are not a completely new phenomenon for welfare agencies, the evaluation of frontline workers now increasingly emphasizes individual performance according to benchmarks—specifically, the share of a caseworker's clients leaving social assistance. The deployment of performance measurement in local office management can be illustrated by looking more closely at two of the agencies in our study, which specified their performance systems in detail.

One agency required caseworkers to select 40 clients from their caseload of 125 to target for removal from social assistance within a year. Perhaps even more significant, the agency was considering making staff wage increases dependent on these exit results. This would mark a considerable, arguably revolutionary, break with traditional wage systems for civil servants, which have long been based on function and seniority. A second agency also introduced performance targets for activation staff. But the caseworkers we interviewed in this agency did not seem to take these targets very seriously. They did not consider the targets to be realistic, and some did not even know what their targets were. Interview respondents complained that they had not been involved in setting the targets, and criticized them as too narrowly focused on social assistance exits, without consideration for qualitative aspects of activation and job placements.

These developments reflect what scholars have criticized as the "implicit claim to political neutrality" of NPM reforms (see chaps. 1 and 2; Brodkin 2007), which, in practice, may influence the very nature of social policy programs (also see Van Berkel, De Graaf, and Sirovátka 2011). In this case, managerial strategies using performance measurement appear to be giving primacy to reducing social assistance caseloads without recognizing other possible objectives regarding social inclusion, economic advancement, and family well-being.

In a recent study, Van der Aa (2012) found that local welfare-office performance-management systems in three large Dutch municipalities were still evolving. Activation workers were confronted with accountability for performance targets including:

- the number of clients placed in jobs, irrespective of the characteristics of those jobs;
- the proportion of individuals in each worker's caseloads engaged in activation pursuits;
- the number of clients referred to specific activation programs;
- the number of sanctions either applied or threatened (both counted toward sanctions performance targets).

According to Van der Aa, agencies varied in their enforcement of performance targets, suggesting the potential for variation in casework practices. Van der Aa concluded that performance management may not make professional activation work impossible, but it does little to promote it.

As previously mentioned, different modes of management may coexist and interact in ways that make the potential effects on frontline work difficult to predict. We found examples in which pressures for standardization, professional discretion, and performance incentives came into conflict. One example involves the use of client profiling by agencies as a means of determining an individual's readiness for work. The profiles are supposed to guide casework decisions regarding activation for each client. However, standardized profiling practices would seem inconsistent with an assessment process utilizing professional discretion. We found that profiling could be used as a tool for professional evaluation of individual client needs; or it could be used as a rote, bureaucratic procedure, effectively reducing the exercise of caseworker discretion.

Another example involves the use of what is referred to as "list work." Contracts with private providers may contain agreements about the number of clients local welfare agencies will refer to them. When spontaneous referrals fall behind targets, managers may direct caseworkers to select additional clients for referral. When confronted with list work, frontline workers effectively are constrained in responding to individual needs. Instead, reaching referral targets becomes the dominant priority in their work. In this sense, professional discretion is bounded by managerial imperatives to reach contract benchmarks.

A third example involves reassertion of hierarchical control to deal with so-called emergencies involving rising social assistance caseloads and supposed public scandals concerning fraud. Fears of emergent administrative problems and warnings of looming deficits in the social assistance budget were used to justify an immediate response. Deficits, in particular, have become increasingly salient as economic and fiscal pressures have led to cuts in the national budget for social and labor market programs. Beyond these visible budgetary responses, Maynard-Moody and Musheno (2000) have argued that in times of crisis, bureaucratic control of frontline workers will increase. List work and use of performance targets to drive down caseloads would be consistent with such control efforts but inconsistent with the drive toward increasing professional discretion.

It seems worth noting that conflicts between bureaucratic and professional modes of practice may exist not only as a matter of governance and management, but also within frontline workers themselves. Bureaucratic practices may continue, in part, because caseworkers find it difficult to cope with increasing autonomy and responsibility and continue traditional approaches. In this sense, bureaucratic practices may be resistant to change to the extent that they are embedded in frontline workers' routines and occupational identities.

It is difficult to know how the management of frontline work will develop in the future, and how these conflicting tendencies will play out. Professionalization provides a strategy for increasing street-level discretion in order to individualize activation practices. Casework professionals can now intervene in how activation processes take shape even when external providers are involved. Alternatively, bureaucratic and hierarchical management would seem to provide strategies for containing discretion and asserting managerial control, especially when emergencies arise. Finally, new managerialism provides strategies for managing the implementation of activation by creating incentives and holding caseworkers responsible for meeting specified performance targets in a discretionary casework environment.

Overall, in a context of budget deficits and cuts, it seems doubtful that conditions will favor successful professionalization of activation work. It is even possible that these conditions could lead to a return to more bureaucratic approaches, or, alternatively, to greater emphasis on performance measurement and other new managerial strategies for controlling discretion.

Conclusion

In this chapter I have argued that the shift of the welfare state from income protection to promoting employability and labor market participation has involved a process of triple activation. This means not only activating the unemployed, but also activating the organizations and frontline staff involved in policy implementation. Analysis of triple activation integrates the insights from social policy, governance, and organizational studies. The picture that emerges from this analysis is dynamic, complex, and replete with contradictions.

As discussed, a key feature of Dutch social assistance reform has involved devolution; that is, increased authority for local welfare agencies over both the content and the organization of service provision. Some of the agencies are themselves devolving more authority to frontline workers. At the same time, the new financial regime for funding social assistance has changed incentives for municipalities by making them pay (literally) for failure to reduce social assistance roles. This has led municipalities to use their managerial authority to deploy strategies that could direct street-level discretion toward the priority of controlling social assistance caseloads. This analysis points to the significance of pressures for national budget cuts in the advancement of activation reform, as these financial pressures are likely to have far-reaching consequences. Ultimately, these pressures affect frontline work in local welfare agencies by shaping and reshaping the ways in which they make activation policy in practice.

I do not attempt to generalize too broadly from the Dutch case, as it differs in certain respects from the reform path taken by other European countries. Activation in the Netherlands has been distinctive because of its far-reaching process of deregulation and decentralization (Van Berkel, De Graaf, and Sirovátka 2011) and its radical initiatives of privatizing and marketizing service provision, although these radical initiatives were partly reversed. This dramatic reversal offers another indication of the distinctiveness of the Dutch experience. In a sense, it would seem to confirm Pollitt and Bouckaert's (2000) view of the Netherlands as a public-management-reform modernizers. But the modernization process has been uneven at best and subject to strategic revision.

This case offers insights that may be used to understand the development of activation reforms in the Netherlands. First, the Dutch case may be understood with reference to specific institutional characteristics. The Dutch tradition is one in which social assistance was a part of the national safety net for the unemployed. It was not only regulated but also funded nationally. The Dutch government abandoned that tradition when it adopted a block-grant system of financing, increasing the financial risks and responsibilities of municipalities as providers of social assistance. While assuming more financial risks, municipalities also gained more room for local policymaking, which they had long been advocating. However, this devolved authority has played out in a context of fiscal and management incentives for municipalities to control social assistance participation, a major concern of the national government.

Second, the Dutch case may be understood with reference to nation-specific public values that are dominant in its political reform discourse. As emphasized in the literature on governance, each mode of governance reflects specific public values (Denhardt and Denhardt 2000). The incentive paradigm that has inspired some of the Dutch governance reforms may be viewed as reflecting the primacy of NPM values of efficiency and effectiveness over traditional bureaucratic values of equality of treatment and political values of transparency and predictability of rights and obligations. Although shifts in public values may not directly influence the work of street-level workers in a deterministic way, they may affect their actions indirectly as translated into managerial strategies and, subsequently, the treatment and social status of clients (Loyens and Maesschalck 2010; Jørgensen, Nørup, and Baadsgaard 2010). Managerial values also may be used to legitimate changing practices, in part, by representing them as nonpolitical.

In this chapter I identified several trends in governance reforms occurring in conjunction with the Dutch reform of social assistance and introduction of activation policies. Governance reforms involved multiple shifts: from bureaucracy to deregulation, from public to private service provision (and back again), from centralization to decentralization, from deprofessionalization to reprofessionalization, from hierarchical to professional modes of practice, from rule-based to incentive-based management, and from managerial strategies exporting and then reimporting discretion.

Clearly, the Dutch path to reform has been far from straightforward, and several strategies that had been adopted were later reversed, at least partially. This makes predicting future developments on the basis of current trends problematic. It also complicates international comparisons, which may look different depending on the point in time at which they are made. If anything, this analysis indicates that one should be careful in applying conceptual frameworks too rigidly: centralization versus decentralization, public versus private provision, or bureaucratic control versus professionalization versus new managerialism. Rather than an "either-or" approach, a "both-and" approach might be more useful in exploring the complex dynamics through which activation reforms are unfolding.

Notes

1. Social assistance is the Dutch program of means-tested income support for poor households.

2. See, for some exceptions, studies by Foster and Hoggett (1999); Wright (2006); Jewell (2007); and Van Berkel, Van der Aa, and Van Gestel (2010).

3. Dutch social assistance is based on households, not individuals.

4. A new social assistance act, called the Work According to Capacity Act, is currently being prepared.

5. "Hard to employ" generally refers to social assistance recipients characterized by long-term unemployment and multiple social problems.

6. Evaluations revealed considerable variation in performance results (Van Berkel 2006).

7. Municipalities receive an annual block grant ("income budget") for social assistance payments from the national government. The central government determines the national social assistance budget. Block grants are then distributed to municipalities according to a model that contains several variables that relate mainly to demographic and labor market characteristics). For details, see the website of the Ministry of Employment and Social Affairs (http://www.gemeenteloket.minszw.nl/dossiers/financieel/financiering/budgetverde ling.html).

8. The Divosa (2008) report details results of the monitor studies of the 2004 Social Assistance Act commissioned by the association of directors of local welfare agencies.

9. "Work first" in the Netherlands is an umbrella concept covering a variety of work-focused activities. According to Sol et al. (2007), work-first projects typically are characterized by an emphasis on work-like activities in a real or simulated work environment, short-term projects, or work-readiness activities, such as coaching. Under the terms of mandatory work first, caseworkers may sanction clients they regard as noncompliant with requirements. For a fuller discussion of how sanctions may be used in practice, see Lens (chap. 14) and Soss, Fording, and Schram (chap. 8) in this volume.

10. Rather than outsourcing full activation trajectories to external providers, municipalities started to outsource specific parts of these trajectories—for example, specific courses or training programs.

11. A group of local welfare agencies started a project in 2011 that was explicitly aimed at professionalizing the work of frontline activation staff.

12. In some instances, caseworkers may require a special certificate to get authority.

7

Active Labor-Market Reform in Denmark

The Role of Governance in Policy Change

FLEMMING LARSEN

D enmark is widely regarded as a "model" example of the Nordic welfare
state. Its highly developed integration of labor-market and social welfare arrangements allows for both social protection and labor-market
flexibility. Denmark is arguably distinctive in the ways in which its labor-market
policies are linked to a broader set of welfare state arrangements, generally
referred to as the "flexicurity state." Although it's difficult to describe the flexicurity concept in brief, generally, it refers to arrangements through which the
state underwrites some of the risks associated with labor-market mobility and
job instability while continually refreshing the human capital of its workforce.
Denmark has received considerable international attention for its remarkable
record of social and economic performance, often ascribed to the Danish flexicurity model (Bredgaard and Larsen 2010; Madsen 2008a; Bredgaard, Larsen,
and Madsen 2006).

Active labor-market policy—or work activation—has been part of these flexicurity arrangements for nearly two decades. However, in the early 2000s, Denmark began modifying its activation program, shifting the emphasis from
human-capital development toward a workfare or work-first model. This departure from the traditional Danish approach to unemployment constitutes a significant change in flexicurity arrangements, reallocating more of the costs of
labor flexibility and job insecurity from government to individuals. Yet this shift
has not been easily or fully achieved, in part because it runs contrary to well-
established principles of social cohesion that are deeply rooted in Danish society
and, arguably, the hallmark of modern Danish politics.

This chapter examines the Danish government's efforts to revise its active labor-market policies. It recognizes two fronts in the political project to advance a work-first approach to activation: changes made through formal policy reforms and changes advanced, less visibly, through governance reforms. Although governance reform is often presented as apolitical and neutral, it is politically consequential when it changes who has political control of implementation processes and how policy is implemented at the street level. My approach builds on a main theme of this volume, focusing on the strategic importance of governance reforms to the activation policy project (see chaps. 1 and 2). While some aspects of the Danish experience are unique to this country, its path to reform also has similarities to those of other European countries. This analysis will consider common trends as well as distinctive features of the Danish reform experience.

This chapter begins by reviewing the development of active labor-market policies in Denmark, placing them in the context of European developments more generally. It next moves from the first wave of policy reform to the second wave of governance reform, examining governance as a strategy for indirectly redefining Denmark's activation program to emphasize work first and social discipline. In analyzing the Danish case, I look first at the narrative offered by government officials to justify governance reforms. Second, I explore key governance changes and how they have altered the organizational structure of influence and incentives. Third, I draw on my empirical research in Danish municipalities to examine ways in which governance reforms have reached down to the municipal level and into street-level practice. I conclude by offering an assessment of these developments and reflections on the still-unfolding politics of Danish activation reform.

The Shift toward Active Labor-Market Policy in Europe

Active labor-market and workfare policies were widely advocated by the OECD and European Union in the 1990s (OECD 1994; European Commission 1993). During the 1990s and early 2000s, formal policy reforms swept across the OECD countries, advancing a transformation from a "passive" to an "active" approach to labor-market and social policies.[1] Typically, income support through social assistance reflected a passive approach; job preparation and placement reflected an active approach. Activation reforms generally built on the perception that the "problem" to be addressed was a deficit within the unemployed: lack of either motivation or incentive to work.

However, the specific elements have varied across OECD countries, in part reflecting important differences in national political, institutional, and cultural contexts (Barbier 2004). For many European countries, traditional policies had aimed at enhancing work competencies and skills and providing income support. However, this approach has been replaced by policies targeting work enforcement and emphasizing rapid insertion into available jobs (Jessup 1993; Lødemel and Trickey 2001; Peck 2001; Torfing 1999, 2004; Larsen et al. 2001; Barbier 2004). Policies adopting a work-first approach generally emphasize the primacy of work through use of quick job offers and programs promoting the fastest possible route to employment, operating on the premise that "any job is better than no job". Other program features include work-ability testing, tough criteria and tests for excusing or delaying work, strong sanctions for breaching work obligations, and only short-term work training, rather than more intensive human-capital-building training and education. The work-first approach has been coupled with reduced availability of income support through social assistance benefits. I refer to this approach as "work first" or "social discipline," as the term "activation" leaves ambiguous exactly what it means "to activate." Using the concept of work first distinguishes one form of activation—human-capital building and support—from another form of activation—work enforcement or social discipline (Larsen 2009).

Introducing Activation to the Danish Flexicurity State

Danish labor market policy involves a range of public benefits, education programs, and work supports. It covers workers eligible for unemployment benefits as well as individuals who do not qualify for unemployment insurance and instead receive social assistance benefits. These labor-market policies are part of the Danish flexicurity model, in which, as I will discuss, the state underwrites the development of a well-trained and agile workforce through its public labor, educational, and social policies, in effect, reducing the risks to individuals resulting from employment insecurity. As part of these arrangements, active labor-market policies have been geared toward helping workers adapt new skills to changing market requirements (a human-capital approach) and supporting labor-market transitions.

In a European context, Denmark is often held up as a model for designing labor-market policies (Bredgaard and Larsen 2010; Madsen 2008b; Bredgaard, Larsen, and Madsen 2006). Denmark follows the Scandinavian tradition of universal services and benefit provision. It also has a public sector that is relatively large by international comparison. In addition, the labor market has traditionally been characterized by limited state intervention (Larsen 2002, 2004). The Danish approach may be regarded as "liberal" in the sense that the state does not intervene in voluntary collective bargaining between trade unions and employers' associations, and job protection for the individual employee is weak (Jørgensen

2002). But, in keeping with a social democratic model, Denmark's policies also are designed to balance the needs of the labor market for flexibility, high job mobility, and periods of unemployment with the needs of individuals for income security and opportunities to build human capital.[2] Denmark's relatively generous social security system for income support and its educational and training opportunities for adults are part of the flexicurity model (Madsen 1999). Since the early 1990s, active labor-market and educational policies for the unemployed have been an important part of this model, in effect constituting the third leg of a "golden triangle."[3] As discussed, these policies help absorb the costs of job insecurity by providing training, education, and income compensation. They also are designed to create incentives for the unemployed to seek work (a deterrent to prolonged unemployment) and to help the unemployed find jobs or build human capital (a qualification effect) (Bredgaard and Larsen 2010; Bredgaard, Larsen, and Madsen 2006; Madsen 2008a).

Despite the international fame of the Danish flexicurity model and the importance attributed to its beneficial effects, the system has undergone significant changes through the introduction of formal policy and governance reforms. Policies mainly targeted toward passive income support (social assistance and unemployment benefits) in the 1970s and 1980s were reoriented toward an active labor-market policy in the early 1990s. Although containing some elements of work first, activation reforms were primarily oriented toward improving the employability of the unemployed using a human-capital approach. From the late 1990s to the early 2000s, formal policies increased emphasis on work-enforcement elements, but still retained strong elements of a human-capital approach.

In 2001, a national election ousted the Social Democrats and brought a right-center government, led by Prime Minister Anders Fogh Rasmussen, to power. Fundamental changes in both formal policy and governance followed. In 2002, policy reforms advanced under the slogan "more people into employment" continued some of the activation measures introduced by the previous government but moved further toward a work-first approach. Officials in the center-right government regarded the prior approach to activation as long-term, inefficient, and expensive. The new objective was to (re)integrate the unemployed as quickly as possible into the labor market.

From Policy to Governance: Analytic Issues

Many researchers have studied the rationales, processes, implications, and classifications of activation instruments, schemes, and programs (Jessup 1993; Lødemel and Trickey 2001; Torfing 1999, 2004). Existing research has largely tended to focus on changes in formal policy design and content, examining program elements and instruments (Lødemel and Trickey 2001; Peck 2001; Andersen, Larsen, and Jensen 2003). These studies sometimes categorize countries according to the degree of work-first elements. However, they overlook how reforms were implemented and, thus, how they really worked in practice.

This analysis takes a different approach that builds on the analytic framework for the volume (see chap. 2). More specifically, it takes account of the distinction between formal policy and organizational or operational reforms (Van Berkel and Borghi 2007, 2008). Formal policy reforms target the content (substance) of legislation, programs, schemes, and instruments for delivering benefits and providing services, among them changes in entitlements, rights and responsibilities, target groups, instruments, and program features. Organizational or operational reforms can be defined as changes in the governance structure for implementation and administration of benefits and service provision, including arrangements for interagency cooperation, decentralization, contracting, performance measurement, and reorganization of service delivery.

Why is this distinction important? Taking the case of Denmark, formal policy reforms featured fairly strong work-first elements. However, tough rules on the books were considerably softened in the course of implementation by local welfare agencies (Larsen et al. 2001). Some implementation researchers have pointed out the problem inherent in taking formal policy as the fixed point when analyzing labor-market and social policy. They argue that, for a number of reasons, the form policies take on the ground is heavily dependent on the street-level organizations (SLOs) closest to policy delivery (see chap. 1 and also Rothstein 1998; Brodkin 1990; Lipsky 1980b).

As discussed in chapter 1 of this book, governance can play an important and strategic role in shaping street-level practices. In fact, many OECD countries (and countries beyond Europe) have enacted wide-ranging operational and governance reforms as part of the activation project (Thuy, Hansen, and Price 2001; Larsen and Van Berkel 2009a; Bredgaard and Larsen 2005; Considine 2001; Sol and Westerveld 2005). As Van Berkel and Borghi (2008, 333) put it: "It is no exaggeration to state that a 'wave' of welfare reforms aimed at substantive changes in social policies has been followed by a second reform wave aimed at reorganising the institutional structures through which service provision take place."

In the first phase of governance reform, a particular target has been the centralized public employment services (PES). Denmark and other European countries gave priority to dismantling the PES and devolving employment and labor market services to decentralized agencies. One method of decentralization involved giving responsibility for employment services to municipalities (as in Denmark, Norway, and Germany). A second method was contracting out employment services (as in Australia and the Netherlands). A third was creating new specialized units placed in decentralized locations, as in the establishment of job centers, one-stop shops, and single-gateway agencies.

But decentralization creates new problems of control and accountability for central government authorities. These have been addressed, in part, by introducing new public management (NPM) reforms as a means of asserting indirect influence over a decentralized service system. NPM reforms have included contracting, performance measurement, benchmarking, management by objectives, and quality management. In some cases, this has been supplemented by old-style reforms, directly regulating the processes of service provision. The old-style reforms have included centrally designed methods and instruments: for example, standardized profiling systems, specified times for contacts, prescribed measures for selected target groups, and so forth. Overall, this hybrid of governance and management approaches can be described as a kind of decentralized centralization that has introduced new ways of doing policy through management, organizational, and implementation reforms.

But there is more to governance reforms, especially the abolition of the PES, than simply improving service delivery. In Denmark and other northern European countries, governance reforms also have been used in ways that undermine corporatist political structures. In the case of Denmark, corporatism has been very strong and embedded in state structures, including the PES, dating back more than one hundred years (Larsen 2002). The PES and other corporatist structures gave tripartite representation to government, employers' associations, and labor unions in councils, committees, and government commissions.[4] Corporatist structures enabled employers' and labor organizations to have a major influence on both policymaking and administration. They also provided a mechanism for consensus building around expansion of welfare state activities.

Corporatist structures often are recognized as crucial to Denmark's distinctive approach to balancing economic and social considerations, in part because they enable labor market organizations (employers' associations and unions) to play a central role in both politics and implementation (Madsen 2008a). This role has come under increasing pressure, partly through governance reforms targeting corporatist arrangements that provided for labor influence in policymaking and administration.

The political and administrative rhetoric used to justify governance reforms is not about politics but about the creation of more efficient (better and cheaper) administrative systems. However, even when they are presented by decision makers as "technical" and "apolitical," research has shown that these and other types of governance reforms may have fundamental and far-reaching implications, not only for political coalitions, but also for service-delivery agencies, frontline workers, and, ultimately, the unemployed. This chapter builds on this approach to governance research, examining whether Denmark's governance reforms have been used to make contested policy changes indirectly—that is, by changing the structures of governance and management and by influencing the practices of the SLOs that effectively make policy as they translate it into practice.

Institutional Structures and Governance Reforms in Denmark

After a first wave of activation reforms was introduced through formal policy-making, the Danish government introduced a second wave of governance and management reforms designed to advance a work-first agenda. Two strategic approaches were used. One involved structural reforms at the national level; specifically, dissolving the PES, which has been a key institution bringing corporatist consensus building to labor-market policy and implementation. The second involved governance and NPM reforms at the municipal level; specifically, using fiscal incentives and performance measurement to encourage implementation practices emphasizing a stronger work-first approach.

To understand this, a brief overview of the Danish labor-market system and some of its major characteristics is needed. From the 1970s until 2009, Denmark had a two-tier labor-market system. The state-run PES, as it functioned until 2009, primarily served businesses and workers covered by unemployment insurance. Municipalities had primary responsibility for welfare-oriented services and for those unemployed who did not qualify for unemployment insurance based on work history. Politically, the PES was significant because unions and employers' associations were part of its administrative structure and, thus, had a strong influence on PES services for the insured unemployed (Larsen 2002, 2004; Klitgaard and Nørgaard 2010). Labor unions also play an important role in the administration of the unemployment insurance system. The unions, usually organized by industry, administer unemployment insurance funds, making payments, checking availability, and enforcing sanctions.[5] They are supervised closely by the National Directorate of Labor.

Seen from the center-right government's perspective, there were two major problems with this system, and specifically with the PES. One was clearly political. As labor-market policy issues became more politicized and subject to criticism, the labor minister was constantly blamed for problems with the PES. The more the government took direct control, the more vulnerable it was to criticism over the PES, which was viewed as providing bureaucratic, inefficient, and ineffective services (Larsen 2009). Another problem was the corporatist structure, which gave considerable power to labor unions, enabling them to protect their members against too-strict work-first initiatives. Also, the unions and employers' associations tended to focus only on core labor, which did not fit well with the work-first project of increasing the number of unemployed (who might be outside of core business sectors and unionized industries) ready for work. Advocates concerned about workers outside the labor union system were critical of these arrangements.

But even if the PES were dismantled, what then? How could the center-right government insure that municipalities would advance its preferred work-first project? Danish municipalities have traditionally had responsibility for providing welfare-oriented services, including labor-market services for those receiving social assistance. They also had a tradition of social work approaches to dealing with the unemployed. How would they operate as implementers of activation policies oriented toward work first? The central government traditionally uses fiscal arrangements to influence municipalities. But municipalities generally retain a high degree of autonomy over the design and implementation of services for social assistance recipients. This has produced considerable variation across municipalities.

From the perspective of the central government, local control enabled municipalities to take an approach to activation that built on their social welfare traditions, rather than advancing the center-right government's shift toward a work-first model. This concern about local implementation was consistent with studies showing that the municipalities' implementation of activation policies tended to be more in line with a human-capital and social integration approach than with a work-first approach. The municipalities implemented the formal policies more "softly" than stated in legislation (Larsen et al. 2001). Many municipalities organized their employment services in traditional ways, with a strong focus on norms of professional social work and wide discretion for front-line workers. These findings, among others, gradually led to a growing conviction among leading government officials that municipalities were an obstacle to their work-first reform agenda.

The Governance Reform Narrative

As discussed, the central government faced serious problems in advancing its work-first agenda, including problems with the PES as a source of political influence for labor organizations and problems with municipalities as potential sources of resistance to the work-first project. Potential resistance to the government's policy agenda that was rooted in the corporatist structure of the PES was largely addressed by dismantling it. Once the PES was dismantled, officials turned their attention to the implementation practices of municipalities. They seemed to recognize that street-level practices could effectively undermine the strictures of work first to reflect the previously dominant human-capital-building and social assistance approaches. In this context, central government officials saw the reform of municipal job centers as "one of the most significant institutional challenges of employment policy in modern times" (Clausen and Smith 2007, 82).

The narrative used to justify the center-right government's strategy of governance reforms provides a window into its thinking. Explaining the government's decision to abolish the PES and devolve authority over employment services to municipalities, the former director of the National Labor Market Authorities (AMS) said:

> There's definitely a wish to put some distance between a minister and problem areas like the employment services. Well, if it's the responsibility of the municipalities to carry out employment policy, then the minister can't be blamed if things fail to work out the way they're supposed to. And that was very much the situation in the ministry—we were blamed, almost on a daily basis, for not doing a good enough job, so yes, there was definitely a wish to distance the minister from all that. . . .
>
> There's also a power aspect of labor market policy, and putting municipalities in charge would cut off the labor market parties from influence, and that has also played a role in the decision to do so.[6]

The minister of employment at the time, Claus Hjort Frederiksen, was particularly outspoken in his criticism of the frontline workers' implementation of municipal activation policies. He accused them of protecting the unemployed from labor-market reintegration by focusing on barriers, social interventions, and their clients' unhappy childhood rather than finding them the quickest possible route back to the labor market (Stigaard et al. 2006, 10). Frederiksen said, "I don't know how many bad social workers there are. But I know that it is a big problem every time a citizen is met by social worker mollycoddling instead of professional advice. An overdose of social understanding creates socially imbalanced results" (Frederiksen 2003a).

The gap between the government's work-first policies and local municipal practices had to be narrowed. In a speech to municipal executives in 2003, the minister of employment made it clear that "the employment system must be designed to ensure that the rules laid down by the elected parliament are complied with. . . . No Minister can live with the fact that [s]he is held accountable for something that [s]he has no influence on. We need consistency between central and local priorities" (Frederiksen 2003b).

A chorus of similar critiques came from leading civil servants in the central labor-market administration. According to the executive head of the ministry of employment, Bo Smith, and a top civil servant, Helle Osmer Clausen,

> There is often a long way from political agreements on labor market reforms to the practical implementation at the operating level. . . . On a number of occasions, implementation seems like a "black box." . . .
>
> The incentive mechanisms in the municipal part of employment policies need to balance diverse considerations, among other things because of local self-governance and municipal priorities. There is a need to do more research on how the intentions of general reforms are "translated" and run through the systems— from the central political level, through local management in the municipalities, and then to the employment and social agencies, and, in the end, to the frontline workers. (Clausen and Smith 2007, 75, 91)

As these statements indicate, once the PES was abolished, central government officials next wanted to gain strategic control over the municipal implementation of labor market policy and, through this, push implementation practices toward work first.

Implementing Governance Reforms

Following the first wave of formal policy reforms, a second wave of governance reforms began to reorganize the institutional structures through which activation policy was produced. As early as 2002, the government's first major labor-market reform ("more people into employment") created a split between purchasers and providers by partly contracting out services for the insured unemployed. The government also declared its intention of setting up new one-stop employment centers as part of a move to create an entirely municipal implementation structure that, in effect, would transfer responsibilities from the PES to municipalities and include a unified benefit system. The proposal quickly ran into strong opposition from the Social Democratic Party, unions, and employers' associations. As discussed, they favored a PES system where they had significant influence on policy and implementation.

After broad political negotiations, the government modified its plan. Beginning in 2007, it agreed to test its job-center design beginning in fourteen locations (out of a total of ninety-one job centers), with evaluation by the central labor-market administration to be completed in 2010. By classifying its plan as an "experiment," the government found a strategy to keep alive a politically disputed proposal (Brodkin and Kaufman 2000). However, in November 2008, long before the evaluation was complete, the government used a finance bill as a legislative vehicle to end the PES and give municipalities control over labor-market services, which were to be delivered through job centers. The measure also placed public financing of the insurance system with the municipalities.

Abolishing the PES not only did away with the bureaucratic centralism of the employment service, but it also decentralized labor-market politics by shifting

administration to the municipal level. Although labor-market councils maintained a corporatist structure, they lost significant influence over policymaking
and administration in this decentralized system and were relegated largely to
monitoring the performance of the job centers. Shifting the financing of unemployment benefits, formerly managed by labor unions, to municipalities was seen
by the unions, among others, as a direct attack on the union-driven insurance
funds and, hence, on the unions themselves.[7] If unions eventually were to lose
control of the insurance funds, this would pose a very serious threat to them, as
the funds constitute one of the most important channels for recruitment of new
members.

Yet, in certain respects, the center-right government's approach to governance reform seems paradoxical. It was a strategy that handed over responsibility
for employment services to municipalities while at the same time regarding
municipalities as the major obstacle to implementing the work-first approach
the government favored. It is here that other aspects of governance reform came
into play. Drawing from the familiar toolbox of NPM strategies used elsewhere
to advance a work-first project (see chaps. 6, 8, and 9 in this volume), the
government introduced a variety of managerial strategies as an indirect way of
asserting its interests. In the Danish case, one may regard these strategies as the
price municipal authorities paid for being "allowed" to take over employment
services.

The NPM dictum of "steering not rowing" has been introduced through new
performance benchmarks, output and outcome measurement, and performance
incentive mechanisms, all targeted toward a stronger work-first approach.
Although local job centers were given the operational responsibility for implementation of employment policy, the central government sought to strengthen
its influence through these instruments. Under new accountability measures, the
ministry of employment sets performance goals.[8] Municipalities, in cooperation
with the local employment council, may add performance objectives to the
municipal plan.

The local job centers are monitored regularly and subject to an annual audit
by the local employment council. If the job centers fail to meet performance
goals, the national minister for employment programs can remove administrative authority from the municipality and contract out services to private providers.[9] Monitoring results are open to public inspection, and include a variety of
data, including items such as punctuality on contacts and employment effects.
These public data allow for comparison among job centers. Public scrutiny provides opportunities that could lead to "naming and shaming," creating additional
incentives for municipal authorities to meet benchmarks. As I will discuss, this
system seems to be having an effect in changing organizational behavior, making
job centers especially attentive to the pursuit of short-term employment.

In addition to standard NPM techniques, managerial reforms adopted a more directive approach. Beginning in the early 2000s, initiatives were launched to standardize profiling and assessment of activation participants. These standardized methods focused primarily on assessing an individual's ability to work, not on discerning social problems that might be relevant to the individual's circumstances. They also gave priority to determining the fastest route to work. Essentially, they were designed to limit the discretion of frontline workers, those social workers most mistrusted by central decision makers. In addition, municipalities separated the work of job centers, responsible for implementing activation, from the work of other social welfare departments providing benefits and social help. The job center had one task: getting people into work. For central-government reformers, this reorganization provided another way to advance a work-first approach at the street level.

In the aftermath of policy and governance reforms, the next question is whether these shifts changed organizational practices and whether they have moved toward a stricter work-first approach.

Reform Effects at the Municipal Level

This section explores the consequences of governance and managerial reforms at the municipal level. Although empirical evidence to date must be regarded as preliminary, it offers a glimpse into the processes through which the work-first project been taking shape in Danish job centers.[10] First, this section examines the perspective of municipal executives, probing their views on the administration of activation programs (Larsen 2009; Larsen et al. 2001). Second, it examines the perspective of street-level staff in municipal job centers, questioning how they perceive their responsibilities, pressures, and practices. This analysis draws on evidence from studies of municipal job centers conducted by myself and my colleagues. This research includes a survey and qualitative interviews with the municipal executives. The analysis also draws on data from ongoing case studies of four municipal job centers initiated in 2010. Data for the case studies were obtained through interviews and observation, targeting staff at both the executive and frontline levels (Jørgensen et al. 2012).

Municipal Executives and the Activation Problem

Data from a survey of municipal job-center executives clearly show that they have shifted their perception of the unemployment problem to be solved from one of building human capital toward one of work enforcement. In 2001, executives reported that their most important objective was to fully consider individual circumstances facing social assistance recipients and to find ways to use training and education to help them qualify for jobs. In 2008, municipal executives gave top priority to imposing activation requirements on individuals, applying sanctions, and using activation as work-ability testing (see table 7.1). In general, executives in 2008 indicated a focus on objectives associated with work first or social disciplining (demands/sanctions, work tests, filling available jobs), with less emphasis on practices aimed at building human capital or promoting social integration (upgrading of skills/training, individual considerations, improvement of quality of life).

In 2008, the clear majority of municipal job-center executives gave priority to assuring that social assistance recipients found work as quickly as possible over improving their employability in the long run. The majority of respondents also prioritized the needs of the labor market for manpower higher than the individual wishes and needs of persons on social assistance (see table 7.2).

Between 2001 and 2008, there were noticeable changes in respondents' perception of the problem to be solved by the employment services. In the earlier period, executives indicated that the main reason unemployed individuals were not participating in an activation program was that they faced problems so severe that the program would not be appropriate. In 2008, the executives attributed

Table 7.1. Municipal job-center executives' priorities for employment services: 2001 and 2008

	Average importance ranking	
Objective	2008 $(n = 50)^a$	2001 $(n = 176)$
To impose requirements on the individual and use sanctions in case of noncompliance	2.8	3.1
To use activation as a work test (availability test)	3.0	3.5
To comply with the needs of the labor market for manpower	3.2	4.7
To use activation for upgrading skills, with an emphasis on training/education	3.3	2.8
To take into account individual considerations to comply with the wishes and intrinsic motivation of the unemployed	3.7	2.6
To improve the quality of life of the individual	5.0	4.3

Source: Data from Larsen (2009).

Note: The survey of municipal job-center executives asked, "Given the fact that employment services often call for different solutions depending on the individual case, how important, in general, do you consider the objectives below to be for your services? (Please prioritize from 1 to 6; 1 being the most important, 2 the second most important, etc.)"

[a] In 2001, there were 275 municipalities, but in 2008, only 91 following the 2007 reorganization of local governments.

Table 7.2.   Municipal job centers' prioritization of the purposes of employment policy
($n = 57$)

A	Agree with A	Somewhat agree with A	Neutral	Somewhat agree with B	Agree with B	B
			%			
The job center prioritizes that persons on social assistance find work as quickly as possible	51	26	18	4	2	The job center prioritizes that persons on social assistance improve their employability in the long run
The job center prioritizes the needs of the labor market for manpower	25	26	28	16	5	The job center prioritizes the individual wishes and needs of persons on social assistance

Source: Adapted from Larsen (2009).

Note: The survey of municipal job-center executives asked, "How does the job center prioritize the various purposes of employment policy? Please assess which statement (A or B) best matches the way the job center carries out its tasks."

nonparticipation largely to lack of administrative resources—that is, the inability of the agency to provide an activation offer to unemployed participants. In 2001, survey respondents complained about problems in finding the right measures for the most vulnerable groups, but this was not regarded as a major problem seven years later. Generally, executives' perception of the problem to be solved seems to have been reduced to one central issue: getting clients working. This is in contrast with more complex views about employment problems offered by earlier respondents, who commented on social and economic factors, human-capital concerns, and complicated social problems that might affect individuals—not just their employability, but also their well-being.

If one can assume that the individuals receiving social assistance have not changed dramatically in their characteristics and needs over this period, then one might reasonably infer that policy and, more importantly, governance reforms have changed the way municipal executives view their job priorities and responsibilities to the unemployed. These responses are generally consistent with a shift in emphasis from a human capital/social need approach to a work first/work discipline approach.

Activation and Street-Level Practices

Several key reforms have been advanced to restructure the practices of activation at the municipal level: reorganization, staffing changes, and introduction of standardized instruments for assessment and job placement. Also, as discussed, municipalities are now subject to performance measures that focus on objectives oriented toward work-first, and they operate under fiscal arrangements that contain incentives to place social assistance recipients in activation programs and into jobs. As a next step in exploring the practices of activation in municipalities, we surveyed and interviewed not only executives, but also frontline staff in order to probe how they viewed changing organizational arrangements and the effects on their work. The following discussion draws on these data.

An important precondition for changing street-level practices is the reorganization of services, moving responsibility for activation from social assistance offices to municipal job centers. The majority of executives indicated that reorganization had led staff to give a stronger priority to placing individuals in jobs, with that focus slightly stronger in cases where they assessed individuals as ready to work. Respondents also indicated that organizational specialization made it more difficult to implement a holistic approach to clients' needs. In the survey, 63 percent of the executives fully or partially agreed with this statement (see table 7.3).

Table 7.3. Municipal executives' assessment of effects of organizational division on job-center staff priorities

More job-oriented implementation	In cases of persons on social assistance assessed to be *ready* for the labor market (%)	In cases of persons on social assistance assessed to be *not ready* for the labor market (%)
Fully agree	49	24
Partially agree	18	28
Neither agree nor disagree	24	26
Partially disagree	10	14
Fully disagree	0	10
Don't know	0	0
Total (*n*)	100 (51)	100 (51)

Source: Adapted from Larsen (2009).

Note: A survey of municipal executives asked, "How do you assess the following statement? The organizational division into a job center and a benefit administration has generally led to a more job-oriented implementation."

The survey and interviews at local job centers also show a change in recruitment of staff, replacing trained social workers with staff trained to do clerical or
administrative work. In general, municipalities have been shifting recruitment
to nonprofessional staff for nearly a decade. This could be seen as a way to
diminish the role of the politically mistrusted social workers. However, the picture varies considerably across municipalities. The four municipalities in our
case studies used different strategies, varying from only recruiting professional
social workers to trying to avoid social workers altogether. Staffing patterns may
also be changed through contracting, using agencies that have a different staff
profile.

Yet another organizational change with potential implications for asserting
indirect control over local practices involved the introduction of NPM instruments focusing on performance and output. Local politicians might have been
expected to resist central initiatives aimed at reducing municipal autonomy.
However, data from this study indicated that since governance reforms were
implemented, they seemed to be paying slightly more attention to activities
associated with work-oriented performance benchmarks than to other types of
services offered to the unemployed (Larsen 2009). This is a new phenomenon.

The data also indicate signs of change in the local employment councils,
which are made up of employers' associations and labor unions. Survey results
demonstrate that they have toned down their expected aversion to transferring
employment services from the PES to municipalities, although they are still
quite critical of their own reduced influence (Bredgaard and Larsen 2009).
Another important change that may be revealed by the data is that measured
outputs have become the dominant criteria for success. This, in effect, changes
the organizational focus from input to output, and the various municipalities,
departments, units, and frontline workers have become very aware of how well
their performance compares. Our case studies clearly show an awareness of the
importance of fulfilling these performance goals at all organizational levels.

It is, however, another indirect control mechanism that has affected municipal implementation the most: the economic incentives attached to the use of
different kinds of activation measures. The state now provides a higher reimbursement to municipalities for benefits paid to unemployed individuals engaged
in activation than for those passively receiving benefits. This has created an
important economic incentive to promote activation. Recently, this incentive
strategy (selective higher reimbursements) also has been used to prioritize specific types of activation measures. Municipalities bear all the costs related to
activation but receive higher reimbursement rates based on the proportion of
individuals engaged in activation. This new financing arrangement has been
associated with a very high level of activation and has put frontline workers
under pressure to start up activation as fast as possible. At the same time, firm

budgetary restrictions apply to programmatic measures and services that can be offered, which, in effect, creates fiscal disincentives for job centers to offer longer periods of training and education. Through their indirect influence, these financing incentives appear to be moving street-level practices (and, thus, policy as practiced) from a human-capital/social-need approach to a work-first/work-discipline approach.

Despite the introduction of NPM strategies that aim at "steering not rowing," government officials have also sought to direct certain street-level practices. As described earlier, a standardized profiling system has been introduced, together with standardized methods to assess what kind of activation measures to offer to the unemployed. Survey data suggest that the prescribed methods have resulted in more standardized services compared to the former more discretionary approach, which enabled staff to take better account of the individual needs of the unemployed (see table 7.4).

The standardization of centrally preferred methods underpins a policy change toward work first. In addition to providing uniform assessment instruments, staff also must observe new rules requiring more regular and frequent contact with each client. This has substantially added to the workload of caseworkers, leaving them less time to work with individual problems and to offer more tailor-made, intensive services. There is evidence from our surveys and case studies indicating that organizational changes have affected staff perceptions of the problems to be solved as well as their strategies and practices. This evidence, although not conclusive, is consistent with a shift toward work first in street-level practice.

However, there is also evidence of some perverse side effects. New processing demands, ranging from increased documentation requirements to added contact

Table 7.4.   Municipal job center executives' assessment of changes in employment services due to creation of job centers

Assessment of visitation and methods	Responses (%)
Much more standardized	9.4
More standardized	71.7
The same as before	15.1
Less standardized	3.8
Much less standardized	0.0
Don't know	0.0
Total	100.0

Source: Adapted from Larsen (2009).

Note: The survey of municipal executives asked, "Has the setting up of local job centers led to changes in services for the unemployed in the following areas? Would you say that visitation (profiling) and methods have become [response categories listed in table]?"

meetings, take time from other casework tasks. That may account, at least in part, for some of the difficulties staff indicate they have experienced in meeting performance benchmarks for placing individuals into activation programs. In the survey of municipal executives, officials tied low activation rates to increasing demands for administrative tasks. Their estimate of how much time a frontline worker spends on administration gives a good illustration of the magnitude of the problem (see table 7.5). Municipal executives estimate that over 80 percent of their frontline workers spend 50 percent or more of their working time on administration. Similarly, time studies carried out by Local Government Denmark (the national association of municipalities) show that frontline workers spend forty-five minutes of every working hour on administration.[11]

Observations from our case studies confirm the picture of caseworkers trying to balance pressures to meet participation targets with pressures to manage a growing burden of administrative tasks. In this context, perhaps it should not be altogether surprising that some frontline workers were quite positive toward standardized assessment tools, expressing relief that they would not bear the burden of discretion in assessing and prioritizing clients. We also saw a tendency toward decoupling (Meyer and Rowan 1977; Brunsson 1989) as a means of coping with growing managerial demands. Some of the frontline workers (often those working with the more vulnerable groups) divided their work between doing what was needed to meet performance targets (e.g., making sure of meeting demands for punctuality in contacts, profiling, documentation, etc.) and reserving time for what they had previously done—namely, other kinds of work that are more responsive to individual client needs.

In these and other ways, one can see emerging from the data a picture of change in the street-level provision of employment services under the rubric of activation policy and governance reforms. Although this picture is, as yet,

Table 7.5. Municipal job-center executives' assessment of share of time spent on administrative tasks

Share of time spent on administration (%)	Responses (%)
76–100	8
51–75	74
26–50	9
0–25	8
Don't know	2
Total	100

Source: Adapted from Larsen (2009).

Note: The survey of municipal job-center executives asked, "How large a share of the frontline workers' total working hours is spent on administrative tasks (reporting, documentation, etc.)?"

incomplete, there are signs that street-level practices may be starting to produce policy on the ground that is moving toward more of a work-first approach. As discussed, this shift has been neither simple nor straightforward, and new types of problems have emerged. The transformation of activation at the street level remains a work in progress.

Danish Activation Reforms: Reflections on the Path Ahead

In Denmark, governance has been an important element in activation reforms, used strategically to move from an approach to labor-market policy emphasizing human-capital building and social protection toward a work-first approach. This can potentially mark a significant alteration of the flexicurity model by reducing the state's role in compensating workers and supporting their adjustment to a flexible labor market.

It is possible that these politically problematic shifts might not have advanced so far had they not been pursued, at least in part, by governance and management reforms that appeared to be far less overtly political than policy reforms. I argue that changing the governance structure of employment services by abolishing the PES and devolving authority to municipalities provided an indirect strategy for reducing the influence of labor-market organizations and deflecting political responsibility for labor-market services from the minister of employment (and thus the center-right government). Governance and management reforms also provided a way to indirectly influence organizational practices and street-level behavior in municipal job centers, producing the hybrid phenomenon of centralized decentralization and leading to a stronger work-first approach to activation.

Strategic use of governance and management reforms in Denmark, as elsewhere, seems to provide a way to transform unpopular and contested policy decisions into a more technical and apolitical form. It offers mechanisms for indirect political control while minimizing the threat of a reaction to that control (Brodkin 1987; chap. 2 in this volume). However, to the extent that this form of indirect policymaking is disguised and invisible to the public, it constitutes a democratic problem.

The Danish case also suggests some of the limitations of this strategy, at least in the context of a country with a deep historical commitment to welfare state policies. In the aftermath of the global recession that began to affect Europe in 2008, the issue of unemployment increased in salience, and the central government's burden to address it intensified. Although the employment minister tried to blame municipal job centers for service deficiencies, there was a veritable media storm in Denmark in 2011 indicating that decentralization may not have

fully succeeded in deflecting political responsibility from the central government. There also was heavy criticism of employment services for forcing the
unemployed into pointless interviews and activation requirements, when jobs
simply are not readily available. Perhaps predictably, if not satisfactorily, the
answer has been a call for more reform.

This analysis suggests that governance reforms were an important part of the
Danish government's project to advance a work-first approach to labor-market
policy and, indirectly, to alter the balance of the flexicurity state. Although there
is evidence suggesting that this strategy has been effective in altering the flexicurity approach, the Danish case also indicates limitations to this project, at
least in the context of a Scandinavian welfare state with strong traditions of
social solidarity and labor organizing. In this context, where there remains room
for resistance and push back, the activation project may best be understood as a
work in progress.

Notes

1. An active approach refers to measures targeted at getting the unemployed into employment. Activation can be pursued either by disciplining measures such as work-ability testing
or by integrative measures such as improvement of skills and employability. A passive
approach refers to income support or compensation provided without active work seeking or
work preparation.

2. The Danish system differentiates between unemployed insured and uninsured persons.
The insured are members of unemployment insurance funds, which are private associations
(often affiliated with the unions) of employees or self-employed persons organized for the
sole purpose of ensuring economic support in the event of unemployment. Unemployment
benefits are, however, largely financed by the state. Unemployed persons receive up to 90
percent of their former income, with a maximum benefit of approximately $3,150 monthly,
and can receive benefits for two years. Those unemployed who are not members of an unemployment fund or those unemployed for more than two years are entitled to receive means-
tested social assistance, which is administered by municipalities. For social assistance recipients over age 25, the monthly benefit in 2011 was approximately $1,900 ($2,500 for those
with children). Individuals must have assets below about $1,900 to qualify for social
assistance.

3. The golden Danish flexicurity triangle is often illustrated as having 3 sides: (1) a very
flexible labor market (with low job security, making it easy to hire and fire), (2) high state-
funded social security for the unemployed, and (3) active labor-market policy aimed at
employability. About 30 percent of the workforce changes jobs every year; 20 percent receive
unemployment benefits or social assistance; and 10 percent are part of active labor-market
programs (Madsen 2008a).

4. Most of the labor market in Denmark is regulated through collective agreements,
requiring limited state regulation. About 80 percent of employees are union members. Most
employers are members of an employers' association.

5. One explanation often put forward to explain the high unionization in Denmark focuses on the unions' administration of the insurance funds. People tend to become members of a union at the same time as they take out unemployment insurance. However, the unions have recently been losing members. There are several possible explanations for this trend, but one could be that the center-right government permitted the establishment of nonunion insurance funds.

6. Lars B. Goldschmidt, Danish Radio, 2008.

7. I would argue that the center-right government used the transfer of authority to municipalities as a tool to weaken corporatist structures. Although insurance funds have been maintained in the new structure, it is hard to imagine that the municipalities will accept, in the long run, that they are to cover expenses while the insurance funds remain in charge of administration.

8. For example, in 2008, the goals included reducing the number of unemployed out of work for more than three months, and getting 25 percent of the unemployed passive for more than one year in a job or training. On average, this group had to be self-supporting 15 percent of the time and in activation 40 percent of the time. In addition, job centers were expected to reduce the number of young unemployed (below age 30) compared to the year before.

9. This step requires consultation with the local or regional employment council or the regional employment authorities, and has not yet been put into practice.

10. A full assessment of reform's consequences poses a methodological challenge, as it can be difficult to isolate and identify impacts arising from operational reforms and impacts from other types of changes. This analysis rests on the assumption of a reciprocal relationship between the mode of organization, the perception of the problems to be solved, and the services realized. However, this goes beyond the inherent understanding in most of the literature on implementation, which tends to neglect the importance of different forms of organizational modes and practices (Rothstein 1998; Matland 1995).

11. See www.kl.dk.

8

Performance Management as a Disciplinary Regime

Street-Level Organizations in a Neoliberal Era of Poverty Governance

Joe Soss, Richard Fording, and Sanford F. Schram

Over the past few decades, neoliberal reforms have redefined the logic of governance in American poverty programs. Neoliberalism is a form of market fundamentalism that, unlike familiar laissez-faire doctrines, does not aim to reduce the state's involvement in economic relations. Instead, it seeks to restructure state operations around market principles, harness state capacities to service markets, and use state interventions to cultivate market rationalities (Brown 2003). At the level of mission, neoliberal welfare reform has entailed a shift away from income support toward efforts to turn the marginalized poor into self-disciplined "worker-citizens" who can be made attractive to low-wage employers (Korteweg 2003). At the level of operations, the neoliberal turn has decentered governance through a combination of policy devolution, privatization, and performance-centered mechanisms of accountability (Kettl 2005). Adopting the neoliberal principles of new public management (NPM), reformers have worked successfully "to replace traditional rule-based, authority-driven processes with market-based, competition-driven tactics" (Kettl 2005, 3).

By dispersing policy control to lower-level jurisdictions and nongovernmental organizations, the neoliberal project has intensified an old administrative challenge: how to ensure that policy agendas get pursued in a coherent and accountable manner. At the same time, the neoliberal turn has rendered many traditional solutions to this challenge less effective. In earlier decades, hierarchical bureaucracies with far-flung operations relied on a variety of tactics to maintain fidelity to agency-wide goals. They carefully selected and trained frontline personnel; they established action categories and clearance procedures to constrain decision making; they used budgets, inspections, and reports to stay abreast of what was happening on the ground; and so on (Kaufman 1960). In an effort to promote localized entrepreneurial innovation, neoliberal reformers eroded such strategies, working to free service providers from the constraints of bureaucratic red tape, procedural monitoring, and standards for hiring and training personnel. Thus, at the same time that central authorities were imposing a bold new agenda on welfare providers, they were weakening the traditional mechanisms that promoted street-level fidelity to a common project.

In this chapter we explore the preeminent neoliberal response to this challenge. "The beginning of the twenty-first century," Donald Moynihan (2008, 3) writes, "finds us in an era of governance by performance management." Indeed, as older methods for securing administrative coherence have been swept away, performance management has emerged as a powerful new disciplinary regime designed to focus disparate actors on a shared bottom line of results. By establishing new monitoring procedures, organized around centrally defined benchmarks, performance systems make frontline activities more legible and susceptible to influence (Scott 1998). By tying rewards and penalties to outcomes, they incentivize preferred behaviors and bring lagging service providers to heel. Under welfare reform, performance measures guide resource allocations at all levels of the system, from federal decisions about state-program funding to local decisions about whether to renew or terminate service contracts (Ridzi 2009).

Proponents of performance management rarely conceptualize it as a disciplinary regime. Typically, they present it as a way to promote efficiency and effectiveness, make better use of objective evidence, and reconcile experimentation with public accountability (Talbot 2005). The implicit promise is that local actors will be freed to go their own ways and then, later, will be judged by their performance and given the information they need to improve. The reality, however, involves a more complex interplay of structure and agency (Moynihan 2008; Radin 2006). The focusing effects of outcome benchmarks, the pressures of competition, the prospects of incurring rewards or penalties, the awareness that one is being monitored: such features of performance management do more than make agents accountable; they reshape agency itself. (On the street-level consequences of performance measurement and managerial reforms more broadly, see chapters 1 and 2 in this volume.)

In this chapter we draw on field research in the Florida Welfare Transition (WT) program to present an empirical critique of performance systems and NPM. We begin by examining organizational behavior. NPM, we show, functions as a disciplinary "grid of intelligibility" that cultivates particular habits of mind (Foucault 1997). But it does so in ways that are often self-defeating.

Unlike many critics of performance management, we do not treat perverse organizational responses as corruptions of NPM that deviate from its "real logic." We argue instead that they are predictable by-products of contradictions that lie at the heart of NPM itself. Echoing Foucault (1980), we suggest that the disciplinary power of NPM is deep and far-reaching yet also fractured, inconsistent, and incomplete.

In the second half of this chapter we show how performance-centered efforts to discipline street-level officials intensify the use of sanctions to discipline welfare recipients. Under welfare reform, sanctions for noncompliance function as a key tool for supervisory efforts to reshape client behavior (Mead 2004; Schram et al. 2009). Most sanction studies have applied econometric models to client characteristics in order to identify the groups that are most likely to be penalized (Wu et al. 2006; Pavetti et al. 2004). To date, such studies have paid little attention to how sanction patterns may be influenced by street-level organizations (SLOs). But sanction decisions are always made in the context of organizational routines and by actors who occupy specific organizational positions. To understand them, one must analyze how efforts to discipline clients are shaped by organizational cultures, structures, and routines.

Taking up this challenge, we draw on three years of field research, including participant observation and in-depth interviews, to analyze how discipline operates on both sides of the desk in the Florida WT program (for details, see Soss, Fording, and Schram 2011). After briefly reviewing statistical evidence that establishes a positive relationship between performance pressures and sanction rates, we draw on the strengths of "deep dish" field research to explain this relationship (Brodkin 2003b). Our analysis casts doubt on the claim that case managers game the system by strategically sanctioning clients to boost their performance numbers. Instead, we show how performance pressures combine with other organizational factors to push case managers toward sanctioning. Our analysis underscores that sanction decisions are more than just individual (case manager) responses to individual (client) misbehaviors. To explain them, we must understand how the work of welfare provision is organized and managed, why it operates as it does, and how organizational structures, routines, and priorities shape disciplinary action.

Performance Pressures and Organizational Behavior: Perversity in the Field

In the Florida WT program, local devolution and privatization emerged alongside one of the nation's leading systems of performance management. Each year, a state board negotiates with each Regional Workforce Board (RWB) to establish region-specific performance goals. Goal-adjusted performance measures are then used to determine state-level evaluations of the regions and RWB evaluations of service providers. Provider "pay points" are tied directly to statewide performance goals, which local contracts often specify in distinctive ways.

Performance in the WT program is tracked on a monthly basis and focused squarely on goals related to work promotion. Results are reported at regular intervals in a competitive format via "the red and green report"—so called because it uses colors to indicate the rankings of the twenty-four regions: red for the bottom six, green for the top six, and white for the twelve in between.[1]

Rankings on the red and green report have significant material consequences. Green scores can qualify a region for substantial funding supplements, while red scores can result in the termination of a local service provider's contract. Between these extremes, providers typically lose pay points and draw unwanted scrutiny when their performance falls below expectations.

NPM predicts that local organizations will respond to this system by innovating in ways that advance statewide goals and improve client services. Devolution will provide the freedoms they need to experiment with promising new approaches. Performance feedback will provide the evidence they need to learn from their own experiments and the best practices of others. Performance-based competition will create incentives for local organizations to make use of this information and adopt program improvements that work.

Previous studies suggest several reasons why organizations may deviate from this script in "rationally perverse" ways. Performance indicators provide ambiguous cues that, in practice, get "selected, interpreted, and used by actors in different ways consistent with their institutional interests" (Moynihan 2008, 9). Positive innovations may fail to emerge because managers do not have the authority to make change, access to learning forums, or effective strategies for reforming the organizational status quo (Moynihan 2008). Performance "tunnel vision" can divert attention from important but unmeasured operations and lead managers to innovate in ways that subvert program goals (Radin 2006). To boost their numbers, providers may engage in creaming practices, focusing their services on less-disadvantaged clients who can be moved above performance thresholds with less investment (Bell and Orr 2002).

Our field research confirms the primacy of performance as an organizing principle for WT implementation. Regional personnel expect to be held accountable for their outcomes. They scrutinize performance reports and keep a close eye on other regions. Most express a strong desire to improve performance through evidence-based reforms. Indeed, local officials routinely describe performance numbers as the heart of the "business model" that organizes service provision in the WT program. In a contract-centered system where performance is exchanged for payments, performance management becomes inseparable from, and is ultimately a form of, revenue management for the for-profit and nonprofit entities that invest in service provision. As one program manager put it, "If we make it [the performance standard] we get paid. Then if we don't, we get zero."

With state officials stressing the need for every region to "make its bogey" (i.e., meet its benchmarks), regional personnel rely heavily on performance measures as guides for action. As one local manager explained, "We're at the bottom of the chain, and we look up to [the state level to] see what's important. And the performance measures are how we know. When you tell me I need to do participation rate, I know what my priorities are. And that's where we spend our time." Another summarized: "This whole process with the [WT] program, it's a number thing. It's about the numbers. Your participation rate, your employment rate . . ."

Performance anxiety is, in this sense, a pervasive feature of organizational culture in the WT program. Its effects on implementation, however, deviate considerably from the optimistic predictions of NPM. Indeed, our interviews point to deep contradictions in NPM that subvert the dynamics of organizational learning and improvement promised by the model.

Consider first the double-edged nature of performance competition and its relation to trust. In theory, competition should encourage regional managers to learn from one another's experiments. Yet it also encourages them to view other regions as competitors who have a stake in outperforming them. Our site visits quickly taught us that the latter dynamic tends to undermine the former. Policy learning and diffusion require a modicum of trust, and this trust can be undermined by highly competitive performance systems. Echoing others we spoke with, one local manager explained that regions try to maintain an edge by guarding their best ideas as "trade secrets" and, in the same interview, asked us not to tell other regions about new techniques being tried at her one-stop. Another explained how high-stakes evaluations undermine learning by fostering suspicions of cheating: "They can't tell you their 'best practices' because their practice is cheating [to win the] competitive game." In these and other ways, competition works at cross-purposes with policy learning. It encourages local actors to distrust the numbers that other regions produce, the best practices they recommend, and the wisdom of sharing their own positive innovations.

Policy learning also founders on a second dynamic that flows from the discursive tensions between devolution and performance management. Statewide performance reports and efforts to publicize best practices function as parts of a discourse of generalization, suggesting that "what works there can work here too." By contrast, the discourse that justifies local devolution and problem solving trumpets the idea that communities have radically different needs, populations, and capacities. Not surprisingly, these two mind-sets clash in the consciousness of the local manager. When presented with success stories from elsewhere, local officials cite a litany of traits that distinguish the region of origin from their own. Managers in rural regions often cite resource differences in this regard, pointing out that "there are best practices that there is no way we can implement or staff." The broader tension, however, is between a discourse that denigrates one-size-fits-all ideas by celebrating local uniqueness and a discourse that treats localities as comparable and seeks to generalize innovations across them. One local official spoke for many when he used the frame of local differences to reject the practice of interregional performance competition: "Philosophically, to me it makes more sense to compare us against us. Don't compare us against Miami. Don't compare us against Orlando."

In addition to these problems, three additional dynamics flow from the fact that local managers hold discretion over how to respond to performance incentives. NPM predicts that performance pressures will encourage local actors to select more effective and efficient program strategies. At the street level, however, managers often select one strategy over another for a more practical reason: from an organizational perspective, it is simply an easier path to pursue.

The best-known form of this response, documented by many studies, is for organizations to count the same old things in brand new ways (Radin 2006). Efforts to improve poverty and employment outcomes are usually seen as arduous campaigns with uncertain consequences for performance numbers. In the short run, it is far easier to change how one counts existing conditions. Thus, local officials report that "people game the numbers all the time" by classifying in creative ways. To illustrate, one regional official explained: "We've got a client who we found out was taking her pastor to church on Sunday. We went out and asked her pastor to sign on saying this was community service. The trick is to find out what people are already doing and find a way to count it as work or community service. This is how you have to do it."

The search for easier paths also underlies a related dynamic that we will call "stream-creaming"—an extension of the conventional creaming strategy described earlier (Bell and Orr 2002). When state officials raise a program's benchmarks, they hope that organizations will work to improve their performance in that program. In an era of service integration, however, providers often hold contracts for several programs at once. As a result, they can stream-cream by shifting their energies to other programs where pay points seem easier to meet. As one local manager told us, "If they are going to make our profit closely tied to something that is so hard to fully obtain, there will be problems." The provider, he explained, would focus its limited resources on efforts to meet the softer pay points in other programs. In addition, it would seek to invest in new programs with more profitable targets. "[My employer] is committed to this welfare industry but they need to make a profit as well. We have been trying to diversify our services and clientele. For instance, we are now working with ex-offenders and things like that. We provide the support system for ex-offenders who are coming out of jail."

Finally, in responding to performance pressures, local organizations also hold discretion over whether to improve services for an existing clientele or, alternatively, reshape the clientele in ways that make it easier to make their bogey. From an organizational perspective, the latter path is usually seen as easier. To illustrate, consider the innovations adopted in what we will call Region A. Early in 2005, Region A officials attended a statewide meeting where their low performance numbers were publicly criticized. Believing that their low numbers resulted from having too many clients who were "not serious enough," Region A officials chose a path of reform designed to trim the caseload down to an easier-to-serve core of clients. The relevant changes went into effect in June 2005 and included the following:

- Intake and orientation procedures were revamped so that applicants would need to attend daily classes for at least one week before having their applications submitted. Forty hours of class attendance were required, and applicants who missed a class or showed up inappropriately dressed were required to start over the following week.
- Intake meetings with applicants were redesigned to emphasize that program requirements were difficult, time-consuming, supported by very limited assistance, and avoidable if applicants chose to pursue only Medicaid and food-stamp benefits.
- The region instituted a more frequent and intensive quality assurance system for monitoring caseworkers' handling of sanctions and work participation.
- The region created a new system for "curing" sanctions. In the past, a sanctioned client could reinstate benefits simply by contacting her caseworker and beginning to document work hours again. Under the new system, all reinstatements had to be approved by a single staff member (known locally as the "Sanction Queen"), who would be available to clients one day each week, for two hours. Sanctioned clients who missed this window would have to wait another week to return.

Staff from Region A reported that these program innovations had major effects on the region's caseload and operations. Our analysis of administrative data corroborates this perception. Between January 2003 and June 2005, the caseload of Region A followed the seasonal dynamics of caseloads throughout the state. After June 2005, however, its caseload fell far more rapidly than caseloads across the state. Indeed, Region A's caseload, which had previously shown greater-than-average responsiveness to seasonal ebbs and flows, now became less responsive than caseloads in other regions. From June 2005 to July 2006, Region A's caseload fell by an astonishing 53 percent.

As a disciplinary regime, then, the performance ethos is powerful yet incomplete. It shapes the thinking of local officials, focuses organizational behavior, and motivates efforts to innovate at the frontlines. Yet its goals are frequently subverted by actors in local organizations who hold substantial discretion in selecting their responses. Performance is the name of the game for local service providers, but it is a game organized by deep contradictions in NPM. Organizations typically respond in ways that have little to do with positive policy learning and program improvement.

Performance Pressures and Sanctioning

The story of Region A suggests that performance pressures can motivate organizations to limit program access for low-income families (Brodkin and Majmundar 2010). Do such pressures also lead service providers to pare their caseloads by sanctioning WT clients off the rolls? Elsewhere, we have presented a variety of statistical analyses that converge on an affirmative answer to this question (Soss, Fording, and Schram 2011). When Florida strengthened its performance system in 2000, sanction rates rose across the state. Under this new system, for-profit providers (who tend to be especially sensitive to pay points) sanction clients at higher rates than other providers. When regions experience declines in their performance rankings, they respond by producing higher sanction rates (and case-closure rates) in the ensuing months. Moreover, these effects tend to be strongest for subgroups of clients—African American and/or less educated—that tend to be perceived as harder-to-serve drags on performance.

With this evidence in hand, we focus in this section on *how* performance pressures influence sanction rates. The most logical candidate for a causal mechanism, and the one most clearly suggested by the literature, is the practice of creaming (Bell and Orr 2002). In this rational-actor narrative, frontline workers use sanctions strategically to rid themselves of low-performing clients, leaving only the cream clients who generate positive numbers. In addition to being well established, this hypothesis fits well with the organizational behaviors described in the preceding section. Indeed, when we started our field research with case managers, we expected to find a creaming dynamic. Our evidence failed to cooperate with this expectation, however. Today, we refer to this account as the "causal story that failed."

Why? To begin with, our interviews made it clear that few case managers adopt the stance of cold calculation presumed by this performance-maximizing model. Most view performance systems and sanctions with deeply conflicted emotions. Almost without exception, they support sanctions in principle because, as one put it, "I think realistically, you have to have teeth in the program to get people to participate." In practice, though, many worry that sanctions punish clients who are, in effect, set up to fail. The clients who confront the toughest problems, they argue, are rarely given the supports they need to meet program requirements. Many echoed the case manager who lamented, "Florida has a punitive system that gets increasingly harsh the more problems a [client] has."

Similarly, most case managers agree that performance should be evaluated but, in practice, see the program's relentless focus on performance as a frustrating barrier to humane and supportive casework: "The way we're able to [stay in business and] help people is by making our measurements on our red and green reports and getting paid, so that we can therefore in return help with childcare and support services. . . . But the more we focus on those [performance goals], the less we're focusing on the candidates. So, it's a catch-22."

As we progressed with our fieldwork, we found it less and less plausible to accept the image of case managers as calculating performance maximizers who intentionally sanction clients to improve their numbers. The creaming account was contradicted in a more fundamental way, however, by a second discovery. Throughout the state, we found broad and deep adherence to one basic belief: in the WT program, high sanction rates lower a region's performance numbers and draw unwanted attention from senior officials. As one program manager explained, "Our region doesn't want to have a sanction rate that's too high. High numbers (of any kind) draw attention to the region, so it had better be something positive." Case managers told a consistent story: "If sanctions get high, they hinder [our numbers]," so supervisors "want you to maintain your sanctions as low as possible." "No career manager *wants* to sanction." Thus, even if case managers operated as pure performance maximizers, their beliefs about means and ends would have made it highly irrational to sanction clients as a creaming strategy.

By demolishing the simplest explanation for our statistical findings, our field research left us with a considerable puzzle. Fortunately, our evidence also pointed to an alternative explanation rooted in organizational dynamics. The key mechanisms that convert performance pressures into higher sanction rates emerge from a conjunction of four factors: (1) the design of WT case management, (2) the performance pressures experienced by case managers, (3) the limited number of tools available to case managers, and (4) case managers' beliefs and frustrations regarding client noncompliance.

WT casework is designed as a highly routinized operation focused on performance-related tasks. As one regional official explained: "If you talk to any case manager here, they will tell you they're not a case manager; they're a technician. They spend about 10 percent of their time on their clients. Their time is about being a technician, and that's the way the program is written. They're doing what they have to do under this system." WT case managers typically describe their workdays as a series of clerical responses to system needs rather than as a proactive process of client engagement. Their daily round consists mostly of efforts to document clients' work-participation hours or pursue sanction procedures when clients lack documentation, such as sending out a "pre-penalty" warning letter, requesting a sanction, or working to bring a sanctioned client back into compliance. Performance documentation and sanctioning are two sides of a single coin, and, together, they stand at the center of the job.

These objective realities are reflected in the subjective focus of frontline workers. Case managers worry about performance almost continually. As one put it, "It's just weird, I mean it really is. And I don't know how to explain how, um, you know, we all run around and we're like, 'where are you at now with your [participation numbers]?' 'Oh, I'm at like 20 percent.' 'Oh man!' So we're all just stressed!" The stress felt by case managers can be traced partly to the fact that they expect performance to matter greatly for their job security and trajectory. Few expect to be fired if their numbers drop. But they are keenly aware that performance equals profit, and declining profits could lead their employer to downsize the staff or sell the operation to another company, whose retention of old employees would be uncertain. In the shorter term, most expect that if they produce weak numbers, they will be subjected to greater supervision in a way that will make their work more stressful and harder to do. One case manager explained, "We [case managers] get our own sanctions. [*laughs*] So, um, you know, that's a big stress. Um, and they also tell us, 'yeah, the entered employment; um, how many jobs are you getting?' . . . I mean, that's just things that are hit every day, fifty percent [work participation], fifty percent!"

Although case managers tend not to see sanctioning as a desirable response to these pressures, they are forced to evaluate sanction-based strategies in relative terms that are defined by a shortage of alternative tools. Case managers are limited in what they can do to raise their numbers, and they are essentially powerless to change clients' opportunities and life conditions. Very few have any formal training as a social worker, and they possess few options for matching clients to services. Opportunities to tailor program requirements to the individual or work intensively on a specific case are so rare that one case manager referred to herself as "Mrs. Cookie Cutter"—in sardonic recognition of the one-size-fits-all approach necessitated by work-first policies and a severely restricted palette of policy tools.

When clients struggle to meet their mandates, case managers typically find that, as one put it, sanctions are "just how the program works." A senior official explained: "Sanctions are the most important process we have in terms of case management and in terms of producing results." In this sense, the primacy of the sanction as a tool for coping with performance pressures emerges by default. In many instances, case managers respond to this realization with a feeling of frustrated resignation. The following quotations illustrate:

> Never mind that Deborah can't read, and she's got a 6th grade education, but you want [her to] go out and get a job at ten bucks an hour. Or, my candidate, who has a substance abuse problem, you know, he keeps drinking on the job, that's why he can't *keep* his job, but [he's] got to go out there and get a job, you know. [. . . So] I think we're more frustrated about meeting our participation rate every single month—that [fifty] percent. . . . It's a big frustration because you're like "I want to make my fifty percent. I don't want to be evaluated at the end of the month and told, "Oh, you didn't make fifty percent." What do you do?

> We try the best not to sanction clients, try to help them overcome barriers. . . . But if we follow regulations and procedures—if they [clients] don't do their part—we have to go by what the program says [and impose that sanction]. . . . The program regulations need to be looked at immediately [at the] highest level and [they need to] give us the tools to help clients to a better outcome.

Discouraged and constrained, case managers must find ways to reconcile competing demands. A small number square this circle by shifting part of the client's burden onto themselves. They put in long hours to establish the activity records needed to satisfy performance goals and avoid a sanction. With little time to spare at the office, they often spend hours at the end of the workday trying to locate clients and secure documentation. As one explained, "My level of sanction is so low. If I were to go by policy [alone], all of [my] caseload would be sanctioned. . . . I go way and beyond [the policy]: a lot of communication, a lot of calling, trying to find where they're at. 'Hey, this is what's going on. If you don't come in, your benefits are going to be stopped.'" Going further, some use "creative counting" strategies to soften the program rules confronted by clients. But such acts of subversion come at a substantial personal cost. Case managers in this group report that they are exhausted, burned out, and disappointed that their job is so often about protecting clients from the program itself.

For most WT case managers, performance pressures are a more controlling organizational reality; the stringent demands on clients are a tide they do not try to swim against. Ultimately, most believe that it is the client alone who is responsible for documenting work activities, and it is the client who must, in some way, be prodded to do so. The problem is that, aside from the threat of sanctions, case managers have few ways to motivate clients. In principle, incentives for good behavior, such as child care vouchers or transportation assistance, offer an alternative tool for influencing clients' calculations regarding desirable behavior. Most such benefits are already available to the clients, however. Thus, discussions that focus on them are, implicitly if not explicitly, about the possibility of a current benefit (or future transitional benefit) being terminated through a sanction. As one official explained, discussions of sanctions are seen as the most available and effective "tool for helping clients see the benefits of sticking with the program in order to get transitional benefits."

Thus, while case managers may want to avoid imposing a sanction, organizational forces channel them toward the threat of a sanction as a way to cajole clients into compliance. When such threats fail, as they often do, case managers quickly find themselves initiating pre-penalty actions as a way to signal that they mean business and the client had better do what is required. At this point, sanction procedures are set in motion. Computer alerts and prompts for routine action kick in, and the caseworker's discretion diminishes. If the client now fails to comply, the case manager is practically forced to move forward with the sanction in a "timely manner." As one explained: "If you have a customer who turns in fifteen [hours] instead of the twenty, at that point in time . . . you have a little flexibility to work it. *But once you start that [pre]penalty . . . process, there's no way to work around that.* It's going to pretty much take its course."

This, then, is the first mechanism linking performance pressures to sanction rates. It is a story of intentional tactics producing unintended outcomes.[2] With few tools at their disposal, caseworkers turn to threats in the hope that compliance will ensue, performance numbers will improve, and a sanction will be averted. Once set on this path, though, they must (however reluctantly) put one foot in front of the other. In a short time, they find themselves imposing a sanction that, in the abstract, they see as a hindrance to high performance.

There is also a second mechanism at work that one might expect few case managers to reveal. In a surprising number of instances, case managers report that they sanction clients out of frustration. Performance pressures contribute to this dynamic in two ways. First, as noted above, they combine with limited tools to produce high levels of frustration at the front lines. Second, the performance system is structured so that evaluations of the case manager depend on client behavior. When clients fail to turn in documents on time, for example, their actions lower the case manager's performance numbers and prompt scrutiny from supervisors. Not surprisingly, clients tend to become the focal point for case managers' frustrations in such instances. (And it is worth recalling here the extent to which case managers believe that their jobs depend on performance numbers.)

In the WT program, the noncompliant client is not just behaving in a way that concerns the case manager; she is doing something to the case manager. As one case manager explained, "The stress is, okay, well *I'm* caring about this, but the customer doesn't care. So then after a while, you still do what you got to do because you need your job, and you got to make your [measured] hours." Another reported: "When it comes to, you know, the problem cases, we get frustrated. I think some people say, 'Yeah, technically I could give her another day [to get her documents in], but you know what, I'm gonna slam it [a sanction] on her.' You know? [*laughs*] . . . It's that whole accountability thing. Because *we* have to be accountable, so I think when you get a customer that doesn't feel that they have to be *as* accountable, you can get frustrated."

This frustration-sanction dynamic was prevalent enough to be openly discussed at statewide training sessions. In discussing sanctions, one trainer began by observing that "some people want to penalize because they're angry with a client. That's not the point." In a private interview afterward, a state-level official elaborated: "There [is] no training about case management or emotional issues. Anger management is a big issue. Case managers snap and then sanction because they're mad."

In sum, the links between performance pressures and sanctioning do not run through the strategic rationality of individual case managers seeking to boost their numbers. They are more deeply embedded in the organization of case management itself. Case managers are positioned as the ultimate repository for the performance pressures that rain down on the front lines. Yet they are given few tools to respond. Lacking alternatives, they turn to the most basic threat they can wield to motivate client compliance. Predictably, the threat leads to a first procedural step, and what was intended as saber rattling turns into a sanction. At the same time, organizational conditions encourage case managers to become frustrated with clients and to perceive an injustice in the fact they are being held accountable while the client is not. In such circumstances, it is not hard to see why they occasionally snap and levy a sanction that, in the cooler light of reasoned reflection, they would prefer not to impose.

Conclusion

In poverty governance today, performance systems are shrouded by free-market images of autonomy, innovation, and efficiency. They are rarely analyzed as disciplinary regimes, yet this is precisely what they are. Indeed, the technologies of discipline that govern case managers are cut from the same neoliberal cloth as the systems designed for their clients. Both rest on incentives for right behavior and penalties for noncompliance; both aim to reshape the motivations of targets so that they will pursue preferred ends as self-regulating subjects; and neither controls behavior completely enough to forestall subversion. Just as welfare clients resist and evade the supervisory regimes of welfare-to-work programs (Gilliom 2001), so too do service providers subvert the goals of performance management. The ubiquity of resistance should not be confused with a weakness of disciplinary power (Foucault 1980). Performance pressures have profound effects on consciousness and behavior at the front lines, and these effects matter greatly for the disciplinary penalties that are meted out to the poor.

Our interviews suggest that welfare reform has initiated a tougher regime of social control, not just for welfare clients, but also for their case managers. Indeed, the high rates of sanctioning in the WT program flow from the power of this organizational regime more than from any expectations case managers have about how sanctions affect clients or performance numbers. Strong performance pressures function both as a form of coercive power that demands responsiveness and as a form of productive power that shapes subjective understandings, perceptions, and choices at the front lines.

Our analysis clearly affirms that SLOs and workers retain significant discretion (Lipsky 1980b; Brodkin 1997). We see it, for example, in the case managers who shift burdens onto themselves in an effort to protect clients, who act on their frustrations by sanctioning in cases where they need not, and who use threats and impositions of sanctions as a way to exert greater control over client behavior. We see it even more clearly in the ways that local program managers pursue strategic but perverse organizational maneuvers in response to performance pressures.

A closer look at these examples also serves to underscore the dependence of individual agency on organizational forces. In Foucault's (1980) terms, one might say that as disciplinary power instigates resistance, it also shapes the mentalities of resistance and the terrains that resistance must traverse. The frustrations that influence case managers' sanction decisions are rooted in the organization of WT casework and the pressures of competitive performance systems. Case managers turn to sanction threats for precisely the reasons emphasized by Lipsky (1980b): because bureaucratic processes push them to use their discretion in ways that lead to rationing, silencing, and disentitlement. Burden-shifting case managers, who work to protect their clients, swim against the organizational tide. But their small numbers and stories of hardship testify to the forces that make it difficult and costly to maintain such a strategy over the long haul. The organizational responses analyzed in the first section of this chapter are facilitated by managerial discretion, to be sure. But as we have seen, they are, for the most part, predictable outcomes of the structures and processes in which officials operate.

In this regard, our analysis raises troubling questions about NPM and the sharp turn toward performance systems in recent years. We are hardly the first to point out that street-level responses to performance measures can be perverse. Our contribution is to show that such problems are more various than the literature has suggested and that they do not arise as forms of deviance that distort the true logic of NPM. To the contrary, goal-subverting organizational responses flow from the internal contradictions of NPM itself—deep tensions among core principles that proponents describe as fitting together seamlessly.

Moreover, as our analysis of case managers reveals, the effects of these contradictions are likely to be understated and misconstrued by scholars who maintain a narrow focus on individual rationality. Case managers expect sanctions to hurt their performance numbers, yet they impose them in response to performance pressures. The specific dynamics involved underscore the importance of attending to the structural power of organizations and the emotional lives of individuals when trying to explain the actions of street-level administrative workers.

NPM suggests to many reformers that they can have their cake and eat it too: centralized control of outcomes *and* local autonomy; generalization of best practices *and* diverse solutions tailored to local needs; private provision *and* public purpose; competition between regions *and* collaboration among regions. It sounds too good to be true, and it is. Reformers would be better served by an open acknowledgment that contradictory features of NPM tend to work at cross-purposes. Competitive performance systems are disciplinary regimes that promote conformity. When reformers prioritize the pursuit of performance-based outcomes, they should expect the benefits of organizational diversity and locally tailored problem solving to be compromised. Conversely, if their priorities focus on local diversity and organizational creativity, they should recognize that performance pressures may need to be eased, at least for a time, to facilitate these goals. Above all, reformers should recognize that performance systems designed to hold SLOs accountable matter greatly for the disciplinary actions that get meted out to the poor. In poverty governance today, efforts to discipline service providers and welfare clients proceed as two sides of a single political project—a neoliberal project centered on market rationality and the bottom line of performing in compliant ways.

Notes

1. During the period of our study, the red and green report included three WT-specific items: the "entered employment rate" among program leavers, the "employment wage rate" based on leavers' average initial wage, and the "welfare return rate" based on the percentage of clients who left for employment but later returned to WT.

2. To be sure, sanction imposition can be seen as an intended feature of the system. Our point here is that, from the case manager's perspective, the sanction is not an intended or desired outcome.

PART IV

Street-Level Organizations and the Practices of Workfare

9

Commodification, Inclusion, or What?

Workfare in Everyday Organizational Life

EVELYN Z. BRODKIN

W elfare states are continually evolving in the context of changes in the economy, society, and the polity. This dynamism became particularly pronounced toward the end of the twentieth century as welfare states appeared to enter a period of transformation reflected, in part, in efforts to contain the provision of welfare and expand participation in work. In the United States, the workfare project has advanced under the rubric of welfare reform.[1]

As a legislative project, welfare reform was highly contentious, some twenty-five years in the making before culminating in the passage of TANF in 1996. This legislative measure marked an end to the New Deal innovation of a federal entitlement to assistance for poor families with children.[2] It reflected a turn in social policymaking, one in which income support would be routinely conditioned on work or (in the arcane language of welfare policy) "work activities." It also meant that welfare could not be relied on as an alternative to market-derived income. The federal government would finance TANF income benefits for only a limited duration, largely (although not entirely) without regard to family poverty or circumstances in the larger economy that might create economic need for longer periods.[3]

Still, the legislation was not completely one-sided. As is often the case in social policymaking, it combined regulatory features with enabling features that offered supports to those seeking to make it in the labor market. TANF and companion welfare-to-work legislation provided funds to states for education and training, child care, transportation subsidies, and other supports manifestly designed to promote and facilitate work. It also allowed extended benefits for a limited number of individuals determined to have barriers to work, such as health needs and caretaking responsibilities.[4]

The law established a framework that policymakers holding different views of welfare reform could find acceptable (Weaver 2000). It contained provisions that offered disadvantaged adults help with entering and staying in the labor market and provided income support during periods of unemployment. In this respect, welfare reform had features associated with a policy of "inclusion." This term, although imprecise, refers both to policy features that provide access to a basic income and those that provide supports for disadvantaged and lower-wage workers. The welfare reform law also contained provisions explicitly limiting the duration of income assistance and making benefits conditional on work or "work effort." These provisions are consistent with a project of commodification.

As discussed in chapter 1, commodification is a concept that gained analytic importance through Gøsta Esping-Andersen's (1990) *Three Worlds of Welfare Capitalism*, in which welfare states were grouped according to the extent to which they decommodified citizens. The term indicated the degree to which states support individual well-being based on citizenship rather than on work effort and, as a consequence, relieve the pressure to work at any cost. Esping-Andersen's analysis distinguished among social democratic, corporatist, and liberal welfare states (moving from most decommodifying to least). The liberal regimes were those (like the United States) that offered the fewest alternatives to market-derived income. Without weighing in here on the subsequent debates this view inspired, the concept of commodification offers a heuristic for conceptualizing the regulatory features of welfare reform and juxtaposing them against those that appear to advance inclusion.[5]

In terms of its formal policy provisions, welfare reform incorporated two rather different policy projects: one had the attributes of a project of inclusion; the other, a project of commodification. Policymakers on either side of the debate could present welfare reform as they preferred it or just blur the lines entirely, as President Bill Clinton did when he famously vowed to "end welfare *as we know it*," inviting listeners to fill in the blanks as to what that meant.

However, the law's formal provisions were only a prelude. After a law is enacted, another stage of policymaking begins. In the next stage, policymaking is less visible and largely indirect, taking place through the street-level practices that mediate policy on the ground (see Brodkin 1990 and chap. 2 in this volume). Although formal policy sets the framework for these practices, it does not fully determine what they will be and how they will evolve. The processes of policy delivery allow space for discretion and, in a sense, require it in order to reconcile the contradictions and ambiguities that legislative bargaining and compromise create.

In the case of TANF, these contradictions were expressed not only in the more obvious policy features that have received the greatest attention (e.g., work requirements and work supports), but also in provisions that made various demands on street-level organizations (SLOs) implementing the law. For example, policy required state welfare agencies to assess and respond to individual needs and capacities and to provide work supports, activities suggestive of inclusion. Other provisions required state welfare agencies to enforce work and subject claimants to an increasing variety of categorical and procedural tests and behavioral requirements, activities suggestive of commodification (Brodkin and Majmundar 2010; Diller 2000).

Presumably, one could review all of TANF's formal provisions and assign them to categories. But this would be a futile exercise, because the provisions alone do not indicate how they really worked. In the past, work requirements were often ignored or eased in day-to-day agency practice (Handler and Hasenfeld 1991). Similarly, income benefits provided by law were not necessarily accessible in practice (Brodkin 1986; Brodkin and Majmundar 2010; Handler and Hollingsworth 1971; Piven and Cloward 1971). Simply put, inscribing either rights or obligations in formal policy does not make it so.

In order to assess whether welfare reform—and the variant of workfare it created—constituted a project of inclusion or commodification (or something else), analysis of formal policy provisions is insufficient. It is necessary to look more closely—beyond formal provisions and stated intentions—to determine how the real world of workfare was constituted in street-level practice.

The empirical objective of this chapter is to illuminate how workfare was constructed in the everyday organizational life of a major urban welfare bureaucracy. The approach offered here is markedly different from much of the familiar policy research that studies welfare-to-work as a policy to be understood either on its own terms (i.e., by measuring changes in caseloads, costs, work hours) or in terms of individuals (e.g., by looking at the behavior or lives of poor women and their families). Instead, this chapter offers an organizational view, one that does not presume what policy *is*, but rather looks at what SLOs *do* in order to illuminate policy as produced and explore its implications. This inquiry asks: What were the practices of workfare; what shaped their evolution; and how did SLOs construct inclusion, commodification, or possibly something else on the ground?

Stacking the Deck? Governance, Management, and the Practices of Workfare

With its mix of policy complexity and delegated discretion, TANF effectively imbued SLOs with a major role in shaping policy. To the extent that the project of reform depended on SLOs, it created a new problem: how to manage the work of policy implementation in a complex and discretionary environment. In this case, Congress used governance and management provisions to address—if indirectly—both the political problem of "What counts?" and the managerial problem of implementation.

How were these provisions used to manage policy work? TANF devolved considerable autonomy to states to set policy and organize practices. But mistrusting states to be tough enough on work, Congress set benchmarks for welfare-to-work participation, specifying a menu of acceptable activities and establishing an escalating participation rate. By the five-year mark, 50 percent of welfare recipients in single-parent households were required to participate in work activities for thirty-five hours per week. Ninety percent of adults heading two-parent households were required to participate in work activities for thirty hours per week.[6] The law also specified the kinds of activities that would count toward meeting these quotas, among them paid work, job seeking, unpaid workfare (in which recipients worked off their welfare benefits at minimum wage or provided child care for other welfare recipients). It also limited the use of education and vocational training as countable activities to meet participation benchmarks.

In addition, TANF rewarded states for reducing their caseloads, in part by providing a financial bonus to states that did so. The law disallowed credit for caseload cuts achieved by imposing new eligibility rules that excluded categories of poor adults. But otherwise, states benefited from cutting caseloads whether by improving the economic prospects of poor families or by pushing people into bad jobs or simply off welfare.

Arguably, these provisions were designed to encourage good programmatic practices and administrative prudence. However, when incentives are unbalanced, encouraging caseload reduction without penalizing or otherwise discouraging wrongful exclusion or poor-quality services, organizational theory would predict that quality is likely to be compromised and that organizational practices will be skewed toward those dimensions of performance that count. The relationship between performance incentives and practices, although indirect, can be pervasive and powerful, as studies in this book demonstrate.

From an organizational perspective, TANF's governance provisions can be viewed as effectively defining the policy goals that mattered, emphasizing accountability for work enforcement and caseload clearance. These provisions were as significant for what they did include as for what they did not. TANF's governance provisions did not hold states accountable for providing the right services to the right people, for assuring access to eligible families, for providing any particular quality of services, or for improving the lives of poor families. In a little-remarked nod to this last concern, there was brief debate in Congress over an amendment to measure TANF's antipoverty effects on children.[7] However, these concerns were not incorporated into the final bill. On the whole, governance provisions emphasized practices more closely associated with a project of commodification than one of inclusion.

It is an empirical question whether governance and managerial arrangements that rewarded caseload reduction and work-activity quotas—largely without reference to how they were achieved—biased policy implementation in ways not recognized in formal law or in the managerial accounting of performance measurement. Consider, for example, that "successful" performance in caseload reduction can be achieved by informally making it more administratively difficult for individuals to get and keep benefits. Clearly, that does not represent the same outcome as caseload reduction achieved by advancing opportunities for individuals to make it in the labor market. Yet measuring performance in terms of caseload reduction and work-activity quotas cannot distinguish between these fundamentally different types of practices.

This raises critical questions for analysis. How did SLOs adapt to new policy and governance arrangements? What did these adaptations mean for the real world of workfare and the production of inclusion, commodification, or something else on the ground?

Research Approach

This inquiry builds on two well-known scholarly traditions. One is associated with organizational research that examines policy delivery at the street level. The study of "street-level bureaucracy" investigates how policy is made through the discretionary behaviors of those at the front lines of policy delivery (Lipsky 1980b). A second tradition is associated with the Chicago school of sociology in that it grounds analysis of social relations in particular settings in order to give it depth and context. In this case, the analysis of policy processes is located in specific organizational settings in order to develop a deeply contextualized understanding of how they are formed and what they do. As discussed in chapter 2, this approach sees SLOs as politically embedded, both reflecting and refracting the larger environment in which they operate.

Empirically, this analysis draws on my organizational ethnographic research in three selected Chicago welfare offices as well as findings from my collaborative quantitative studies of organizational practices (Brodkin and Majmundar 2010; Brodkin, Fuqua, and Waxman 2005). The Chicago case was selected not to represent all welfare agencies, but to probe everyday life in a big-city welfare agency responsible for the vast majority of the state's welfare caseloads and serving urban clients—a population whose poverty was arguably at the heart of welfare reform. Field research was conducted in three welfare offices purpose-fully selected to focus on locations serving areas with concentrated urban pov-erty, while varying in theoretically relevant organizational elements, including office size, race/ethnicity of welfare recipients, rate of caseload decline in the first year after welfare reform, and neighborhood.[8] Intensive field research con-tinued over a three-year period (1999–2001) with follow-up visits and inter-views in the subsequent two years.

The research utilized methods of semistructured and open-ended interviews, observation, and, on occasion, participant observation. This included shadowing caseworkers through their days and simply hanging around in order to observe routine organizational and case-management activities. It also included exten-sive observations of caseworker-client interactions that were part of the pro-cesses of assessment and eligibility review, training sessions, job clubs, and management meetings. In addition, interviews were conducted with state-level managers, as well as the regional-level managers responsible for each of the local offices studied and the top three to five management staff members in each office.[9] Other data sources include agency and business documents, case materi-als from legal challenges and complaints, administrative data and reports, and evidence from evaluation and research studies.[10]

The analysis uses the extended case method, in which "the significance of a case relates to what it tells us about the world in which it is embedded" (Bura-woy 1998, 281). The first-order objective of an organizational ethnography is to reconstruct agency practice in terms of its own internal logic. This involves a systematic examination of both the conditions of work and the content of prac-tice, moving heuristically between the two in an effort to explain the particular form that implementation takes in specific settings. The second-order objective is to relate these practices to the larger political context in which they are embedded. In this case, the objective is to consider the street-level construction of workfare and whether it advanced a broader project of either inclusion or commodification.

Workfare in Everyday Organizational Life

To briefly set the context for this analysis: Everyday life in a Chicago welfare office is difficult to describe and, for some, perhaps, difficult to imagine.[11] For caseworkers, there were the endless piles of paperwork, lines of clients waiting to be seen, supervisors demanding to be satisfied, balky computer and telephone systems to contend with, and periodic retraining in the nuts and bolts of case management as rules and procedures changed. For clients, there were the hours of waiting in rows of plastic chairs in often overheated or overcooled buildings;

the repeated demands to appear at the welfare office and to provide documents proving various aspects of their status; the job-club lectures about how to smile, shake hands, and show a good attitude toward employers; and periodic negotiations over what must and can be done.

Within local welfare offices, participation rates and caseload reduction were closely watched, consistent with performance requirements incorporated into TANF law. In interviews and observations, managerial staff in local welfare offices often referred to unremitting pressure from state-level superiors to meet performance benchmarks. Said one manager, "We'll all either live or die with these results." Another commented, "My sphere of influence depends on the numbers. If they're bad, I'll have a lot of explaining to do." Said a third, "It's all about the numbers. We play games to make the numbers."

It is in this context, where policy and managerial reforms intersected, that managers and frontline staff engaged in the activities that came to constitute the real world of workfare. The following discussion focuses on four types of practices that had particular significance for shaping that world and creating commodification or inclusion in everyday organizational life.

Administrative Practices: Informal Barriers to Income Support

Organizations operate as informal gatekeepers, developing modes of operation that affect the ease or difficulty of claims making. Operational practices—both formal and informal—can add hidden costs to claims making to the extent that they are complicated, confusing, or cumbersome. Individuals implicitly recognize these costs when they complain of being "tied up in red tape" or given the "bureaucratic run around" (Moynihan and Herd 2010). These types of hidden organizational costs can have systematic effects, resulting in administrative exclusion—that is, nonparticipation attributable to extralegal organizational factors rather than formal provisions of law or individual preference (Brodkin and Majmundar 2010). To the extent that otherwise-eligible citizens are excluded from participation by these organizational practices, citizens lose access to cash assistance that provides an alternative—or sometimes a subsidy—to paid labor. Like formal eligibility rules (including time limits), exclusion constitutes the blunt edge of commodification. However, unlike formal rules, administrative exclusion constitutes a largely hidden and extralegal form of commodification, making it difficult not only to observe, but also to challenge.

Barriers to access are sometimes intentional, but not necessarily so. They may occur as a by-product of decisions made on other grounds. In the TANF case, governance provisions favoring caseload reduction created state-level incentives to underinvest, advancing and assuring access to benefits for eligible, needy families. Other things being equal, underinvestment in access would be rational, whether purposeful or an inadvertent consequence of decisions to direct limited resources to other priorities. As long as the minimum requirements of law and due process were met, additional investments that would increase the capacity of street-level staff to respond to claims and individual need would constitute an inefficient use of resources.

In Chicago, underinvestment was evident in inadequate paper-management systems, malfunctioning telephones, and inadequate computer systems. These types of problems were documented and repeatedly criticized by federal agency reviewers as well as caseworkers and their union.[12] Given work tasks that involved high caseloads and complicated processing requirements, infrastructure limitations created conditions at the street level in which individual responsiveness was likely to be quite burdensome for caseworkers and to come with few, if any, organizational rewards. As a corollary, the more complex and difficult the case, the higher the caseworker burden, making conditions for responsiveness to individual needs and circumstances even less favorable. Simply stated, difficult working conditions and limited administrative resources make it harder to be individually responsive to clients. Given these resource limitations, one would expect street-level work to adapt by developing informal practices that minimized casework burdens (e.g., time, effort, etc.), while maximizing measured performance.

Cost shifting is one common type of street-level adaptation to managing the burdens of case management under conditions of administrative underinvestment. Consider that records management is a major task for caseworkers, who must obtain, record, retain, and frequently update numerous documents establishing aspects of family status, compliance with work rules, educational progress, and so forth (Lurie 2006; Diller 2000; Brodkin and Majmundar 2010). Without a relatively sophisticated system for computerizing records, caseworkers frequently misplaced documents or had difficulty locating them when needed. Missing records put caseworkers at risk of negative performance reviews when their files were inspected for compliance with documentation requirements. These conditions favored street-level adaptations that shifted the cost of document management to clients when possible.

For example, one common adaption was to require claimants to resubmit missing records. The potential cost to claimants of replacing documents could be relatively minor. But it could be more substantial when clients depended for documentation on the cooperation of third parties such as employers, landlords, or doctors, who were not easily accessible or well disposed to requests for replacement documents. More problematic, caseworkers could avoid the risk of negative performance reviews by automatically sanctioning or terminating clients for noncompliance when documents were missing rather than asking—and waiting—for replacements. Inappropriate sanctions or terminations were not monitored by local, state, or federal performance metrics. One study showed that case-processing difficulties—including problems of administrative disorganization and confusion—accounted for 72 percent of reported administrative problems (Brodkin, Fuqua, and Waxman 2005).

Another type of street-level adaptation involved time-management practices that increased caseworker efficiency in claims processing, but as a by-product increased the effective costs of claiming for clients. Observations revealed that some caseworkers routinely scheduled multiple clients for the same appointment time. They explained that they did this so they would not waste time if a client was late or failed to appear, but would always have a ready pool of cases to process. This may have improved processing efficiency for caseworkers, but it also added time costs for claimants. For some, waiting amounted to a relatively minor inconvenience. But for others—for example, claimants who had appointments with doctors or potential employers or needed to pick children up from school—unexpected waits were more problematic.

This could put claimants at risk of losing benefits for noncompliance if they were not correctly recorded as appearing for scheduled appointments or if they needed to leave before they could be seen. This risk was not trivial, at least in two of the larger offices observed, because procedures for entering the offices did not work properly. In fact, caseworkers themselves were frustrated by malfunctioning intake processes, because they lost time when they were not informed that clients were waiting in the lobby. This was so common that some caseworkers routinely told clients to bring money for the public telephone so they could call them on arrival. But these efforts also could be thwarted because the telephone systems did not function properly, and clients phoning from the lobby might be unable to reach their caseworker or leave a message.

These types of informal cost-shifting and time-management adaptations are significant when they effectively become structured into routine practice as a logical adaptation to underinvestment in administrative infrastructure. It is not possible to know the full extent of these and other, similar adaptations because they occur out of sight of managerial accountability instruments. However, caseworkers themselves, at times, accused their managers of purposefully increasing the frequency of appointments in the expectation that some clients were likely to be late or miss appointments, permitting them to be removed from their caseloads.[13]

The routine types of hassle, red tape, and mismanagement associated with underinvestment matter because they make benefits hard to get and to keep. These factors were associated with caseload decline, not only in Chicago (Brodkin, Fuqua, and Waxman 2005), but also nationally (Brodkin and Majmundar 2010). By preventing the acquisition of social assistance through informal, extra-legal means, these practices of administrative exclusion effectively functioned as mechanisms of commodification, perhaps even double commodification. They denied poor families access not only to cash assistance, but also to the training and social support features of workfare that ostensibly advance inclusion.

Simplification, Reductionism, and Access to Supportive Services

As discussed, street-level practices associated with achieving participation rates and caseload reduction were closely monitored. This occurred not only at the local office level, but also in smaller units of four to seven caseworkers, where supervisors reviewed performance metrics regularly, commonly intensifying surveillance and pushing for improvement when caseworkers fell short. In this context, caseworkers used their discretion to devise adaptive strategies that reflected a street-level calculus of costs and constraints.[14] These strategies effectively reduced the cost of complex tasks such as assessing, sorting, and supporting individuals, tasks that were ostensibly part of a policy design aimed at human-capital development and labor-market inclusion. One street-level adaptation involved a variety of reductionist strategies that lowered the cost of what is familiarly known as "meeting the numbers." These strategies included simplification, categorization, and redefinition of the casework task to enhance processing efficiency. These patterned adaptations did not need to be conscious or purposeful in order to have systematic effects—that is, positive effects on processing efficiency, as well as negative effects in terms of responsiveness to need and wrongful exclusion.

Reductionist adaptations enabled caseworkers to expedite processes requiring them to assess individual client needs and devise programmatic plans to fit them. For example, one caseworker saved time by preparing assessments in advance of meeting her clients. Another caseworker, a specialist in a referral unit for clients with drug and alcohol problems, demonstrated how she expedited the process of determining barriers to work and service referrals, permitting an observer to sit in on the assessment process. With each client she quickly went down the written checklist of questions—"Do you have an abuse problem?"—ticking boxes. She then, almost instantly, came up with a program referral. Asked how she could manage such a complicated task so quickly, she responded that she selected programs on the basis of zip code. When asked whether other elements of fit entered into consideration, she said that she knew little about either the programs or the individuals, but assured the observer that it was best for clients to attend programs nearest to their homes.

Although specific strategies varied, speed-over-need adaptations generally functioned to maximize processing efficiency. The logic of such practices was illuminated in extended observations of one caseworker, the most celebrated in his office, recognized by managers for his exceptional productivity. This case-worker (who I will refer to as Mr. Frank) consistently held the top position in the "Fifty Percent Club," an honor conferred on caseworkers who exceeded performance standards by achieving work-participation rates of 50 percent or higher. Observation provided an opportunity to ascertain how he achieved that success. In a sense, he was a master of strategies that enabled him to simplify complex job tasks (such as assessments and referrals), limit demands for individualized responsiveness, and suppress potential complaints.[15]

First, Mr. Frank achieved scheduling efficiency by arranging all appointments for only two days of each week (leaving other days free for paperwork) and scheduling each of his clients (on average about ten per day) for the same hour of 9:00 a.m. This strategy enabled him to shift the cost of waiting for appointments from him to his clients. Given a clientele composed largely of single mothers, there were those for whom waiting meant they might not be able to pick up their children at school. Those who did not remain were subject to penalties for noncompliance and termination of benefits. Mr. Frank at times advised clients to bring money for the pay telephone in order to call him from the waiting room. But he was rarely available to answer the phone, and the office lacked a functioning message system.

In addition to cost shifting, Mr. Frank also developed simplification strategies that enhanced efficiency in the assessment process. He discouraged claimants who tried to present complicated personal issues to him, in part by asserting that their problems were outside his domain (regardless of whether that was the case). He used informal decision rules that saved time and allowed him to ration scarce services. For example, one week he referred nearly every client to a single welfare-to-work service provider. When asked why he made the same referral for each client, he replied that he sent them to his "favorite" program, his favorite being the one that submitted paperwork to him on time, enabling him to process casework more expeditiously.

Asked if that was the right match for each client, Mr. Frank readily acknowledged that he did not know. He explained that he regarded these placements as an informal test. Those who met this test proved they "deserved" an opportunity later to move into a more suitable program. Those who complained or did not comply he regarded as undeserving. Essentially, Mr. Frank demonstrated the classic street-level strategy of redefining his clients to fit his processing routine. By this strategy, those demanding responsiveness to their individual situations were likely to be labeled as troublesome.[16] In his own words: "We send 'problem people' to 'work first.'" Work first was unpaid work assignments, positions that most clients disliked and some argued were unfair. For Mr. Frank, clients who accepted these assignments demonstrated that they were deserving, and those who complained were a problem. "It's up to you," he told one client who objected to the assignment. "You cooperate or you don't."

Mr. Frank readily acknowledged that he assigned individuals to service providers that he knew did not deliver on their promises. He described one agency, which told clients that after forty days of unpaid work they would be placed in paid positions. But "they're still in work first for six to nine months." When asked why he continued to use this agency, he explained, "That's a safety valve to lower your caseload." Compliance would raise his participation rate; noncompliance would reduce his caseload. Either contributed to his efforts to excel in measured performance, and he did. Mr. Frank added that the hardest thing about his job was cutting people's benefits when they did not comply with his decisions. He explained that "it was really hard at first. I was thinking about these poor children without food. . . . But it comes down to whose job do I like more—theirs or mine?"

No single example can capture the variety of street-level adaptations favoring speed over need. However, this case is instructive in revealing how street-level practices responded to organizationally structured opportunities and constraints. Singled out by management for his excellent performance, Mr. Frank not only demonstrated but articulated the logic of street-level work that prevailed in everyday organizational life. It was a logic largely unbalanced by countervailing incentives regarding access, responsiveness, and appropriateness of caseworker judgments about services and needs. It also demonstrated a practice logic that was skewed against practices that might advance inclusion through well-targeted, quality labor-market training and other initiatives. While these informal practices were functional for the welfare agency and the state government in saving money and meeting benchmarks, they were dysfunctional for welfare recipients seeking to make it in the labor market or trying to maintain access to income benefits provided by law.

Rituals, Symbolism, and Realities: The Case of Job Clubs

Street-level work involves more than paper pushing or eligibility reviews. Caseworkers also are expected to function as labor-market intermediaries and job-search coaches. Although many states contract out these types of services, the first step toward either services or employment is participation in local-office job clubs, where the welfare-to-work process begins.

Under TANF governance provisions, participation in job clubs counted toward federal work-participation benchmarks. Federal law set participation hours and required that participants search for jobs, but otherwise did not specify what job clubs should do. In Chicago, operational discretion largely was delegated to job-club staff. There were no formal criteria that qualified case-workers for job-club positions. From the point of view of caseworkers, these positions were desirable because they allowed for greater autonomy and less paperwork than standard casework positions.

Once staff were assigned to these positions, what were the conditions under which job-club practices took shape? First, resources were limited. Generally, leaders received a room to meet in, access to the department's general database of employers, and, at times, a TV and video player. They did not receive special training in the provision of services for job seekers, yet had discretion in design-ing programmatic activities that would take place in job-club sessions. Second, they were subject to management oversight focusing on compliance with atten-dance and job-search requirements, both of which were necessary in order for job-club participation to count toward the agency's participation benchmarks.

Observation in scores of job-club sessions suggested that, on the whole, case-worker practices under these circumstances were idiosyncratic, dependent on available resources and the skills and inclination of job-club leaders. In a context in which staff did not have access to a steady supply of suitable jobs or a clear technology for supporting job-seeking efforts, they developed strategies that enabled them to manage their responsibilities, in part by developing ritualized activities that filled the time, met performance benchmarks, and possibly offered affective benefits of hope and support for some participants. That said, these rituals could be strikingly disconnected from the realities of the lower-wage labor market that was the primary employment source for welfare recipients.[17]

For example, at one job-club session, a group of women, mostly minority and unskilled, were told to watch and discuss a film about searching for a job. The film featured young, white, male professionals preparing to interview for white-collar business jobs. Job seekers were advised to buy a good wool suit and to have a stationer print their resumes on high-quality paper. While women (mostly African American or Latino) in sweatsuits watched and discussed the film in one room of the welfare office, in another room, employers from freight-service companies were interviewing other recipients for packing and shipping jobs. One company recruiter described her hiring criteria this way: "I don't care if they wear nose rings and have tattoos all over their bodies. If they can be at our building at 5 a.m. and lift 60 pounds, I'll hire them." However, the company found few recruits, in part because the shipping center was in a suburb about one hour by car from the welfare office and unreachable by public transportation.

Ritualization could take many forms. In another welfare office, a job-club leader fashioned herself into an Oprah-like dispenser of self-help wisdom and inspirational personal stories. Participants could be seen emerging from her ses-sions pumped up and chanting positive slogans ("We can do it!"). Despite the obvious enthusiasm of the participants, it was not clear that the types of job-club wisdom dispensed in these sessions, mostly about appearance and personal characteristics (sometimes referred to as "soft skills"), were necessarily relevant to their employment prospects. Job-club staff did not receive any systematic feedback regarding the quality or effectiveness of their efforts. The only performance that mattered was that linked to benchmarks for client attendance and number of job applications submitted.

The disjuncture between the ritualized world of the job club and the real world of lower-wage work appears, at first glance, to illustrate a standard implementation problem, in which lower-level irrationality and discretion undermine higher-level objectives. However, this view ignores the terms of governance that make such practices rational for both the street-level worker and the organization itself. Given the limited resources under which job-club staff operated and the skewed performance benchmarks for which they were accountable, ritualization at the street level was an adaptive strategy. Arguably, this strategy was not only adaptive at the individual (caseworker) level, but also at the agency level (and possibly beyond), to the extent that it appeared to provide help to job seekers—in effect, deploying "myth and ceremony" to obscure the absence of material support (Hasenfeld 2000).

In this sense, job clubs may be regarded as more symbolic than practical in their function, substituting rituals of uncertain value for practices more likely to contribute to human-capital development. Symbolically, they appear to engage in efforts to advance inclusion, while, instead, reaffirming the problematic moral status of those receiving cash aid without work (Hasenfeld 2000; Handler and Hasenfeld 1991).[18] To the extent that the practices of job clubs generally developed in a context of resource constraints and lack of accountability for value added, one would have to conclude that their everyday practices functioned in ways more consistent with a project of commodification than one of inclusion.

Delegitimating Claims on the State

A project of commodification can be said to advance when policies and practices reduce the ability of citizens to make claims on the state for protection from market vulnerability and receive income support that allows, at minimum, for the basic necessities of life. Commodification may be produced through informal organizational practices that function to delegitimate claimants and claims making, in part by redefining claimants from citizens in need (entitled to responsiveness from the state) to dependent (and potentially inauthentic) claimants, subject to caseworker discipline and sanctions.[19]

Delegitimation may not be a matter of conscious strategy. Rather, it may be a by-product of the street-level adaptation to work demands in the context of limited resources and skewed performance incentives. In this case, as discussed, street-level practitioners informally adapted to organizational conditions, in part by limiting access; they adjusted to resource limitations by using strategies such as simplification and ritualization. However, these strategies alone could not adequately suppress the demand side of workload equation. Moreover, they had the potential to create cognitive dissonance for caseworkers who may have wanted to do more to help, but found they could not, creating the potential for street-level resistance to managerial pressures.[20] It is in this context that delegitimation emerged as an additional adaptive strategy.

Usually this kind of subtle adaptation must be inferred indirectly from extended field research. But on rare occasions it was possible to observe informal processes of delegitimation taking shape more directly and actively encouraged by management, although certainly not portrayed or understood in these terms. Observation of local-office sessions called "staffings" (a term borrowed from the medical world for meetings in which medical professionals jointly review key cases) provided a window into this process. At staffings, welfare office managers and supervisors met with a professional consultant (who had a PhD in social work) to review selected cases, specifically targeting those that were not contributing to participation benchmarks.

At one staffing the consultant presented the agency's formal casework model, called "the pipeline," which she described as a "tool to determine client's needs." In a rather Orwellian spin, the pipeline was actually used as a tool to convert clients with problems into problem clients. It sorted them into three categories representing their position in the welfare-to-work process. They were either

- *lost*—"avoids contact with service providers, angry and resentful"
- *stuck*—"follows only the letter of the plan, easily discouraged"; or
- *flowing*—"is on time for appointments, enthusiastically participates."

In a rare formalization of client redefinition, the agency used the pipeline to explain why clients weren't working in terms of their own personal deficiencies in belief, attitude, or behavior, not in terms of their skills, health, or family issues, the availability of job opportunities, or the difficulties of managing work and family in the lower-wage labor market. Clients who were deemed at risk of imminent failure to make it through the process were informally referred to as "waste."

The view of clients as deviants to be brought into line was reinforced in staffings where casework supervisors were called to account for clients who were not meeting work-participation requirements. In virtually each case, supervisors who claimed their caseworkers' clients could not work because they were homeless or mentally ill or had some other serious problem were pressed to reconsider these clients as suspect at best and unwilling to comply at worst. This included cases in which the formal record documented serious health or mental problems. When a supervisor attempted to argue that a client with a documented mental illness could not work, the staffing leader insisted, "If you can't do anything, that means you're in a vegetative state. There are no medical exemptions—only barriers."

Staffings were conducted in ways that instructed street-level supervisors and their caseworkers to redefine both the task and the client, a strategy that is ordinarily employed in less-visible form. In effect, staffings defined the task of casework not as one of assessing or responding to individual needs and circumstances, but as one of pushing clients through the pipeline and placing blame for failure largely on the clients themselves. At staffings unit supervisors were called to account for cases that did not contribute to performance benchmarks. They were instructed to regard claims of individual need with suspicion and nonworking claimants with skepticism.[21] At one session the staffing leader passed around the file of a recipient who had received an exemption from work requirements because she was homeless (an exemption permitted by law). The leader challenged the group to look at the photo in the file. "Does she look homeless to you?" she demanded.

The sessions made clear that supervisors and their caseworkers could—and would—be called on the carpet for excusing individuals from work requirements, even if those excuses were arguably permitted—even ostensibly required—under good-cause exemptions in the law. Supervisors brought this approach to their casework units, through means of instruction, surveillance, and pressure on caseworkers to justify any case that did not contribute to participation benchmarks. For caseworkers, the option to consider clients' problems and offer exemptions became that much harder.

This is not to say that street-level responsiveness to clients or resistance to management were entirely precluded. Some caseworkers were responsive, and even bent the rules for favored clients. But they operated under conditions that generally favored a less responsive, even a more punitive approach. One test of sorts of this proposition is to see how caseworkers responded to individuals they found especially sympathetic or deserving of help. In one encounter, a caseworker burst into tears as she prepared to sanction a client whose child had cerebral palsy and had been struggling to sit erect in a stroller while her mother was interviewed about her noncompliance with work requirements. The mother had missed some welfare-to-work classes because she had to make emergency trips to the health clinic with her child. The caseworker privately expressed anguish to an observer, but was nonetheless reluctant to grant an exception or even bring the matter to her supervisor.

In another instance, a caseworker expressed concerns about a client who seemed willing but unable to conduct the required number of job searches each week or show up for meetings on time. The caseworker was distressed that she had sanctioned the client for noncompliance, and worried that the woman had seemed fatigued, sad, and in ill health. An observer suggested that these could be symptoms of clinical depression, which would qualify for exemption and referral to a mental health unit.[22] The caseworker expressed surprise at the suggestion, but, thinking out loud, said that she might have latitude to refer this one case because otherwise her "numbers" were high.

These disturbing examples are striking given that welfare law permits, even requires, exemptions in these cases. But these features of law were less relevant to street-level practice than governance provisions measuring work participation and caseload benchmarks. Of course, the patterns of street-level practices described here might have been disrupted if there were substantial counterpressure by citizen-claimants that altered the choice calculus for caseworkers. However, opportunities to assert an alternative conception of citizenship rights have traditionally been quite limited in welfare settings (in this volume, see Adler, chap. 13; Lens, chap. 14; also see Felstiner, Abel, and Sarat 1980; Levine 2013; Soss 2000). Far more relevant to everyday practice were the general terms of TANF governance, which were largely indifferent to dimensions of performance related to responsiveness to claimant needs or attentiveness to service quality.

Assessing the Real World of Workfare

Welfare reform and its workfare provisions were highly contested as a matter of explicit legislative policymaking. Making the case for welfare reform, proponents argued that it offered a strategy for bringing disadvantaged citizens into the market economy and out of marginalized status; in effect, that it was a policy of inclusion. Opponents argued that workfare provisions would "regulate the poor" (Piven and Cloward 1971) and either drive them into a labor market where they would face economic hardship and insecurity or simply drive them to destitution. From that perspective, welfare reform constituted an instrument of commodification. TANF's formal provisions could be marshaled in support of either view. They limited income benefits and imposed work requirements. But they also introduced new work supports and maintained assistance (if temporarily) for those judged to face special barriers that prevented employment.

This analysis brings an organizational perspective to this debate, directly examining the street-level practices through which the real world of workfare was constructed. The approach adopted here permits analysis to probe beneath categorical policy terms, managerial metrics, and even the ways in which street-level practitioners and beneficiaries perceive their experiences. This close examination of street-level practices in one big-city agency and at one (extended) point in time may thus limit generalization in certain respects. But it also reveals how common, structural features shaped the practices of workfare and how street-level workfare practices developed at the intersection of formal policy provisions, organizational arrangements, and managerial instruments. One would expect different conditions to produce different practices. However, the common elements of workfare as a policy strategy and the extensive use of new managerial instruments as an administrative strategy are not unique to this case, as the studies in this book demonstrate.

The patterns of practice highlighted here were not fully ordained by formal policy and rules, but they were shaped, if less visibly, by governance and managerial arrangements. Performance measurement was virtually ubiquitous and infused into the very fabric of organizational arrangements and practices. These arrangements indirectly but systematically fostered practices that emphasized welfare reform's commodifying features and undermined its supportive ones. This imbalance was exacerbated by the absence of counterpressures sufficient to mitigate reform's most harmful, regulatory effects. On balance, administrative appeals, legal challenges, and other forms of advocacy, although important, have tended to be limited and case specific (Lens, chap. 14), while managerialism exerts a broad and systemic influence.

This study's portrait of the real world of workfare is more consistent with a project of commodification than one of inclusion. It also reveals how the practices of commodification take shape in everyday organizational life. Formal policies set the stage but informal practices seal the deal. This is especially problematic because informal practices are not readily visible or easy to discern. Nor are they captured in the limited language of administrative metrics.

This analysis highlights the problematic nature of political accountability when there is a disjuncture between what policy purports to do and what it actually does. Too often, when welfare-to-work and other types of poverty programs do not improve the economic and social well-being of the poor, policymakers blame the poor themselves. Perhaps they didn't try hard enough or weren't sufficiently compliant. However, this look inside the practices of workfare tells a different story. It is one in which poor adults seeking assistance have little control over what they get and whether it has any real value. This is not to say that all programs are badly run or that no one gets services of value. Indeed, there may be some programs that beat the odds, although most likely because of conditions are that are specific and situational.

But the overall record of welfare reform—or US-style workfare—is troubling, at best. One result is unambiguous: welfare caseloads dropped dramatically across the United States. In the first five years after welfare reform, the number of individuals on the welfare rolls declined 57 percent. At the ten-year mark, caseloads were down by 64 percent.[23] Caseloads rose slightly in the aftermath of the US recession, but not nearly as much as rising unemployment would have indicated (Pavetti, Trisi, and Schott 2011).

If a process of commodification took place, one would expect to see a reduction in state-provided income as an alternative to market-derived income. In fact, in 1996, before the advent of welfare reform, 68 percent of poor families with children received cash assistance through welfare. By 2010, only 27 percent of poor families received benefits from TANF, and the value of those benefits had declined as well (Trisi and Pavetti 2012). This does not mean that the United States spent less money under TANF. Rather, it shifted its spending, making fewer payments to poor families and more to service providers. At TANF's start, 73.1 percent of spending went to the poor; twenty years later, only 44 percent did. When one looks only at total spending as the measure of social welfare support, this remarkable redistribution is rendered invisible.

Diminished access to income assistance occurred not only or even primarily through the imposition of time limits, welfare reform's most visible and highly contested feature. Caseload reduction (for those who remained poor enough to qualify for assistance) also advanced less visibly through informal organizational practices that made benefits harder to get and to keep, in part by subjecting claimants to administrative hazards that they could not surmount. Analysts who treat sanctions as if they were simple tools for penalizing shirkers do not understand how sanctions and attributions of noncompliance are constructed in street-level practice. In public bureaucracies and contracted agencies, sanctions and benefit terminations provided a relatively easy-to-use tool for reaching the performance benchmarks that were forever bearing down on street-level practitioners.

This analysis of a public welfare agency, when compared with Soss, Fording, and Schram's analysis of contracted agencies (chap. 8), indicates that in both settings the structural conditions of work have made it more likely that caseworkers will choose to cancel benefits rather than find ways to document good-cause exemptions. From a rational choice perspective, it is logical for caseworkers to avoid administrative activities that are costly to them in time and effort (e.g., processing exemptions). It also is rational for caseworkers to avoid grappling with the complicated problems that beset some of those individuals facing sanctions. In some circumstances, caseworkers have to make fairly heroic efforts in order to take the more responsive course, making it all the more remarkable when they do. Although analysts often refer to the importance of organizational "culture" or "values," a street-level view illuminates how organizational and managerial arrangements shape available practice choices. As

Celeste Watkins-Hayes shows in chapter 10, the structural conditions that wrap both caseworkers and their clients in red tape may be more significant than personal preferences, including racial affinity, in influencing what caseworkers do.

If welfare reform advanced a project of inclusion, in its broadest sense, one would expect it not only to provide alternatives to market-derived income, but also to improve prospects for making it in the market through employment. Perhaps this second aspect of the workfare project is not captured by the commodification-inclusion dichotomy, because it involves improving well-being through labor-market participation, not just providing nonmarket income. So, what about work? Did welfare reform advance economic inclusion by supporting labor-market participation?

Certainly, more welfare recipients entered the job market after welfare reform than before. But sophisticated analyses examining the effects of workfare suggest different outcomes for differently situated segments of the population (Greenberg and Cebulla 2008; Grogger and Karoly 2005). Generally, those who were among the best off (i.e., those with high school education and previous work experience) were more likely than others to leave welfare for work, at least during the economic boom years of the late 1990s. However, even then, their wage rates placed them only just above the poverty line, assuming that work was available to them on a full-time basis and their hours were consistent.[24] A middle group of recipients appear to have moved in and out of poverty as they churned between lower-wage jobs and welfare. The third group, those who were among the most disadvantaged, were at greatest risk of ending up with no work and no welfare.

A 2005 report concluded that "program group members themselves seemed to gain little from being assigned to most welfare-to-work programs" (Greenberg, Cebulla, and Bouchet 2005, 121). Furthermore, program activities such as basic education or work experience (i.e., unpaid work) "did not have a consistent positive effect on impacts and, in some cases, were negative. . . . Average annual earnings benefits for welfare-to-work participants amounted to about $500 at best." Remarkably, the assessment concluded that "the effects of a typical welfare-to-work program are extremely modest. *Although these programs are probably worth running* . . . by themselves they will do little to reduce the size of welfare rolls or improve the lives of most persons assigned to them" (ibid.; emphasis added).

A street-level view suggests the limitations of analyzing workfare in terms of nominal policy categories, focusing on participation in activities such as training or job clubs. What actually goes on under the rubric of these labels is both variable and uncertain. Moreover, the street-level sorting practices that place individuals in different types of activities, as exemplified by the strategies of the remarkable Mr. Frank, cast doubt on idealized policy rhetoric about "tailor-made" programs and "individual assessments." In the real world of workfare, individuals may find themselves sorted into available program slots regardless of the potential value or suitability of those programs. This may help explain, at least in part, why evaluations consistently demonstrate such mediocre and equivocal results. When cost-benefit analyses make the numerator cost and the denominator savings (from reduced benefit payments), policymakers are likely to be satisfied that workfare is a success. However, if the denominator were instead economic advancement, security, or well-being, the picture would look quite different.

In the United States, the post–welfare reform picture is not simply one of commodification. It is also one of increasing precariousness and poverty both for those relegated to contingent and lower-wage jobs and for those outside the labor market for any extended time. While access to welfare more or less kept poor families afloat prior to welfare reform, the purging of caseloads has occurred in tandem with extreme deprivation. The proportion of families living in deep poverty, defined as household income below half of the poverty line, has climbed higher since welfare reform. This trend preceded the recession and has worsened in its wake. In 2011, some 44 percent of the poor lived in deep poverty and the overall poverty rate was 15 percent. In addition, growth in income inequality has continued, a trend that welfare policy was too modest a program to have caused, but certainly did not mitigate.

One cannot attribute all of these broad trends to the advent of workfare and declining access to cash assistance. Changes in the economy and tax policy likely are larger factors in these shifts. But it does seem fair to conclude that workfare has done little to advance a project of inclusion in the United States, if that means bringing poor families out of a status of marginalization and economic instability.

This picture is at odds with prevailing views of welfare reform as a policy success (Haskins 2002). However, it is consistent with indicators of deepening poverty and inequality, and with a variety of qualitative analyses, including chapters in this volume, that reveal a real world of workfare that is more reductionist than robust, more commodifying than inclusive. Admittedly, generalization is difficult in the face of devolution, which has discharged workfare's production to a diverse array of organizations, each with its own clientele, activities, and results. Arguably, devolution and privatization have contributed to blurring the lines of responsibility at the same time that managerial emphasis on caseload reduction and work-participation benchmarks have obscured meaningful policy feedback (Pierson 1994) that might take account of the kinds of informal practices highlighted here.

That is why it is important for analysis to link patterns of practice that emerge in specific organizational settings to broader governance and managerial arrangements that transcend those settings. The arrangements described in this chapter largely provided the appearance of accountability although, in fact, they left welfare agencies virtually unaccountable for the quality of service provision and for assuring needy families access to benefits the law provides. This unbalanced approach to welfare administration, while it did not directly assert a policy bias, indirectly skewed street-level practices, exacerbating workfare's already considerable commodifying tendencies.

This analysis underscores that the transformation of the welfare state, and political projects of inclusion and commodification, cannot be adequately understood by examining formal policies alone or outcomes that are only loosely linked to them, although both are clearly important. It is also necessary to examine the organizational practices of the welfare state—how SLOs construct policy in practice—in order to more adequately expose, assess, and potentially reform the mechanisms that create the terms of inclusion and commodification on the ground.

Notes

The author is grateful for research support for this project from the National Science Foundation (grant nos. SES-0129643 and 129643), the Ford Foundation, and the Open Society Institute.

1. As noted in chapter 1, I use the term "reform" because it has become part of the language of the workfare project in the United States. I do not use it to imply "improvement." Rather, I hope that by illuminating the real world of reform this analysis contributes to a different understanding of "reformed welfare."

2. Previously, under the terms of AFDC, the federal government provided an open-ended guarantee to states that it would reimburse part of the cost of their welfare payments. It set no time limits on the duration of benefits it guaranteed. The term "entitlement" refers to this guarantee.

3. Among TANF's key features are that it ended the federal guarantee of income support and placed a lifetime five-year limit on assistance; it imposed work requirements as a condition for receiving assistance, with adults required to participate in work activities within a maximum of two years of receiving assistance; and it capped federal expenditures, providing a $16 billion block grant over five years. For a more detailed look at the legislative process and the law's details, see Weaver (2000).

4. Individual states may vary in the terms they set for extending time limits, and some attach work requirements to those extensions.

5. According to Esping-Andersen (1990, 21–22), "De-commodification occurs when a service is rendered as a matter of right, and when a person can maintain a livelihood without reliance on the market."

6. These benchmarks substantially increased when TANF was reauthorized in the Deficit Reduction Act of 2005. Under these revised provisions, states were required to engage at least 50 percent of their assistance caseloads in a specific list of countable work activities for at least 30 hours a week (20 hours a week for single parents with a child under 6), or face financial penalties. There is a separate requirement that 90 percent of two-parent families be engaged in work activities for 35 hours a week (55 hours of work is required for two-parent households receiving child care subsidies).

7. In debate on this question in the House, Rep. Benjamin Cardin (D-MD) argued, "If child poverty goes up, we have failed." Rep. Nancy Johnson (R-CT) acknowledged that the amendment raised an important concern. "This is something we want to achieve, to see women and children do better in America," she said. But she emphasized that "if you use poverty as a goal, you will reduce motivation for achieving other goals." The Cardin Amendment was defeated in committee by a 5–8 vote. See "Two House Subcommittees Approve Companion Welfare Reform Bills," on the Women's Policy website, accessed June 20, 2012, www.womenspolicy.org/site/News2?page = NewsArticle&id = 5593.

8. For details, see Brodkin (2011a).

9. For more on this methodology and its rationale, see Brodkin (2003b).

10. The study used a triangulation method to cross-check different forms of data with each other (Denzin 1989), subjecting inconsistent findings to special scrutiny through successive, iterative analysis.

11. Portions of this discussion are adapted from "Policy Work: Street-Level Organizations under New Managerialism" (Brodkin 2011a). The author is grateful to the *Journal of Public Administration Research and Theory* and Oxford University Press for permission to use this content.

12. One federal review described disarray in the welfare office, malfunctioning computers, and missing case records. It also highlighted the physical conditions, which federal inspectors castigated as "a barrier to participation since the poor condition of the entrance and waiting room is offensive and disrespectful and can send a negative message to anyone who walks in the door." U.S. Department of Agriculture, Food and Nutrition Service 2000, *TANF/Medicaid State Review: Illinois.*

In an American Federation of State, County, and Municipal Employees survey, caseworkers complained of increasing workloads and inadequate administrative infrastructure, including antiquated telephone and computer systems, as well as lack of access to up-to-date procedural manuals. American Federation of State, County, and Municipal Employees, Council 31, *Overworked and Underserved: A Report on the Status of the Illinois TANF Program for Caseworkers and Clients*, Chicago, IL, January 1999.

13. Caseworkers reported management pressures to reduce caseloads through these types of informal and extralegal strategies at a hearing organized by their union, the Service Employees International Union. One caseworker reported that she had been told to violate rules regarding adequate notice as part of a more general campaign to use this strategy to reduce caseloads. "Caseworker Rights Board Hearings," *Illinois Welfare News*, June 1999.

14. As I have elaborated elsewhere, "Street-level practitioners will respond to an individual calculus of costs and benefits that derive from the ratio of resource availability to demand burden (R:D) as moderated by incentives. According to this calculus, one can assume that caseworkers will select action A over B when A is less costly and more rewarding. It follows

that management strategies that change the informal calculus of costs and benefits will result in different patterns of discretionary choice" (Brodkin 2011a, i259).

15. For a fuller discussion of these strategies, see Lipsky 1980b. On their application and consequences, see also Brodkin (1997) and Lens (chap. 14 in this volume).

16. On trouble and tests for trouble, see, generally, Maynard-Moody and Musheno (2003) and Miller (1983).

17. Regarding the disjuncture between welfare-to-work and the lower-wage labor market, see Edin and Lein (1997), Lambert and Henly (chap. 5 in this volume), and Zatz (2006b).

18. Handler and Hasenfeld (1991, 11) argue that "because much greater emphasis is placed on the symbolic than on the substantive consequences of welfare policy, its implementation tends to focus on structural features designed to affirm the distinctions between deserving and undeserving poor, and to certify eligibility for welfare benefits. We term these features myths and ceremonies because their main function is to confirm the dominant cultural norms about the poor."

19. For an insightful treatment of this issue in a different context, see Dubois (2010).

20. See Lipsky (1980b) for a general discussion of the tendency of street-level workers to redefine both their tasks and their clients. In this case, the pressures to demonstrate performance intensified after an initial period of sharp caseload decline, generally understood as moving many of the most work-ready clients off the caseload. At that point, as one manager explained, "We're left with cats and dogs now."

21. Hasenfeld (2000, 337) refers to this as the moral construction of clients.

22. The Mayo Clinic lists these among the symptoms of clinical depression. See "Depression (Major Depression): Symptoms," February 10, 2012, www.mayoclinic.com/health/depression/DS00175/DSECTION = symptoms.

23. Some states virtually purged caseloads: Wyoming and Idaho proudly announced reductions of 88.9 and 85.1 percent. Even states with large urban populations cut caseloads by one-half to three-quarters.

24. The assumption of a stable full-time job with consistent hours is highly problematic in the lower-wage labor market. See Lambert and Henly (chap. 5 in this volume).

10

Race, Respect, and Red Tape

Inside the Black Box of Racially Representative Bureaucracies

CELESTE WATKINS-HAYES

US welfare agencies operate as access points for social benefits as well as enforcers of an expansive set of rules and requirements designed to limit reliance on public assistance, fulfill work requirements, and minimize fraud and errors. Scholars have shown that historically welfare has also functioned as a racialized system of social provision that reinforces rather than mitigates racial and ethnic inequalities (Lewis 2000; Lieberman 2001; Neubeck and Cazenave 2001; Schram, Soss, and Fording 2003). Such judgments about welfare systems must undergo continual reassessment, especially given the decrease in overtly discriminatory policies and practices in recent decades and the increased presence of racial minorities in policymaking and administrative roles. Recent research recognizes racial minorities' increasingly significant role as gatekeepers to social benefits and mediators of public resources in human service organizations (Schram et al. 2009; Watkins-Hayes 2009).

These developments complicate traditional narratives about bureaucracy, raising questions about what happens when previously excluded populations become agents of state authority. This chapter explores how welfare agencies mediate race and ethnicity by examining both sides of the desk, eliciting the perspectives of caseworkers as well as clients. Two key questions guide the analysis. First, how do racial minorities negotiate their racial and ethnic status in the routine practices of street-level organizations (SLOs)? Second, what does this reveal about how racial and ethnic identities are interpreted and deployed within multiracial welfare offices? This examination illuminates existing theories of

167

racial dynamics by asking whether and how racial and ethnic identity matters in street-level interactions between black and Latino caseworkers and clients.[1]

Two theoretical frameworks—racially representative bureaucracy theory and street-level bureaucracy theory—seek to explain how black and Latino bureaucrats and clients interpret and negotiate racial and ethnic identity. Racially representative bureaucracy theory predicts that the demographic composition of the bureaucracy directly and indirectly shapes client outcomes. Perhaps the mere presence of staff from socially disadvantaged groups benefits clients from those groups, or perhaps these bureaucrats make consequential decisions informed by their social group memberships. "Passive" or "symbolic" representation denotes the presence of racial minorities on staff, while "active" or "substantive" representation denotes measurable "decision making behavior on the part of a specific group of civil servants which tends to affect systematically the resource allocation of a specific group of citizens" (Hindera 1993b, 419; also see Hindera 1993a; Meier 1993; Meier and O'Toole 2006; Meier and Stewart 1992; Naff 2001). Representative bureaucracy theory predicts that racial affinity will produce distinct patterns of interaction between clients and caseworkers sharing racial and ethnic minority membership, perhaps in ways that clients recognize and value.

Street-level bureaucracy theory implies that organizational actors enjoy opportunities to exercise considerable discretion. However, the theory also recognizes that organizational conditions bear down on frontline employees, creating tension between agency demands and client needs. Caseworkers use bureaucratic discretion to negotiate these opposing pulls. When we consider how the racial composition of the workforce affects organizational dynamics, street-level bureaucracy theory requires us to consider organizational structures, policies, and cultures. It predicts that these factors will shape the use of discretion, perhaps trumping racial affinities.

This chapter assesses these theories by analyzing intraracial dynamics between minority caseworkers and clients within welfare offices. The analysis uses interview data collected from twenty women and men who recently received cash or food-stamp benefits from the Massachusetts Department of Transitional Assistance (MDTA). It also includes interview data from seventeen black and Latino caseworkers from the same office. My purpose is to explore client and caseworker perceptions of their interactions and use their accounts to consider how race is employed in these encounters. This work aims to shed light on the content of racial relationships at the street level and contribute to understanding of how racial interactions affect the policy experience.

This chapter begins with a discussion of representative bureaucracy and street-level bureaucracy theories. After describing the data-collection methods and sources, it examines the racial narratives offered by caseworkers and clients.

The data also reveal a bureaucratic narrative for organizational interactions, suggesting that a strong bureaucratic structure restricts meaningful engagement between clients and caseworkers. I conclude by arguing that racial diversity in street-level bureaucracies (SLBs) may not work as representative bureaucracy theory suggests. Although it can enhance organizational dynamics, this effect may be mitigated by organizational conditions and intragroup politics within minority communities. As I will elaborate, agency staff diversity alone may be insufficient to assure responsiveness to diverse client populations.

Race in Street-Level Bureaucracies: Changing Models and New Questions

Racial and ethnic minorities increasingly staff US human service agencies. For example, blacks made up just 10.9 percent of the total labor force in 2006, but they constituted one-fourth of those determining eligibility for public benefits and services (US Bureau of Labor Statistics 2007). As the new faces of such organizations, black and Latino bureaucrats articulate agency goals and expectations, broker services, and implement policies (Lewis 2000; Pattillo 2007; Watkins-Hayes 2009). Their presence in public agencies represents a significant departure from the historic record of racial exclusion and requires reexamining how social welfare policies and services are formulated and reworked on the ground.

Both street-level bureaucracy and racially representative bureaucracy theories seek to understand how, through the bureaucrat-client relationship, organizational power arrangements permit or restrict access to public resources. The standard view of SLBs is perhaps best represented in classic texts by Lipsky (1980b), Blau (1972), and Hasenfeld (1972), which laid the foundation for organizational research into the efforts of contemporary welfare agencies to implement welfare-to-work requirements. Discretion serves as a critical tool, allowing street-level bureaucrats to minimize or maximize the economic or social support that clients receive and the surveillance to which they are subjected. As such, street-level bureaucracy theory addresses "what influences, and especially what systematizes, the exercise of discretion, producing informal organizational routines that effectively constitute policy on the ground" (Brodkin 2011b, i199). The discretion of street-level bureaucrats must be understood within a context of organizational incentives and constraints and take account of both internal and external influences (Watkins-Hayes 2009).

Racially representative bureaucracy theory, while acknowledging the influence of structures and policies, ultimately attributes to bureaucrats the capacity to significantly shape organizational outcomes. The ideal is to create "representative political institutions" that draw from all sectors of society (Dolan and Rosenbloom 2003; Kingsley 1944). Individuals of the same social background are thought to share a common history; similar life experiences, values, and political interests; and a collective social identity. The theory suggests that historically marginalized groups will receive a fairer hearing if staffers are drawn from similar groups. Evidence supporting this thesis can be found in studies such as Thielemann and Stewart's (1996) research showing that AIDS patients preferred receiving services from members of their ethnic group or gender.

But neither theory alone fully explains the complexities of intraracial dynamics within public agencies. The representative bureaucracy framework may fail to take adequate account of the political, social, and economic diversity of racial communities. Sociologists have identified a range of commonalities and differences characterizing relations between the black middle class and its poorer counterparts (DuBois 1995; Drake and Cayton 1993; Frazier 1997; Landry 1988; Pattillo 2007). They argue that the public representation of black interests has been and remains reflective primarily of the goals of the most privileged (i.e., middle or upper class, heterosexual, black males). This challenges assumptions about how group interests might be articulated within a public organization (Cohen 1999; Gaines 1996; Ginwright 2002; Reed 1999). Others have challenged the assumption of an all-encompassing pan-ethnic Latino political agenda (Jones-Correa and Leal 1996; Masuoka 2006; Segura and Rodrigues 2006; Stokes 2003), concluding that the notion of race- and ethnicity-based "representation" is fraught with qualifiers, contradictions, and contingencies. In addition, the representative bureaucracy literature focuses mainly on how aggregate percentages shape agency outcomes, so discussions of personal interactions rarely occur. This obscures the view into the black box of racially representative bureaucracies. We cannot see the processes at play or learn how either party interprets them.

SLB research acknowledges the inequalities suffered by blacks and other minorities at the hands of white public servants, and has shown how discretion historically has worked against clients from marginalized groups (Lieberman 2001; Lipsky 1980b; Neubeck and Cazenave 2001; Gooden 1998; Schram, Soss, and Fording 2003; Schram et al. 2009). Similar patterns have emerged in countries such as Germany and England, as migrants experience institutional discrimination even though welfare-office policies explicitly promote avoidance of such treatment (chap. 11 in this volume; Lewis 2000). In the United States, discrimination against blacks and Hispanics through the denial of benefits, the disparate enforcement of rules, excessive regulation of their work and domestic lives in exchange for benefits, and their exclusion from the employee ranks of welfare offices was routine in these organizations throughout much of the twentieth century (Lieberman 2001; Neubeck and Cazenave 2001). Discriminatory policies and practices were challenged by powerful, grassroots social movements, leading to laws that prohibited overt discrimination and introduced affirmative action as a remedy. In the 1970s and 1980s, there was a marked increase in the hiring of racial minorities. This calls for an updated understanding of the role of race in public bureaucracies and, more specifically, in the bureaucrat-client relationship. In previous work (Watkins-Hayes 2009), I have identified a "racialized professionalism" among street-level bureaucrats who seek to integrate race and other social identities into their work. I found several ways in which race shapes organizational processes, with power being deployed differentially depending on both the racial and class identities of the clients and bureaucrats involved, bureaucrats' investments in racialized professionalism, and the orientation of the organization.

Can these two theories—street-level bureaucracy and racially representative bureaucracy theory—be reconciled? Street-level studies focus on organizational *processes*, while representative bureaucracy studies emphasize *outcomes*. This chapter suggests that racial representation can be a bureaucratic outcome, an ingredient shaping discretionary bureaucratic processes, *and* a racial project. A process-focused interpretation of racial representation produces a more nuanced story about how bureaucratic actors straddle the line between organizational expectations and social group norms. Moreover, a street-level approach situates bureaucratic power within a context of organizational constraints. It enables exploration into what I call "processes of representation" and how they are influenced by agency demands and organizational conditions. It reveals the multiple and intersectional ways in which social identities collide with organizational dynamics.

Data and Methods

I explore these issues using interview data collected from a study of welfare reform in the United States, focusing on the implementation of the TANF program. TANF provides time-limited cash assistance to low-income families and in-kind resources that are directly tied to work. Although welfare caseloads have fallen dramatically since the policy was implemented in 1997, welfare offices continue to interact with large numbers of low-income households seeking other benefits, most notably food assistance. As the gatekeeper to these and other benefit programs, welfare offices are still very much involved in the lives of low-income families.[2]

This chapter draws on data from interviews I conducted in 2008 with seventeen women and three men receiving income support from the MDTA. Fourteen respondents are Latina and six are black.[3] MDTA clients were eligible to participate in the study if they (a) had received cash or food-stamp benefits in the twelve months prior to recruitment, (b) had participated in at least two face-to-face meetings with an MDTA caseworker in the last twelve months, (c) were English speaking, (d) were living in the Boston area, and (e) were over the age of 18. Individuals were recruited from a variety of social service agencies and subsidized housing complexes, and by word of mouth. All names have been changed to protect confidentiality. The tape-recorded and transcribed interviews were coded to reveal emergent themes and analyzed using HyperResearch qualitative analysis software.

This chapter also draws on data I collected in an earlier study, which included caseworkers currently working at one of the MDTA offices used by client interviewees (Watkins-Hayes 2009). This site is one of two remaining offices in one of Massachusetts's biggest cities. The earlier project investigated factors shaping policy delivery in the wake of welfare reform and included two rounds of fieldwork in 2001 and 2006 (Watkins-Hayes 2009). I draw on interviews conducted with fifteen caseworkers—eight black and seven Latino—and two black supervisors.[4] Because many of the caseworkers interviewed in 2001 and 2006 were discussed by clients in their 2008 interviews, caseworker and client perspectives can be analyzed together.[5]

This analysis is a small-n study, a type of study that is ideal for exploring social experiences and mechanisms likely to operate in other places and contexts as well as for building theoretical models to be tested in future work. As others have noted (Meier and Hawes 2009), it is difficult to observe the active representation of racial group interests within a bureaucracy, especially when the organization explicitly affirms its commitment to equality of services. I conducted in-depth interviews to obtain insights into processes of representation by probing the attitudinal and behavioral building blocks that enable (or limit) active racial representation.

"An Understanding of Where I'm Coming From": Clients Talk about Race in Postreform Welfare Offices

Low-income individuals interviewed for this study routinely identified welfare offices as sites of assistance. They tried to discern quickly whether officials would facilitate or hinder their efforts to meet their families' short- and long-term needs. Commonality and connection between caseworkers and clients may ease the inherent tension in these interactions, especially in light of welfare reform's stringent eligibility requirements. Racially representative bureaucracy theory expects black and Latino bureaucrats and clients to leverage their shared histories and present-day experiences of racial subjugation in a way that helps clients effectively negotiate the human service bureaucracy.

One-third of client respondents recalled incidents in which they believed that race mattered in a relationship with any caseworker of any race. The rather small number of clients who talked about race in the bureaucracy suggests that these moments were perceived as elements of rather than central issues in their experiences. Five clients talked about moments that seemed to be informed by intraracial solidarity or discord.[6]

For example, Jackie, a twenty-eight-year-old black mother of three, reflected on a pivotal relationship with her caseworker Teresa, also a black woman. Although she appreciated that this caseworker performed her job well—procuring Jackie's benefits efficiently, explaining the rules carefully, and alerting Jackie when she needed to update her case file—it was their interpersonal connection that Jackie valued the most. Teresa exhibited a unique combination of personal warmth and blunt honesty. Jackie's first interactions with Teresa set the stage: "When you're young, you have the sass: 'I don't care what they say.' Teresa was always telling me, 'You know you're not gonna get far with that attitude. This is what we need to do, and this is where I can help you.' It helps when you have support. Those moments . . . they've stuck with me."

Teresa offered an even stronger intervention during the intake interview when Jackie admitted that she was unsure who the father of her oldest child was and would therefore be unable to provide much information about him:[7]

> I just was honest and told 'em, "I really didn't know. It was between two people . . ." Teresa was kinda understanding. She just took as much information as she could and gave me a lecture through it all, "Being a young woman . . ." She honestly thought she was more of a mom figure, "You grow from your mistakes . . . you don't wanna . . . be just out there running around and just hanging out. It's time to go back and get your education, and it's time to be a mom." It was things like that, it was positive.

The combination of the messenger's social characteristics, the style in which the message was delivered, and Jackie's personal history made Teresa's strong guiding hand appealing. After her mother passed away the previous year, Jackie found it increasingly difficult to stay motivated in her general equivalency diploma (GED) classes, so she appreciated Teresa's intervention. "I was just coming to a lotta obstacles, hitting a lotta walls," she explained. "It was like I was up to my limit with everything. . . . I didn't seem to be accomplishing anything." The fact that such stern words were coming from a woman who reminded Jackie of her mother likely made a difference in exactly what could be said:

> I think a white woman could've said the same thing. But . . . it was more of the same race, too. I think that she felt that she *could* say it. She was talking from . . .

being a MDTA worker . . . being a mom . . . being a sista.[8] Basically . . . she didn't want to see me keep going the route that I was going. . . . "As a young African American woman, you know, we tend to have it a little harder. This is what you need to be doing. This is where you need to go. We don't need to have this situation happen to where you don't know who [the father of your child is]." You know, she just was more of a positive . . . role model. . . . I really liked her. She just set her job aside and [gave] a lecture; and the lecture kind of helped. Because when you don't have a mom around anymore, sometimes when people . . . just . . . play that role or to try to guide you in the better direction, you appreciate that. I was really grateful. . . . She kinda got me started in the first place on a better path, going down a road to where I was able to obtain a career.

It was under Teresa's direction that Jackie finished her GED and pursued medical office training, leading to a hospital job that lasted five years. This case history ran as predicted by racially representative bureaucracy theory. Shared social group membership between a client and a bureaucrat directly or indirectly enabled the norms, expectations, and sense of collective identity of marginalized group members to filter into the organization. Teresa's response and Jackie's interpretation of her intervention demonstrate the promise of racially representative organizations: to deliver important resources in a transaction informed by affective affinity and grounded in the cultural knowledge of the actors involved.[9]

Contrary to what representative bureaucracy theory might lead one to expect, however, not all social interactions between clients and caseworkers from the same racial minority groups were understood by clients as moments of racial solidarity. While Jackie viewed interactions with her caseworker as probing but welcome mentoring, others believed that such racial commonality worked against them. For example, Reena, a Puerto Rican mother of six, described several experiences in which Latina bureaucrats seemed to create more distance, and even to express hostility, when working with her. She reasoned that they did so to protect their own professional standing. After all, minority bureaucrats also come from disadvantaged social positions and must protect their status as employees (Lewis 2000; Watkins-Hayes 2009). Reena recalled an incident that she believed was shaped by racial and ethnic commonality:

I feel, in some cases, your own race discriminates against you too. I went to translate for somebody, and I noticed that [the caseworker] wasn't being gentle to the lady's problem. . . . She was very rough, 'cause I just feel that she was more worried about her position in the agency . . . than being kinder with her own race. I feel that she thought, if she gives in a little bit more, be nicer, you know, [her bosses] will be like, "Oh, she was nice 'cause they're your race or whatever." So she put on this hardcore [attitude]. It was just so funny, because . . . we know somebody else that's not our race that has that same situation, same worker, and got better results than my friend did. I just feel that, 'cause they're so worried about losing their job or [people] saying that they're choosing favoritism, that they're harder with their own race than with other races.

Whatever explains this caseworker's apparent aloofness, Reena's perception was that racial minorities must be *more* detached and strict with racemate clients than with other clients. This suggests that for some clients diverse welfare offices maintain rather than break down existing social hierarchies. Despite the presence of Puerto Rican caseworkers, Reena saw whites as firmly in control of the system. Minorities exercise some control over allocating resources but are ultimately limited in power and must be hypervigilant lest they appear biased, even if it means enforcing the strictest boundaries with racially similar clients. As I will discuss, caseworkers share this perception of themselves as "middlemen" (Pattillo 2007). While the reasons may vary in individual cases, social boundaries are often formed between black and Latino bureaucrats and racemate clients, challenging assumptions about representative bureaucracy theory.

What informs clients' beliefs about proper intraracial conduct within racially representative bureaucracies? A small but analytically significant group of client respondents hoped that a connection with caseworkers from their racial group would translate into a sympathetic ear (and helping hand) and, in an often-used phrase, "an understanding of where I'm coming from." As Jackie explained, Teresa's social characteristics as a higher-status member of Jackie's racial group helped her to convey her message more powerfully than a white woman might have. In Reena's case, her caseworker's lack of empathy felt like an even deeper betrayal given their shared ethnic background. As Ana, a 23-year-old Puerto Rican mother of one, explained, "I thought I was gonna relate easier to those black and Hispanic [caseworkers] because I'm black Hispanic, you know." Andre, a 25-year-old black male, relied on a previous experience with a case manager at a job-training program to inform his expectations about his food-stamp caseworker: "It's just the way that we interacted with each other and him being a black male, and certain things he has had in his life . . . challenges, struggles, and obstacles. So when you can sit down and communicate with somebody on the same level . . . [about] what you've been through, you know, this is not like this person is reading this out of a book. They know by personal experience as far as being a black man."

Wanting a caseworker who shares one's racial background had less to do with wanting special privileges and more to do with wanting bureaucratic protection from harsh treatment or from insensitivity to how race, class, and gender converge to limit opportunities in life. Shannon, an African American mother of two, revealed her misgivings about her white caseworker, with whom she had gotten off to a rocky start:

I wish she would have understood my situation, you know. . . . I felt she didn't care, that she's not in the situation, so it really didn't bother her. And I don't know how many white people are on food stamps, but I just felt . . . like she really didn't care . . . didn't care that my kids were starving. . . . If she were put in my shoes, I don't think she would have felt the same way. I just felt like . . . her being a woman and me being a woman and her having kids and me as well . . . how could you not care for someone that's in a bad situation?

Shannon's belief that her caseworker lacked empathy because of her class and racial background represented a clearly marked boundary. She hoped in vain to find common ground based on gender. In this sense, clients like Shannon carried expectations into the office about how social group memberships should function within the bureaucracy and shape the caseworker-client dynamic. Asked if she would have expected a different result had her caseworker been black, Shannon asserted, "I believe so . . . I just feel that they'll understand [my situation] more than a white person would."

These interviews yield insights into the dynamics of racial representation. Some clients expected racial commonality to result in empathetic case management grounded in a common social experience. Yet the intersection of caseworkers' racial, class, and bureaucratic interests was much more complex. Of those clients who perceived their caseworkers to be engaging with them through racial commonality, some read these encounters as welcome interventions on the part of racemates, others as heavy-handed maneuvers by relatively privileged members of their communities. This suggests that representative bureaucracy theory may overlook processes of racial representation that can variously ease or reinforce inherent tensions between bureaucrats and clients. The next section explores how black and Latino caseworkers see the significance of race in their relationships with clients.

Engagement in a World of Constraints: Caseworkers Talk about Race in Postreform Welfare Offices

Evidence suggests that race shapes the outlooks and values that black and Latino welfare caseworkers bring to the welfare system (Riccucci and Meyers 2004; Lewis 2000; Watkins-Hayes 2009). Caseworkers' beliefs about clients' opportunities and constraints are influenced in part by their own understanding of racial stratification and its impact on economic opportunity. There is evidence to suggest that these beliefs affect organizational service-delivery processes. In earlier research (Watkins-Hayes 2009), I found that black and Latino welfare caseworkers and supervisors actively deployed race (and class and gender) by shaping the content and tone of their interactions with black and Latina clients, reflecting both key priorities in welfare reform implementation and intragroup politics. They leveraged racial commonality to communicate the social goals and political motives of welfare policy to racemate clients and deployed occupational authority and social status to shape client behavior.

Almost all of the bureaucrats in this study had experienced both economic and racial disadvantage and drew upon the perception that they had once walked in clients' shoes. They expressed the belief that they brought a unique sensibility to service delivery and interactions with same-race clients. Sundra, a caseworker and former welfare recipient, explained: "To me, my background gives me a better avenue of understanding where my clients are truly coming from. I know what it's like to sit in that chair. . . . It's not that much different sitting over here, just more paperwork. . . . You truly understand because you have sat on that side of the table and asked somebody to give you a slice of bread, too. . . . You know how that makes you feel if the person isn't responding to what you're asking for. Or that you're being demeaned even by asking them for it."

Sundra's empathy permitted her to deploy her history strategically to forge a symbolic connection and legitimer her approach. Still, Sundra's messages to clients aligned very tightly with a policy orientation that emphasizes work enforcement and independence from government assistance. In this sense, she implicitly used race and explicitly used class to underscore, rather than undermine, policy. Her racial, class, and organizational positions worked together to inform her approach to service delivery:

> I don't share [that I was on welfare] with all my clients. But sometimes when I see a woman being stuck, and not knowing where she wants to go, or she sees all kinds of roadblocks, I say, "I understand what you mean because I had to make a decision like this at one time too. Whatever is there, use it to the best of your ability." Or I'll say, "I understand your struggle because I'm of the same struggle. . . . But if you keep persevering, you can make a change. But you've got to want it and work for it and be able to seize the opportunity when it does happen for you."

Black and Latino bureaucrats said that, in spite of their experiential understanding of racial subjugation and economic instability, their interventions rarely went beyond offering words of encouragement. They maintained that a racially representative bureaucracy should not deploy race to pursue particular outcomes. They worried about both fairness and their own professional standing. Loretta, a Colombian woman who occasionally advised Latina clients "as if I am their mother," asserted that she nevertheless placed greater emphasis on her role as a bureaucrat. "Sometimes clients who are Spanish," she explained, "expect that I'm going to be on their side because we are Spanish. And I'm not. You can be

Chinese, Arabic, Russian—to me you're a client. . . . I have to think about my job before anything else." Reginald, a black administrator, was even more direct as he acknowledged limits on what black caseworkers can actually do to help black clients: "Black folks can't talk about [race to their black clients], except under their breath, behind the backs of their supervisors. They might get [black clients] to more honestly state their concerns, but [black caseworkers] don't have the power, outside of their ability to motivate people . . . to get people out of poverty. But they do have something very powerful . . . and that is . . . a life that was advanced through education and job experience, and can serve as an example."

This suggests that street-level bureaucrats view their racial identities as symbolic assets to be managed within a bureaucratic and political environment over which they have little control (Meier and Morton 2010). Their ideals of racial representation face significant organizational challenges and constraints. Eligibility rules and paperwork requirements are extensive, and caseworkers must juggle these as they funnel clients into job-search and training programs, address clients' movement on and off the rolls, impose sanctions, and try to respond to special needs. Riccucci et al. (2004, 438) are not alone in finding that "front-line workers in welfare offices continue to believe that traditional eligibility determination concerns are the most important goals at their agencies." Organizational scholars argue that such structural parameters make it difficult for caseworkers and clients to forge any kind of connection, much less one based on common experiences (see chaps. 2, 8, 9, and 14 in this volume). Barbara, a caseworker with decades of experience, explained, "The quantity of time you had to spend with a client before welfare reform, you don't have that anymore. . . . There's a sense of urgency . . . with clients that wasn't there before."

Black and Latino caseworkers work under pressure from an agency that expects efficiency, accuracy, and compliance with specific performance targets; clients who expect a certain level of service; racemate clients who seek a sympathetic understanding of the issues they confront; and caseworkers' expectations of themselves as racial representatives. Despite the symbiosis of race and poverty that informs caseworkers' sensibilities, they are generally unwilling to jeopardize their standing in an organization or challenge management. This suggests that, within processes of racial representation, race and other social group memberships can both inform caseworkers' understandings of their work and be actively deployed in service delivery in order to legitimate their practices and gain compliance from clients. Yet bureaucratic conditions may constrain them in representing those with whom they might identify racially. Caseworkers' self-conceptions are not necessarily shared by clients. As discussed next, clients generally interpret a bureaucratically constrained, arm's-length approach to racial representation as a sign of aloofness and disconnection. In fact, most clients believe that the color that matters most is red: the disempowering reality of bureaucratic red tape.

The Most Powerful Color in the Bureaucracy: Red (Tape)

Respondents agreed that racial diversity in welfare offices symbolizes inclusion and openness. However, very few clients interviewed for this study saw race as a defining factor in their interactions with caseworkers. Their experiences in welfare offices were most clearly defined by their caseworkers' power to address their immediate and longer-term economic concerns and by the quality of their treatment. After Rosario, a Puerto Rican mother of two, reeled off a litany of bad interactions with caseworkers, she reflected, "Do I think things would be different if I had a Puerto Rican caseworker? No. Because it all depends on how the person thinks and sees things and how they try to contribute to you." Similarly, Louise, an African American mother of one, was asked whether and how her relationship with her black female caseworker was shaped by their shared background. She shrugged: "It's not, not really. Can't trust any of them down there at the welfare office." Bureaucrats are bureaucrats, these clients reasoned, working on the opposite side of the service equation.

Clients blamed the heavily formalized structure of their interactions for limiting opportunities for tailored exchanges with their caseworkers. Despite declines in welfare caseloads overall, individual caseloads average over one hundred, giving caseworkers little time to address anything beyond eligibility status and job-search or training activities. Food-stamp-only clients receive even less personalized attention from caseworkers who are responsible for literally hundreds of such families. Some caseworkers exercise discretion to occasionally shoehorn in intensive conversations with clients (Watkins-Hayes 2009). According to most respondents, however, most caseworkers focus on completing the necessary paperwork and moving on to the next task (Blau 1972; Brodkin 1997 and chap. 9 in this volume; Hays 2003; Lipsky 1980b; Soss 2002).

Some clients are downright distrustful of how extraneous information they provide to caseworkers might be used. As Tanya, an African American mother of two, explained, the most important thing is to "just try to get through it as quickly as possible and get the hell out of there. Because the longer you stay, the longer they have time to probe you. Just tell me what I need to do and let me go." Silence becomes an organizational survival strategy, so common connections—race-based or otherwise—rarely emerge. Leila, a black, 19-year-old mother from a Puerto Rican family, had struggled to connect with her caseworker, Alona: "I don't talk much at all. . . . I feel like if I talk a lot she's gonna cut [my benefits] off. Like, if she asks me a question, I'm gonna tell her [the answer] and then go to details. And just by her facial reaction, she'll hear something that will be bad. Or while I'm talking, she's like grabbing things and doing all this paperwork. And I'm like, 'Okay, aren't you supposed to listen?' I know you don't have to look at me to listen, but . . . that's rude, going through papers."

Clients generally see their caseworkers not as bearers of racially based empathy but as state agents who can either provide the necessary resources to help them take care of their families or subject them to blistering scrutiny and block their access to benefits (Brodkin 2011a; Brodkin and Majmundar 2010). Intraracial solidarity is trumped by the burden of time, the magnitude of the paperwork and surveillance involved, and the paucity of and postreform limits on benefits. Andre, who described his expectation of a connection with his food-stamp caseworker, explained why such a relationship is now a near impossibility: "I think being in a role like that, [caseworkers] are under a lot of stress and pressure. They really are overworked. So I think as far as when they bring somebody in their office, 'Okay, this is what you got to do.' In and out, [because] there's a lot of people waiting on you. So . . . he was on the speed." Most clients described having civil but detached relationships with caseworkers. Many could not recall their caseworkers' names. They generally viewed caseworkers as untrustworthy unless presented with strong evidence to the contrary. As Jackie explained, "When you're . . . dealing with certain [caseworkers of any race], they just throw you stress. They just throw you off because you're down on your luck and . . . looking for help."

Clients lamented that the indignities of poverty threatened to inflect all their interactions with caseworkers. They generally believed that their impoverished, relatively powerless status created the greatest potential for abuse from caseworkers. They most often correlated negative treatment they suffered with disrespect because of their status as recipients. Jackie said this about a black caseworker to whom she was assigned after Teresa: "In how I've been treated, I wouldn't say it was race or anything. My caseworker just seemed like she was just bitter. You know, just didn't wanna do her job. I can see how anybody else would say it was a race thing. But it felt more like the education thing, like I'm just another statistic walking in. . . . When I would call, I just always got a little sass from her, that tension I felt between she and I."

As clients' sense of social vulnerability due to their impoverished status meets the words and deeds of bureaucrats who seem to control their fate, they seek to maintain their dignity. Andre mused about his latest food-stamp caseworker, a white male:

> When you have dealt with more than one person in social services, you see if the sincerity is there. And it makes a tremendous difference when . . . they care,

because you're supposed to have compassion and it's not so much about the money. It's supposed to be about, "Okay I'm in a position where I can help people, I have these resources and I can connect them with other people." I would say, with my caseworker, even though he's busy, his professionalism [is good]. He seems like he really cares because I called him to let him know "Okay, I have a job now," and he's like, "Oh, well, congratulations! I hope everything works out."

Over two-thirds of respondents, among them Rita, a Puerto Rican mother of six, expressed views similar to Andre's: "I don't have no preference whether [the caseworker] is a man or a female, black or white . . . as long as they treat me with respect, then I treat them with respect." How this respect was defined by clients varied little. Respondents highlighted norms of courtesy (friendliness, accessibility, attentiveness), but also wanted caseworkers to avoid treating them as perpetual outsiders who had no reasonable claim to public benefits. The concluding section considers how this stated desire for respect relates to racially representative bureaucracy and street-level bureaucracy theories.

Conclusion

Centuries of economic, political, and social suppression of blacks and Hispanics by the white majority have engendered a durable arrangement of racial hierarchies in the United States. Social movements, hard-won legislative protections, and changing racial attitudes have opened the opportunity structure while adding new complexities to our understanding of the significance of race, class, and gender within social welfare bureaucracies.

Only one-third of black and Latina clients in this study identified race as a salient feature in their interactions with caseworkers, and an even smaller proportion of these respondents talked about moments that they thought were informed by intraracial solidarity or discord. Black and Latina clients who sensed racial overtones in their interactions with same-race staff members did not interpret these encounters monolithically. They read them variously as pointed but welcome interventions by race mates who assisted them in negotiating the welfare system or as heavy-handed maneuvering by relatively privileged members of their racial communities.

These are puzzling findings given the racialized history and politics of the welfare system (Neubeck and Cazenave 2001) and the respondents' widespread agreement that having a racially diverse workforce in welfare offices is symbolically important to them. Racially representative bureaucracy theory posits a positive effect when the workforce reflects the demographic diversity of its clientele. Agency actions based on intraracial dynamics should benefit minority clients and reduce institutionalized racial disadvantages. The findings presented in this chapter suggest that this is not necessarily the case.

First, racially representative bureaucracy theory underestimates the multiple and intersectional ways in which race and other group memberships inform interactions. Processes of representation are informed by the class and bureaucratic interests of caseworkers of color in ways that can both ease and reinforce inherent tensions between bureaucrats and clients. Racial connections between them can produce positive interactions and positive outcomes for clients who are members of marginalized groups through brokering, tailored advice, and empathic understanding. However, these relationships can also produce adverse effects driven by the class-based need of street-level bureaucrats to prove their own professional legitimacy. This analysis shows that race, class, and organizational politics intersect to inform the behaviors of bureaucrats of color. Their choices about where to place their alliances may or may not produce racial representation.

Second, the theory fails to recognize that bureaucratic constraints can limit intragroup connections and ultimately trump racial representation. Although racial diversity potentially enables social group commonality to shape responsiveness, such affinities do not automatically occur. The potential for racial responsiveness depends, in part, on organizational factors. Under certain conditions, racial representation may be quite costly to minority bureaucrats, placing their professional standing at risk. My study suggests that bureaucratic environments characterized by red tape are likely to undermine racial representation by generating strong boundaries in bureaucrat-client interactions, even between racemates. In addition, representation is less likely to occur in organizations where minority employees feel compelled to act to protect their hard-won access to employment. Such organizational conditions confound the processes of representation. This helps to explain why, despite social group commonality, clients and bureaucrats express varying interpretations and understandings of racial representation in welfare agencies.

This study reveals a tension between the desire of caseworkers to leverage their social backgrounds when working with clients and the structural requirements of street-level work in agencies characterized by demands for efficiency, formality, and client surveillance. From the client perspective, caseworkers are seen as routinely evading and even suppressing client demands. When clients complain about red tape, they often are describing what they see as draconian rules and impersonality in service delivery (Moynihan and Herd 2010). Under these conditions, caseworkers are likely to experience limited engagement with clients, possibly precluding effective racial representation. In that sense, the stated preference of caseworkers to achieve deeper engagement is denied by organizational structure.

In short, race is mediated through organizational dynamics, but not necessarily as representative bureaucracy theory predicts. Clients express a desire for respect as the critical currency. Whether such respect is operationalized through minimal intrusion or maximum engagement, clients seemed to be advocating, at the least, for a level of neutrality that does not further problematize them. To clients, respect therefore marks an organization as representative of their interests regardless of their caseworkers' racial identity.

I do not dispute the importance or legitimacy of racially diverse staffing in bureaucracies. Rather, I draw attention to the organizational conditions that may work in opposition to the objectives of diversity. Depending on those conditions, passive representation has the potential to improve treatment of minority clients, tempering racial tensions within the organization. Meier and Hawes (2009, 272) stress that racial representation is supported by "the normative position that representative bureaucracies are a positive good, that such bureaucracies either provide symbolic reassurance to citizens of the representativeness of government, or more important, that such bureaucracies will actually implement policies in a different way." However, this chapter suggests that diversity alone may not be enough. Processes of racial representation also are structured by organizational conditions and intragroup politics, making it important that reformers be mindful of the complexities of diversity in specific organizational settings.

Notes

This work was supported by the National Science Foundation (grant no. 0512018). The author is grateful to interviewees for their participation and candor.

1. I refer to respondents as black *and* Latino, although recognizing that these categories, at times, might overlap. None of the Latino caseworkers and only two of the Latina clients in my study identified themselves by both race and ethnicity.

2. Welfare agencies are key points of entry to benefits for lower-income individuals, including TANF, food stamps (now provided under SNAP), and Medicaid, a national program providing health insurance to low-income families.

3. Place of family origin is noted in the case of the Latina respondents, all of whom are first- or second-generation migrants from Puerto Rico or immigrants from Central or South America.

4. In January 2006, 39.3 percent of family heads in the office's caseload were black, 37.3 percent were Hispanic, 18.6 percent were white, and 3.7 percent were Asian. At that time, the TANF casework staff included twelve whites, eight blacks, nine Latinos, and three Asians. The office staff also included six white and two black supervisors.

5. Limited staff turnover in these offices helped to facilitate this.

6. This chapter does not explore differences between black and Latino bureaucrats and clients because few were found. With a larger sample, however, one might be able to determine how racial representation differs across different minority groups.

7. Providing information about absent parents is a requirement of welfare eligibility and is used to allow the state to recoup child support from absent parents.

8. "Sista," or "sister," is a common term among blacks to describe black women and is often meant to signal a sense of racial community.

9. This example demonstrates how a distinct and unspoken layer of politics, simultaneously supportive and regulatory, informs interactions between bureaucrats and clients during the process of racial representation. Recent work suggests that many low-income women see motherhood as an opportunity to demonstrate worth, regardless of their economic circumstances or the viability of the relationship with the father (Edin and Kefales 2005). Furthermore, poor women have often felt it is in their interests to be somewhat confrontational in public bureaucracies (Nadesen 2005; Orleck 2005). Teresa's advice to Jackie about her sexual history and her conduct in a bureaucracy evinces a very different set of assumptions, likely informed by her class status and organizational position as a bureaucrat. The advice coincides with, rather than contradicts, the normative principles of welfare reform and the expectations of the organization.

11

Good Intentions and Institutional Blindness

Migrant Populations and the Implementation of German Activation Policy

MARTIN BRUSSIG AND MATTHIAS KNUTH

G ermany has the largest share of immigrants among the larger European countries.[1] This presents an enormous challenge: how to address the exclusion and marginalization of migrants from the labor market. Following increasing national unemployment in the course of successive business cycles, in 2005 Germany introduced major labor-market reforms using activation services and work requirements as central policy instruments. These policy initiatives, known as the Hartz reforms, extended work-activation requirements, not only to the native German population, but also to migrant populations. Migrants comprise more than one-quarter of those made subject to activation requirements. Yet, as we will discuss, neither the formal provisions of activation policy nor administrative reforms designed to implement them contemplated the special circumstances facing migrants in the labor market.

This chapter focuses on Germany's migrant populations as a special case for understanding the policies and practices of activation. It analyzes the relationship between activation reforms and migrant populations from two perspectives. First, from a policy perspective, it draws attention to a mismatch between key features of activation policy and the migrant experience and considers what this mismatch means for the implementation of activation requirements. Second, from an organizational perspective, it examines how Germany's activation bureaucracy addressed—or failed to acknowledge—differences between migrant and native populations. This perspective highlights a paradox that emerges out of the German bureaucracy's tendency to operate according to Weberian principles—that is, a commitment to rules and their equal application—even when dealing with groups of unequal standing and circumstances. Although a bureaucratic approach that emphasizes equal treatment under the law aims to avoid intentional discrimination, it can produce institutional discrimination in effect by failing to adjust to the specific circumstances of the migrant population.

The main argument of this chapter is that the bureaucratic practices of activation are likely to disadvantage migrant job seekers when there is a mismatch between formal policy, informal practices, and the specific circumstances of migrant populations. We begin by providing background on German activation reforms and migrant populations. In the second section we look more closely at characteristics and experiences of migrant populations that are subject to activation requirements. The third section explores the mismatch between activation requirements and the special circumstances of German migrants. This lays the foundation for the fourth section, in which we analyze what happens in job centers, where the activation bureaucracy and migrants meet. We conclude with observations about the perverse effects of what we see as "institutional blindness"; that is, activation's failure to formally recognize or informally respond to the special circumstances of Germany's migrant populations.

Activation Reforms in Germany: The Special Case of Migrants

Although Germany tends not to perceive itself as a country of immigrants, its history has seen considerable immigration, emigration, and internal migration (Bade 2002). After World War II, over 12 million refugees and displaced persons flooded into West Germany, followed by nearly 4 million East Germans until the border was sealed in 1961. Between 1955 and 1973, so-called guest workers were recruited from southern Europe and later also from Turkey, partially replacing the labor supply lost by the closing of the eastern German border. Recruitment from southern Europe largely ceased after oil-price shocks jolted the economy in 1973, yet the number of nonnational residents living in Germany continued to grow, fueled largely by family reunification, asylum, and war refugees. The subsequent decline in manufacturing, including the off-shoring of manufacturing jobs, meant that those who had once come to fill jobs in lower-skilled industries experienced increasing difficulties in the labor market.

A second wave of immigration occurred after the breakup of the Soviet Union. During the 1990s, ethnic German repatriates (the descendants of eighteenth-century settlers) as well as non-Germans from the former Soviet Union and Eastern and Southeastern Europe arrived to encounter a tight labor market.[2] Consequently, Germany's now sizable foreign-born population has a disproportionate rate of unemployment. Since the 1970s, unemployment among migrants has grown faster than that of German nationals, reaching a level more than double that of nationals by 2005.[3] Migrant populations now constitute a significant sector of the unemployed and, thus, a sector subject to the work requirements of activation.

What is known about these migrant populations and how they are affected by activation policy? Generally, the literature on migration and on migrant communities in developed countries has focused on motivations, mechanisms, and patterns of migration, on stages and pathways of integration and assimilation, on migration and naturalization policies, as well as on discrimination, disadvantage, and poverty among migrants and conflicts between ethnic groups.[4] The literature on activation (or welfare-to-work) has specifically addressed lone parents (Knijn, Martin, and Millar 2007; Schwarzkopf 2009), young people (Beale, Bloss, and Thomas 2008), people with impaired health (Carcillo and Grubb 2006; Stafford et al. 2007; Kemp and Davidson 2010; Brussig and Knuth 2010a), and older workers (Brussig and Knuth 2010b). But with a few exceptions (Schneider, Fischer, and Kovacheva 2008; Andersen 2007), the activation literature has largely failed to address migrants as a population of interest. Overall, relatively little is known about how activation reforms have affected them.

Germany's Activation Reforms: Policy Shifts

Until the end of 2004, Germany had two benefits for unemployed individuals who had exhausted work-based unemployment insurance. "Unemployment assistance" was the wage-replacing but means-tested follow-on benefit for those exceeding the twelve-month limit of unemployment insurance. "Social assistance" was the needs-based, flat-rate benefit of last resort for those who did not qualify for work-based unemployment benefits. The so-called Hartz reforms of 2005 merged these two benefits into one, called Unemployment Benefit II (UB II). UB II is a flat-rate benefit with work obligations attached for each household member deemed fit to work. It provides income support for individuals and families who have exhausted or do not qualify for unemployment insurance. This reform was highly contested because it implied that former workers, after losing their jobs and exhausting their eligibility for work-based unemployment benefits, would no longer enjoy a status-maintaining breadwinner benefit.[5] Opposition to this policy shift became a factor in the emergence of a new left-wing party (Die Linke) and the defeat of the Schröder government in 2005 (Knuth 2009).

The Hartz reforms laid out the framework for a new activation regime. Despite considerable debate over its provisions, migrants received little if any explicit attention (Hartz Commission 2002). This omission is significant given that migrants were more likely than the native-born population to be affected by activation reforms and more likely to occupy a marginalized position in the labor market (Kaltenborn and Wielage 2010).[6] It is striking that both the political and the academic discourse on activation or welfare-to-work has largely failed to address what is the biggest single target group of these policies in Germany as well as some other European countries.

The unemployment rate increased immediately after the Hartz reforms, appearing to contradict reformers' promise of reducing unemployment through a stricter activation regime. However, other factors drove the unemployment rate increase: namely, (1) a poor economic climate, (2) an increase in unemployment registration (but not unemployment itself), as social assistance beneficiaries were now required to register, and (3) new registration requirements for the nonworking spouses of UB II beneficiaries. Together, these factors produced an unemployment rate for nonnatives that was more than twice the rate for native Germans.[7] It seems fair to say that the labor market problems of migrant populations became more visible.

Germany's Activation Reforms: Organizational and Governance Changes

As in other countries adopting activation reforms (including those discussed in this volume), the Hartz reforms incorporated changes in both policy and governance. A key goal involved changing the traditional hierarchical and rules-based organization of the German public employment services (PES) by introducing new public management-style (NPM) reforms.[8] Governance reforms imposed performance targets on the federal PES while also promising greater flexibility and innovation, making for a rather complicated mix of centralized and discretionary arrangements.

A second managerial reform envisioned "single gateways" for all job seekers. In practice, creating a single gateway meant combining the work of the federal PES with the work of municipal social assistance agencies. This evoked path dependencies that were difficult to overcome (Knuth 2009). It led to the development of a second tier of employment services for UB II beneficiaries, with municipalities involved in the provision of benefits and activation services. Resulting from parliamentary compromise, two models of service delivery were implemented in parallel and declared an experiment. In one, municipalities formed consortia with the federal PES. In a second model, municipalities became the sole providers for UB II participants. In both models, benefits and services are administered in job centers that are organizationally separate from the first-tier employment services.

One argument used in favor of municipal implementation of the new benefit and activation regime was based on its alleged closeness to the needs of local populations. However, as we will discuss, municipal job centers (whether run by consortia or the municipality alone) have hardly had more to offer than the traditional federal PES when it comes to addressing the special circumstances of migrant populations. The administrative practices of municipal job centers and the training of their predominantly native staff are permeated by the same Weberian spirit found in the federal PES.

After the Hartz reforms, the Federal Ministry of Labour and Social Affairs commissioned a study on the effects of the new benefit and activation regime on recipients with migrant backgrounds. This study was conducted by a consortium of five institutes and led by the authors. This chapter draws on data from this study. It examines the status of migrants to Germany who are recipients of UB II. The findings are based on qualitative case studies in sixteen job centers and on a beneficiary telephone panel survey in two waves of approximately 25,000 respondents each. The sample for the telephone survey was drawn from recipients in September 2006; the two waves of interviews were conducted in the winters of 2006–7 and 2007–8, respectively. The second interview was timed approximately twelve months after the first.[9]

Migrant Populations and the Challenges of Activation: Characteristics of the Migrant Population

There is no single definition of migrant populations that is used consistently in policy analysis. For this study we defined residents of Germany with a migrant background in ways that highlight characteristics with potential labor-market relevance. Migrants include:

- persons without German citizenship[10];
- nationals born abroad and with at least one parent also born abroad[11];
- nationals born in Germany with at least one parent born abroad and whose preferred family language is not German[12].

According to these definitions, well above one-quarter (28.6 percent) of UB II recipients have a migrant background. Of those recipients defined as having a migrant background, two-thirds reported that they mostly used languages other than German at home.

We identified five subgroups of migrants receiving UB II benefits, taking postwar Germany's immigration history into account and aiming at constructing groups sufficiently large for multivariate analyses (see table 11.1). The subgroups include:

- beneficiaries of Turkish origin (including Kurds and other ethnic groups resident in Turkey);
- beneficiaries from southern European countries from which guest workers were once recruited (Greece, Italy, Spain, Portugal, and the former Yugoslavia and its successor states)[13];
- beneficiaries from middle and eastern European countries including the whole of the Soviet Union or Commonwealth of Independent States (CIS), but excluding ethnic German repatriates;
- beneficiaries recognized as ethnic German repatriates (mostly from Soviet Union/CIS, Romania, and Poland);
- beneficiaries from the "rest of the world"—a heterogeneous category of small minority populations, largely coming from the Middle East, Southeast Asia, and Africa, but also from old and new EU member states that are not in the previous two groups.

Middle and eastern Europeans (including those from the CIS) are the largest group among the benefit recipients. This is somewhat surprising given the widely held perception that Germany's nonnative population is still dominated by guest workers from Turkey and southern Europe. Adding ethnic German repatriates who came from the same middle and eastern European areas, migrants from this part of the world make up nearly half of the population receiving UB II. Although substantial in the population at large, these two

Table 11.1. Groups of origin and migrant backgrounds among UB II recipients (%)

Nationality/region of origin	Non-Germans	Born abroad[a]	Family language other than German[b]	Total benefit recipients with migrant background
Turkey	28.3	20.5	27.5	23.0
Southern Europe	16.0	7.9	9.7	10.9
Ethnic German repatriates	0.7[c]	18.7	16.1	16.5
Middle and Eastern Europe/CIS	35.5	33.8	32.5	30.2
Rest of the world	19.6	19.1	14.2	19.4
Total	100.1	100.0	100.0	100.0

Source: Customer telephone survey, extrapolated for the whole of Germany; authors' calculations.

[a] The individual and at least one parent were born abroad.

[b] Language use was only asked for if at least one parent was born abroad. Multiple counting was allowed.

[c] Less than 30 cases.

groups are actually overrepresented among recipients of UB II.[14] The second-largest group of benefit recipients is Turks, followed by migrants from the rest of the world. Southern Europeans are the smallest group.

Is There a Mismatch between Policy and Populations?

As these data suggest, migrants come from diverse backgrounds and bring with them diverse characteristics and experiences. In the following discussion we draw attention to three significant ways in which activation policy and practice fail to take account of this diversity.

The "Recognition Gap": Credentials and the Assessment of Human Capital

German public discourse tends to attribute elevated rates of unemployment and welfare receipt among the migrant population to lack of human capital (Grundig and Pohl 2006). However, during the guest worker era, formal vocational qualifications hardly mattered because recruitment was aimed at filling low-skill entry-level and marginal jobs. According to official statistics, half of the migrant population has no formal vocational qualification (Konsortium Bildungsbericht-erstattung 2006). This is critically important in a labor-market environment characterized by a very broad vocational segment, where certification is the ticket to employment and where school tracks and grades serve as gatekeepers to vocational training.[15] In this context, lack of education and certification implies a high risk of labor-market exclusion. However, official statistics, including the unemployment statistics of the PES, show only those vocational or academic qualifications that have been acquired or formally recognized in Germany.

Our survey data of UB II recipients allow us to assess the "recognition gap"—that is, the difference between qualifications acquired in the respondents' countries of origin and qualifications recognized in Germany. This is not to say that all qualifications are necessarily worthy of formal recognition as equivalent to German vocational or academic degrees. It does mean, however, that categorizing trained individuals as unskilled in official statistics is misleading and that treating them as such in job-brokering services wastes human potential.

As shown in table 11.2, taking into account qualifications acquired abroad considerably reduces the share of migrant UB II recipients who can be regarded as unskilled.[16] In all groups of origin, most qualifications acquired abroad are not recognized in Germany and, thus, are formally worthless on the German labor market. This stands out in particular among those who came from middle or eastern Europe (including the CIS), whether as ethnic German repatriates or

Table 11.2. Reported vs. recognized vocational or academic qualifications: Percentage of UB II recipients by group (respondents 25 years and over)

	Nonmigrants		Migrants		Migrants by group of origin				
	M	F	M	F	Turkey	Southern Europe	Ethnic German repatriates	Middle and Eastern Europe/ CIS	Rest of the world
No qualification acquired	20.4	26.6	34.5	50.5	74.1	58.3	24.3	27.7	37.8
Qualification acquired in Germany	—	—	30.2	27.7	8.2	4.3	38.2	45.2	33.0
Qualification acquired abroad and recognized in Germany	—	—	12.5	10.5	3.5[a]	2.8[a]	15.0	19.8	8.4
Qualification acquired in Germany	79.6	73.4	22.8	11.4	14.2	34.6	22.5	7.4	20.9
Total	100	100	100	100	100	100	100	100	100

Source: Customer telephone survey, extrapolated for the whole of Germany; authors' calculations.
Note: M = males; F = females. Rounding up of fractional numbers results in totals slightly above 100% in three columns.
[a] Fewer than 30 respondents.

as foreigners. Equally conspicuous are the high proportions not reporting any qualification among those of Turkish or southern European origin. In addition, the gender gap in qualifications is much larger among migrants than in the native population. The percentage of women with a migrant background who do not have work or educational credentials (whether recognized or unrecognized) is almost double the percentage among native women.

Using panel survey data, we test the effects of qualification status on taking up paid work, controlling both for regional context and for individual sociodemographic characteristics.[17] Recognition of qualifications matters. The propensity for taking up work was found to be similar for those with qualifications acquired abroad but not recognized in Germany and those with no qualifications. By contrast, individuals with an officially recognized foreign qualification have a 50 percent higher propensity of taking up work than those without recognition, a rate similar to that of individuals with qualifications acquired in Germany (see figure 11.1).

It might be questioned whether these findings from UB II beneficiaries can be generalized to the migrant population at large. Based on a survey of migrants

Figure 11.1.   Rates of paid work participation within one year by qualification (respondents 25 years and over)

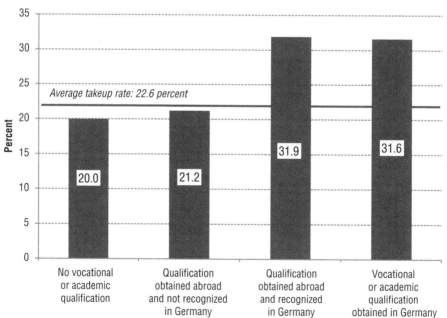

Source: Customer telephone survey, extrapolated for the whole of Germany: authors' calculations.

from the former Soviet Union, some of whom were ethnic German expatriates, Kogan (2012) finds similar positive effects of the recognition of qualifications on integration into employment and on the status level of employment. Those who do not care to have their qualifications recognized take up employment faster but remain at lower levels of the labor market. Those who do apply for recognition but are turned down are the worst off.

Arrangements for recognizing credentials in Germany are quite complex. In Germany's federal governance structure, the *Länder* (somewhat similar to US states) oversee general academic education. Germany's system of vocational training is entrusted to chambers, corporatist bodies that regulate professions and occupations.[18] Responsibility for recognizing qualifications obtained abroad is institutionally fragmented, with variations among the individual Länder.[19] The total number of authorities responsible for the recognition of vocational or academic qualifications is estimated at nearly four hundred. Navigating this system can be quite difficult, with uncertainty as to whether one can even find a contact person who will assume responsibility (Englmann and Müller 2007). Until April 2012, there was no universal legal entitlement to formal assessment of qualifications obtained abroad. However, new legislation created to fill this gap covers only those occupations for which the federation has legal responsibility; concurrent legislation by the sixteen federal states has yet to be enacted. Moreover, European regulation does require recognition for roughly sixty selected occupations and professions.[20] Some chambers issue informal assessments of skills equivalence for occupations with unrestricted access, but these assessments are made on a voluntary basis.

All of this is very difficult to understand, even for experts, let alone newcomers to the country who may be unfamiliar with its institutional setup and have limited command of the German language. It is here that the role of job centers as street-level organizations (SLOs) assumes critical importance in mediating between formal policy provisions and the specific needs and circumstances of individuals (see chaps. 1 and 2 in this volume). Migrants with non-German credentials and limited German-language skills need professional advice and guidance; that is, they need caseworkers who exercise discretion in ways that are responsive to their diverse circumstances. Ideally, recipients of UB II should get this guidance from their case managers in local job centers. However, our interviews with frontline staff indicate that the average case manager may be just as confused by the system as recipients and therefore may be of little help. As one frontline adviser put it: "This is incredibly complicated. . . . This is not really on my personal agenda. I have not bothered to memorize all that since it is regionally different" (interview 14–6-PAP_Ü25).

Nor did administrative systems facilitate caseworkers in responding to diverse types of credentials. The IT systems in use at job centers at the time of this study reflected the vocational structure of the German labor market and did not allow for recognition of noncertified skills. For example, academically trained construction engineers without formal recognition of their diplomas could only be coded as "building hands." In this way, the human capital of migrants is devalued rather than recognized and developed. From a street-level perspective, the IT system constitutes a structural constraint in that it fails to provide resources that would facilitate responsiveness to the special circumstances of migrants. Without those resources, it becomes costly for individual caseworkers to find ways to adjust to the migrants' diverse needs.

Our empirical results demonstrate the consequences of these practices for the UB II system. If migrants' qualifications were formally recognized, their chances of taking up employment and quitting the benefit might well improve. When job centers fail to address the recognition gap, migrants are less likely to be successful in the labor market.

The "Language Gap": German-Language Proficiency and Labor-Market Opportunities

In Germany, language constitutes a significant problem for migrant populations seeking employment. Generally, immigration to Germany is not structured by former colonial ties. Few people choose Germany as a target for migration because of cultural or linguistic affinity. This seems to make language more of a barrier to labor-market integration than in former colonial powers like the United Kingdom, France, and Spain.

Our data indicate that the majority of migrant UB II recipients do not use German as their preferred language. This is also true for both ethnic German repatriates and for naturalized citizens with migrant backgrounds. The use of non-German mother tongues in people's private spheres does not necessarily exclude bilingualism; but in practice it often does. One-third of respondents reported problems conversing in German, and more than half reported difficulties writing a letter in German. Functional illiteracy was not a topic of this research, but it is known to be relevant among women from Turkish villages, who often have only a few years of schooling. Differences among migrant groups are considerable (see table 11.3). Ethnic German repatriates, on average, rate their language proficiency higher than their non-German counterparts from the same regions, but still lower than southern Europeans and, most notably, women of southern European origin.

In terms of activation policy, the primary response to German-language deficiencies has been to offer language training. However, referrals to language courses are problematic in two respects. First, job centers make referrals but do

Table 11.3. Problems with oral/written communication by groups of migrant
UB II recipients (%)

	All migrant recipients	Turkey	Southern Europe	Ethnic German repatriates	Middle and Eastern Europe/CIS	Rest of the world
All						
Oral	33.7	39.2	8.9	33.3	44.1	19.3
Written	54.9	60.4	26.5	52.6	68.9	37.2
Males:						
Oral	36.4	34.0	12.2	37.7	58.3	26.4
Written	54.9	55.7	36.0	53.0	70.8	47.3
Females:						
Oral	31.4	44.2	5.9	28.2	37.5	11.3
Written	54.9	64.9	17.7	52.1	68.1	25.8

Source: Customer telephone survey, extrapolated for the whole of Germany; authors' calculations.

Note: Table shows percentages of respondents reporting that oral/written communication in German is "rather difficult" or "very difficult," as opposed to "rather easy" or "very easy."

not themselves control what kind of training individuals will receive. German-language courses are administered by the Immigration and Refugee Authority (Bundesamt für Migration und Flüchtlinge), which aims training at level B1 of the Common European Framework of Reference for Languages. However, level B1 is insufficient for success on the German labor market except in very menial jobs.[21] It is certainly insufficient in any service job requiring interaction with customers.

Second, irrespective of the level of training, UB II recipients do not seem to gain much from participating in these courses, based on caseworkers' reports and self-reports.[22] This may be in part because the courses are offered in classroom settings that are intimidating to participants with little or unsuccessful school experience. Language exercises embedded in a training-on-the-job setting seem to be more effective (Deeke 2011). In short, as was the case with the recognition gap, efforts to address the language gap have not been adapted to the specific needs and circumstances of migrant populations.

The "Culture Gap": Activation Requirements and the Breadwinner Role Model

By imposing work obligations on adults, regardless of gender or marital role, UB II implies an "adult worker model" (Annesley 2007). This is not in full harmony with the German family model, which still partially supports a single (implicitly male) breadwinner role (Gottfried and O'Reilly 2002). In addition, activation requirements may not be in harmony with migrant family models and can conflict with their traditional gender roles. In surveys of UB II participants, we probed views on gender and family roles and their relationship to work requirements. Independent of gender, around 90 percent of UB II respondents regarded personal participation in work as important even if financial needs could be met through the family. However, some subgroups—notably, women from middle and eastern Europe and men from the rest of the world—were less likely to favor work over traditional family roles (see table 11.4).

Generally, migrants profess more traditional attitudes about family roles than native Germans. In addition, on average, men profess more traditionalism than women of the same group of origin.[23] The gender gap regarding the breadwinner model is largest among southern Europeans, followed by respondents of Turkish origin. Turkish women indicate the greatest reluctance to work while their children are still small (and thus, implicitly, to entrust their children to someone else's care). In this respect they appear more traditionally minded than Turkish men. Males from middle and eastern Europe (including the CIS) show the highest preference among all male migrants for the male-breadwinner model. Female ethnic German repatriates show the highest preference for the male-breadwinner model relative to female migrants generally.[24] To the extent that there is a culture gap regarding work and family roles, it raises questions about how the activation bureaucracy responds to those for whom work requirements run contrary to deeply embedded patterns of familial relations.

The Practices of Activation: Job Centers and Activation Experience

As discussed, migrant populations face significant difficulties in the German labor market, in part because of "gaps." We found a gap between migrants' possession of credentials certifying human capital and their recognition in Germany, as well as, to some extent, a mismatch between human capital and a changing labor market with decreasing demand for lower-skilled workers. In addition, we found that migrant populations may be disadvantaged in the labor market because of language and cultural gaps. These gaps affect different migrant populations in different ways. For example, Turkish migrant workers and their descendants have been hit especially hard by the restructuring of the German labor market and the decline in lower-skilled manufacturing jobs. They also express traditional views regarding gender and familial roles that are at odds with activation-policy requirements. Human-capital and language gaps may multiply the disadvantages migrants face in competing for places in the labor market.

Table 11.4. Views on work and breadwinner role models (percent of respondents agreeing with statement)

	"Participating in work is important in its own right even if financial needs are met through the family."			"In marriage or partnership the male partner should be the principal breadwinner of the family."		
	All	M	F	All	M	F
Nonmigrants	94.3	93.8	94.8	33.4	40.3	26.3
Migrants from:						
Turkey	93.5	93.7	93.2	62.8	71.8	54.5
Southern Europe	94.3	94.1	94.5	61.4	75.9	47.6
Ethnic German repatriates	94.3	96.2	92.1	69.5	75.5	62.7
Middle and Eastern Europe/CIS	87.7	95.2	84.5	63.5	78.0	57.5
Rest of the world	87.1	83.1	92.2	53.8	61.4	44.1

	"Mothers should stay at home at least until the children enter school."			"The observation of religious commandments is also important to me in my work."		
	All	M	F	All	M	F
Germans without migrant background	53.3	58.5	48.1	25.9	25.3	26.5
Turkey	77.7	74.8	80.3	49.3	50.4	48.2
Southern Europe	67.0	83.6	51.8	37.4	37.2	37.5
Ethnic German repatriates	62.3	60.7	64.3	36.9	33.4	41.2
Middle and Eastern Europe/CIS	63.2	65.6	62.3	36.2	32.0	37.9
Rest of the world	58.1	67.3	46.4	47.2	53.9	38.7

Source: Customer telephone survey, extrapoated for the whole of Germany; authors' calculations.

Note: Table shows percentages by group of indivduals who responded to statements with "agree" or "somewhat agree," as opposed to "disagree" or "somewhat disagree."

These gaps and the diversity among migrant groups create challenges for job centers, the SLOs responsible for putting activation into practice. In the following sections we explore their responses to these challenges, examining data that shed light on how these organizations, in effect, mediate between formal policies of activation and the diverse needs and experiences of migrants receiving UB II.

Casework in Job Centers

Interviewees in our job-center case studies (both local managers and frontline caseworkers) insisted on their allegiance to principles of equal treatment and nondiscriminatory practices. They did not indicate a special concern for the status of migrant groups in the activation process. Rather, job-center staff tended to see their jobs as involved in social and employment policies that just happened to engage high percentages of migrants.

Job-center staff are themselves relatively homogeneous. Although the percentage of job-center staff with a migrant background is uncertain, it has been estimated at about 3 percent (IAQ et al. 2008). This undoubtedly reflects the traditional exclusion of nonnationals from civil-servant status. European regulation now requires that civil-servant status be opened to Europeans, and civil-servant status is no longer predominant among job-center staff, but recruitment patterns appear to have hardly changed. While the creation of job centers opened a window of recruitment opportunities, it was not used strategically to increase staff diversity. We are mindful that, as Watkins-Hayes points out (chap. 10 in this volume), bureaucratic diversity does not necessarily assure responsiveness to minority populations. However, we could find no evidence that managers sought to develop any strategies that might improve responsiveness to migrants, such as assigning ombudspersons to investigate the migrants' experiences or targeting "care workers" to migrant populations. In fact, caseworkers responsible for "care work" (essentially a social work–type function) have limited capacity to respond to the special needs of migrant populations, given that they also carry a large burden of administrative work, similar to that of other caseworkers.

As previously discussed, one-third of UB II recipients with migrant backgrounds report problems in oral communication in German. Our research indicates that staff in job centers see the responsibility for overcoming language problems exclusively as the burden of their clients, or "customers," as they are called. It is seen as acceptable that customers bring their children as interpreters even during school hours. The legal principle that German is the official language of administration is misinterpreted by many case managers as even forbidding them to use foreign language skills they may have. Under the circumstances, it should not be entirely surprising that, for migrants, the initial visit to the job center may end with no action, although the resulting delay in benefit processing is likely to aggravate their financial distress. Interviews also suggest that communication problems hinder the development of a trustful working relationship with case managers.

The federal employment agency website does provide translations of forms, checklists, and guides for applicants in the two most important languages of migrant beneficiaries, Turkish and Russian. However, locating this information requires navigating through five screens, each of them in German only. Those who have attempted to use the website have expressed frustration that it is difficult to follow or remember, even for those who do understand German. Interestingly, most case managers interviewed in job centers were unaware of the existence of these materials. Some expressed disbelief that translated forms existed at all, noting that "German is the official language."

Despite these problems, UB II participants with migrant backgrounds by and large expressed higher satisfaction than native participants. Migrants were less likely than natives to report that they were "getting treatment inferior to others" and more likely to report "getting treatment superior to others." Decomposing the data tells a somewhat different story. About 20 percent of Turkish migrants—of both sexes—reported that they got treatment inferior to others, and they were less satisfied with the staff than were other migrant groups. For reasons to be explored further, intercultural tensions seem to be concentrated among Turkish migrants, a finding at least superficially consistent with their marginalized status in German society.

Activation of Job Seekers with Migrant Backgrounds

German activation reforms promised modernized and better employment services and more efforts to bring the unemployed into the labor market—that is, more activation (Hartz Commission 2002). Our standardized survey of UB II beneficiaries inquired about selected activating events, among them the number of job-center interviews, the coverage of certain issues in these interviews, the completion of a back-to-work agreement, receipt of a job offer (or an offer for apprenticeship, in the case of youths), and threats and incidence of financial sanctions.

Beneficiaries with migrant backgrounds, in general, reported similar frequency of activating events as other recipients; in fact, slightly more (see table 11.5). But these events were less likely to be directed at human-capital investment and more at requiring work first and threatening or imposing sanctions. Roughly three-quarters of the respondents had at least one job-center interview within the year; however, they concluded fewer back-to-work agreements than nonmigrants. Interviews suggest that problems with comprehension may be a

Table 11.5.   Indicators of activation by group of origin (%)

	Nonmigrants	Turkey	Southern Europe	Ethnic German repatriates	Middle and Eastern Europe/CIS	Rest of the world
Interview with case manager	73.0	74.6	70.0	79.2	75.2	73.4
Valid B2W agreement	44.7	26.3	31.4	23.6	26.0	25.4
Job or apprenticeship offer	19.2	26.2	25.5	17.8	17.1	24.3

Source: Customer telephone survey, second wave, extrapolated for the whole of Germany; authors' calculations.

Note: Interview with case manager = at least one interview during preceding year. Valid B2W agreement = back-to-work agreement concluded during previous year or older agreement still valid. Job or apprenticeship offer = full-time or part-time job or apprenticeship offer made during preceding year.

factor. Some case managers said that they would refrain from concluding a back-to-work agreement if they were not sure the client understood the agreement. Migrants were referred less frequently than nonmigrants to certain activities, such as education, training, or make-work jobs. This may suggest that fewer monetary investments are made in their human capital or in efforts to help them locate paid work.

In addition, some migrant groups were more likely than nonmigrants to receive job or apprenticeship offers, rather than human-capital building opportunities. This was the case for southern Europeans of both genders, middle and eastern European men, Turkish women, and women from the rest of the world. It thus appears that, generally, migrants were subject to a more straightforward work-first regime than nonmigrants.

One of the professed objectives of reform was the introduction of a stricter sanction regime, in the form of reduced benefits for defined periods. The survey asked respondents about sanction threats (i.e., whether a case manager mentioned sanctions as a possible consequence of noncompliance) and about whether imposed sanctions had been justified. The propensity of being shown the "sticks" in the activation process did not differ greatly among groups of origin, although middle and eastern Europeans reported somewhat fewer sanction threats. However, the incidence of sanctions actually imposed shows great variation (see table 11.6.) At the extremes, the ratio of execution (reported sanctions imposed over reported threats of sanctions) is 17 percent for male ethnic German repatriates and 97 percent for females of Turkish origin. The ratio of execution is also high for Turkish men, for men from the rest of the world, and for southern European women.

Table 11.6. Sanction indicators, by group of origin and gender (%)

	Nonmigrants	Turkey	Southern Europe	Ethnic German repatriates	Middle and Eastern Europe/CIS	Rest of the world
All respondents						
Threatened with sanction	27.7	29.9	30.0	25.6	17.8	28.9
Sanction actually imposed	11.5	24.8	17.9	4.6	5.7	18.3
Ratio of execution	.42	.83	.66	.18	.32	.63
"Sanction not justified"	72.6	79.2	75.6	75.0	45.6	65.7
Males						
Threatened with sanction	28.5	36.4	38.7	28.1	22.2	32.1
Sanction actually imposed	12.5	26.7	18.6	4.7	7.8	23.1
Ratio of execution	.44	.73	.48	.17	.35	.72
"Sanction not justified"	69.5	71.4	88.0	80.5	62.2	74.5
Females						
Threatened with sanction	26.9	23.7	22.1	23.0	15.9	24.8
Sanction actually imposed	10.5	23.1	17.3	4.5	4.8	12.4
Ratio of execution	.39	.97	.78	.20	.30	.50
"Sanction not justified"	76.4	88.5	61.1	68.9	34.2	45.8

Source: Customer telephone survey, extrapolated for the whole of Germany; authors' calculations.

The majority of those sanctioned said that the sanctions were not justified. But here again, the variation between groups of origin is striking. Women from middle and eastern Europe indicated both a low incidence of sanctions and the highest acceptance of them. By contrast, Turkish women and southern European men show a higher incidence of sanctions and almost 90 percent nonacceptance of them.

Our sanctions data indicate that casework practices in job centers may disadvantage migrant populations in a variety of ways that neither informal discretion nor formal processes of redress and mediation remedy. For example, although caseworkers threaten to impose sanctions for infractions of the rules, they may use their discretion to consider excuses for noncompliance or expressions of willingness to comply with the rules. There is also a written hearing procedure. Our data indicate inequality in incidence of sanctions; they were most likely to be imposed on migrants from Turkey and southern European men. Survey responses also indicate differences in the extent to which migrant groups regarded sanctions as unjustified, with highest rates of dissatisfaction reported by southern European men and Turkish women. Interestingly, objections to sanctions also were relatively high among repatriated German men.

How can we understand the migrant experience of activation? Our data are subject to alternative interpretations. One possibility is that case managers may consider certain groups of origin less trustworthy than others and may thus be less prepared to accept their claims for benefits and services or for exemptions from specific work rules which would amount to statistical discrimination on ethnic grounds. A second possibility is that certain groups may be less able than others to understand letters sent to them and to comprehend the rules to which they are subject. If noncompliance because of incomprehension results in a higher sanction risk for this group, this could be characterized as indirect or institutional discrimination (Feagin and Feagin 1978; Gomolla and Radtke 2009). In this case, institutional discrimination would result not from purpose-fully discriminatory practices but from equal treatment in the face of systemati-cally unequal circumstances. A third possibility is that individuals understand the rules and the potential consequences of noncompliance but value the moral and psychological costs of compliance higher than the financial costs of incur-ring a sanction. In this case, conflicts between traditional cultures and the adult worker model of activation policy might not constitute purposeful discrimina-tion, yet might produce discrimination in effect.

These important differences pose a challenge that German job centers are not prepared to meet in any strategic and coordinated way. The experience of Muslim women is particularly instructive. Interviews with job-center staff sug-gest that women of Muslim origin may be unable to translate the idea of the adult worker model into their family reality. They may be unable to reconcile work offered to them with their very notion of motherhood or with their moral and religious obligations. Caseworker interviews shed light on this problem:

> This husband always comes here with his wife wearing a headscarf and he thinks that she is nothing but stupid anyway and this is also what she thinks of herself. . . . Well, now again I have formally obliged her to go there [to a job interview]. . . . Well, it only works the sanction way. (Interview 02-2-FM_Ü25)

I had two such cases this morning. Those were two mothers who had done no job search whatsoever during the last months, and both justified themselves by saying: I did not know that I have to look for jobs. . . . If this happens again, both will have to get a 30 percent sanction at the least. (Interview 11-3-PAP_Ü25)

Well, these young Arab girls are very often accompanied by their father . . . and they talk to each other in their mother tongue and I don't know what about. . . . Just the other week such a girl was here, totally intimidated, with her father here and she is really scared. (Interview 02-4-FM_U25)

A 16- or 17-year-old Turkish girl was told to take up vocational training and a few days later her mother is down here with her case manager and starts crying . . . because her daughter has been obliged to do what does not fit into the family pattern at all. The daughter does not go out to work—full stop. That is not envisioned at all. The daughter is to stay at home, no question about that. (Interview 01-4-AGV)

These quotes illustrate the fundamental dilemma job-center staff face when dealing with migrant women of certain origins. If they apply formal rules equally to native and Muslim women, the end result will be a sanction but no job for the Muslim women. If, however, they were to respect role models from different cultures, they would be using discretion in their interpretation of the law, possibly even contradicting it. In this sense, they would be violating the principle of equal treatment under the law. To complicate matters further, one might regard them as implicitly collaborating in keeping migrant women in their culturally constructed gender roles, with all the limitations those imply. Given the Weberian traditions of German bureaucracy, an alternative form of casework, one that might tap and support women's own quest for independence in subtle and non-disruptive ways, would require a degree of discretionary practice—and cultural awareness—that may lie beyond the structural constraints and normative traditions of job-center work.

More broadly, our data suggest that, regardless of the apparent uniformity of activation's formal policy provisions, in practice, selected migrant populations—especially non-European migrants—may experience a harsher form of activation than others. They receive fewer educational and work-support services, tougher work-first requirements, and more threats and incidence of sanctions.

Activation and Migrant Populations

As in other parts of Europe, migrant backgrounds negatively affect job opportunities in Germany. The composition of the migrant population in Germany, the changing labor-market structure, and the system for certifying educational credentials exacerbate the obstacles facing migrants in the labor market. In an economy where demand for lower-skilled manufacturing workers has declined and service-sector jobs have increased, gaps in human capital, recognition of education and training credentials, and language skills present formidable obstacles to economic integration. Similarly, cultural gaps, especially differences regarding family and gender roles, complicate the implementation of activation policy that is largely predicated on assumptions about prevailing values and traditions.

Our analysis shows that job centers are not well prepared to address the specific needs and circumstances facing diverse populations of migrants. Diversity among the staff is very low, and little effort has been made to improve responsiveness to migrants by increasing staff diversity or cultural sensitivity or by engaging specialists in migrant advocacy. Linguistic communication problems are largely left to migrants to solve themselves. Neither activation policy nor street-level practices in job centers are organized to assist migrants in getting their qualifications recognized. More commonly, caseworkers responsible for job brokering simply treat migrant beneficiaries as unskilled. Rather than addressing the diverse circumstances of migrant beneficiaries, job-center staff are more likely to emphasize nondiscrimination and equal treatment. In the classic bureaucratic tradition, they give preference to equality of treatment over responsiveness to individuals.

Yet there are some puzzles in our empirical findings. Although our data suggest that interactions between job-center staff and migrants are fraught with inequality and operate to the disadvantage of groups from Turkey and southern Europe, we also find relatively high rates of self-reported satisfaction by migrants and limited complaints. In addition, our extensive interviews with job-center staff have yielded little evidence of purposefully or explicitly discriminatory attitudes or practices. How might we account for the apparent disjuncture between our findings of unequal treatment and indicators of relative satisfaction and limited complaints? Our examination of evidence from other research suggests that this issue must be treated with caution, as both staff self-reports and client survey responses can understate systemic problems. As one study has indicated, recipient satisfaction surveys may be overly positive, due to limited information about legal rights and a tendency to distinguish individual caseworkers from the system as a whole (Soss 1999).

Moreover, on closer inspection, our data do indicate subgroup variations in reported satisfaction that are consistent with the more troubling picture of unequal treatment that our data reveal. In particular, Turkish migrants appear as an outlier in some dimensions of satisfaction and are overrepresented among those subject to the punishment of sanctions. Clearly, one must take care to account for variation in the experiences and responses of diverse migrant groups.

We would argue that our findings suggest that in the German welfare bureaucracy nominally equal treatment of persons with unequal backgrounds and circumstances can have the effect of deepening existing inequalities. Contrary to
their apparent good intentions and their espousal of institutional blindness, the
street-level routines of job-center bureaucrats reveal de facto forms of institutional discrimination. These practices effectively reinforce existing inequalities
by (1) treating vocational or academic qualifications not recognized in Germany
as nonexistent (particularly disadvantaging middle and eastern Europeans); (2)
disregarding the special human-capital and language-training needs of migrants
in favor of a need-blind work-first approach; and (3) applying a formalized
sanction regime equally to groups whose ability to respond adequately is
unequally distributed and whose cultural and familial traditions are disregarded.
It is here, especially, that Turkish migrants lose out.

The German style of bureaucratic activation may appear superficially less
discriminatory than a more overtly discretionary street-level bureaucracy in
which caseworkers may have more visible opportunities to transform personal
prejudice into discriminating behavior. However, we have shown that the German bureaucracy has produced discrimination in effect, largely because it is not
well prepared to effectively assist claimants in overcoming the gaps that constitute labor-market barriers specific to migrant backgrounds or to recognize cultural differences. We also have shown that the punitive sanctions regime weighs
most heavily on migrant subgroups from Turkey and southern Europe.

What are the prospects for addressing these gaps and social differences more
effectively? There is no easy and obvious solution to the extent that the adult-
worker model implicit in the activation regime is in conflict with the family
roles of migrant groups. More research and conceptual work is needed to understand how activation and welfare-to-work policies can effectively address diverse
needs, especially the needs of women in more traditional family roles. The tensions between bureaucratic routine and the needs of diverse populations and
between care work and paid work are issues that go beyond the German case, as
other chapters in this book illustrate. The case of migrants subject to Germany's
activation regime demonstrates how these tensions play out in a specific political
and organizational context. It also demonstrates how, in this context, the practices of activation may exacerbate, rather than relieve, economic and social
inequality.

Notes

1. In 2009, a "migrant background" was ascribed to 19.2 percent of Germany's population according to the definition of the Federal Bureau of Statistics (Statistisches Bundesamt
2010). Among this population, 12.9 percent (or 10.6 million) were foreign born, and 6.2

percent had at least one foreign-born parent; 10.3 percent were German citizens, and 8.8 percent were nonnationals. According to OECD 2008, the European countries with higher percentages of foreign-born population were Luxemburg (34.8 percent, or 160,000), Switzerland (24.1 percent, or 1.8 million), Ireland (14.4 percent, or 601,000), and Austria (14.1 percent, or 1.6 million).

2. The outnumbering of nonnationals by Germans with a "migrant background" (see n. 1) is primarily due to the automatic recognition of German nationality to repatriates, and is due to a lesser extent to naturalization, which has only been facilitated since 2000. It should be noted, however, that in terms of their limited command of the German language or recognized skills, repatriates have much in common with other groups of immigrants.

3. According to the administrative count of the Federal Employment Agency, unemployment rates were 6.4 percent for nationals and 14.6 per cent for nonnationals in May 2011; see Bundesagentur für Arbeit (2011). Unemployment rates for those with a migrant background are only available according to international standards (based on the International Labour Organization's [ILO's] definition of unemployment): 6.2 percent for natives and 12.7 percent for those with a migrant background.

4. There has been concern about alleged "welfare migration" (Borjas 1999; Boeri 2009; Boeri, Hanson, and McCormick 2002; Razin and Sadka 2004), recently refuted for Britain and Ireland by Corrigan (2010), and about the undermining of solidarity among the native population if perceived outsiders reap its benefits (Mau and Burkhardt 2009; Van Oorschot 2010; Stichnoth 2010).

5. In a 2007 survey, majorities of the population, including the unemployed, thought that unemployment insurance should be based on former wages, although this was no longer the case for the majority of the unemployed (Becker and Hallein-Benze 2009).

6. In 2009, only 26 percent of unemployed migrants received unemployment insurance benefits, compared to 41 percent of natives. Migrants are less likely to have jobs that qualify for unemployment insurance or to survive in them long enough to qualify.

7. See n. 3.

8. On preliminary assessments of governance reforms, see Federal Ministry of Labour and Social Affairs (2006); Hielscher and Ochs (2009); Knuth and Larsen (2009).

9. Most of the interviews were conducted as part of a comparative evaluation of two competing models of service delivery (Brussig and Knuth 2009). Since the fundamental design of this project consisted of a pairwise comparison of territorial units with different governance, the survey sample was drawn from only those 154 territorial units (out of a total of around 440) that had been sampled for interregional comparison. The data were weighted using a countrywide survey of recipients of UB II for reference (Trappmann et al. 2007). Descriptive tables in this chapter report extrapolated values.

10. Persons with several citizenships of which one is German were treated as nationals but may qualify as having a migrant background by virtue of the other two criteria.

11. This second clause excludes persons born of German parents during a temporary stay abroad.

12. Territorial definitions refer to the time of birth; from 1945 to 1990, they include Eastern and Western occupation zones and later both German states. The reference to preferred language excludes from this definition children from multiethnic families whose cultural and educational background is predominantly German.

13. This is not to imply that all people in this category actually came as guest workers or are children of guest workers. Many from the territories of the former Yugoslavia came as

war refugees. But further differentiation would result in groups too small for meaningful analysis.

14. The recipiency rate (the percentage of the respective population receiving UB II) is 8 percent for natives and 19 percent for those with a migrant background. Broken down by migrant groups, the rate is 28 percent for middle and eastern Europeans (including ethnic Germans), 19 percent for those of Turkish origin, 12 percent for those from southern Europe, and 13 percent for migrants from the rest of the world (Brussig, Kaltenborn, and Wielage 2010). The recipiency rate for ethnic German repatriates could not be determined.

15. Even though the German dual (apprenticeship plus public schooling) system of vocational training shows some signs of decline, more than 50 percent of each birth cohort still enters this system.

16. Persons under 25 were excluded because their vocational training may still be upcoming or ongoing.

17. Because of space restrictions, the model is not reported here; we present only a descriptive comparison in figure 11.1.

18. Chambers are legal, corporative bodies whose members are in specific occupational categories—e.g., self-employed craftsmen, workers in manufacturing and commerce (the largest chambers), lawyers, medical doctors, pharmacists. They have regulative functions with regard to the access to and conduct of their respective professions or occupations. Trade unions also participate in administering occupational exams.

19. To complicate matters further, hospital nurses and other nonacademic health care professionals, as well as child care professionals, are trained in schools run by their respective Land, with differing curricula and occupational titles.

20. These are occupations and professions in the fields of health care and legal services, but also craftspeople whose work is regulated by safety standards, such as electricians. Ethnic German repatriates enjoy a general recognition privilege. But according to the data shown in table 11.2, this seems not to help them much.

21. Level B1 is designed to provide the following proficiencies: "Understands main points in clear standard language where familiar subjects related to work, school, leisure, etc. are concerned. Able to manage most situations encountered when traveling in the area where the language is spoken. Able to express oneself coherently in a simple manner on familiar topics and areas of personal interest. Able to report experiences and incidents, describe aspirations and aims, and explain and justify plans and opinions" (Trim et al. 2009; author's translation).

22. In interviews, job-center staff indicated that language command had not improved when clients returned from language courses. In the telephone survey, clients who reported improved language skills very rarely attributed the improvements to participation in language courses.

23. This is not specific to benefit recipients but was also found in a survey of the population at large (Cornelißen 2005, 308).

24. These findings should be treated carefully with regard to their relevance for people's actual behavior. We tested the relationship between survey responses and respondents' propensity to take up work, controlling for regional and personal characteristics. We found that agreeing with the statement that "mothers should stay at home at least until the children enter school" had significant negative effects on work participation only for Germans without migrant backgrounds.

12

Frontline Workers
as Intermediaries

The Changing Landscape of Disability and
Employment Services in Australia

GREGORY MARSTON

Recent welfare reform in Australia has been constructed around the now-familiar principle of paid work and willingness to work as the funda-mental markers of social citizenship. Beginning with the long-term unemployed in Australia in the mid-1990s, the scope of welfare reform has now extended to include people with a disability—which is a category of recipients of income support that has been growing. From the national government's point of view, this growth is a financial concern, as it seeks to move as many people as possible into paid work to support the costs of an aging population (DEWR 2006). In doing so, the government has changed the meaning of disability in terms of eligibility for financial support from the state. At the same time, it has redefined the role of people with a disability with regard to work and the role of the state with regard to the disabled. This has been a matter of some political contention in Australia.

This conflict has played out at different levels of the sociopolitical system. At the policy level, it has involved a struggle to define disability as a policy category, especially with reference to one's obligation and capacity to work. At the per-sonal level, it has involved a struggle to define the social status and identity of the disabled (as citizens, workers, and social participants). At the organizational level, it has involved a struggle to negotiate the conflicting principles of work mandates versus responsiveness to the special needs and circumstances of people with a disability. In this struggle, street-level caseworkers are the intermediaries. Their practices are important in negotiating disability as a policy and sociolegal category—particularly in the context of welfare reforms that require people with a disability to work. This intermediary role has the potential to pose ethical conflicts, as practitioners find themselves juggling the dual charges of responding to needs and enforcing welfare-to-work compliance. In other words, they find themselves caught in the middle of a clash between needs-based and work-based modes of resource distribution and social citizenship.

This chapter reviews each of these elements of struggle over Australia's welfare state reforms. It begins by discussing the main elements of policy reform, including those related to disability. It brings into this discussion the political history of disability as a social category and efforts by people with a disability to shape that status. It also recognizes that the changing conception of disability as a sociolegal status is only partly determined by individuals or by formal policy change. This chapter uses data from interviews to probe the struggle over the changing status of disability from the perspective of beneficiaries and the street-level workers who must assign status under the terms of the new welfare reforms. It examines conflicts and ethical dilemmas in the specific context of disability employment service organizations, subject to new contract and performance requirements.

It is my contention that these local spaces are where social citizenship rights and responsibilities are negotiated and where modes of welfare governance have become both coercive and voluntary at the same time (Cruikshank 1999). I am particularly interested in the mediating role that organizational norms and service-user identities have on the worker-citizenship relationship. Some organizations, for example, may make a public virtue out of what they consider to be a healthy disrespect for official policy pronouncements, or at least are able to successfully manage competing demands and expectations, such as bottom-up and top-down accountabilities (driven by clients' needs and by government funding requirements, respectively).

The mediating functions of street-level workers in frontline organizations helps us to think critically about what Evelyn Brodkin refers to as "policy as produced," which is a perspective that helps the observer appreciate that policies are shaped and reshaped through the friction of personal-professional values and the broader politics of policy change within concrete organizational settings (see chap. 2 in this volume). It is a particular aspect of this organizational friction that is the focus here; specifically, the sociolegal category of disability and its contested meanings within discourses of social need, self-advocacy, and paid work. Before exploring these issues empirically, the first section of the chapter presents some of the policy background and context.

Context

In July 2006, the federal government in Australia, then led by Prime Minister John Howard, implemented welfare-to-work policies for several social security cohorts, including people with a disability. These reforms were the latest in a decade of policy changes that were introduced in the name of activating citizens through what the government referred to as "mutual obligation" policies. One of the major policy assumptions that informed the design of the 2006 welfare-to-work policy changes was that many people were faking their disability in order to qualify for the Disability Support Pension (DSP). Prior to 2006, a medical practitioner was required to support a person's application for the pension. The government believed there was collusion between some medical professionals and citizens to ensure that people qualified for the DSP. With the 2006 welfare-to-work changes a new assessment process was designed, and the power to make a decision about whether someone was work capable was outsourced to allied health professionals who were contracted to conduct a job-capacity assessment (JCA).

Despite these administrative changes, the numbers of people eligible to claim a disability pension increased after 2006. People with a disability are one of the largest groups of income-support recipients in Australia. It is estimated that over a three-year period, from June 2007 to June 2010, the number of DSP recipients in Australia grew by almost 11 percent, to around 800,000 recipients, compared with around 690,000 in 2006.

Part of this increase can be explained by recent changes in eligibility for the aged pension in Australia, which forced people to remain on the DSP for a longer period before being transferred to the aged pension. Nonetheless, this increase in the overall rate is still significant, particularly since a key assumption of the 2006 welfare-to-work policy changes in Australia had been that the numbers of people on the DSP would decrease as they moved into paid work as a result of activation policies. In a 2009 speech, the federal minister for housing, community services, and indigenous affairs acknowledged the failure of the 2006 welfare-to-work policies to shift people into the workforce: "Unfortunately the disability support pension has become a destination payment. . . . Clearly the policy challenge we face is to determine why existing policies are failing Australians with a disability."[1]

The 2006 welfare-to-work policy changes represented a new direction for people with a disability and for the Disability Employment Network (DEN) (Macali 2006). Employment services for people with a disability in Australia have for the last thirty years been delivered via the DEN, which was since renamed the Disability Employment Service (DES) in 2010. The service model of DES is based on contracting arrangements between the federal government as purchaser and a multitude of for-profit and nonprofit provider organizations (Carroll and Steane 2002). There is significant diversity among DES providers in terms of size, age of the provider, and type of service. Most services are generalist, assisting people with a range of different disabilities. Other services specialize in assisting people with a particular disability, the most common being intellectual disability, psychiatric disability, and physical disability, although there are small numbers of providers in a range of other specializations (Wade and Bell 2003, 7). DEN providers operate in all Australian states and territories, and in metropolitan, regional, rural, and remote settings.

The welfare-to-work reforms presented a challenge to the way in which the DEN had traditionally operated, because the nature of the professional support relationship changed from being based on voluntary assistance to a mode of engagement with clients based on elements of compulsion and coercion. One of the contractual duties associated with welfare-to-work case management is monitoring the conduct of clients to ensure they comply with their activity agreements, which may involve engaging in various job-search activities and maintaining regular contact with employment service providers. As Abello and MacDonald (2002) indicate, employment consultants are required not only to assist people in finding suitable employment but also to take on a policing and compliance role, alongside the traditional focus on employment brokerage and support. In other words, employment consultants are asked to manage a new dual role of being a soft cop as well as a human service worker supporting people in becoming self-determining agents.

In the broader context of mainstream employment services it is important to note that Australia has adopted a full purchaser-provider split, meaning that organizations compete via a tender process to provide services as agents of the government (Struyven 2004). This new system, referred to as the Job Network, was established to replace the former Commonwealth Employment Service in 1998, which was a public employment service provided by public employees. The changes to the funding model of the DEN in 2006 were understood as a move to bring this part of the sector into line with the competitive quasi-market model of mainstream employment services. There was a lot of fear within the disability employment sector about what this change would mean for the quality of the service the employees provided and the means of engaging with clients (Macali 2006). These fears were substantiated by independent evidence that the mainstream Job Network regularly sacrificed effectiveness for efficiency and was unable to provide meaningful services to the most disadvantaged, particularly the long-term unemployed (Marston and McDonald 2006).

Much has been written about the influence market models have on social service delivery, and I do not intend to say more about that here. My interest is more in the tensions that this clash of paradigms produces in practice, which is the space where welfare citizenship is made and remade. It is at this level of analysis that we are able to see how managerial reforms govern both workers and clients, according to the same logic. As Schram et al. (2010, 746) succinctly put it: "Today, with the new public management firmly entrenched, the personnel of the welfare system are subjected to a neoliberal disciplinary regime so that they will ensure that clients of the welfare system are subjected to the same."

Using competitive contracts to deliver traditional government services can theoretically result in positive gains by providing innovative services at minimal cost, so long as the quality of service provision is not compromised (Webster and Harding 2000). However, this also can create a level of dissatisfaction among nonprofit organizations, particularly in cases where government simply invites organizations to "accept the terms of a deal it has already drafted" instead of negotiating "as equals the terms of an agreement" (Hancock 2006, 55). In other words, contractual welfare reforms become a case of "centralized decentralization"—the state does not "roll back" but instead "rolls out" its organizational rationalities for nonprofit organizations to adopt (Schram et al. 2010). They are urged to accept if they wish to continue to receive government funding.

Researchers note that the overwhelming response to perceived failures in the welfare system (i.e., increases in disability expenditures and number of recipients) is to develop and implement bureaucratic solutions, introducing more and more systems, assessments, procedures, and guidelines in the sector (Schram et al. 2010). Eardley (2002, 301) believes that the creation of the Job Network (and now the DEN) represents a "significant challenge for non-profit, community based agencies . . . accustomed to working in partnership with government on a grant-for-services basis" who are now "faced with full-scale competition." New compliance-monitoring requirements place disability organizations (and, essentially, the people who constitute these organizations) under greater surveillance in order to "normalize, stabilize and optimize work related activities" (Dean 1999, 174) and "maximise labour market participation" (Daguerre and Etherington 2009, 16).

There are other forces shaping the practice of workers at the front lines, such as professional norms. Workers' beliefs and biases about the target population have been found to play an important role in shaping how decisions are made on the ground (Maynard-Moody and Musheno 2003). These beliefs about the target population can themselves be influenced by the cultural legacy of social movements that have historically attempted to publicly and often vigorously address various forms of stigmatization, or what Nancy Fraser (1989) refers to as "misrecognition." These political projects shape human service education and the conduct of professionals in the field. For example, the disability rights movement in Australia has been very active in challenging charitable conceptions of how people with a disability should be treated by state and nonprofit organizations. This movement, informed by what is commonly known as a "social model of disability," has rallied against a construction of people with a disability as subjects only worthy of pity and paternalism. It has also demanded equal treatment for people with a disability in accessing social goods and services. This social movement has been successful over the past thirty years in having principles of equal treatment enshrined in antidiscrimination law in Australia and other countries, among them the United Kingdom and the United States.

While many disability advocates and people with a disability demand access to open employment as a social right, there has also been a demand by some within this social movement for recognition of the right not to work—that is, to receive ongoing support from the state and to engage with the labor market from a position of autonomy and independence. The following personal reflection by a female artist with a physical disability captures this ethos very eloquently, as well as illustrating the tension between productive social norms and nonmarket markers of self-identity:

> The very first thing that people ask me when I say I am a painter is "Do you sell your work? Are you supporting yourself?" I actually do sell my work, but I do not support myself from these sales. I hate this question and I feel ashamed no matter how I answer it. This is because I always feel like this question is a test; a test to see whether my lifestyle and hobby are legitimate. . . . Much of the empowering rhetoric in disability movements is about becoming employed and about having equal access to mainstream society. Capitalism has at its root the idea of an individual's worth being intrinsically linked to their production value. Many, though by no means all, disabled people will never be good workers in the capitalist sense: if you cannot move or speak, it is hard to succeed in a mainstream career. There is a small but significant percentage of the disabled population that has "made it" and has achieved economic equality working as professionals, lawyers, artists, professors, and writers. They are a fortunate minority and the work they do is important. (Taylor 2004: 1)

This personal and powerful demand for the decommodification of labor is directly oppositional to the logic of welfare-to-work that operates on the basis of paternalism. Asserting the value of autonomy and alternative modes of citizenship and participation has the potential to destabilize the naturalness of the welfare-to-work policy narrative and other path-dependent policy assumptions that are joined together to justify contemporary welfare-to-work initiatives. In symbolic and material terms, what is at stake in these debates is the contested meaning of disability and impairment and the expressed right of people with a disability to determine the means and ends of their participation in society in a way that is consistent with the value of individual autonomy. The above quote also alludes to the fundamental ambiguity in the disability employment discourse as to whether people with a disability deserve access to open employment because it provides an entrée to social standing and capability building, but do not have to achieve a level of employment that would allow them to economically support themselves, if indeed the goal of such employment is economic self-sufficiency (Yeatman 2000).

A distinctive strength of disability-led approaches to participation is that they seek to make a distinction between autonomy and independence. At the same time we need to recognize that welfare-to-work policies seek to collapse this distinction. As Jayasuri (2001, 58) argues in his criticism of the maximal choice of autonomy and economic independence that pervades welfare-to-work policies, "It fails to recognise that individual autonomy requires that we acknowledge that individuals make choices within the context of institutional arrangements or structures, some of which may work to inhibit the exercise of choice. Contractualist welfare programs, through the insistence on economic independence as the defining attribute of individual autonomy, fail to acknowledge how a system of domination or subordination—which cuts across the public/private divide—influences the shape of individual autonomy."

These contrasting logics of individual autonomy set up a tension in the sociolegal category of disability and impairment as it is played out in social policy debates and disability employment organizations. Traditionally, if you were defined by the state as being unable to work, then you were defined as being "in need." Thus, during early capitalism people with an impairment were classified as belonging to the category of the deserving poor and were made eligible for state assistance. As the demand for labor has increased, there is now a new set of pressures to categorize some of this same group as being "work capable."

In the Australian case, the federal government in 2006 reduced the work test from being able to work thirty hours per week to being able to work fifteen hours, in an attempt to move greater numbers of people into paid work rather than onto the DSP. The government has more recently updated the impairment tables that are used by the income-support agency Centrelink in assessing what weighting to give different impairments in judging whether an individual can meet the eligibility requirements for the DSP. A test of the new tables found that four out of every ten people who qualified for the DSP in 2011 would not qualify under the new regime. After the new rules take effect in 2012, the government estimates it will save some $35 million per year.[2]

These changes to eligibility criteria for the DSP in Australia, under the auspices of welfare reform, highlight how the sociolegal category of disability is contentious and ambiguous. It also highlights how disability has become a structural boundary category between work-based and needs-based distribution systems, a binary that Oliver (1990, 41) argues has often been used in an oppressive and stigmatizing way against disabled people. This critical viewpoint is similar to Deborah Stone's (1984) thesis in *The Disabled State* that the disability category constitutes a movable boundary that is manipulated by the state to regulate access to social welfare benefits. Stone also contends that this determination of disability has become increasingly medicalized over time. The "social model of disability" arose in response to this medicalization of disability.

The social model of disability suggests that the previously taken-for-granted, naturalistic category of disability may, in reality, be an artificial and exclusionary social construction that penalizes people with an impairment who do not conform to mainstream expectations of appearance, behavior, and/or economic performance (Tregaskis 2002). This theory of disability has been a powerful force for change, shaping both the self-organization of people with a disability and the espoused goals and practices of professional support organizations working with people with a disability, including employment agencies.

It is this form of social and cultural politics that adds a level of analytical depth to the case of disability and employment services in Australia, as it helps to highlight the intersection of different markers of identity as they are constituted and contested at the level of the organization. How citizens position themselves in this mix of cultural and organizational politics is also highly relevant to our understanding of how policy operates through subjects located in particular organizational contexts. People with a disability, for example, may seek to privilege their disability in making a claim for a disability pension. On the other hand, the state, through the implementation of welfare-to-work policies, may be understood as attempting to erase such differences and to see this group as principally just another group of citizens requiring work activation. How frontline workers interpret the imperatives of self-sufficiency and work first in welfare-to-work policies is an important normative and empirical question. The next part of this chapter examines street-level organizations (SLOs) as policy mediators (see chap. 2 in this volume), exploring how they have mediated changes in pension policy for the disabled.

Methods and Purpose of the Study

Data were obtained through qualitative interviews of eighty people with a disability. They either received a disability pension (the DSP) or had been transferred to Newstart (the unemployment benefit) during the 2008–9 period. The purpose of this study was to better understand the experiences of people with a disability in their attempts to access the paid labor market following implementation of the 2006 welfare-to-work reforms.

Many studies have examined ways to increase labor-market integration of people with a disability and have made recommendations including job monitoring in work environments (Roulstone and Warren 2006); affirmative action (Raskin 1994); job coaching (Hoekstra et al. 2004); social capital development to build social networks to overcome employment difficulties (Potts 2005); and customized employment (Griffin and Keeton 2009). However, many of these policy prescriptions often miss the actual lived experiences of people with a disability accessing welfare benefits, nor do they question some of the assumptions inherent in the welfare reforms. In addressing this gap the specific aims of this project were to:

- investigate the experiences of people with a disability in the context of policy change, particularly the welfare-to-work policy changes of 2006;
- document and analyze the effects of the changes on people with a disability and service providers;
- analyze the major ethical issues associated with these reforms, including examining how compulsory employment and training is being taken up by workers, and the new roles and responsibilities people with a disability are now expected to fulfill.

Participants came from both urban and rural areas across Australia and identified themselves as having a range of disabilities; among them, physical and intellectual disabilities, psychiatric and psychological conditions, behavioral disorders, autism, and acquired brain injury. The first round of face-to-face semistructured interviews traced participants' life histories—their current and past employment, their housing, the quality of their relationships with family and welfare workers, the factors inhibiting their participation in work or finding work, their experience of the JCA process, and their aspirations for the future. The second round of interviews, twelve months later, focused on changes—specifically, the impact of the new service delivery model on enhancing employment and their reflections on employment experiences.

Reflexivity and responsiveness were critical tools for this research, in terms of both acknowledging the participants' active role in shaping their lives and making full use of participants' frames of reference where possible—*their* language, *their* schemes, and *their* themes. The first part of the discussion considers citizen responses to the ethical tensions of welfare-to-work, while the second part explores how workers managed their dual role.

Job-Capacity Assessments— Operationalizing Welfare-to-Work

In her critique of neoliberal governance of welfare in the twenty-first century, Dowse (2009, 576) argues that such a system brings a culture that seeks to identify those who are deemed unlikely, unable, or in need of assistance to attain "productive" working status. The JCA is one such strategy, introduced in 2006, to define people with a disability in terms of their capacity to work. Since this time, individuals have been assessed to establish whether they are able to work a minimum of fifteen hours per week. If the job-capacity assessor concludes that an individual is able to work this minimum number of hours, the individual receives unemployment benefits, the Newstart allowance. The individual must sign an activity agreement that spells out his or her obligations and notes the possibility of sanctions if he or she fails to comply.

While most participants in the study believed that the government has a right to assess their circumstances, many challenged both the assessment process and the assumptions underlying it. Paul, a 38-year-old Brisbane resident with HIV and clinical depression, spoke for many when he asserted that the JCA assumes that recipients of the DSP are untruthful about their circumstances: "They [the government] assume that the person getting a disability pension isn't truthful about what has happened in their life. They assume that the person is using the system to do whatever they want. For example, they still make me bring in medical certificates even though I have the later stages of HIV. Hasn't anyone told them that there is no cure?"

The JCA process attempts to distinguish whether an individual's disability is based on choice or chance (bad luck, accident, etc.) and attaches benefits or burden based on this assessment. For Paul, the new assessment process added "cultural insult to economic injury," to use Nancy Fraser's (1997) expression connecting the politics of identity with economic redistribution. Paul resisted the assumed identity of "untruthful subject." Part of the frustration that Paul expressed was also related to the sense that no one took the time to listen; hence the last part of his utterance, "Hasn't anyone told them there is no cure?" Voice and communicative action are important dimensions of respect for autonomy. As Yeatman (2000, 195) argues, the "who-ness" of any individual is not something that can be assessed in terms of the individual's socialized capacities to work; rather, the who-ness comes into being only as it is disclosed to others and, through this relationship, to the individual. This is why two-way communicative action is critically important at the front lines of social services.

In contrast, the JCA process is a one-way exercise in clinical assessment that privileges expert medical knowledge and provides the Australian government with a way of rationalizing compensation and deciding who gets what assistance. As mentioned in the previous section, the conduct of these assessments did not result in a reduction in the number of people claiming the DSP, which meant that the vast majority of people applying met the eligibility criteria for the pension, even under the harsher work-test rules. Recent analysis shows that people who were moved onto the lower payment rate of the unemployment benefit were often financially worse-off because they did not get promised jobs. Among people with a disability, 67 percent experienced no change, 29 percent were financially worse-off, and 3 percent were better-off. Income losses were estimated at up to $99 a week (Davidson 2011).

Participants also questioned the actual JCA process, which placed them in the medical model of disability and assessed them according to their individual level of impairment rather than the inclusiveness of social institutions or avail-ability of employment opportunities. Resisting the medical model of disability has been a key battleground for policy activists and citizens alike who insist on a social theory of disability. What is being resisted here is the expert medical knowledge that devalues everyday knowledge and lived experience, as high-lighted by 27-year-old Madeline, diagnosed as legally blind when she was in high school: "Everyday life decisions are vested in the hands of people who have very little understanding of the everyday reality of disabled people's lives. They may understand the physical or psychological illness, but this doesn't mean they know about our working lives and how much we are able to work." Ralph, a 34-year-old man from Brisbane, explained further: "She was an OT [occupational therapist] that did the assessment. I thought, 'What do you know about my mental health? Do you know what it's like to experience schizophrenia?' I don't think it was fair that she did my assessment. Don't get me wrong, she's probably an excellent OT, but I don't need an OT."

Participants' comments reveal that the assessment confuses disability with being sick (Oliver and Barnes 1998). Participants also experienced a sense of insecurity caused by being continually assessed. The possible loss of income and associated benefits because of changes to the DSP was a major source of anxiety. Leonard, a 35-year-old Brisbane resident who lives with an acquired brain injury, explained: "It's a fear that they will say, 'You're capable of working 25 hours a week' without considering the lack of supports I have, the tiredness, and that my disability isn't constant. I don't think entering into this assessment puts me in a safe place. I may be worse-off."

Bernard was a 31-year-old man from Brisbane living with paraplegia. He had higher-education qualifications, worked full-time, and offered strong opinions about the welfare-to-work reforms and the insecurities they could bring. He explained: "They [the government] place value on things that may not be what I value. Then they exercise control over you. Like they say, 'Here's some money, come and take it and there's more coming next week, but I'm not telling you when it's going to stop coming.' Then they change the rules and the money stops or there is a threat of it not coming . . . and then they expect us to justify why we need the money again and again and expect that we're just going to do it without any thought. It's relentless assessments and surveillance."

Bernard's comments shed light on the processes that subject people to prac-tices designed to shape compliance with a market logic. At the heart of this surveillance is a system designed to keep recipients "jumping through hoops" (according to Nelson, a 54-year-old respondent with impaired vision). Jolly (2003) argued that this surveillance process contributes to the ontological ambi-guity of impairment by ignoring the disabling aspects and barriers that prevent people with a disability from developing their abilities. Like many in this study,

33-year-old Jacinta discussed how this process affected her ability to access and maintain a continuity of care from her DEN service: "I hate how they've told me, 'You can only be with one employment agency for 18 months . . . and then we have to shift you on to somewhere else.' I was with one disability agency for eight years and they were great, and then they gave me the 'heave ho' because everyone was like, 'I don't think you're ever going to get a job, and you've been on the books for too long.'"

For Madeline, the quality of relationships she had with her employment consultants significantly changed after the 2006 reforms:

> When I was just out of school I didn't always have allocated times to see my job person. It was like, "Let's have a coffee and talk about your life, how we can support you." And even though it was an employment agency, we didn't always have to focus on employment if that wasn't the main thing. Since the introduction of case-based funding they now have to account for every single hour I'm with them. They also have a finite period of time to have you in a job and if the money runs out before you're in a job—oh well, tough to you.

Madeline's comment suggests how the practices of reform seem to be framing inclusion in terms of productivity and contribution, rather than self-fulfillment or quality of life (Dowse 2009, 573). It indicates that workers have had to make a shift in their practices and how they think about their work. How much control workers have over their tasks, whether they make assessments on the basis of need and respect for citizens' autonomy, and how they decide whether to recommend financial sanctions are issues of practice that highlight the frontline challenges associated with the transition to the new model of disability employment services.

Mediating the Social Identity of Disability in Employment Services

Previous studies on the effects of contracting out employment services through the Job Network in Australia have shown that nonprofit organizations have adopted the financial strategies and competitive spirit of their for-profit competitors, arguably affecting the practices, and, ultimately, the social mission of many of these organizations (Considine 2003; Ramia and Carney 2003; see also chap. 8 in this volume on the effects of contracting in the United States). Interview data provided insights into how conditions and practices had changed for disability employment workers. Increasing administrative burdens was a recurring theme. Workers typically described a workday that was reactive and clerical, focused on the performance-driven tasks of documenting clients' work-activity hours and entering the results into the data-tracking system. Workers noted that the time spent on paperwork and complying with these new administrative procedures often outstripped time spent working directly with families and children.

Chrissy, a worker in the disability field for sixteen years and the manager of a large Brisbane DEN service for the previous six years, talked about increased bureaucratic procedures: "Trying to deliver a quality service has been impacted by lots of new rules. All of a sudden administration became the focus, like 'We have to tick all our boxes' because the industry became self-regulated. Monitoring changed a lot. It was sort of like, 'You will do your own claims for your funding, and if you don't claim them all [all recipients], you lose money, and that's your problem, not ours.' So there was a big shift in our approach to working with clients . . . more outcomes driven. We have to get them a job at any cost."

Dale, a Western Australian worker in the disability field for eleven years, similarly stated: "So it was almost like we had to develop these systems, 'Have you done your claims yet?' At staff meetings we developed a team jar. If people didn't do their claims they'd have to donate to the team jar for our social things. We had to find ways to make sure that we did all the administration and paperwork."

Jason, an inner-city disability services worker in Melbourne, discussed the new business model of disability services: "And you can see all the employment consultants were sitting at their desks behind their computers, claim, claim, claim . . . document, document, document . . . write your progress notes; put it on GEMA [a computer system], do this, do that, do that . . . evidence, evidence, we have to have evidence for everything in the files because when DEWR [the Department of Employment and Workplace Relations] come they have to see what we've been doing so we'd have to try and manage that as best as possible. So yes, the changes had a huge impact. And it takes up so much time now being in the business of moving people into work."

For caseworkers, following the procedures potentially meant increased accountability and consistency of service delivery (the ability to say, "I have followed policy and procedures"). But caseworkers also expressed concern that the welfare of recipients might not be protected or fulfilled. Workers discussed "losing a number of clients as a result of these changes in their practices. As Dale explained: "So we've lost a number of clients because we've had to say, 'They are going to assess your pension,' 'Oh well I don't want to look for a job then,' so it's sort of hindering people who want to get out there and look for a job and the clients we used to work with, the ones that were here by choice now are . . . going to get their pension reviewed." Jason offered a similar perspective, observing that the new procedures sent a warning message to potential clients:

"Okay, you can come to our service, but you need to go through this process, please keep in mind this may trigger a review of your pension."

It is clear from workers' comments that they see their roles changing, limiting their opportunities to engage in building supportive relationships with clients that respect autonomy and meaningful choices. Much of the support work with clients, a primary motivation for many frontline workers who enter the disability welfare field, is no longer the direct responsibility of DEN workers and agencies. As Dale noted:

> I guess the most challenging thing is having done this for so long, previous clients I used to work with in the old world were on DSP and they were here because they wanted to be here, no one told them to come here, they were just looking for a job and they could come here. Now the people I'm working with are told to come here and that they must get a job or their pension will get taken away or their Newstart allowance. It's very hard to support people in that way who are told they have to do something so that's probably more challenging, the changing clientele that we have. They are here because they are told to be here and that's more difficult to work with.

Dale's quote highlights the problem of working with involuntary clients, who may not disagree with policy goals regarding work, but who resist the paternalism associated with this approach. Some caseworkers invoked a more traditional needs-based discourse in discussing the perceived harshness of the new policies and the contradiction between enforcing compliance and having regard for personal autonomy. Sue, a frontline worker in a small nongovernment employment service provider, highlights this contradiction in the following statement

> I've got nothing against mutual obligation, it's a good thing but you need human beings dealing with it with compassion . . . when you're dealing with certain disability groups the implications of not meeting your obligations are not always apparent to some people, despite you explaining that to them . . . I mean it's too complicated for them to understand and, of course, they just often wear the breach on the chin because they can't offer a reasonable explanation . . . I think the people that are most vulnerable are the ones that are going to get hurt by this.

As discussed, control and a capacity for autonomy have been key issues in constructing professional modes of engaging with people with a disability. The workers themselves become enmeshed in techniques of surveillance and measurement aimed at limiting access to public resources rather than ensuring inclusion and access to programs (Meekosha and Dowse 2007). This disciplinary role becomes very explicit when they recommend a financial sanction against a client (see chap. 8 in this volume).

The ethical dilemma they express emerges, in part, from the structuring effects of welfare-to-work contracts. Decision making has become more complex and fraught with competing objectives. McBeath and Webb (2002, 1016) suggest that "the kind of moral agent best fitted to working under the conditions of a complex social system is that offered by virtue ethics, which places emphasis upon judgment, experience, understanding, reflection and disposition." Street-level workers, unlike those at the top of hierarchical organizational structures, do not see citizens as "abstractions but as individuals," and, therefore, their relationships with their clients are often "personal and emotional, rarely cold and rational" (Maynard-Moody and Musheno 2000, 334). In short, caseworkers are caught between their professional identities, including a commitment to ethical principles of justice and respect, and the demands of contract work under the terms of welfare reform that press them to assume a more disciplinary role.

In drawing together the threads of this discussion it is useful to think about the themes in terms of continuities and discontinuities in welfare governance. The continuities include an intensification of eligibility requirements for benefits, paternalism toward people with a disability at the level of national social policy, and the application of market discipline in activating subjects. Poverty continues to be seen predominantly as a moral failing, but now the category of those who suffer this failing has been expanded to include people with a disability. There is also continuity in terms of contestation about how to classify incapacity to work and, more broadly, the sociolegal definition of disability. In her study, Stone (1984) shows that as far back as the early 1900s in a range of national contexts, medical and legal experts have been disagreeing about how to define "incapacity" for the purposes of determining eligibility for sickness benefits and disability pensions. In contemporary contexts, it remains a politically charged policy and organizational environment, due to the resource implications for the state and the implications for the social identity of those individuals recognized or not recognized by shifting boundaries between ability and disability.

The discontinuities that arise from the empirical study are more localized and focus on the shift from voluntarism to compulsion in worker-citizenship relationships and a competitive funding model for disability employment service providers, as well as intensification of medical and social scientific expertise in surveillance of people with a disability. The dominance of this medical discourse undermines the social model of disability, which has historically been important in mobilizing the social movement for disability rights.

Conclusion

Australia's controversial 2006 welfare-to-work changes have had a mixed result in terms of policy production on the front lines. Clearly, the pressure to achieve a job outcome in a short period of time placed unprecedented sets of pressures on workers and nongovernment organizations that have been traditionally been more focused on a voluntary mode of engagement. Common to all worker responses in this study was a concern about how compulsion had changed the relationship between workers and clients, as well as a complaint about the increased administrative burden associated with contractual welfare and client compliance. People with a disability were forced to negotiate new models of activation during this period of policy change. Previously this group of citizens was under the umbrella of an enabling model of activation; they had a greater capacity to determine their own pathway to a greater degree of economic independence. However, with the 2006 changes they faced a new work test and a possible sanction if they failed to comply with activation requirements.

Having made this distinction, it would be a mistake to assume that the former model of activation was completely voluntary and the post-2006 welfare-to-work policy changes were completely coercive. In the post-2006 system, not everyone has to be sanctioned in order to participate, and similarly, prior to the reforms being introduced, not everyone who sought assistance from disability employment was there of their own free will. Feelings of personal guilt about not conforming to social norms about paid work, encouragement from family and friends, and fear of poverty are all forms of motivation that do not easily fit into the category of either coercion or individual autonomy.

Arguably, the success of welfare-to-work and its rapid adoption by many countries have come about precisely because it taps into powerful cultural narratives about successful selves and moral conduct—it is a policy frame centered on individual transformation that works to obscure structural barriers to employment for people with a disability. The conflation of economic independence with individual autonomy is one of the political success stories of welfare-to-work policies. However, it is important to recognize that for a person with a disability, the definition of self-sufficiency can be more directly concerned with communicative action and control over basic personal services, rather than physical self-sufficiency or economic independence (Taylor 2004; Yeatman 2000).

One thing the empirical research suggests is that autonomy continues to be a key battleground in the local disability employment office, particularly as welfare-to-work policies make individual agency and social identity key sites of contestation—for both workers and clients. What people can decide for themselves in terms of their welfare and well-being versus how much is decided for them by others is both a personal and political struggle.

This study also raises questions about the organizational costs and benefits of reforms that may make practice more difficult and fraught. There may be hidden costs; for example, the most ethical caseworkers might withdraw their services because they felt morally compromised by their role. Others might remain, but feel dissatisfied and disenfranchised by heightened administrative burdens that limit their ability to interact with clients, listen to their needs, and find them a possible pathway to a better future of work or study. This conclusion is similar to that reached by Celeste Watkins-Hayes (chap. 10 in this volume), who finds that "the stated preference of caseworkers to achieve deeper engagement is effectively denied by organizational structure."

Using an organizational lens exposes the contradictions and complexities of policy as it is produced on the ground. In the case of Australian disability policy, it reveals how policy and governance are bearing down on street-level staff, changing their relationship to their work and to their clients. Without consideration of the ways in which reforms are reshaping local organizational contexts, the public discourse about welfare-to-work initiatives would continue to be about overall numbers and percentages of those on and off welfare and in and out of a job. From that perspective, both citizens and workers on the ground are somewhat meaningless abstractions from the real challenges and obstacles to social participation. That is why, as Brodkin (chap. 9) argues, "it is important for analysis to link patterns of practice that emerge in specific organizational settings to larger features of governance that transcend those settings." We must have an eye for both the particular and the universal in order to understand how changes in welfare policy are mediated by the practices of SLOs and what they mean for those working in them and the results they produce.

Notes

Some of the material used in this chapter was previously published in a peer-reviewed article (Thornton and Marston 2009). I would like to thank the editors of the *Australian Journal of Social Issues* for allowing me to use that material for this chapter.

1. Jenny Macklin, "Per Capita Policy Exchange 2009: Valuing the Future; Policymaking for the Long Term," speech, http://jennymacklin.fahcsia.gov.au/node/1229.

2. "Major Crackdown on Disability Support Pension," Pro Bono News Australia, August 1, 2011, www.probonoaustralia.com.au/news/2011/08/major-crackdown-disability-support-pension.

PART V

Administrative Justice

Challenging Workfare Practices

13

Conditionality, Sanctions, and the Weakness of Redress Mechanisms in the British "New Deal"

MICHAEL ADLER

T his chapter analyzes the implications of the New Deal in the United Kingdom for the accountability of officials and for the rights of redress of job seekers. As context for this analysis, it also reviews the development of social security provisions for the unemployed, which include social assistance as well as social insurance benefits. In the United Kingdom, there has been a shift from a more passive approach, in which the main function of social security is to prevent hardship, toward a more active approach, in which the main function of social security is to activate unemployed people and get them back into work. This shift has involved the integration of social security policies and employment policies, which were formerly relatively autonomous policy areas. Although policies for the unemployed have always combined passive and active features, a largely passive approach was in the ascendancy for the first forty years after World War II, while a more active approach has increased in importance over the last twenty-five years.

The first part of this chapter offers an account of UK policy developments and highlights two key changes: (1) the increasing use of conditionality and its application to groups previously excused from work requirements, and (2) the increasing use of sanctions for noncompliance and their application to an increasing number of beneficiaries. Conditionality is central to activation. As discussed, it is now applied to those who, because of child care responsibilities, illness, or disability, were formerly regarded as outside the labor market.

The second part of the chapter attempts to make sense of these developments. It explores the shift away from a more bureaucratic and legalistic type of decision making toward a more professional and managerial one, and discusses the implications of this shift for rights of redress and for accountability.[1] It concludes that it is increasingly difficult for job seekers to challenge sanctions that are imposed on them or the advice and help they are given, and that street-level staff are insufficiently accountable for what they do.

From a Passive to an Active Approach to Social Security

It is sometimes said of the Beveridge Report, which laid the foundations for the British welfare state, that it reflected a passive approach to social security.[2] This is because its main aim was to respond to the circumstances of people's lives rather than to change their behavior. In the case of those who are capable of work, an active approach would have aimed to get them back to work or to prepare them for work and discourage them from relying on benefits.

However, an active approach began to take hold in the late 1980s under the Conservative governments of Margaret Thatcher and John Major. It was considerably extended under the Labour governments of Tony Blair and Gordon Brown. Since 2010, it has been promoted, with great enthusiasm, by a coalition government led by David Cameron.

Following the example of the Reagan administration in the United States, in the early 1980s the Tory Party government, led by Margaret Thatcher, adopted an increasingly neoliberal approach to policy. Employment rights were curtailed and benefit levels reduced. Over the 15-year course of her administration, the government's approach to the unemployed and the welfare state changed even more dramatically. The overall aim of policy became that of reducing so-called welfare dependency, restricting benefit eligibility and closely policing the job-seeking behavior of the unemployed.

New legislation redefined the position of those who were out of work. Most unemployed 16- and 17-year-olds lost the right to means-tested Income Support. Instead, they were offered a place on a Youth Training Scheme (YTS). In addition, the benefit claims of those above that age, in particular the long-term unemployed, were scrutinized more rigorously. The previous requirement that claimants should be "available for work" was replaced by a stronger requirement that they should be "actively seeking work." The legislation also called for everyone who had been unemployed for six months to be given an interview, provided with advice and information about training, and encouraged to agree on a course of action that would get them back into work.

In 1995, Prime Minister John Major's Tory government put in place an even stricter benefits regime. Activity requirements were imposed on claimants who failed to secure employment, and caseworkers could impose sanctions on those they assessed as failing to satisfy them. However, carrots were used as well as sticks. Benefits for the low paid, known as "in-work benefits," were promoted and claimants were given an in-work benefit assessment, examining their eligibility for Family Credit (for those with dependent children), Housing Benefit (for tenants), and Council Tax Benefit (for those who pay council tax), alongside a review of their job-seeking activities.[3] These measures were intended to ameliorate the unemployment trap and encourage individuals to take low-paid jobs of the sort that were increasingly being generated in the deregulated labor market.[4] The number of low-income households claiming Family Credit exceeded five hundred thousand in 1994. More than 2 percent of the workforce had their wages supplemented in this way.

In 1996, the Major government introduced the Jobseeker's Allowance (JSA). JSA provided a single benefit with unified rules in place of the combination of contributory Unemployment Benefit and means-tested Income Support. It emphasized the responsibility of the unemployed to take advantage of every opportunity offered to return to work. Everyone in receipt of JSA was required to enter a "job seeker's agreement" that specified the detailed weekly steps they were expected to take in looking for work. They also were assigned a personal adviser (PA) whose role was to provide individualized and continuous support for job seekers. Advisers also were responsible for monitoring compliance with the job seeker's agreement at fortnightly intervals. Officials were given the power to impose sanctions for work-related misdemeanors, such as failure to apply for or refusal to accept a job vacancy. They were also given a new power to issue a "job seeker's direction," which required those in receipt of JSA to look for jobs in particular ways, take specific steps to "improve their employability," or take part in a training scheme. Advisers were empowered to impose sanctions on those who did not meet their requirements.

When the Labour Party returned to government with Tony Blair as prime minister in 1997, it did not attempt to turn back the clock but set out to develop a new "third way" that incorporated some of the neoliberal ideas that had been put in place by the Conservatives, while ostensibly maintaining a social democratic commitment to social justice (Giddens 1998). Its centerpiece was the New Deal, a set of policies that the new government announced in its first budget in 1997.[5] The avowed aim of these policies was to do everything possible to get young people, the long-term unemployed, and single parents into work, in the belief that, for those who are able, work is the best guarantor of welfare.

A distinction was made between two categories of the unemployed. The first category included those deemed able to work. The principle of activation was applied to them, and they were to be helped and/or cajoled into work by one of six New Deal programs distinguished by age group, caretaking responsibilities, duration of unemployment, and disability status. The second category included those regarded as excused from work. They continued to receive unconditional support in the form of social security benefits. The principle of activation was not applied to them at this stage, although, as discussed below, it was extended to some of them later on. A key feature of the New Deal, which distinguished it from previous initiatives, was the provision of support ostensibly tailored to the needs and circumstances of each of its client groups. Programs were directed to target groups (e.g., young people and lone parents) with a number of specific features provided within each program.

As in other countries discussed in this volume, policy reforms were accompanied by administrative reorganization (see chap. 1). Administratively, New Deal reforms established a new agency known as Jobcentre Plus, created in 2002 through a merger of the Employment Service, which operated job centers, and the Benefits Agency, which ran social security offices. The new agency was given responsibility for paying benefits to the unemployed *and* getting them back into the labor market, either directly by getting them into work or indirectly by providing training to improve their employability. Its establishment reflected a new mode of joined-up government—in which departments are expected to communicate with each other and to act together effectively, efficiently, and in a coherent fashion. This was a central plank of the first Blair government's program for public-sector reform. At the street level, the merger was associated with the introduction of individualized service, in which PAs would meet claimants to discuss their work aspirations and options; assist them in searching for jobs; explore their training needs and the availability of training programs; advise them on child care and the availability of specialist services, such as services for those with drug or alcohol dependency; and calculate whether they would be better-off in work or on benefits (Stafford 2003, 221; Stafford and Kellard 2007).

The Post-2007 Round of Welfare Reforms

Most people appeared to support the government's commitment to securing employment for those who are out of work.[6] Moreover, there is some evidence that the measures introduced by the government may have contributed to the relatively high employment rates and the relatively low levels of unemployment in the United Kingdom, at least prior to the economic crises beginning in 2008.[7] However, it is clear that the government's approach under Blair and then his Labour Party successor as prime minister, Gordon Brown, led to some excessively authoritarian policies and practices. The government's obsession with social security fraud (Sainsbury 2003) and the widespread use of television advertising, which encourages the public to treat those in receipt of social security with suspicion, reinforces the efforts of social security staff to get claimants off benefit and into work.[8] As a result, at the street level, claimants who are not really capable of work may be pressured into seeking work and subjected to sanctions when they fail to obtain it. This emphasis on work also may lead to the stigmatizing of people on benefits.

Many aspects of the regime to get unemployed people in receipt of JSA back into work, such as the requirement of frequent attendance at work-focused interviews (WFIs), have more recently been extended to those who, because of child care responsibilities, illness, or disability, are not in employment. This extension of the activation regime was intended to produce a shift in the boundary between those who can and those who cannot work. The government also assumed that it would lead to a substantial reduction in the number of single parents and people registered as sick and disabled who were on benefits.[9]

Under the Welfare Reform Act of 2007, policies were introduced with the aim of getting 1 million of the 2.7 million claimants who had been in receipt of Incapacity Benefit back into work. Incapacity Benefit, and Income Support paid on grounds of incapacity, were abolished for new claimants in October 2008 and replaced by an Employment and Support Allowance (ESA) with a much stricter test of disability.[10] Most claimants are now required to complete a lengthy questionnaire about their condition and its effect on their ability to work and to attend a work-focused health-related assessment to assess their capability for work-related activities. Those who are deemed incapable of work are provided with a "support component," while those who are deemed capable receive a "work-related activity component" and are required to participate in a series of five interviews with a PA. Claimants who are assessed as not being able to take part in any work-related activity (the minority who are most severely disabled) may voluntarily participate in work activities but are not required to do so. However, claimants who are assessed as being capable of taking part in some form of work-related activity (the majority who are less severely disabled) may be subject to sanctions if they do not follow all steps required of them and are not deemed by their caseworkers to have good cause for an exception (DWP 2008).

As noted, the principle of activation was first applied to the unemployed who claimed JSA and has more recently been applied to the long-term sick and disabled who claim ESA. Subsequently, the government appears to be concerned that these activation measures may not have succeeded in getting problem drug users back into work. Under the Welfare Reform Act of 2009, those who claim ESA are now required to answer questions about their drug use. Those who do not declare that they are drug users but are suspected "on reasonable grounds" of drug dependency or a "propensity to misuse drugs" may be required to undergo a "substance-related assessment." Those who fail to comply with this requirement "without good cause" may be required to undergo a test to ascertain the presence of drugs in the body.[11]

Where the assessment suggests that claimants have a pattern of drug use that "requires and may be susceptible to treatment" and affects their job prospects, they will have to formulate a "rehabilitation plan" with a specialist employment adviser. This will specify the steps they are expected to take in order to "to stabilise their drug dependency, move towards recovery, tackle the problems they face and get into work." Claimants will normally be bound by the plan for fifty-two weeks and will be expected to "submit to treatment by or under the direction of a person having the necessary qualifications or experience," participate in interviews or assessments at places and times specified in the plan, and take any other specified steps. Sanctions may be imposed for noncompliance with any of the above requirements.[12]

The extension of activation measures to drug users raises two important issues. First, there is the issue of diminishing marginal returns. Applying activation measures to this group is unlikely to be effective—of the two groups that activation measures have been applied to, the long-term sick and disabled are harder to activate than the healthy unemployed. This raises the question of whether it makes any sense to pursue activation policies for groups like problem drug users. Second is the appropriateness of activation measures during a period of high unemployment. When the New Deal was first introduced, UK unemployment was at 6 percent and falling. But by mid-2009 it had risen to 8 percent, and has remained at about that level since, measuring 7.8 percent at the beginning of 2013. In this context, one might think that for drug users the prospects of finding a job are negligible both in absolute terms and relative to those who do not have a drug habit.

Drug users and the long-term sick and disabled are not the only claimants to have been affected by the shift toward greater conditionality and the increased use of sanctions. Lone parents on Income Support are now required to participate in WFIs. Since April 2008, they have had to undergo regular interviews every six months. Lone parents who wish to take up the offer of greater support to move toward employment can volunteer for the New Deal for Lone Parents program, which aims to help them improve job readiness and employment opportunities and "gain independence through working."

The Welfare Reform Act of 2009 took this process further. It set out a framework for abolishing Income Support and moving beneficiaries to JSA or to ESA. This applies to lone parents whose youngest child is age 7 or older—those who are able to work are being transferred to JSA and those who are sick or disabled to ESA. Those deemed able to work are subject to a conditionality regime ostensibly tailored to the individual's personal circumstances, so that preparation for work becomes a natural progression rather than a sudden step up. Lone parents are required to undertake differing levels of activity, depending on the age of their youngest child. Where the child is less than 1, no activity is required;

where the child is between 1 and 3, the parent must attend a WFI at regular intervals; and where the child is between 3 and 7, the parent is required to undertake work-related activity. Deviation from these requirements without good cause can result in sanctions.

Rethinking the Balance between Rights and Responsibilities

Underpinning the New Deal is a shift in the way government understands the relationship between the state and the claimant. The government has referred to this as "a change in the contract between the state and the individual" (Department of Social Security 1998), which involves the granting of new rights for claimants in return for the acceptance of new responsibilities. The new rights include the right to expect government to guarantee the availability of good-quality job-search advice, training opportunities, and employment (in a normal, unsubsidized job or in a job subsidized by the state).[13] The new responsibilities involve an obligation to take full advantage of these opportunities. A hand up rather than a handout is the new mantra: work rather than benefits is seen as the main route to social security, and the New Deal is central to this strategy.[14]

Supporters of a passive approach to social security regard income benefits as an unconditional right—that is, as something that citizens should be able to claim without conditions attached. On the other hand, supporters of an active approach are critical of the emphasis on rights, arguing that a something-for-nothing approach results in people making demands against the state without feeling any obligation to contribute to society.

Clearly, conditionality, in the sense of attaching activation conditions to the receipt of benefits, is becoming more widespread in the United Kingdom. After being applied first to the unemployed, it is now being applied to the long-term sick and disabled and to lone parents. Greater numbers of sanctions are being imposed and greater numbers of people are being subjected to them. Thus, the sanctions net is becoming wider and deeper. The next sections take a closer look at the new sanctions regime and its implications for administrative justice in the UK benefits system.

Reform and Administration of the New Sanctions Regime

As discussed, the New Deal stepped up the use and enforcement of more punitive elements of the earlier legacy (Bryson 2003, 82). For example, work-focused interviews (known as "restart" interviews), which had been introduced in 1986, are now required for all long-term unemployed claimants. In addition, attendance at work-focused training courses became a condition of entitlement to benefits. As in other countries that promoted activation, conditionality is enforced by the application of sanctions—financial penalties for individuals on benefits. Under compulsory New Deal programs, sanctions may be imposed for failure to attend interviews or training courses without good cause.[15] These include the "full family sanction," which applies to all benefits claimed by the household, not only to the individual deemed to have violated the rules.

Prior to the introduction of JSA, the traditional sanctions—for work-related misdemeanors—could be applied for variable periods of up to twenty-six weeks (Wikeley and Ogus 2005, 373). By contrast, the new sanctions are fixed in length. For example, claimants who breach a jobseeker's direction are disqualified from benefits for a fixed period of two weeks or, in the event of a further breach within the next twelve months, for four weeks (Wikeley and Ogus 2005, 375). Moreover, since the introduction of the various New Deals, sanctions that were formerly applied only to work have been extended to cover mandatory participation in training schemes and employment programs.

Between April 2000 and August 2005, 936,029 sanctions were imposed on unemployed claimants, corresponding to a rate of 172,805 sanctions per year.[16] Of this total, 131,575 (77 percent) were variable-length sanctions relating to the circumstances in which claimants left their previous employment or refused an offer of employment. Another 39,658 (23 percent) were fixed-length sanctions imposed for failing to meet training or job-search requirements. Claimants who disagreed with the imposition of a sanction could ask for the decision to be reconsidered and/or could appeal. Between April 2000 and August 2005, 10–15 percent of sanctions decisions were reconsidered in this way (Peters and Joyce 2006, 36).

Reconsidering Conditionality and the Growth of Sanctions

In July 2008, the secretary of state for work and pensions commissioned Paul Gregg, an economist from the University of Bristol, to undertake a wide-ranging review of conditionality and sanctions and to examine how more people could be transferred from benefits into work. The Gregg Report (Gregg 2008) recommended that all claimants should be allocated to one of three broad groups:

1. "Work-ready," for those deemed immediately job ready, making them subject to standard job-search requirements similar to those of the JSA.
2. "Progression to Work," where an immediate return to work is not appropriate but where, with appropriate intervention, there is "a genuine possibility" of a return to work.

3. "No Conditionality," for those with a serious health condition or disability, lone parents with a child under age 1, and selected caretakers, excusing them from work-related activities or taking steps to find work.

The report presents data, reproduced in table 13.1, on the incidence of referrals from PAs to sector decision makers and on disallowance rates for one year ending in August 2008.[17] In this period, there were more than 800,000 referrals, and more than 500,000 sanctions were imposed on unemployed claimants—considerably more than the average in the preceding years. This is partly because of the imposition of 227,000 referrals and sanctions for "failure to attend an interview or appointment." It also appears that the sanctions regime as a whole became more punitive.

According to the Gregg Report, sanctions are needed to underpin the obligations expected of claimants (Gregg 2008, 12). The report claims that, although the use of sanctions to enforce conditionality had been "quite successful," it could be improved. It argued that the sanctions regime was too complex and too difficult to understand, and that it was too time-consuming and too costly to operate. It recommended that it could be improved by:

- aligning the imposition of a sanction more closely with the behavior that triggers the sanction and devolving decision making for some key decisions to frontline staff (i.e., from sector decision makers to PAs);
- improving claimants' awareness and knowledge of what is required of them by introducing an early warning system for those at risk of being sanctioned, a stronger set of rules around attendance at mandatory meetings, and a move toward a system of fixed fines;
- dealing more effectively with repeat offenders by introducing a clear and simple sanction-escalation procedure for failure to attend an interview or appointment without good cause

The report indicates that approximately 18,500 sanctions appeals were received by the Tribunals Service in 2007–8 and that about 7,500 cases—less than 1 percent of the number of sanctions imposed—were heard by a tribunal, with around one-quarter being decided in favor of the claimant (Gregg 2008, 69).

The Gregg Report is a rather one-sided document in that it focuses on claimants' obligations to meet requirements imposed on them by New Deal staff. It is completely silent about the obligations of staff and whether or not they are successful in getting claimants—in particular, hard-to-help claimants—back into work or into training.[18] It is likewise silent on what claimants can do if they think the sanctions imposed on them are unreasonable or if they are dissatisfied

Table 13.1.   Referrals from PAs to sector decision makers, disallowance rates, and number of sanctions imposed over twelve months ending August 2008

Reason for referral	No. of referrals	Disallowance rate (%)	No. of sanctions
Failure to attend an interview or appointment	324,587	70	*227,210*
Leaving a job voluntarily	233,857	54	*126,282*
Misconduct	76,706	44	*33,751*
Actively seeking employment	71,479	87	*62,186*
Other (including jobseeker's directions and jobseeker's allowance agreements)	48,842	66	*32,236*
Refusal of employment	43,000	71	*30,530*
Availability questions	19,377	64	*12,401*
Overall	817,848	*64*	*524,596*

Source: Based on Gregg (2008, 71); author's calculations in italics.

with what the staff have, or have not, done for them.[19] Although the report's commitment to greater transparency is to be welcomed, the devolution of responsibility for imposing sanctions from centralized decision makers (sector decision makers) to frontline staff (PAs) is, as I seek to demonstrate, extremely problematic. It raises important questions about administrative justice and the organizational pursuit of redress.

Welfare Reform, the New Deal, and Administrative Justice

This chapter now turns to an examination of the implications of the New Deal for the accountability of officials and for claimants' right to redress.

Normative Models of Administrative Justice

I begin by identifying and comparing normative models of administrative justice, defined in terms of the justice inherent in administrative decision making. These models are "competitive" rather than "mutually exclusive" (Mashaw 1983, 23) and reflect the concerns and bargaining strengths of institutional actors who have an interest in promoting them. Table 13.2 sets out the six competing models of administrative justice that are encountered in routine administrative decision making today, and characterizes them in terms of their mode of decision making, legitimating goal, mode of accountability, and mode of redress.[20]

Since the six normative models of administrative justice are competitive rather than mutually exclusive, trade-offs can be made among them, and the more dominant one model is, the less dominant the others will be. The trade-offs that are actually made—and likewise those that could have been made—

Table 13.2. Six normative models of administrative justice

Model	Mode of decision making	Legitimating goal	Mode of accountability	Mode of redress
Bureaucratic	Applying rules	Accuracy	Hierarchical	Administrative review
Professional	Applying knowledge	Public service	Interpersonal	Second opinion, complaint to a professional body, or merits review
Legal	Asserting rights	Legality	Independent	Appeal to a court or tribunal (public law)
Managerial	Managerial autonomy	Improved performance	Performance indicators and audit	None, except adverse publicity or complaints that result in sanctions on management
Consumerist	Consumer participation	Consumer satisfaction	Consumer charters	Voice and/or compensation through consumer charters
Market	Matching supply and demand	Economic efficiency	Competition	Exit and/or court action (private law)

typically reflect the concerns and bargaining strengths of civil servants and officials in the case of the bureaucratic model; professionals and street-level bureaucrats (Lipsky 1980b) in the professional model; lawyers and court and tribunal personnel in the legal model; managers and auditors in the managerial model; consumers and members of the public in the consumerist model; and private-sector providers in the market model. The outcome of the power struggle between these institutional actors determines the outcomes of trade-offs between the different models of administrative justice with which they are associated and, thus, the overall administrative justice associated with administrative decision making in that context.

Organizational Changes in Adjudicating Casework

The next step is to consider the impact of some of the changes outlined in this chapter for the trade-offs between different normative models and, thus, for administrative justice in social security. Despite rhetoric that assumes benefits users operate as consumers would in a market, there is little evidence that this is, in fact, the case in the United Kingdom (Lister 2001). As demonstrated in other chapters in this volume (see chapters 7–12), benefits users have more in common with the involuntary (and, thus, disempowered) individuals described by Lipsky (1980), than with consumers, who can use their purchasing power to make choices about goods and services. Therefore, this discussion will focus on the bureaucratic, professional, legal, and managerial models of administrative justice.[21]

When Baldwin, Wikeley, and Young (1992) undertook their study of adjudication in social security, the key decision makers were the adjudication officers.[22] This is no longer the case. Adjudication officers were abolished under the Social Security Act of 1998. When Jobcentre Plus was established, one of its aims was to create a unified workforce from staff who previously worked for either the Benefits Agency or the Employment Service. It is my contention that the key member of the staff in Jobcentre Plus is now the PA, who manages a caseload of job seekers and has considerable discretion in carrying out this task. The decline of the adjudication officer and the rise of the PA reflects a shift from a predominantly bureaucratic to a more professional model of administrative decision making.[23] Sainsbury (2008, 33) has drawn attention to the high degree of discretion that PAs exercise in advising and supporting sick and disabled claimants, although he also acknowledges the influence of the bureaucratic model on their decision making.[24] Van Berkel and Valkenberg (2007) link discretion with the personalized forms of intervention nominally associated with activation programs.

Adjudication officers, as front-line caseworkers, were, at least notionally, independent, but in practice accountable to their line managers. In contrast, the new managerial regime of performance measurement shapes the work of PAs, who now staff the front lines. They are subject to various forms of performance management and are expected to give priority to meeting a variety of nationally and locally set targets.[25] This change reflects an increase in importance of the managerial model of administrative decision making. At the same time, the ending of the adjudication officers' independent status and the abolition of the role of the chief adjudication officer in 1998 have undoubtedly led to a reduction in the importance of the legal model of administrative decision making. Claimants' appeal rights have been weakened by the removal of jurisdiction from appeal tribunals[26] and the introduction of "paper" hearings.[27]

These changes suggest that the bureaucratic and legal models of decision making have decreased in importance while the professional and managerial models of decision making have increased in importance. The next section considers the implications of these changes for rights of redress and accountability.

Rights of Redress and Accountability

In their study of adjudication in social security, Baldwin, Wikeley, and Young (1992, 65–67) describe what used to happen when a claimant attempted to challenge a benefits decision. The claimant could either request a review of the initial decision or lodge an appeal. In the case of contributory benefits, reviews were conducted by the official who made the initial decision. In the case of means-tested benefits, the appeals process formally provided for a hearing conducted by a specialist and heard by an independent social security tribunal. However, in practice, an appeal first would trigger an informal review to establish whether the initial decision should stand. This would often lead to a formal review. If, after a formal review, the claimant's complaint was validated, that would be the end of the matter. But if it was rejected or only partially accepted, the case would proceed to a tribunal.

These two procedures (reviews and appeals) constitute the characteristic modes of redress associated with bureaucratic and legal models of decision making (see far-right column in table 13.2). For example, a formal appeals process is characteristic of the United States (see chap. 14 in this volume). The characteristic modes of redress associated with the professional and managerial models of decision making are much less well developed. Table 13.2 indicates that redress in the professional model occurs through either a second opinion, a complaint to a professional body, or a "merits review" by a tribunal.[28] Although the first two mechanisms are usually available when the decision maker is a professional, this is rarely the case when the decision maker is a semiprofessional or a "street-level bureaucrat."[29] In such cases, it is unlikely that a second opinion will be an option or that there will be a professional body that could investigate the complaint. The third mechanism, a merits review, is poorly developed in the United Kingdom, although common elsewhere—for example, in Australia.[30] Table 13.2 also indicates that there is no effective mode of redress associated with the managerial model and that the only option available to someone who wishes to challenge a decision is to create adverse publicity or make a complaint that puts pressure on management.

In the United Kingdom, the shift from a bureaucratic and legal model to a professional and managerial model of decision making has made it extremely difficult for anyone who is required to take part in the New Deal programs to challenge sanctions or complain about the advice and help they receive.[31] Yet, in Jobcentre Plus, PAs have many characteristics associated with street-level bureaucrats[32] and wield a great deal of discretionary power. Moreover, it is not always clear which of their actions actually constitutes a decision (Sainsbury 2008, 334).

Arguably, many PAs do their jobs well, or at least try to, and assessed levels of user satisfaction are high.[33] However, it does not follow that Jobcentre Plus provides a good service.[34] The DWP uses three indicators to assess standards of decision making (payment accuracy, claim clearance rates, and official error) by individual members of staff, but it was not able to provide individualized data for members of staff working in Jobcentre Plus.[35] It should also be noted that the collection of individualized data on standards of performance relating to activation does not appear to be on the DWP's agenda. But, in any event, these indicators do not measure the content or quality of agency practices or their value to service users.

Under the new sanctions regime, front-line discretion has powerful consequences. Jobcentre Plus staff can impose sanctions not only on claimants, but also on their families. They make judgments about a variety of infractions, among them what constitutes a violation of the job seeker's agreement. Yet, in practice, the possibilities for administrative justice are truncated. As discussed, tribunals hear very few appeals against the imposition of sanctions (Gregg 2008, 69). Just why this is the case is not at all clear. However, one consequence is that it allows the members of staff who impose sanctions to be effectively immune from challenge. A revitalized appeal process could provide an important corrective to the incorrect application of street-level discretion. But, as far as the imposition of sanctions is concerned, the practice of independent adjudication and appeal has pretty much disappeared. Consequently, street-level staff are not properly accountable for their decision making either through internal or external audit or through rigorous processes of appeal and redress.

Implications for the Sanctions Regime

New Deal policies and practices have brought with them shifts from a more passive type of intervention to a more active type of intervention and from a primarily bureaucratic and legalistic type of decision making to a primarily professional and managerial one. These shifts are fraught with problems. The first is problematic because there is a real danger that those who are not really fit for work are being required to look for employment and being penalized—and feel a sense of failure—when they are unable to find it. The second shift is problematic because, although Jobcentre Plus staff exercise a great deal of power over those who are looking for work, it is increasingly difficult for job seekers to challenge what they do or do not do for them.

I would argue that, whatever the merits of welfare-to-work, it should not be implemented without due regard to justice and fairness. Does it have to be so difficult to hold staff to account and challenge what they do? The answer is surely no.

I first consider the imposition of sanctions. The Gregg Report (Gregg 2008) argued that the sanctions regime was too complex and difficult to understand, and that it was too time-consuming and costly to operate. It recommended that it could be improved by aligning the imposition of sanctions more closely with the behavior that triggers them (greater proportionality); devolving decision making for some key decisions to frontline staff; improving claimants' awareness and knowledge of what is required of them; moving, in the longer term, toward a system of fixed penalties; and introducing a clear and simple sanction-escalation procedure for failures to attend interviews or appointments without good cause. Three of these recommendations (proportionality, information, and progression) would almost certainly increase the justice and fairness of first-instance decision making. The other two (devolution and fixed penalties) would probably have the opposite effect. The three positive recommendations all involve the promulgation of rules and guidelines and would strengthen bureaucratic influences on decision making. So too would the introduction of fixed penalties. However, fixed penalties are a very blunt instrument and take little account of individual circumstances, such as whether or not the claimant could claim good cause for his or her behavior. Likewise, more devolved decision making would strengthen professionalism and lead to greater variation and arbitrariness. Thus, three of Gregg's recommendations would enhance administrative justice while two would not.

As far as bringing accountability to the staff for sanction decisions, the most effective way of achieving this would involve the adoption of the US practice providing for access to a hearing before benefits can be reduced. The major difference between the United Kingdom, where very few claimants appeal sanctions, and the United States, where—following the Supreme Court decision in *Goldberg v. Kelly* (397 U.S. 254)—all claimants must have an opportunity to appeal before a sanction is imposed, is that decision makers in the United Kingdom are effectively unaccountable while those in the United States are, in theory and, to some extent, in practice, held to account.[36] (For a discussion of administrative justice in the United States, see chap. 14.) Such a change would involve a strengthening of legality.

I now turn to what is involved in holding PAs, who play the leading role in implementing the New Deal, to account.

What is required is the development of a set of good-practice rules and guidelines for staff, which define their duties and specify the limits on their discretionary powers; a requirement for written statements to be issued at various points in the process; and a right of review and appeal for job seekers disputing the decisions of PAs. Although it would appear that individual-level monitoring of staff standards of performance is still a long way off, measures that involve enhancements to bureaucracy (in the form of additional rules and guidelines) and legality (in the form of enhanced rights of appeal) should make it possible both to improve the quality of activation and to more effectively to hold staff to account. Although Brodkin (2011a) is skeptical about the extent to which rules and guidelines structure the discretion of street-level bureaucrats, it is the contention of this chapter that these measures cannot fail to make the actions of staff, and in particular of PAs, more consistent than they would otherwise have been.

Conclusions

The analysis in this chapter has many similarities to critiques of activation practices presented in this book, particularly in confirming the critical role of street-level organizations (SLOs) in the workfare/activation regime. It also builds on Van Aerschot's (2011) critique of activation in Denmark, Finland, and Sweden, where he, too, argues that frontline staff and their managers effectively determine how activation is implemented. He suggests that in the Nordic countries, SLOs, in a sense use discretion to prioritize their own goals, while the legal paradigms that are supposed to protect clients do not function very well. As a result, the individual rights of the unemployed who are subject to activation are not well protected. Van Aerschot concludes that a more equal balance of power between clients and activation staff calls for the individual rights of the unemployed to be taken more seriously. That conclusion applies equally to the United Kingdom.

It may appear as if the argument advanced here conflicts with the argument made by Lens in chapter 14, who points out that the potential of hearings to secure redress and administrative justice is often not realized. Lens attributes this, first, to the preoccupation of hearings with procedural issues, which obscures substantive disputes; second, to case-by-case redress, which prevents improvements to frontline practices that could benefit others; and, third, to the failure of many administrative law judges to adopt an independent stance. These are valid and important criticisms, which I do not wish to dispute. However, I take it that Lens is not arguing that, because of their shortcomings, hearings should be abolished or that everyone would be better-off without them. Her argument suggests, rather, that they are not perfect and could be improved.

The model of administrative justice that has been deployed in this chapter takes a similar position. It sees the justice of administrative decision making in terms of trade-offs between competing models of how administrative decisions should be made and argues that a different set of trade-offs would lead to enhancement of administrative justice. It quite explicitly rejects the view that different models are mutually exclusive and that one has to choose among them. The conclusion of the chapter is that, as far as the imposition of sanctions and the weakness of redress in British New Deal programs are concerned, the existing trade-offs are out of kilter and need to be rebalanced.

Notes

This chapter is based on a previously published work titled "The Justice Implications of Activation Policy in the UK" (Adler 2008), which appeared in Sara Stendahl, Thomas Erhag, and Stamatia Devetzi, eds., *A European Work-First Welfare State*. © Michael Adler, Sara Stendahl, Thomas Erhag, Stamatia Devetzi, and Gothenburg University. Used by permission. Earlier versions of this chapter were presented at the School of Social Service Administration Centennial Symposium in Chicago in May 2009, at a RESQ Workshop in Duisburg in November 2009, and at the Law and Society Association Conference in Chicago in May 2010. The author would like to thank those who commented on the paper.

1. John Clarke (2004, 14) has cautioned against "telling history as a unilinear shift from one thing to another," but, by using the qualifying adjectives "more" and "less," I have been careful in this chapter not to do so.

2. This characterization has been vigorously challenged, in particular by my Edinburgh colleague, Adrian Sinfield, who has argued that social security policy in the United Kingdom, and elsewhere, has always involved a mixture of active (labor market) and passive (income replacement) measures. See, e.g., Sinfield (2001). I accept that this is the case but would, nonetheless, argue that the balance between active and passive measures has changed, and this is the argument that is advanced in this chapter.

3. These are all means-tested benefits for low-income households. Family Credit, which was replaced by Working Families Tax Credit in 1999, was a tax credit paid to working families who were responsible for at least one child under 16 (or under 19 if in full-time education) if the applicant or the applicant's partner (if he or she had one) worked for sixteen hours or more per week. Housing Benefit is for low-income households who may either be on benefits or in work and who need financial help to pay all or part of their rent. Council Tax Benefit is likewise for low-income households who may be on benefits or in work and need financial help to pay all or part of their council tax, which is a local tax on domestic property that is paid by everyone who owns or rents their accommodations.

4. The "unemployment trap" refers to the lack of financial incentives for unemployed people to return to work. It is caused by high replacement rates, i.e., by incomes for the unemployed that approach (and in a few cases exceed) the incomes they did or could obtain from work.

5. For an excellent review of the measures introduced by successive governments since 1997, see Wright (2009).

6. According to the latest British Social Attitudes Survey, sympathy toward benefit claimants has apparently evaporated, along with support for redistributive tax-and-spend policies, over the past twenty years, with Labour governing (from 1997 to 2009) during a period of significant hardening of attitudes toward the poor. See Park et al. (2011).

7. See National Audit Office (2006, summary). From July 2000 to June 2008, monthly unemployment rates in the United Kingdom (based on the ILO measure) fluctuated between 4.7 and 5.5 percent. By August 2009, following the banking crisis, the unemployment rate in the United Kingdom had risen to 7.9 percent, the highest since April 1997. It has remained at that level since then. Comparative figures were 10.0 percent for the sixteen-nation euro region and 9.5 percent for the United States.

8. See Grover (2005). Members of the public are encouraged to report cases of benefit fraud to the National Benefit Fraud Hotline, and the Department for Work and Pensions

(DWP) employs over three thousand fraud investigators to look into allegations of fraud and apprehend those who are involved.

9. For an account of these developments, and of the shift from a passive to an active approach in the provision of social security for those with sickness and disability, see Sainsbury (2009). For an account of the failure of similar developments to achieve their objectives in Sweden, see Hetzler (2009).

10. The new work-capability assessment test aims to assess what an individual *can* do, rather than what he or she cannot do, and considers a person's capacities such as his or her ability to use a computer keyboard or mouse. In a trial of the new test involving claimants in Aberdeen and Burnley who were in receipt of Incapacity Benefit, Severe Disablement Allowance, and Income Support paid on the grounds of illness or disability, 29.6 percent were found to be fit to work, 31.3 percent were eligible for ESA unconditionally, and the remaining 39.0 percent were placed in the work-related activity group. They were required to attend six WFIs as a condition of receiving ESA. One-third of the unsuccessful applicants who subsequently appealed had the decision overturned. See "Welfare Reform Bill: Parliamentary Briefing; Second Reading," Full Fact, March 9, 2011, http://fullfact.org/files/2011/03/Welfare_Reform_Bill_2R_Briefing.pdf.

11. John Harris, "Back to the Workhouse," *Guardian* (London), June 8, 2012.

12. ESA is reduced by 50 percent of the work-related activity component for the first four weeks and 100 percent after that.

13. However, there has been no discussion of how these new rights could be enforced.

14. The new strategy contains a number of other components; e.g., the introduction of a national minimum wage and much greater emphasis on in-work benefits delivered through tax credits. For accounts of the new strategy, see Millar (2003a) and Adler (2004).

15. The New Deals for young people and for those age 25 and over have always been compulsory, while those for the partners of the unemployed and those age 50 and over have always been voluntary. The New Deals for lone parents and disabled people were initially voluntary, but an element of compulsion is now being introduced.

16. Author's calculation based on Peters and Joyce (2006, table D2).

17. Sector decision makers are staff members in Jobcentre Plus who are responsible for implementing the sanctions regime.

18. There is likewise no discussion in the report of whether the European Convention on Human Rights and other international conventions impose any constraints on what the New Deal authorities can require from claimants in return for the help that they are given. For an example of such a discussion in Denmark, see Ketscher (2007).

19. On the difficulties of enforcing the welfare state side of the welfare contract, see Brodkin (1997 and chap. 9 in this volume) and Lens (chap. 14 in this volume).

20. Table 13.2, which is based on Adler (2010), differs in a number of minor ways from versions that appear in earlier publications.

21. Jobcentre Plus no longer has exclusive implementation responsibility. Under the Flexible New Deal introduced in March 2009, support and assistance for long-term unemployed people is now provided by private contractors who are paid according to their success in getting people into work. This system of payment by results is, however, bound to discourage contractors from putting much effort into working with hard-to-place claimants. The use of private contractors to implement the New Deal follows the recommendation of an independent review, commissioned for the DWP (Freud 2007). However, it should be noted that,

under the new contracted-out regime, sector decision makers are still responsible for the imposition of sanctions.

22. Adjudication officers were members of staff who performed statutory functions in deciding claims for social security benefits but were required to do so independently of the minister. Thus, they were bureaucrats with judicial responsibilities, whose position was similar to that of administrative law judges in the United States (see ch. 14 in this volume).

23. In Australia, where activation measures had already been contracted out to private- and voluntary-sector providers, Carney (2005) identified a shift from a bureaucratic mode of decision making, which emphasized rules and procedures, to a market mode of decision making, which emphasizes discretion.

24. It should be noted that Sainsbury does not accept that managerialism, consumerism, or the market constitute distinct models of administrative justice.

25. In April 2006, Jobcentre Plus adopted the job-outcome target as its primary performance measure. This records the number of people moving off benefits and into work at the district level. However, it cannot be used to assess the performance of individual offices or advisers and, because it lags behind the current date by a few months, is of little use for day-to-day management. Jobcentre Plus has also developed a set of internal performance measures for assessing the performance of individual PAs, which focus on inputs, such as the content and quality of interviews, and actions taken, rather than outputs. Unlike the output measures, they do not discourage advisers from working with hard-to-place claimants. For details, see National Audit Office (2006, pars. 44–45). As Brodkin (2011a, i273) points out, choosing what to measure and what not to measure is a fundamentally political matter.

26. The Social Fund was a means-tested scheme, administered by Jobcentre Plus, that provided grants and repayable loans to people on low incomes who had no other resources. It was set up under the Social Security Act of 1986 as a replacement for Single Payments. As a general rule, recipients of grants and loans needed to be getting income-related benefits like Income Support, income-related ESA, income-related JSA, or Pension Credit. The Social Fund provided regulated payments as of right in a number of specified circumstances: e.g., Sure Start Maternity Grants; Funeral Payments and Winter Fuel Payments; and "discretionary payments," paid following an assessment of need, such as Community Care Grants (which helped with expenses like furniture, clothing, and household equipment), Budgeting Loans (which helped pay for essential items like furniture, household equipment, or clothing), and Crisis Loans (which helped pay for items after an emergency or a disaster like a fire or flood). See descriptions of these payments at "Social Fund," Turn2Us, http://www.turn2 us.org.uk/information__resources/benefits/social_fund.aspx.

Although claimants could no longer appeal to a tribunal against the refusal of an application for a discretionary payment, they could ask for the decision to be reviewed by the Independent Review Service. Under the Welfare Reform Act of 2012, the Social Fund was abolished and replaced by a scheme administered by local authorities. A reduced level of funding was made available to local authorities in England and the devolved administrations in Scotland and Wales to provide such assistance in their areas "as they saw fit."

27. Appellants can choose whether to have an oral hearing, at which they can put forward their case and ask and answer questions, or a paper hearing, which is heard in their absence and decided on the basis of paper submissions. Success rates for oral hearings are substantially higher than for paper hearings. Between April 1, 2009, and August 31, 2009, 39 percent of cases were cleared in favor of the appellant; where appellants opted for an oral hearing, this rose to 48 percent (House of Commons Work and Pensions Committee 2010, par. 148).

28. "Merits review" refers to the process in which a tribunal reconsiders the facts and the law and policy aspects of the original decision and determines the "correct and preferable" decision. It is sometimes described as "stepping into the shoes" of the first-instance decision maker.

29. A "semiprofessional" is someone, like a librarian, who works in an occupation that has some but not all the characteristics of a profession. See Etzioni (1969). A "street-level bureaucrat" is an official, like a policeman on the beat, who works without direct supervision and is required to make on-the-spot decisions by exercising his or her judgment. See Lipsky (1980b).

30. For a discussion of the potential and limits of merits review in Australia, see Cane (2009).

31. Sainsbury (2008) makes this point in relation to claimants of Incapacity Benefit. In Australia, Carney (2005) has noted that it has likewise become difficult to challenge the imposition of sanctions and the quality of the activation measures that are available.

32. Wright (2006) has used Lipsky's theory of street-level bureaucracy to analyze the ways in which the staff in a Jobcentre placed claimants into administrative and moral categories and traced the consequences of these processes for the services they received. Her study, which was carried out in 1998 (i.e., before the merger of the Benefits Agency with the Employment Service into Jobcentre Plus), drew attention to the discretion exercised by staff. She notes that, as a result of subsequent policy developments, the importance of discretion has undoubtedly increased since then.

33. According to the National Audit Office (2006, pars. 21 and 31), Jobcentre Plus's customer survey shows that 77 percent of job seekers and 90 percent of employers are satisfied with its performance.

34. Many commentators have pointed to the fact that surveys showing high levels of satisfaction and in-depth interviews revealing subordination are contradictory but, as Soss (1999, 79–87) points out, satisfaction and subordination may coexist with each other like two sides of the same coin. According to Soss, clients distinguish between the agency and the particular workers they encounter, and between workers as individuals and the client-worker relationship. This enables them, at one and the same time, to feel degraded by agency procedures, subordinated in their relationships with workers, and satisfied with the performance of individual workers.

35. The published data only refer to benefits administered by the Pensions, Disability, and Careers Service. See House of Commons Work and Pensions Committee (2010, par. 29).

36. However, as Lens (ch. 14 in this volume) demonstrates, this is only true if their case is heard by an "adjudicator judge"; i.e., a judge who facilitates challenges to bureaucratic decision making. "Bureaucratic judges," who adopt the mind-set of the bureaucratic decision maker, tend to rubber-stamp first-instance decisions about matters such as the imposition of sanctions.

14

Redress and Accountability in US Welfare Agencies

VICKI LENS

T he governmental distribution of welfare benefits is more than a monetary exchange. It is also a transaction with consequences for the relationship between citizens and the state. When the government provides
welfare benefits, it is obligated to do so fairly and equitably, not just economically or efficiently (Frederickson 2005). Under US law, recipients of cash assistance are entitled to certain legal protections, including the right to challenge
a denial, discontinuance, or reduction of benefits in an administrative forum,
commonly referred to as a fair hearing. This chapter will examine fair hearings
as an organizational mechanism for securing administrative justice in the implementation of workfare policy. It draws on sociolegal and street-level theory to
raise questions about how fair hearings operate in practice and what that means
for the ability of citizens subject to workfare to obtain redress for government
error or arbitrariness.

This chapter draws on original research on the fair hearing process in two
counties in a northeastern state of the United States. It begins with a brief
history and description of the role of fair hearings in the administration of public
assistance. This is followed by a discussion of sociolegal and organizational
approaches to understanding law and administrative justice. It then turns to
findings from my field research to illuminate how these hearings work in practice and what that means for administrative justice under a workfare regime.

The Fair Hearing Process

Fair hearings have been required since the inception of the Aid to Dependent
Children (ADC) program in 1935, the first federal public-assistance program

for poor families. They were intended primarily to correct individual errors made by welfare agencies and also to standardize the administration of benefits as county-level agencies came under state supervision for the first time. They were rarely used during the first several decades of the ADC program, in part because they were provided after the termination of benefits, too late to help clients ward off the immediate harm caused by the cessation of benefits. That changed in 1970 with the US Supreme Court decision in *Goldberg v. Kelly* (397 U.S. 254), which held that states were required to provide recipients with hearings before the termination of benefits under the due process clause of the Constitution. The court found that the statutory scheme that granted welfare benefits was a form of property that could not be taken away without procedural safeguards that protected the recipient from arbitrary government action. In constructing what protections were required, the court imported many of the features of adversarial judicial proceedings, including the provision of timely and adequate notice, a chance to argue the case orally, the opportunity to confront and cross-examine witnesses, and a written decision.

Notwithstanding these features, hearings are more informal than court proceedings. Unlike most legal proceedings, the parties are not routinely represented by counsel. The agency is typically represented by an employee, often specially trained as a fair hearing representative, while appellants are rarely represented by legal counsel or advocates (Baldacci 2007). While under an adversarial system judges are not expected to play an investigatory role, but to remain passive and neutral (Baldacci 2007), at hearings there is more leeway. For example, in the state where the study was conducted regulations generally permit the fair hearing examiner (called an administrative law judge) to assist the appellant in eliciting documents and testimony, especially when the appellant is having difficulty questioning a witness. Rules governing the submission of evidence are also less strict than in court proceedings; for example, the regulations provide that the technical rules of evidence need not apply.

In about half the states, hearings are part of the same state welfare bureaucracy that administers benefits, but they are charged with regulatory and supervisory oversight of local welfare agencies (Brodoff 2008). Thus, unlike in more formal judicial systems, where the distinction between prosecutors and judges is clear, the identity of administrative judges is blurred. They are employed by the welfare bureaucracy, but also expected to act neutrally and independently of the bureaucracy when rendering a decision. In sum, hearings are both a creature of the bureaucracy and autonomous from it. As a judicial institution nestled within a bureaucracy, it calls for examination through two theoretical lenses: a sociolegal approach that seeks to understand how law, and concepts such as due process, are constituted and constructed on the ground, and an organizational approach that seeks to understand the role of street-level bureaucrats, in this instance the administrative law judges, as they decide whether an agency has acted arbitrarily or in error.

Theoretical Framework

The decision to institutionalize concepts such as due process within the welfare bureaucracy was a response to organizational arrangements that permitted case-workers wide discretion when granting or denying benefits. Between 1935, when ADC was passed, and the 1960s, welfare bureaucracies operated on a social work model, with caseworkers guided by flexible standards and with grants tailored to individual needs (Simon 1983). Such wide discretion made it difficult to insure administrative justice, which has both substantive and proce-dural dimensions. The former requires that individuals get the benefits they are entitled to under the law, while the latter requires a fair process for determining eligibility for those benefits (Adler 2010). The social work model left too many decisions in the hands of caseworkers, whose individual biases and attitudes toward clients led to the unequal and arbitrary distribution of benefits (Handler and Hollingsworth 1970).

To restrain individual bias and prejudice, protect individual rights, and pro-mote uniformity, a system of legal formality was instituted. Constructed on substantive rules and procedures, this system aims for the fair and equitable distribution of benefits by applying formal sets of rules, rather than complex interpretive judgments about a particular individual's entitlement to benefits. Its mode of operation—what Mashaw (1983) calls "bureaucratic rationality"—is to implement governmental objectives by processing information accurately, efficiently, and consistently (see also Adler 2003, 2006, and chap. 13 in this volume).

However, as Simon (1983) suggests, such a formalized system contains the seeds of its own destruction. It leaves little room to accommodate differences, often substituting mechanistic and literal application of the rules for more indi-vidualized determinations. Rather than insuring fairness, formal rules and stan-dardized procedures can constrain and restrict, and invite workers to mechanically and literally apply the rules rather than attend to the larger goals and aspirations underlying them. A program's goals and objectives may be undermined, and replaced with a preoccupation with the minutiae of bureau-cracy. Rules may be translated in confusing and complicated ways, making the cost of claiming too high, resulting in administrative exclusion (Brodkin and Majmundar 2010). Such a system, rather than insuring uniformity and fairness, can wrongly exclude eligible participants from receiving benefits (Hasenfeld 2000; Bane and Ellwood 1994; Brodkin 1986; Soss 2002).

In a sense, workfare policies invite such exclusion. Workfare provides for the imposition of sanctions, or a reduction or discontinuance of benefits, when a participant is found to be in violation of a work rule. A subjective and factually complex decision about participants' willingness to work or suitability for work activities takes time and skill, which are often in short supply in welfare bureaucracies (Diller 2000). A mechanical application of the rules is often the preferred path, with workers eschewing holistic assessments and instead viewing the imposition of sanctions as a clerical task (Lens 2006, 2008). When this occurs, caseworkers (or in some cases automated computer systems) merely record attendance at work-related appointments, with a single missed appointment functioning as a proxy for more complex individualized judgments. Similarly, participants may be sanctioned for minor violations of the work rules, while obstacles or barriers to work are overlooked or ignored by caseworkers. In these ways, the most disadvantaged participants may be excluded from programs instead of being supported as they seek self-sufficiency.

The fair hearing system is supposed to correct such errors, with administrative law judges mediating between frontline workers and citizens and insuring that they are only excluded because they are ineligible, not because of organizational factors. Organizationally, hearings are situated apart from the front lines and the everyday workings of the bureaucracy. They provide an opportunity for a fresh look at eligibility. Unlike frontline decision making, which operates under incentives favoring mechanistic and wholesale judgments, fair hearings ostensibly are built around the individual, requiring the judge to respond to the specific facts and circumstances embodied in a case. Judicial and administrative discretion also differ from one another. While rules can restrain both workers and judges, the latter have the capacity to exercise their professional judgment in ways that consider the larger goals and objectives underlying the rules. Such professionalization is often cited as an antidote to the often-mechanized judgments of lower-level and unskilled workers (Simon 1983). Arguably, judges are better prepared to make an individualized and complex decision in determining whether a participant is able or unwilling to work, whether an individual needs work supports, and whether the agency has provided them.

However, as sociolegal scholars have noted, law on the ground often looks very different than law on the books (Silbey 2005). Legal proceedings also are subject to individual and organizational stresses and strains, and are shaped as much by the environment as by formal rules and procedures. As decades of research by sociolegal scholars has shown, "legal action both reflect[s] and reproduce[s] other features and institutions of social life" (Silbey 2005, 325). This includes replicating the powerlessness of the "have-nots" in society, with aspirational notions of due process and the containment of arbitrary power often not realizing fruition on the ground (Galanter 1974; Kritzer and Silbey 2003).

When, as described above, the relevant state actors are a hybrid of the judicial and the bureaucratic systems, the potential for leakage between the two is even greater than within more independent and formal court systems. It is possible that judges who occupy positions within the bureaucracy could be steeped in the norms and expectations of bureaucratic decision making and, thus, replicate rather than check its worst excesses. They may view themselves not as adjudicators of disputes and a bulwark against arbitrary state action, but as engaged in the "systematic and affirmative implementation of certain prescribed legislative policies" (Mashaw 1974, 780).

This chapter examines the role of fair hearings as arbiters of policy and practice and its implications for redress within the context of work-activation policies and, more broadly, administrative justice. It addresses two key questions. First, what kinds of disputes are adjudicated? As reviewers of decisions made elsewhere, appeals systems must play the cards they are dealt. Thus, any inquiry into the role and function of hearings must begin with an examination of the nature of the disputes that make their way into the hearing room. A second key question is: How do judges adjudicate disputes? The judge, as the key player with the discretion to determine how the dispute will be adjudicated, decides how the tension between bureaucratic and judicial decision making will be navigated.

Methodology

This study draws on data from two different fair hearing units located in a state in the northeast of the United States, one suburban and one urban. Both units are part of the same state welfare bureaucracy and hence governed by the same rules and procedures. I chose a large, urban and a smaller, suburban unit in order to compare fair hearing appeals in locations that differed in terms of caseload and staff size. This provided an opportunity to explore whether the "mass-processing" demands associated with a large, complex bureaucracy would result in different types and volume of appeals than those arising in a smaller, nonurban setting. The urban welfare agency approved nearly 250,000 cases for assistance in a year; the suburban agency, about 12,000. The urban agency handled about 76,000 fair hearings in a year; the suburban agency, about 1,000. The comparison allows exploration into whether these organizational differences in size and location produced differences in fair hearing complaints, both in number and in content. The comparison also provides a way of controlling for organizational differences when examining how fair hearings are adjudicated. This strategy makes it possible to get a better sense of features that are common to the adjudication process generally versus those that are related to the specific features of urban or suburban welfare offices.

Seventy hearings were observed in the suburban unit and 144 hearings in the urban unit. Of these hearings, 71 (19 in the suburban area and 52 in the urban area) involved work-activation issues. The observations in the suburban unit were conducted during 2007 and 2008, for a total of four months during this time period. The observations in the urban unit were conducted in 2009 over a three-month period. I conducted all of the hearing observations and observed all of the judges (seven) who were assigned to the suburban unit. In the urban unit I also conducted all the hearing observations, which consisted of observations of thirteen judges, out of the seventy-five assigned to the urban unit.

In the suburban unit I did not use any formal selection process when deciding which cases to hear. On those days when there was a single calendar, I observed cases in the order in which they were heard. On those days when there were two calendars, and hence two judges hearing cases, I chose hearings based on which appellant appeared first and was ready to proceed. In the urban unit, there were approximately thirty-five judges hearing cases on any given day, with calendars assigned by subject matter (e.g., food stamps, general public assistance, medical programs). I was assigned by the supervising judge to observe a particular judge based on a combination of factors, including the judge's availability and willingness to participate and the nature of the cases he or she was presiding over on the day I observed. For example, I would commonly request that I be assigned to "regular hearings" involving public assistance cases rather than food-stamp cases. In between hearings in both units I conducted informal interviews with the judges and, to a lesser extent, the agency representatives.

In-depth, semistructured interviews were also conducted with seventy-nine participants who had utilized the fair hearing system, twenty-nine of whom resided in the suburban area, and fifty in the urban area. The interviews took place between 2006 and 2009 and were conducted by myself and several research assistants. Of these interviews, thirty-two were with appellants whose hearings I had observed; the rest were with appellants whose hearings I did not observe, who were recruited through local social service agencies. Of the interviews, thirty-four in the urban area and thirty-one in the suburban area involved work-activation issues.

The Nature and Quality of Disputes

The vast majority of work-related appeals occurred in response to a sanction for failing to attend work-related appointments or activities. Many of these disputes involved procedural errors—either the appellant's or the agency's. For example, appellants disputed receiving proper notice of a work activity or complained about being thwarted when trying to contact the agency about a mandated work appointment. The agency, for its part, complained that appellants did not follow reporting and notification requirements. The focus on procedural errors is a direct consequence of the ways in which bureaucracies have implemented the work rules. As Brodkin and Majmundar (2010, 831) have observed, "complicated work requirements, irrespective of their substantive intent, added a new layer of procedural steps—and procedural discretion—to welfare claiming." Disputes involving procedural error thus dominated the hearing room, and had substantial implications for the ways in which disputed errors were addressed, particularly in the urban area.

The contrast between the urban and suburban units graphically demonstrated how bureaucratic practices below influenced the processing of disputes above. Participants in both areas complained of wrongfully imposed sanctions. However, in the urban unit the agency routinely committed basic procedural errors when imposing sanctions. Thus, the vast majority of work-sanctions cases were resolved by the urban agency's withdrawing the sanction because of these errors. In contrast, in the suburban unit, fair hearings challenging sanctions were less likely to involve procedural errors and were more likely to result in a full hearing of the issues.

Thus, in the urban unit this meant that work-rule cases were not fully adjudicated. Once the agency representatives realized—either on their own after reviewing the file or sometimes after pointed questioning from the judge—that proper procedures were not followed, they withdrew the notice, restoring the appellant's grant. The procedural irregularities were of the type likely to occur when systems designed to process large numbers of cases break down. These irregularities included, for example, defective notices that failed to advise appellants of the basis for the sanction or contradicted the case record, missing documents in the file, and improperly addressed notices. In the urban office, where agency error occupied central stage, the deference fair hearing judges might otherwise give to official records was discarded because such records were routinely incomplete or riddled with mistakes.

At first glance the urban hearing unit's emphasis on procedural regularity, which usually disadvantages welfare participants by creating barriers to receiving aid, advantaged appellants. In contrast to the suburban unit, urban appellants were more successful, winning 80 percent of work-related hearings compared to a 45 percent success rate in the suburban area. However, such victories were often only temporary, because the agency was not prevented from issuing a new notice sanctioning the appellant for the same alleged infraction. Nor did this guarantee that the agency would follow the proper procedures in future sanctions cases. In fact, it was not unusual for appellants to become repeat players in the fair hearing room (or as some staff derisively called them, "frequent flyers"), contesting another, often defective, notice reducing or discontinuing aid. Under these circumstances, hearings functioned less as a judicial space for adjudicating disputes than as a routine stop in the bureaucratic gauntlet appellants had to navigate to retain their benefits. Put another way, hearings became part of the game, not a way to stop the game.

Legal procedures that emphasized an opportunity to testify and present evidence were more likely to be short-circuited in the urban unit. Most hearings involving defective notices took only a few minutes to resolve, in contrast to the suburban unit, where the average hearing took thirty minutes. While nominally more efficient, these abbreviated hearings often failed to offer the rudiments of legal due process, including an opportunity to be heard, present evidence, and question adversaries. In observed fair hearings, the judge and agency representative at times communicated in shorthand bureaucratese, with the agency representative simply naming code 21 or code 24 (the codes for withdrawing a notice) and the judge promptly agreeing. Participants had no role to play or reason to talk. They often expressed surprise at the brevity of the hearing, and some were confused as to what had occurred. In follow-up interviews, even though they had won, they expressed disappointment that the judge had not looked at the documents they brought to prove their case.

Arguably, an opportunity to be heard is less necessary when a dispute is resolved favorably. However, the quick and routine resolution of disputes by agency withdrawals limited the hearing system's ability to fully adjudicate disputes over the work rules. Because appellants never testified about the circumstances surrounding the sanction, questions about how and why the agency imposed work sanctions, including what evidence it relied on and what factors it considered (or not), were left unexamined. Matters at the crux of work disputes, such as the appropriateness of assignments or the availability of supports or resources to address obstacles to work, were also never addressed. Nor were the consequences of the agency's actions, including the deprivations and hardships created by the threat or reality of discontinuance of benefits. Much as in interactions on the front lines, appellants' individual and immediate needs were sanitized, transformed into disputes over paperwork and process rather than substance and need. Hearings became absorbed into the bureaucracy, only temporarily correcting procedural errors while failing to uncover and scrutinize the substantive conflicts underlying work rules.

In contrast, in the suburban unit the agency virtually always met the threshold procedural requirements when issuing reduction or denial notices. With something to review beyond procedural irregularities, the suburban unit (and the urban unit, in those work-sanction cases not resolved by a withdrawal) could potentially function more as a traditional legal space, requiring the participation of both the agency and the appellants and a review of the substantive facts. Under these circumstances, fair hearings have the potential for a fuller adjudication of the issues and conflicts underlying the work rules. However, whether this potential was realized depended, in part, on how fair hearing judges used their discretion when presiding over hearings.

Styles of Judging

Although fair hearing judges in both the urban and suburban counties operated under the same legal rules, the discretionary and professional nature of judging leaves room for diverse styles to emerge. These diverse styles had different consequences for the role hearings played within the welfare system. On one end of the spectrum is a style of judging I call "bureaucratic." Bureaucratic-style judges essentially replicated and reproduced the approach of frontline agency staff, characterized by preoccupation with procedural regularity and compliance. On the opposite end of the spectrum are judges I call "adjudicators." Judges that functioned primarily as adjudicators had a distinctive judicial identity, employing legal rules and norms to scrutinize both parties, while also at times using the law and legal procedures to correct power imbalances and reform the bureaucracy, much as envisioned in *Goldberg*. Using this typology of judicial styles provides a framework for assessing the important role of discretion in the adjudication of fair hearings.

Judges as Bureaucrats

As discussed above, fair hearings are part of the bureaucracy they judge. Although they are structured as adversarial proceedings, there is ample space for judges to shape interactions and use their discretion in considering challenges to agency practice. The observations of hearings revealed cases in which work sanctions were applied broadly and stringently, with little or no attempt to distinguish the unwilling from the unable, or a technical violation from a more serious infraction. Consistent with studies on the application of sanctions in New York and other states (see Lens 2006, 2008), a single missed appointment was viewed as a proxy for participants' overall work behaviors. Procedural violations, such as a failure to notify the correct worker or agency if a work activity was missed, often substituted for more nuanced assessments. In general, bureaucratic judges were apt to hew to this narrow and reductive view, using the rules of evidence regarding relevancy and adequacy to prevent a fuller picture from emerging, thus shielding such practices from scrutiny.

An illustrative case involved an appellant challenging a work sanction for failing to attend a work appointment during her final months of pregnancy. At the hearing, the appellant explained her absence by telling the judge about the birth of her child, including that her labor was induced because of preeclampsia, a serious medical condition. She produced as evidence two notes from her doctor dated four days prior to the birth. The doctor's notes indicated that at the time she was thirty-five weeks pregnant and "urgently" needed an appointment. The judge did not regard this evidence of her condition as relevant, explaining that "the only appointment we really want to focus on at this moment is the April 28 appointment with the city." That was the appointment the appellant failed to keep. The judge noted that the doctors' letters were dated May 14, after the missed appointment, questioning whether she had seen a doctor on the day of her scheduled appointment.

The appellant responded that she did seek medical help on that date, but that she saw the triage nurses, not the doctor. She said that it was difficult to get notes from triage nurses. The rest of the hearing focused on her failure to bring written documentation of this medical visit, with the judge repeatedly chiding her for not doing so. An excerpt of this dialogue follows:

> JUDGE. Knowing you had the fair hearing today, why didn't you just go in prior to that to get a letter from the hospital and then you wouldn't have a problem today?
>
> APPELLANT. Uh, I had my daughter on the 18th. . . . My daughter was two weeks in the hospital which I have paperwork for, also, on that.
>
> JUDGE. Alright. I, I believe you. But, if you, if you, listen—I'm saying this because it seems to me it would be better for you had you come in with a letter from the hospital saying you were seen on that date. Now, regardless of when you gave birth, regardless of the fact that your daughter stayed in the hospital for a week or two, you've been out of the hospital for a while. And, if you knew you were coming in today, why didn't you go to [the hospital] yesterday or the day before or the day before and just get a letter saying that you were seen on April 28?

As the hearing concluded the judge told her, "You can't come into a fair hearing and say you were seen by a doctor and not bring written documentation that you were there. Because the letters you're showing me don't say anything about April 28."

Embedded in the dialogue between the judge and the appellant are conflicting beliefs about the meaning of relevancy. As a legal concept, relevancy pertains to evidence that proves a fact significant to the case. In adversarial proceedings, each side is responsible for proving its case through the introduction of documents and testimony, which all must be relevant to the facts in dispute. The judge narrowed the circle of relevancy to the single date of April 28, when the appellant did not appear for her scheduled work appointment. He deemed as irrelevant anything that occurred before or after that date.

The appellant's circle of relevancy was much broader and continuous, encompassing a several-month period covering a complicated pregnancy and the birth of her child. To her, these events formed an unbroken thread that explained her behavior, including the missed work appointment. In contrast to the judge's more fragmented focus, the appellant painted with a broader brush. She experienced her pregnancy and its complications as one continuous event. In her view, a note from her physician dated a few weeks after the missed appointment, attesting to her urgent need for an appointment, followed by a premature birth only a few days later, explained her overall medical condition during the last stages of her pregnancy and justified the missed work appointment.

The judge and appellant also had differing views on the nature of proof and the assessment of credibility. To the judge proof meant written, "official" proof, from a third party (here, a medical professional), indicating that the appellant sought medical assistance on the date of her missed work appointment. He regarded her own testimony as insufficient, even though he explicitly stated "I believe you" when she described the events before and after giving birth to her child.

In this case, the judge functioned much as frontline workers do, seeking the right piece of paperwork to document an absence. There was no flexibility or nuance or attention to context, or threading of the appellant's testimony together with her proffered proof to see if they constituted a coherent whole. The judge asked for nothing more or less than what's routinely demanded on the front lines, telling the appellant she "can't come to a fair hearing" without it. Her fuller and richer explanation of why she had difficulty attending her work appointment was deemed irrelevant, even though the judge claimed to believe it. In this context, the defining and distinguishing feature of hearings—the opportunity to appear in person to present testimony and argue one's case— appeared to have little meaning or import. In style and substance the encounter was more bureaucratic than judicial, as the judge used his discretion to reduce the dispute to a single date and the appellant's failure to provide "official" documentation.

Generally, hearings presided over by judges that adopted a bureaucratic approach followed a common path. They focused more on the appellant's perceived failures than on the agency's. For example, appellants' allegations that the agency habitually neglected to return phone calls, a fact relevant to work-rule violations when absences must be reported, were ignored, although appellants were directed to call if they could not make an appointment. In contrast, appellants' actions were scrutinized very closely, with bureaucratic judges, like frontline workers, routinely requiring third-party documentation rather than accepting appellants' statements concerning events within their personal knowledge.

Observations of fair hearings indicated that skepticism toward appellants was expressed as personal disapproval, with judges emphasizing narratives of personal irresponsibility. As Super (2005) observes, underlying the mandate to work is the assumption that a failure to work is the fault of the individual and curable by him or her, with work-activation policies thus operating as an explicit and enforceable moral test. A regime based on legal formality, administered with a veneer of procedural regularity and uniformity, can mask moral judgments (Simon 1983). Such judgments are diluted when rules are applied seemingly impersonally. Although hearings ostensibly offer redress for rules that are not fairly applied, in practice they can pose a risk for participants. When bureaucratic-style judges preside over fair hearings, they may use their discretion to make negative or skeptical judgments about the character of the appellants, criticize their behavior, and even explicitly question appellants' ability to appropriately manage their daily lives.

An illustrative case involved a 43-year-old woman, living in an emergency shelter and suffering from shingles, AIDS, asthma, and orthopedic problems. She had a history of repeated hospitalizations, and a recent attempt at work ended because of her physical impairments. The woman challenged a sanction for missing an appointment at the Department of Labor (DOL), the agency that provides welfare-to-work services, claiming she had good cause for missing the appointment due to transportation problems. At the hearing, she explained that when she realized that the bus she had planned to take would get her to the DOL twenty minutes late for her appointment, she called the DOL and was told not to come. After this explanation, the following dialogue ensued:

JUDGE. Have you gone there [to the DOL] before?

APPELLANT. No, this is new to me. I was working and got sick.

JUDGE. How much time did you have between the notice and the date of the appointment?

APPELLANT. [couldn't remember]

JUDGE. When you did receive it [the notice] why didn't you make an effort to find out before the date how to get there?

APPELLANT. Every morning I wake up sick, in pain, the landlord checks on me. It takes me a while to get going.

JUDGE. I want some clarity. You were rambling. You didn't call before because you got sick in the morning?

APPELLANT. Yes. But I didn't know it would take so long.

JUDGE. Do you travel by bus usually?

APPELLANT. Yes.

JUDGE. So don't you know to check before how long it will take?

APPELLANT. I didn't know it would take so long. The route [the bus] sent me on [62] went past out to R_____and back to C_____. All my other [bus] trips are right there. I have to walk fifteen minutes to church to use the telephone.

JUDGE. Glad you clarified this. It was a bit incredible that you couldn't get up and call from your house.

APPELLANT. There is no phone in the house [emergency shelter] where I'm staying.

Through her questioning, the judge framed the issue as one of personal responsibility, questioning how conscientiously the appellant handled the transportation arrangements. She injected skepticism and criticism into her questioning, first by telling her, "I want some clarity. You were rambling," and then by commenting, "It was incredible that you couldn't get up and call." The focus was not on the obstacles the appellant confronted every day (illness, living in a shelter with no immediate means of communication) but on her ability to plan, with the judge suggesting that she waited too long when she checked the bus routes the morning of her DOL appointment. The judge could have used her discretion to question whether the DOL should have accommodated the appellant by permitting her to arrive twenty minutes late to her appointment. But she did not.

In sum, fair hearings presided over by judges adopting a bureaucratic approach are less an opportunity for appellants to present or successfully explain the events leading to a sanction than a place for bureaucratic officials to ask for the same documents deemed relevant on the front lines. The focus is on insuring compliance with the agency's procedures, rather than considering whether sanctions are just in the individual case. As such, they become a vehicle for imposing an additional level of surveillance on participants. Paradoxically, in these examples the mechanical application of sanctions on the front lines is replaced with a more individualized assessment, but one that emphasizes the appellants' perceived personal flaws, rather than the agency's possible mistakes.

Interviews with appellants indicated that they experience such hearings much as they do their frontline interactions. As one appellant described his encounter with such a judge, "It's like a chicken processing plant. They cut your head off and put you on the conveyor. That's what they want. They don't want any conversation." He further elaborated, "I also understood how in connection the agency person and the judge was. I mean they were teamed together." During such hearings, some appellants found it difficult to talk and present their cases. As one appellant described his experience, "I felt like I was being downgraded. . . . It made me feel defeated right then and there." Put simply, a space designed to give voice to appellants instead silenced them.

Judges as Adjudicators

On the other end of the spectrum were judges who hewed more closely to judicial norms and procedures. The question is whether judges adopting this approach provided different opportunities for appellants to challenge agency practices and, thus, produced different outcomes for administrative justice. Because welfare hearings are situated within the larger welfare bureaucracy, appellants often distrust the neutrality of the judge and view him or her as just another government welfare official. Moreover, the adversaries in the hearing room are not equal; as inside players with access to bureaucratic files and a superior knowledge of the law, agency representatives have considerably more power and knowledge than appellants.

Observations of fair hearings indicated that judges adopting an adjudicator approach may be able to surmount, or at least minimize, the obstacles facing appellants in the fair hearing process. Common to adjudicator-style judges were efforts to emphasize their neutrality and level the playing field. From the outset, they tried to make the process more transparent and less intimidating. An instructive example involved the required opening statement, used by the judges to explain the process. Some judges stuck to the dry legalistic tone of the script, repeating it as if they have said it hundreds of times (which they have), and communicating a message of indifference rather than respect for the process. The following is one such example of this approach, delivered by a judge speaking very quickly and without looking at the appellant.

> My name is_____. I'm the hearing officer. I've been assigned to hear the case. Today we'll make a record. You'll get a decision. Both sides can ask questions. You can make statements, you can provide documents if you have them. After the hearing's over, the record will go to_____and the Commissioner will issue a decision. If you did ask the agency for documents for today's hearing and they didn't give them to you, let me know.

In contrast, adjudicator judges were more apt to personalize the script to make it more understandable and to put appellants at ease. They also used it to educate appellants and hence alter the power imbalance between the repeat player in the room, the agency representative, and those appellants who might be less sophisticated and less well-educated. The following is an example, with the appellant's responses in parentheses:

Let's first explain how hearings work, and then we'll introduce everybody around the table here, and then we'll get into the heart of matter. First of all, as far as hearings, hearings go this way. Each side presents their case through their testimony and whatever documents you want to submit. (Uh huh.) Each of you will have an opportunity to question each other back and forth, and of course, I get involved in questioning also. (Okay.) Then, everything, including the tape recording, the entire record of it is sent up to the Commissioner, who reviews it again. (Uh huh.) He makes a decision on it and sends that decision to you by mail. (Okay.) If you've requested any documents from the city, for today's hearing, and the city failed to provide them to you, I need you to bring that issue to my attention right away. Because that's very important in the law. (Okay. Okay.) Okay? The gentleman seated across from you is the city's representative. [Both parties identify themselves for the record.]

With these types of issues—all the ones you have here—reductions and discontinuing, there's a thing in the law called the burden of proof. And, what it means is that's the person who has the responsibility to go first and prove that they have a valid case before the other side contests something wrong with it. (Right.) That burden is on Mr. B. for today. Okay? Because, all your issues are those types of that the city has the burden first. So, I'm gonna be asking him to go first. (Okay.) Keep in mind, he doesn't know you personally. So, he's not gonna testify. There's nothing he can testify to. He's gonna produce his case by handing over a series of documents to me and the same set of documents to you. (Okay.) So that we all have the same exact set. (Okay.) Yours are for you to keep. Mine, I'll review and I'll send up to the Commissioner. Keep in mind that all these papers have a lot of your personal information on them. Don't be casual about them when you take them. (Alright.) If you're gonna get rid of them, shred them, because you don't want the public to get any access to your personal information.

Now, before we start that, I want to get a couple of things as far as background. Keep in mind, I'm a neutral,_____State judge, looking at your dispute with_____. So, I don't know a lot about your case. You're gonna have to be, you're gonna have to be my teacher. You're gonna have to give me as best an explanation, a detailed an explanation as you can so I get the full picture. (Okay.) And, if you brought documents, don't be shy about pulling them out. They help fill in the blanks. A little bit of background helps me also with the case itself. I'm gonna do a quick questionnaire with you and then we'll let Mr. B. present his case.

Through his opening statement, the judge explained, in easy-to-understand terms, and beginning and ending with the inclusive "we," everything from the process (who speaks when, how decisions are made and communicated), to the identity and status of the parties, to legal terms, such as "burden of proof." He established his neutrality, distinguishing himself from the agency by stating "I'm a neutral,_____State judge, looking at your dispute with_____. So, I don't know a lot about your case." By telling the appellant "You're gonna have to be my teacher," he communicated the value of her input, and encouraged her participation. He did the same for any documentary proof she might have, telling her, "Don't be shy about pulling them out. They help fill in the blanks." As he talked the judge looked directly at the appellant, who responded at intervals by nodding and saying "okay" or "all right," thus signaling she was listening and engaged.

Adjudicator judges were less likely to accept the agency's version of the case and more likely to examine it than judges who adopted a more bureaucratic approach. Adjudicators tended to be more vigorous fact finders, employing a distinctly judicial style of equal-opportunity skepticism, scrutinizing both the agency and the appellant's case. Their style of questioning was neutral; unlike bureaucratic judges their questions were more open-ended and didn't assume a particular set of facts. For example, when questioning an appellant about an alleged missed work appointment, one judge asked, "Did you go to the appointment?" rather than "Why didn't you go to the appointment?" This gave the appellant a clean slate to tell her story and signaled that all versions of the event, including the agency's, were open to question.

In observations, adjudicator hearings tended to unfold as the facts developed, with no uniform narrative dominating from hearing to hearing. While bureaucratic judges often advanced narratives of personal responsibility and/or procedural compliance, adjudicator judges had no one set narrative. They tended to focus on the facts of the case rather than on the appellant's character or personal habits.

Adjudicators did not tend to conform to the standards of acceptable proof used by caseworkers and were more flexible about accepting personal testimony in lieu of third-party documentation. In an illustrative case, one appellant claimed she missed her work appointment because she and her children were ill. At the hearing, the agency asked whether she had documentation of the illness. When she did not, the judge interceded to ask a series of questions eliciting a detailed story of family illnesses:

JUDGE. I want to ask a couple of questions, if I may, for starters. With the kids, let's start with that. Did you take them to a doctor?
APPELLANT. I took them to the doctor, uh, before the appointment date. So . . .
JUDGE. When did you?
APPELLANT. Uh, that was a Saturday. I think I took them that Thursday because they were complaining about stomach and, you know, the whole swine flu thing. I was just, you know, very concerned about that.
AGENCY. So, the condition got worse?

APPELLANT. No. It didn't get worse. I just took 'em to the doctor as soon [inaudible] about . . .

JUDGE. What's the doctor's name?

APPELLANT. Uh, Dr. V_____.

JUDGE. Okay. And, what did Dr. V_____give them or what did he say?

APPELLANT. She said, uh, just to treat, to treat it, this is before they were sick with, uh, you know, stomach and everything, she said to treat it like a regular cold. You know, [inaudible] 'cause . . .

JUDGE. She didn't prescribe any medication?

APPELLANT. She didn't give 'em, she told me to give 'em like Motrin and, you know, whatever.

JUDGE. Okay.

APPELLANT. Uh, she advised me not to take them to the hospital because it's not sick, you know, only to take them if their condition gets worse, because if they're not sick with that, takin' them to the hospital will put them at risk of getting sick.

JUDGE. And, by Monday, you had it, you said, correct?

APPELLANT. Yes, by Monday I was sick, sick with my stomach. I was throwing up. I was not feeling well.

In contrast to the example of the bureaucratic judge above, this judge did not reiterate the demand for third-party documentation or question why the appellant did not bring it with her. He relied instead on the conventional legal format for eliciting testimony, asking short, concise questions arranged chronologically. The questioning was fact intensive and designed to elicit a contextual and detailed narrative from which to judge credibility. It was devoid of the personal judgments that characterized the tone and style of bureaucratic judges.

Adjudicator judges, at times, veered into advocacy for the appellant. Rather than present a united front with the agency, as often occurred in hearings presided over by bureaucratic judges, adjudicator judges were more likely to assist appellants in making their cases. In an illustrative example, a young woman who was sanctioned for not attending a work assessment claimed she was working an overnight shift that day. At the hearing, the agency representative claimed that the caseworker contacted the employer and was told the appellant had quit several weeks before. Skeptical of the agency, the judge reviewed the agency file during the hearing and found evidence favorable to the appellant. The documents indicated that the appellant had been working the overnight shift and had submitted pay stubs to the agency. The judge asserted that the proof "flies in the face" of the agency's assertions. The agency representative then pursued another tactic, suggesting that the appellant purposely made her assessment appointment when she knew she was working and unable to attend. The judge blocked that line of argument, asking, "Now, is that relevant?"

In these subtle ways, adjudicator judges created a distinctly judicial space. They created an environment where different versions of the same event can emerge, as the adversarial process is designed to do. As one appellant described his encounter with such a judge, "He didn't just brush me off. He let me speak. He let me explain. He sat there and listened to everything I had to say." At times adjudicators did more than listen to appellants; they helped them make their cases, taking advantage of fair hearing regulations, as described above, that encourage judges to assist appellants who are having difficulty presenting their case. The particular nature of welfare hearings, involving deeply unequal adversaries, sometimes invites this more activist style of judging as the judge seeks to protect appellants from more powerful state actors.

Conclusion

This chapter has examined whether and under what circumstances the fair hearing process provides an opportunity to challenge agency practices, achieve redress, and advance administrative justice. The research findings presented in this chapter indicate that the potential of hearings to secure redress and achieve administrative justice is often not realized. It also suggests some of the factors that limit the value of the fair hearing process. For one thing, poor procedural practices on the front lines may displace concerns over nonprocedural issues, in effect limiting the substantive scope of adjudication. In fair hearings dominated by procedural error, this study indicates that substantive challenges to agency practices—for example, challenges regarding caseworker judgments leading to a sanction—are likely to remain unexamined. In addition, fair hearings may offer appellants only a temporary victory while doing little or nothing to prevent similar errors, even within one appellant's own case, in the future. Paradoxically, for a hearing system to function properly, frontline practices must be reformed to prevent procedural errors from suppressing the adjudication of substantive disputes. For hearings to be fully effective frontline practices must be competent enough to allow substantive disputes to emerge. This is especially the case in large, urban bureaucracies, where the procedures put in place to enable them to process large numbers of cases may generate mistakes that clog the fair hearing system, but that, ultimately, remain unresolved by it at a system level.

Those disputes ripe for adjudication can also be bureaucratized by judges. Bureaucratic-style judges do relatively little to distinguish hearings from the welfare bureaucracy over which they stand in judgment. Instead, they function more in a ministerial role, applying the same reductive and mechanistic view of relevancy and proof as on the front lines. They arguably leave appellants worse off for challenging the bureaucracy because they subject appellants to one more bureaucratic barrier while also exacerbating the stigma and powerlessness of welfare interactions.

However, the inevitability of bureaucratic judges is belied by the existence of adjudicator judges. As observed in fair hearings, adjudicator judges can create legal spaces where less-powerful appellants can effectively challenge bureaucratic decision making. Such judges utilize the inherently discretionary and professional nature of judging—a feature of all judicial systems and one that encourages diversity of judicial styles—to carve out a distinct judicial identity that allows appellants to expose and correct agency error. Such judges make full use of the adversarial process, which is a form of decision making that encourages "complex judgment, decentralization, and professionalism" (Simon 1983, 983). When individual facts and circumstances are ignored on the front lines, hearings provide an important counterweight if presided over by adjudicators. As Adler notes in this volume, the right to appeal a decision is essential, especially under newly fashioned welfare-to-work regimes that emphasize professionalized and managerial roles for caseworkers rather than a more legalistic type of decision making (see chap. 13). But the use of such mechanisms is limited unless and until a judicial rather than a bureaucratic stance predominates. To understand how and why judges adopt specific styles further research is needed, including examination of the influence of bureaucratic structures and processes, role formation and identification, and socialization.

This close examination of the fair hearing process indicates that there may be limits to the usefulness of even well-run adversarial proceedings. Hearings cannot alter what some critics see as the harsh terms of a law that makes income assistance conditional on work and places time limits on cash aid (Handler and Hasenfeld 2007). In this context, fair hearings may be conducted in ways that "coat the system with a veneer of procedural fairness which may serve to deflect attention from the severe and rigid nature" of the laws (Baldwin, Wikeley, and Young 1992, 23). They rarely promote systemwide change, even when individual decisions are error signals for more systemic problems (White 1990). It is equally clear, however, that in the day-to-day struggle to survive, hearings are often the only recourse for individually aggrieved appellants.

Note

This study was supported by a grant from the National Science Foundation (no. 0849193).

PART VI

Conclusion

15

Work and the Welfare State Reconsidered

Street-Level Organizations and the Global Workfare Project

EVELYN Z. BRODKIN

In this volume we have sought to introduce a new perspective to the study of welfare state policies and politics, one that directs analytic attention to the street-level organizations (SLOs) at the operational core of the welfare state. Turning the focus from policy to practice, this volume makes visible the variety of ways in which workfare-style policies operate in everyday organizational life. It also reveals how governance and management reforms have functioned as a second track for policy change, steering workfare practices on the ground toward greater social regulation and less support for the unemployed and disadvantaged.

In bringing a street-level perspective to the study of welfare state politics, we build on and extend Pierson's (1994) important insights about the strategic significance of visibility—or perhaps more importantly, invisibility—to welfare state retrenchment. We show that, beyond policies on the page, adjustments to the welfare state's boundaries can be made indirectly through alterations in the organization of policy delivery and street-level practices. We bring these developments out of the shadows, directly interrogating the role of SLOs in order to shed new light on how workfare is reshaping the boundaries between work and the welfare state.

To be clear, we recognize that formal policies of workfare matter; they set the workfare project in motion. But policies do not, by themselves, determine how this project operates and what takes place day-to-day under its rubric. A street-level perspective illuminates the *missing middle*—the opaque spaces between formal policy provisions and social outcomes in which the essential work of the welfare state and its policies takes place.

In this volume we illuminate how organizations mediate the policy experiences of the poor, marginalized, and unemployed who are subject to workfare and activation. We show that, in ways that often fall beneath the radar of administrative metrics or evaluation studies, street-level practices effectively determine whether individuals will have access to services that can help them make it in the market, whether they will be pressed into labor at disadvantageous terms, or whether they will be left to fend for themselves against daunting odds.

This book also brings a comparative perspective to bear, recognizing that the workfare project now extends around the world. As a global project, workfare-style arrangements have developed along common lines. However, there are important differences in paths and politics leading, on the one hand, to US-style workfare, and, on the other, to European-style activation (chap. 4). American workfare generally is characterized by its market and regulatory emphasis, with severe restrictions on welfare and strong demands for work. The varied policies of European activation are more difficult to characterize, but, as a general matter, place greater emphasis on support for labor and fewer (although increasing) restrictions on welfare.

Yet, as we have argued, formal policies tell only part of the story. Despite differences in national policies and politics, we find that many countries have adopted a common set of governance and managerial initiatives, initiatives that have become closely intertwined with the workfare project and, effectively, formed its second track. Although implementation has been uneven, governance and management strategies have tended to move in a common direction, quietly pushing back the welfare state's boundaries and enlarging the zone in which market principles prevail.

This chapter reviews the book's key findings as a point of departure for reconsidering the workfare project and highlighting how a street-level perspective informs analysis of welfare state politics and polices.

Workfare in Practice: The Role of Governance and Management Reform

Unlike the policies of workfare, which are by now fairly well examined, the governance and managerial reforms that constitute workfare's second track have received less systematic attention. Yet they have played an important part in the workfare project's evolution, a part that our research brings from the analytic sidelines to the forefront. Governance and management initiatives tend to appear manifestly nonpolitical. However, we reveal them to be deeply political, altering the welfare state's boundaries in ways that are difficult to see and to trace and, thus, less likely to provoke controversy than more visible forms of policymaking.

Studies in this volume underscore the strategic importance of visibility and traceability in welfare state politics (Pierson 1994). In addition, they also suggest that some governance and management reforms stay better cloaked in the veil of administrative invisibility than others. Perhaps the most apparent—and controversial—governance reform has involved European efforts to dismantle the public employment services (PES). The PES were the operational arm of activation in many EU countries (Larsen and Van Berkel 2009b). Under the rubric of devolution and modernization, countries began to dismantle these agencies and transfer managerial and operational responsibilities for activation to regional, municipal, and, in some cases, private entities. In his analysis of the Danish case, Flemming Larsen (chap. 7) argues that there was an underlying political dimension to this manifestly nonpolitical reform. As partners in the Danish PES, labor groups had been able to oversee activation's implementation. This provided labor with opportunities to support practices that emphasized activation's enabling features and limited its regulatory ones. Dismantling the PES reduced labor's influence, opening the door to a more regulatory style of activation. Perhaps it should not be entirely surprising that organized labor fought back (albeit with limited success) when the agencies through which it exercised policy influence were targeted for elimination.

Other types of reorganization have followed a more complicated path, as Rik Van Berkel shows in the case of ongoing battles over devolution, decentralization, and contracting in the Netherlands (chap. 6). In contrast to efforts to reorganize the PES out of the activation business, Van Berkel's research suggests that these other governance reforms may be less likely to provoke coherent political opposition. Certainly, public sector workers who are the immediate targets of reform may resist efforts to impose new managerial controls. Indeed, Van Berkel depicts a simmering interbureaucratic struggle that has made the advance of Dutch governance reforms uneven and uncertain. Yet governance and managerial concerns tend to generate limited political interest, rarely extending beyond the public sector employees directly affected.

It is noteworthy that, on the whole, these conflicts over changes in the organization of policy delivery in Europe were fairly modest relative to disagreements about legislative policy initiatives. But even these relatively well-contained conflicts stand in contrast to US experience. In the United States, widespread privatization and contracting of workfare programs have met with relatively little organized resistance (Sanger 2003; Sol and Westerveld 2005). This difference may derive, at least in part, from the fact that these shifts advanced incrementally in the United States, more often occurring through increases in contracting rather than overt dismantling of public sector agencies or anything similar to the elimination of the PES in Europe. The US experience also undoubtedly reflects the relative weakness of organized labor and public sector workers in America, mitigating the potential for mobilizing opposition to an expanding contracting regime, despite its implications for public sector provision. The political dynamics of governance reform in the United States (or, arguably, its unpolitics) may also be related to the relatively weak public support for both government and the public sector that is characteristic of contemporary US politics, as Michael Lipsky highlights in chapter 3.

If reorganization has provoked resistance in some countries, managerial strategies deploying performance measurement and various performance-based financial incentives have advanced with substantially less controversy. Performance schemes are now nearly ubiquitous, used to manage SLOs in many policy areas in countries around the world. Performance measurement can have powerful effects when it deeply penetrates street-level practice. But that does not mean it operates as neatly as its advocates would have it. Studies in this volume show that performance schemes intersect with localized organizational conditions to produce below-the-radar street-level adaptations that, effectively, become the real worlds of workfare and activation.

For example, my organizational ethnography of a big-city welfare agency in the United States (chap. 9) shows that performance measurement insinuated itself into the very interstices of street-level discretion. Although measurement instruments were used in ways manifestly intended to improve accountability, in practice, they created incentives systematically favoring caseload cuts over counseling and favoring suspicion over support. The chapter also shows how workfare practices are effectively hollowed out when caseworkers have limited capacity to support claimants, by providing either income assistance or services that could help them make it in the labor market.

The potentially powerful effects of performance-based management are underscored by Soss, Fording, and Schram in their investigation of contracted workfare agencies in Florida (chap. 8). Their study, in conjunction with chapter 9, provides a rare opportunity to compare workfare practices in a public agency with those in a private, contracted setting. In both public and private organizations, the practices of workfare were more problematic than policy on the books would indicate. In both cases, performance pressures, in a context of limited resources, created an environment in which street-level staff were constrained in how they could enable workfare participants and nearly unrestricted in how they could regulate them. These findings raise the possibility that, under certain circumstances, public-private distinctions may be less consequential than managerial arrangements, a matter that calls for further research.

Workfare in Practice: Inequality, Marginalization, and Street-Level Organizations

For those who would argue that the policies of workfare and activation are vehicles for social integration or inclusion, studies in part IV reveal a very different picture of how they work on the ground. They suggest that, in practice, they may reinforce inequality and marginalization, albeit in ways that are largely hidden from view. Celeste Watkins-Hayes (chap. 10) provides insights into how race and ethnicity are mediated in US welfare offices. She finds an organizational environment with limited prospects for responsiveness and meaningful exchange, even where, theoretically, one might have expected racial and ethnic affinity to produce responsiveness between racemates. The Watkins-Hayes study, similar to those previously discussed, demonstrates the power of organizational conditions to shape the informal practices that effectively create the policy experiences of marginalized populations. Watkins-Hayes shows organizational pressures bearing down on street-level practitioners, even to the point of displacing otherwise powerful racial affinities.

Looking at a different country and population, in chapter 11, Martin Brussig and Matthias Knuth investigate how street-level practices shaped the activation experiences of migrants to Germany. They reveal that informal practices in German job centers have tended to reinforce the marginalization of migrants, especially highly marginalized immigrants from Turkey, while ostensibly seeking to advance their integration. They find that German activation practices generally operate to the disadvantage of migrants—and, perhaps, women migrants in particular—despite manifest fealty to norms of equal treatment.

Gregory Marston, in chapter 12, looks beyond race, ethnicity, and nationality to consider disability as a distinct status. He examines how this status is negotiated in street-level practice under Australia's welfare-to-work regime. His research reveals how emerging practices are informally eroding policy's more enabling features and reducing opportunities for citizens to exercise self-determination in navigating the boundaries between work and welfare. Together, these studies demonstrate the critical importance of adopting a three-dimensional view of SLOs (chap. 2) in order to make visible how their practices shape status distinctions, citizenship, and social integration or, alternatively, marginalization.

Workfare in Practice: The Limitations of Administrative Justice

Certainly, it is unreasonable to expect workfare and activation to operate without error or flaw. Public agencies may address problems by providing mechanisms for review and redress. To the extent that administrative justice mechanisms are reasonably accessible and put remedies in place, they have the potential to mitigate some of the problematic street-level practices detailed in this book. In part V, two contributors investigate this possibility, examining how administrative justice works in the United Kingdom and United States. Their findings suggest that, at least in these two countries, justice for those inappropriately or unfairly treated by the practices of workfare cannot be assured.

Michael Adler, in chapter 13, assesses the conditions necessary to secure administrative justice in SLOs implementing workfare under the British New Deal. His study indicates limited opportunities for workfare participants to obtain recourse and redress. In addition, Adler is particularly critical of governance reforms that give job center managers authority to assess grievances in their own agencies. He contends that, by eliminating independent adjudicators, these governance reforms stack the deck against individuals who seek redress. Adler suggests that administrative justice functions more effectively in the United States, because welfare agency judges operate with greater autonomy.

However, Vicki Lens offers a different view. In chapter 14, she closely examines the appeals process in a major US welfare agency and finds that judicial autonomy is insufficient to assure administrative justice. She contends that other organizational factors and styles of judging profoundly affect the possibilities for individual redress. Paradoxically, she also discovers that administrative justice functions least effectively where it is most needed. Lens's analysis shows that adjudication processes in the agencies most bedeviled by procedural and bureaucratic problems were least likely to address substantive issues of fairness in the workfare's administration. Beyond individual redress, Lens finds that the practices of adjudication provide few opportunities for advancing systemic reforms that could promote fairness and accuracy beyond single cases.

Street-Level Organizations and the Workfare Project

In this book we have provided an inside look into the global workfare project, taking analysis beyond the readily visible policies of workfare and activation to examine street-level practices that too often escape scrutiny. We find that these practices are changing the boundaries between work and the welfare state, but often in hidden ways. We also find that governance and managerial reforms have become an important track for indirectly steering the street-level production of workfare, in the process eroding workfare's potentially enabling dimensions and intensifying its regulatory functions.

We recognize that there are important baseline differences in the way the workfare project has developed in different parts of the world, with significant distinctions between European-style activation (especially in the northern social democratic states) and US-style workfare in the more liberal states (among them, the United States, Australia, and the United Kingdom). These differences make all the more striking our discovery that, irrespective of regime type, countries appear to be following similar paths toward governance and managerial reform. These administrative reforms may seem, on their face, best left to technocrats and management experts. But we challenge that view. Analyses in this book demonstrate that governance and managerial strategies should be understood as politically significant, because they reshape the boundaries between work and the welfare state by indirect means.

We show how these strategies—including the reorganization of the PES, devolution, contracting, and performance measurement—influence street-level practices. We find that they have changed where discretion is located and how it is exercised. In a variety of ways, we see managerial regimes of control squeezing out space for discretion that might enable responsiveness to claims for welfare and labor market assistance. At the same time, these regimes appear to be creating ever-stronger incentives to pressure the poor and unemployed into bad jobs or simply deny them social benefits. To be sure, these regulatory types of practice are strongest in the United States. But studies in this book indicate that managerial and governance strategies have begun to influence practices elsewhere, invisibly but powerfully functioning in ways that seem consistent with a neoliberal agenda of rolling back the welfare state. To make this functional argument is not to say that these strategies are necessarily advanced with anti-welfarist intentions; although we do not rule out intentionality.[1]

Our point is that the consequences of these strategies are deeply political. They provide a path to welfare state change and retrenchment that limits transparency, visibility, and traceability—precisely the characteristics Pierson (1994) associates with policy designs meant to obscure potentially unpopular political actions. Governance and managerial reforms are politically significant because they provide an avenue for changing the boundaries of the welfare state while simultaneously limiting the visibility of these changes and, thus, the prospects for political mobilization and resistance. Our findings make an important addition to the tactical menu of retrenchment strategies that Pierson identified.

This book underscores the importance of bringing research on SLOs to the study of welfare state policy and politics. It points toward an agenda for the next generation of research that builds on a three-dimensional view of SLOs and extends analysis across a wider variety of policy domains. Our findings also point toward the importance of advancing critical governance and management studies that illuminate the less well observed effects of the so-called new public management on SLOs at the operational core of the state.

The Future of Work and the Welfare State

This book is not the first to cast doubt on the workfare project, and it is unlikely to be the last. It is distinctive, however, in bringing a street-level perspective to examination of this project and directly investigating workfare practices in varied national and organizational settings. Studies in this book demonstrate that the workfare project has developed unevenly, with marked differences between US-style workfare and European forms of activation. But by focusing on workfare in practice, they also reveal emerging common tendencies that suggest a more general movement toward rearranging the boundaries between work and the welfare state, advancing the former and rolling back the latter.[2]

Our analysis also shows that the workfare project is rife with tensions and contradictions derived, in part, from underlying tensions and contradictions in the relationship between the market and the welfare state. Work is necessary to the welfare state, fueling processes of production and underwriting economic development and growth. But work in the paid labor market is insufficient to assure either individual economic security or the well-being of the broader society. As a general matter, markets, when unregulated, produce inequality, offering an avenue of advancement for some, hardship for others, and uncertainty for many.

In recent decades, structural economic shifts have exacerbated these problems. For many, the possibilities for earning economic security through work have diminished as contingent and flexible work arrangements have increased. The development of more flexible labor markets, already well advanced in the United States, is becoming more widespread, extending to countries that have traditionally had more highly regulated labor markets. The consequences for workers are profound. Susan Lambert and Julia Henly's research on lower-wage jobs (chapter 5) indicates that the prospects for achieving economic security and advancement through work are highly doubtful for those at the lower reaches of the labor market. Beyond the hardships of prolonged unemployment in a recession-battered economies, the realities of the lower-wage workplace are daunting even for those fortunate enough to land a job. Even the most motivated and dedicated workers may be confronted with uncertain hours, varying wages, high turnover, and out-of-reach benefits. Although these types of jobs may be more prevalent in the United States, they are now found throughout the developed world.

Recently, these labor market trends, coupled with the global recession and prolonged economic crises, have increased both unemployment and the share of contingent jobs in the labor market. Arguably, these developments would suggest a reconsideration of the workfare project, particularly US-style workfare. After all, where are the jobs? Yet as fiscal pressures on the state have intensified, so, too, have pressures on the poor, marginalized, and unemployed. This is most apparent in the liberal regimes.

In the United States, restrictions on welfare benefits continue to attract political support, and there is little evidence of emerging opposition to the workfare project. Perhaps this is a predictable playing-out of the two welfare state narratives Michael Lipsky describes in chapter 3. As Lipsky puts it, narratives that provide a technical rationale for social and labor market policies have proven no match for an ascendant antistate narrative that now seems to dominate US political discourse. Further, the absence of discernible interest in reconsidering the workfare project may reflect the aversion of Democratic Party politicians to reopening the welfare policy wars they regarded as an impediment to efforts to expand and solidify an electoral coalition extending beyond the party's traditional liberal base.[3]

The harder edge of the workfare project also has continued to advance—even intensify—in the United Kingdom, although millions are suffering from the effects of prolonged recession. It is in this context that the Cameron government stepped up its workfare demands in 2011 and 2012, extending them more widely and requiring more Ronald Reagan–style workfare (i.e., unpaid work under the notion that you should "work for your benefits"). However, by 2013, as these efforts intensified in the United Kingdom, there was some evidence of a reaction against them. Emerging anti-workfare sentiment was exacerbated by government reports of mismanagement in its "mandatory work activity programme" (UK Department for Work and Pensions 2012) and reflected in judicial decisions challenging unpaid work placements (Henley 2013).[4] It is significant that workfare's most observable regulatory mechanisms have aroused political resistance, while regulatory practices advanced less visibly through governance and management reforms have not.

Outside the liberal regimes, it is more difficult to characterize European responses to workfare under changing economic conditions. There is considerable variation in how countries have experienced global economic disruptions and how they have used welfare and labor market policies to respond. A strong welfare state tradition, especially in northern Europe, retains considerable political support. Yet, despite national differences, over time, the workfare project has become institutionally embedded, part of the policy and organizational architecture of countries around the world.

As we have detailed, the practices of workfare developing within this architecture are varied and subject to shifting influences; most notably, those asserted through governance and management reforms. Certainly, some workfare practices offer the unemployed opportunities to retool their skills and support those working in the more precarious sectors of the labor market. But other practices are advancing a harder and more regulatory approach, reducing alternatives to work at any cost.

Of particular concern is this book's findings that governance and managerial reforms appear to be quietly shifting street-level practices away from social support and investment and toward greater social regulation.[5] Over time, these shifts could continue to reshape the workfare project, even if formal policy features remained largely unchanged. Paradoxically, governance and management reforms may have the greatest political utility in incrementally tightening welfare guarantees and increasing pressures on workers where overt policy shifts would more likely provoke opposition. This underscores the case for taking close account of new governance and managerial regimes, which provide strategies for welfare state retrenchment that mitigate the political risks inherent in more visible strategies.

Workfare is a global project with direct significance for the poor, marginalized, and unemployed. Beyond its impact on individuals, this project has broad political significance because it is redrawing the boundaries between work and the welfare state, changing the state's role in buffering the consequences of market-derived inequalities and economic vulnerabilities. In this book we have offered an approach to research that recognizes the pivotal role of SLOs in mediating policy and political change. We have used this approach to make visible otherwise invisible processes that are altering the boundaries between work and the welfare state, increasing the precariousness of life for the unemployed and those living at the economic margins. As this project evolves, it will be crucial to understand not only what the policies of workfare *say*, but also what they *do*.

Notes

1. From a functional perspective, we see workfare operating in practice as if it were intended to regulate workers and the unemployed and roll back welfare state protections. This neither requires intentionality nor does it preclude it.

2. I borrow the term "tendencies" from Kildal, who also notes that "the primacy of work has always been central to Scandinavian welfare legislation. . . . The most distinctive difference between the new and old work approach is . . . the introduction of a quite new kind of requirement: a duty to work in return for benefits in the lowest tier of the income maintenance system" (2001, 6).

3. In contrast, Republican politicians at times have seen strategic advantages in promoting the welfare wars as a way of expanding and solidifying their base among white, working-class voters (Weaver 2000).

4. See John Henley, "Victory of the unsung hero in the workfare battle," *Guardian* (London) February 13, 2013. See also Daniel Boffey, "Welfare Bill Won't Work, Key Advisers

Tell Iain Duncan Smith," *Observer* (London), September 15, 2012; John Harris, "Back to the Workhouse," *Guardian* (London), June 8, 2012.

5. Jean-Claude Barbier, a critic of the activation project, suggests that analysis will ultimately show that "the whole 'activation industry' of the past 20 years has eventually not fulfilled its promises, except traditional cost-containment goals and the uncertain containment of what the Scandinavians call 'marginalization,' while the ideological shift has perhaps at the same time destabilised many individuals across our nations, some more than others in some countries" (2010, 12).

REFERENCES

Abello, David, and Helen MacDonald. 2002. "Job Network: Changing Community Sector Values." *Drawing Board: An Australian Review of Public Affairs* 3 (1): 51–63.

Acs, Gregory, Norma B. Coe, Keith Watson, and Robert I. Lerman. 1998. *Does Work Pay? An Analysis of the Work Incentives under TANF.* Washington, DC: Urban Institute.

Acs, Gregory, and Pamela J. Loprest. 2001. *Final Synthesis Report of Findings from ASPE's "Leavers" Grants.* Washington, DC: Urban Institute. www.urban.org/url.cfm?ID = 410809.

Adler, Michael. 2003. "A Socio-legal Approach to Administrative Justice." *Law and Policy* 25 (4): 323–52.

———. 2004. "Combining Welfare to Work Measures with Tax Credits: A New Hybrid Approach to Social Security in the UK." *International Social Security Review* 57 (2): 87–106.

———. 2006. "Fairness in Context." *Journal of Law and Society* 33 (4): 615–38.

———. 2008. "The Justice Implications of Activation Policy in the UK." In *A European Work-First Welfare State*, edited by Sara Stendahl, Thomas Erhag, and Stamatia Devetzi, 95–131. Gothenburg: Centre for European Research, University of Gothenburg.

———. 2010. "Understanding and Analysing Administrative Justice." In *Administrative Justice in Context*, edited by Michael Adler. Oxford: Hart.

Allison, Graham. 1971. *Essence of Decision: Explaining the Cuban Missile Crisis.* Boston: Little, Brown.

Andersen, Jørgen Goul. 2007. "Restricting Access to Social Protection for Immigrants in the Danish Welfare State." *Benefits* 15 (3): 257–69.

Andersen, Jørgen Goul, Christian Albreckt Larsen, and Jan Bendix Jensen. 2003. *Marginalisering og velfærdspolitik—Arbejdsløshed, jobchancer og trivsel.* Copenhagen: Frydenlund.

Annesley, Claire. 2007. "Lisbon and Social Europe: Towards a European 'Adult Worker Model' Welfare System." *Journal of European Social Policy* 17 (3): 195–205.

REFERENCES

Appelbaum, Eileen, Annette Bernhardt, and Richard Murnane. 2003. "Low-Wage America: An Overview." In *Low-Wage America: How Employers Are Reshaping Opportunity in the Workplace*, edited by Eileen Appelbaum, Annette Bernhardt, and Richard Murnane, 1–32. New York: Russell Sage Foundation.

Arnold, R. Douglas. 1990. *The Logic of Congressional Action.* New Haven, CT: Yale University Press.

Bade, Klaus J. 2002. *Europa in Bewegung: Migration vom späten 18. Jahrhundert bis zur Gegenwart.* Munich: Beck.

Baldacci, Paris R. 2007. "A Full and Fair Hearing: The Role of the ALJ in Assisting the Pro Se Litigant." *Journal of the National Association of Administrative Law Judiciary* 27 (2): 447–95.

Baldwin, John, Nick Wikeley, and Richard Young. 1992. *Judging Social Security.* Oxford: Clarendon.

Bane, Mary Jo, and David T. Ellwood. 1994. *Welfare Realities: From Rhetoric to Reform.* Cambridge, MA: Harvard University Press.

Barbier, Jean-Claude. 2004. "Systems of Social Protection in Europe: Two Contrasted Paths to Activation and Maybe a Third." In *Labor and Employment Regulation in Europe*, edited by Jens Lind, Herman Knudsen, and Henning Jørgensen. New York: Peter Lang.

———. 2005. "When Words Matter: Dealing Anew with Cross-national Comparison." In *Politiques sociales/Social Policy: Enjeux méthodologiques et epistémologiques des comparisons internationales*, edited by Jean-Claude Barbier and Marie-Thérèse Letablier. Brussels: Peter Lang.

———. 2007. "From Political Strategy to Analytical Research and Back to Politics, a Sociological Approach of 'Flexicurity.'" In *Flexicurity and Beyond*, edited by Henning Jørgensen and Per Kongshøj Madsen. Copenhagen: DJØF.

———. 2010. "The Activation of Social Protection for the Last 10 Years: Was It a Complete Failure?" Paper presented at the 6th Annual International Policy and Research Conference on Social Security. Luxembourg.

Bartels, Larry M. 2006. "Is the Water Rising? Reflections on Inequality and American Democracy." *PS: Political Science and Politics* 39 (1): 39–42.

Batt, Rosemary, David Holman, and Ursula Holtgrewe. 2009. "The Globalization of Service Work: Comparative Institutional Perspectives on Call Centers; Introduction to a Special Issue of *ILRR*." *Industrial and Labor Relations Review* 62 (4): 453–88.

Beale, Ian, Claire Bloss, and Andrew Thomas. 2008. *The Longer-Term Impacts of the New Deal for Young People.* London: Department for Work and Pensions.

Becker, Jens, and Geraldine Hallein-Benze. 2009. "Einstellungen in der Bevölkerung: Wie Hartz IV beurteilt wird." *Soziale Sicherheit* 6:205–10.

Bell, Stephen H., and Larry L. Orr. 2002. "Screening (and Creaming?) Applicants to Job Training Programs: The AFDC Homemaker–Home Health Aide Demonstrations." *Labour Economics* 9 (2): 279–301.

Bernhardt, Annette, Heather Boushey, Laura Dresser, and Chris Tilly, eds. 2008. *The Gloves-Off Economy: Workplace Standards at the Bottom of America's Labor Market*. Champaign, IL: Labor and Employment Relations Association.

Bernhardt, Annette, Martina Morris, Mark S. Handcock, and Marc A. Scott. 2001. *Divergent Paths: Economic Mobility in the New American Labor Market*. New York: Russell Sage Foundation.

Berry, Jeffrey. 1999. *The New Liberalism: The Rising Power of Citizen Groups*. Washington, DC: Brookings Institution Press.

Blank, Rebecca M. 2002. "Evaluating Welfare Reform in the United States." *Journal of Economic Literature* 40 (4): 1105–66.

Blau, Peter M. 1972. *The Dynamics of Bureaucracy: A Study of Interpersonal Relations in Two Government Agencies*. Rev. ed. Chicago: University of Chicago Press. First published 1955.

Blumenthal, Sidney. 1986. *The Rise of the Counter-establishment*. New York: Times Books.

Boeri, Tito. 2009. *Immigration to the Land of Redistribution*. IZA discussion paper Vol. 4273. Bonn: Forschungsinstitut zur Zukunft der Arbeit.

Boeri, Tito, Gordon H. Hanson, and Barry McCormick, eds. 2002. *Immigration Policy and the Welfare System: A Report for the Fondazione Rodolfo Debenedetti*. Oxford: Oxford University Press.

Bonoli, Giuliano, and David Natali. 2011. *The Politics of the New Welfare States in Western Europe*. Florence: European University Institute, Robert Schuman Centre for Advanced Studies.

Borjas, George J. 1999. "Immigration and Welfare-Magnets." *Journal of Labor Economics* 17 (4): 607–37.

Bredgaard, Thomas, and Flemming Larsen, eds. 2005. *Employment Policy from Different Angles*. Copenhagen: Djoef-Forlaget.

———. 2007. "Implementing Public Employment Policy: What Happens When Non-public Agencies Take Over?" *International Journal of Sociology and Social Policy* 27 (7/8): 287–301.

———. 2009. *Regionale og lokale beskæftigelsesråd—I spændingsfeltet mellem stat og kommune* [Regional and local employment councils in the cross field of state and municipality]. Aalborg: Aalborg Universitetsforlag.

———. 2010. "External and Internal Flexicurity: Comparing Denmark and Japan." *Comparative Labor Law and Policy Journal* 31 (4): 745–72.

Bredgaard, Thomas, Flemming Larsen, and Per Kongshoj Madsen. 2006. "Opportunities and Challenges for Flexicurity—the Danish Example." *Transfer: European Review of Labour and Research* 12 (1): 61–83.

Brehm, John, and Scott Gates. 1999. *Working, Shirking, and Sabotage: Bureaucratic Response to a Democratic Public*. Ann Arbor: University of Michigan Press.

Brodkin, Evelyn Z. 1986. *The False Promise of Administrative Reform: Implementing Quality Control in Welfare*. Philadelphia: Temple University Press.

———. 1987. "Policy Politics: If We Can't Govern, Can We Manage?" *Political Science Quarterly* 102 (4): 571–87.

———. 1990. "Implementation as Policy Politics." In *Implementation and the Policy Process: Opening Up the Black Box*, edited by Dennis Palumbo and Donald Calista. Westport, CT: Greenwood.

———. 1997. "Inside the Welfare Contract: Discretion and Accountability in State Welfare Administration." *Social Service Review* 71 (1): 1–33.

———. 2003a. "Requiem for Welfare." *Dissent* 50 (1): 29–37.

———. 2003b. "Street-Level Research: Policy at the Front Lines." In *Policy into Action: Implementation Research and Welfare Reform*, edited by Thomas Corbett and Mary Clane Lennon. Washington, DC: Urban Institute.

———. 2007. "Bureaucracy Redux: Management Reformism and the Welfare State." *Journal of Public Administration and Theory* 17 (1): 1–17.

———. 2009. "The Politics and Governance of Workfare in the US." In *The New Governance and Implementation of Labour-Market Policies*, edited by Larsen and Van Berkel, 139–63.

———. 2011a. "Policy Work: Street-Level Organizations under New Managerialism." *Journal of Public Administration Research and Theory* 21, supplement 2: i253–i277.

———. 2011b. "Putting Street-Level Organizations First: New Directions for Social Policy and Management Research." *Journal of Public Administration Research and Theory* 21, supplement 2: i199–i201.

———. 2012. "Reflections on Street-Level Bureaucracy: Past, Present, and Future." *Public Administration Review* 72 (6): 940–49.

Brodkin, Evelyn Z., Colleen Fuqua, and Elaine Waxman. 2005. *Accessing the Safety Net: Administrative Barriers to Public Benefits in Metropolitan Chicago*. Chicago: Public Benefits Hotline Research Project.

Brodkin, Evelyn Z., and Alexander Kaufman. 2000. "Policy Experiments and Poverty Politics." *Social Service Review* 74 (4): 507–32.

Brodkin, Evelyn Z., and Flemming Larsen. 2013. "Changing Boundaries: The Policies of Workfare in the US and Europe." *Poverty and Public Policy* 5 (1): 37–47.

Brodkin, Evelyn Z., and Malay Majmundar. 2010. "Administrative Exclusion: Organizations and the Hidden Costs of Welfare Claiming." *Journal of Public Administration Research and Theory* 20 (4): 827–48.

Brodoff, Lisa. 2008. "Lifting Burdens: Proof, Social Justice, and Public Assistance Administrative Hearings." *New York University Review of Law and Social Change* 32 (2): 131–89.

Brown, Wendy. 2003. "Neo-liberalism and the End of Liberal Democracy." *Theory and Event* 7 (1): 1–21.

Bundesagentur für Arbeit (2011) Arbeitslose nach Strukturmerkmalen. Bestand, Bewegungen und regionaler Vergleich. Deutschland. Juni 2011. Nürnberg: Bundesagentur für Arbeit.

Brunsson, Nils. 1989. *The Organization of Hypocrisy: Talk, Decisions and Actions in Organizations.* Chichester: John Wiley & Sons.

Brussig, Martin, Bruno Kaltenborn, and Nina Wielage. 2010. "Hartz IV-Empfängerinnen mit Migrationshintergrund: Definition und Struktur." In *Arbeitsmarktintegration und Integrationspolitik—zur notwendigen Verknüpfung zweier Politikfelder: Eine Untersuchung über SGB II-Leistungsbeziehende mit Migrationshintergrund,* edited by Matthias Knuth, 43–59. Baden-Baden: Nomos Verlagsgesellschaft.

Brussig, Martin, and Matthias Knuth. 2009. "Alternative Styles and Roles for Local Governments in Implementing Activation Policies in Germany." In *New Governance and Implementation,* Larsen and Van Berkel, 69–93.

———. 2010a. "Activation! Or De-activation? Intensity and Effects of Activating Strategies among Older Recipients of Minimum Income Benefits in Germany. Paper presented at the CARMA conference, Copenhagen.

———. 2010b. "Rise Up and Work! Workless People with Impaired Health under Germany's New Activation Regime." *Social Policy and Society* 9 (3): 311–23.

Bryson, Alex. 2003. "From Welfare to Workfare." In *Understanding Social Security,* Millar.

Burawoy, Michael. 1998. "The Extended Case Method." *Sociological Theory* 16 (1): 4–33.

Burt, Martha, and Demetra Nightingale. 2009. *Repairing the U.S. Social Safety Net.* Washington, DC: Urban Institute.

Cane, Peter. 2009. *Administrative Tribunals and Adjudication.* Oxford: Hart.

Cantor, David, Jane Waldfogel, Jeff Kerwin, Mareena McKinley Wright, Kerry Levin, John Rauch, Tracey Hagerty, and Martha Stapleton Kudela. 2001. *Balancing the Needs of Families and Employers: Family and Medical Leave Surveys, 2000 Update.* Rockville, MD: Westat.

Carcillo, Stéphane, and David Grubb. 2006. *From Inactivity to Work: The Role of Active Labour Market Policies.* OECD Social, Employment and Migration Working Papers, Organisation for Economic Co-operation and Development, Paris.

Carney, Terry. 2005. "Not the Old Way, Not the Third Way, But the OECD/US Way: Welfare Sanctions and Active Welfare in Australia." *Journal of Social Security Law* 12 (2): 57–80.

Carré, Françoise, and Chris Tilly. 2008. "America's Biggest Low-Wage Industry: Continuity and Change in Retail Jobs." Occasional Paper 22, Center for Social Policy Publications, University of Massachusetts, Boston. http://scholarworks.umb.edu/csp_pubs/22.

Carroll, Peter, and Peter Steane. 2002. "Australia, the New Public Management and the New Millennium." In *New Public Management: Current Trends and Future Prospects,* edited by Kate McLaughlin, Stephen P. Osborne, and Ewan Ferlie. London: Routledge.

Caudill, Harry. 1963. *Night Comes to the Cumberlands.* Boston: Little, Brown.

Citro, Constance F., and Robert T. Michael, eds. 1995. *Measuring Poverty: A New Approach*. Washington, DC: National Academies Press.

Clarke, John. 2004. *Changing Welfare, Changing States: New Directions in Social Policy*. London: Sage.

Clasen, Jochen, and Daniel Clegg. 2006. "Beyond Activation: Reforming European Unemployment Protection Systems in Post-industrial Labour Markets." *European Societies* 8 (4): 527–53.

Clausen, Helle Osmer, and Bo Smith. 2007. "Arbejdsmarkedsreformer—fra ide til implementering." In *Når politik bliver til virkelighed—Festskrift til Søren Winter*, edited by Vibeke Lehmann Nielsen and Niels Ploug. Copenhagen: Social forskningsinstituttet.

Cohen, Cathy J. 1999. *The Boundaries of Blackness: AIDS and the Breakdown of Black Politics*. Chicago: University of Chicago Press.

Considine, Mark. 2000. "Selling the Unemployed: The Performance of Firms and Non-profits in the New Australian 'Market' for Unemployment Assistance." *Social Policy and Administration* 34 (3): 274–95.

———. 2001. *Enterprising States: The Public Management of Welfare-to-Work*. Cambridge: Cambridge University Press.

———. 2003. "Governance and Competition: The Role of Non-profit Organizations in the Delivery of Public Services." *Australian Journal of Political Science* 38 (1): 63–77.

———. 2005. "The Reform That Never Ends: Quasi-Markets and Employment Services in Australia." In *Contractualism in Employment Services*, Sol and Westerveld.

Cook, Peter, and Harlan Beckley. 2001. "Discrediting Neo-liberalism: The Social Democratic Welfare State of the Netherlands." Working paper, Washington and Lee University, Lexington, VA.

Cornelißen, Walfraud, ed. 2005. *Gender-Datenreport*. Müchen: Bundesministerium für Familie, Senioren, Frauen und Jugend.

Corra, Alex, and Mirjam Plantinga. 2009. "New Modes of Governance in the Dutch Reintegration Market: Analyzing the Process of Contracting Out." In *Activation and Security*. Brno, Czech Republic.

Corrigan, Owen. 2010. "Migrants, Welfare Systems and Social Citizenship in Ireland and Britain: Users or Abusers?" *Journal of Social Policy* 39 (3): 415–37.

Cruikshank, Barbara. 1999. *The Will to Empower: Democratic Citizens and Other Subjects*. Ithaca, NY: Cornell University Press.

Daguerre, Anne, and David Etherington. 2009. *Active Labour Market Policies in International Context: What Works Best? Lessons for the UK*. London: Department for Work and Pensions.

Dahl, Robert A. 1956. *A Preface to Democratic Theory*. Chicago: University of Chicago Press.

Davidson, Peter. 2011. "Did 'Welfare to Work' Raise or Lower the Incomes of Sole Parents and People with Disabilities?" Paper presented at the Australian Social Policy Conference, University of New South Wales, Sydney.

Dean, Mitchell. 1999. *Governmentality: Power and Rule in Modern Society.* London: Sage.

Deeke, Axel. 2011. "Berufsbezogene Sprachförderung und berufliche Weiterbildung von Arbeitslosen mit Migrationshintergrund—eine Verbleibs- und Wirkungsanalyse." In *Migration als Chance: Ein Beitrag der beruflichen Bildung*, edited by Mona Granato. Bielefeld: Bertelsmann.

De Graaf, Willibrord, and Tomas Sirovátka. 2011. "Governance and Effects of Activation Policies." Paper presented at the ESPAnet Research Conference, Valencia, Spain.

De Koning, Jaap. 2009. "Reforms in Dutch Active Labour Policy during the Last 20 Years: An Evaluation." Working Paper 2009/2, SEOR, Rotterdam.

Denhardt, Robert B., and Janet Vinzant Denhardt. 2000. "The New Public Service: Serving Rather Than Steering." *Public Administration Review* 60 (6): 549–59.

Denzin, Norman K. 1989. *The Research Act: A Theoretical Introduction to Sociological Methods.* 3rd ed. Englewood Cliffs, NJ: Prentice Hall.

Department of Social Security. 1998. *New Ambitions for Our Country: A New Contract for Welfare.* London: Stationery Office.

DEWR (Department of Employment and Workplace Relations). 2006. *Disability Employment Network Uncapped Stream: Programme Procedures, 2006–2009.* Canberra: Australian Government.

Dias, Janice J., and Steven Maynard-Moody. 2007. "For Profit Welfare: Contracts, Conflicts, and the Performance Paradox." *Journal of Public Administration Research and Theory* 17 (2): 189–211.

Diller, Matthew. 2000. "The Revolution in Welfare Administration: Rules, Discretion, and Entrepreneurial Government." *New York University Law Review* 75 (5): 1121–220.

Divosa. 2005. *WWB monitor: Een jaar Wet Werk en Bijstand.* Utrecht: Divosa.

———. 2006. *WWB monitor, 2006: Meer perspectief voor mensen; Twee jaar Wet Werk en Bijstand.* Utrecht: Divosa.

———. 2007. *Divosa monitor, 2007: Verschil maken; Drie jaar Wet Werk en Bijstand.* Utrecht: Divosa.

———. 2008. *Divosa monitor, 2008: Worstelen met invloed; Vier jaar Wet Werk en Bijstand.* Utrecht: Divosa.

———. 2009. *Divosa monitor, 2009: Meer dan ooit; Sociale diensten en participatiebevordering.* Utrecht: Divosa.

Dolan, Julie, and David Rosenbloom. 2003. *Representative Bureaucracy: Classic Readings and Continuing Controversies.* Armonk, NY: M. E. Sharpe.

Dowse, Leanne. 2009. "'Some People Are Never Going to Be Able to Do That': Challenges for People with Intellectual Disability in the 21st Century." *Disability and Society* 24 (5): 571–84.

Drake, Sinclair, and Horace Cayton. 1993. *Black Metropolis: A Study of Negro Life in a Northern City.* Chicago: University of Chicago Press. First published 1945.

Dubois, Vincent. 2010. *The Bureaucrat and the Poor: Encounters in French Welfare Offices.* Burlington, VT: Ashgate.

DuBois, W. E. B. 1995. *The Philadelphia Negro: A Social Study*. Philadelphia: University of Pennsylvania Press. First published 1899.

Duncan, Greg, Aletha Huston, and Thomas Weisner. 2007. *Higher Ground: New Hope for the Working Poor and Their Children*. New York: Russell Sage Foundation.

Eardley, Tony. 2002. "Mutual Obligation and the Job Network: The Effect of Competition on the Role of Non-profit Employment Services." *Australian Journal of Social Issues* 37 (3): 301–14.

Edelman, Murray. 1964. *The Symbolic Uses of Politics*. Urbana: University of Illinois Press.

Edin, Kathryn, and Maria Kefales. 2005. *Promises I Can Keep: Why Poor Women Put Motherhood before Marriage*. Berkeley: University of California Press.

Edin, Kathryn, and Laura Lein. 1997. *Making Ends Meet: How Single Mothers Survive Welfare and Low-Wage Work*. New York: Sage.

Ellwood, David. 1988. *Poor Support: Poverty in the American Family*. New York: Basic Books.

Englmann, Bettina, and Martina Müller. 2007. *Brain Waste: Die Anerkennung von ausländischen Qualifikationen in Deutschland*. Augsburg: Global Competences. www.berufliche-anerkennung.de/brainwaste.pdf.

Esping-Andersen, Gøsta. 1990. *The Three Worlds of Welfare Capitalism*. Princeton, NJ: Princeton University Press.

———. 2002. *Why We Need a New Welfare State*. Oxford: Oxford University Press.

———. 2006. "Three Worlds of Welfare Capitalism." In *The Welfare State Reader*, edited by Christopher Pierson and Frances G. Castles, 160–75. Malden, MA: Polity.

Etzioni, Amitai, ed. 1969. *The Semi-professions and Their Organization*. New York: Free Press.

European Commission. 1993. *Growth, Competitiveness, and Employment: The Challenges and Ways Forward into the 21st Century*.

Feagin, Joe R., and Clairece B. Feagin. 1978. *Discrimination American style: Institutional Racism and Sexism*. Englewood Cliffs, NJ: Prentice Hall.

Federal Ministry of Labour and Social Affairs. 2006. *The Effectiveness of Modern Services on the Labour Market: Report of the Federal Ministry of Labour and Social Affairs on the Impact of the Implementation of the Proposals by the Commission for Modern Services on the Labour Market*. Berlin.

Felstiner, William, Richard Abel, and Austin Sarat. 1980. "The Emergence and Transformation of Disputes: Naming, Blaming, Claiming . . ." *Law and Society Review* 15 (3): 631–54.

Filion, Kai. 2009. *Minimum Wage Issue Guide*. Washington, DC: Economic Policy Institute. www.epi.org/publications/entry/issue_guide_on_minimum_wage/.

Ford Foundation. 1989. *The Common Good: Social Welfare and the American Future*. New York: Ford Foundation.

Forslung, Anders, Daniela Froberg, and Linus Lindqvist. 2004. "The Swedish Activity Guarantee." OECD Social, Employment and Migration Working Paper 16, Organisation for Economic Co-operation and Development, Paris.

Foster, Deborah, and Paul Hoggett. 1999. "Change in the Benefits Agency: Empowering the Exhausted Worker?" *Work, Employment and Society* 13 (1): 19–39.

Foucault, Michel. 1980. "Power and Strategies." In *Power/Knowledge—Selected Interviews and Other Writings, 1972–1977*, edited by Colin Gordon, 134–45. Brighton: Harvester.

———. 1997. *Discipline and Punish: The Birth of the Prison*. New York: Vintage. First published 1975.

Fraser, Nancy. 1989. *Unruly Practices: Power, Discourse, and Gender in Contemporary Social Theory*. Minneapolis: University of Minnesota Press.

———. 1997. *Justice Interruptus: Critical Reflections on the "Postsocialist" Condition*. New York: Routledge.

Frazier, E. Franklin. 1997. *The Black Bourgeoisie*. New York: Free Press. First published 1957.

Frederickson, H. George. 2005. "The State of Social Equity in American Public Administration." *National Civic Review* 94 (4): 31–38.

Frederiksen, Claus Hjort. 2003a. Speech delivered at annual meeting of the Danish Association of Social Workers, Nyborg, Denmark, September 29.

———. 2003b. Speech delivered at annual meeting of Municipal Social Services Directors, Aarhus, Denmark, October 27.

Freud, David. 2007. *Reducing Dependency, Increasing Opportunity: Options for the Future of Welfare to Work*. London: Stationery Office. www.dwp.gov.uk/docs/welfarereview.pdf.

Friedlander, Daniel, and Gary Burtless. 1995. *Five Years After: The Long-Term Effects of Welfare-to-Work Programs*. New York: Russell Sage Foundation.

Furniss, Norman, and Timothy Tilton. 1977. *The Case for the Welfare State: From Social Security to Social Equality*. Bloomington: Indiana University Press.

Gaines, Kevin. 1996. *Uplifting the Race: Black Leadership, Politics, and Culture in the Twentieth Century*. Chapel Hill: University of North Carolina Press.

Galanter, Marc. 1974. "Why the 'Haves' Come Out Ahead: Speculations on the Limits of Legal Change." *Law and Society Review* 9 (1): 95–160.

Galtier, Bénédicte. 1999. *Les temps partiels: Entre emplois choisis et emplois "faute de mieux."* Économie et Statistique 321–22. Paris: INSEE. www.insee.fr/en/ffc/docs_ffc/is44_321–322.pdf.

Giddens, Anthony. 1998. *The Third Way*. Cambridge: Polity.

Gilbert, Neil. 2002. *Transformation of the Welfare State: The Silent Surrender of Public Responsibility*. New York: Oxford University Press.

Gilens, Martin. 2005. "Inequality and Democratic Responsiveness." *Public Opinion Quarterly* 69 (5): 778–896.

Gilliom, John. 2001. *Overseers of the Poor: Resistance, Surveillance, and the Limits of Privacy.* Chicago: University of Chicago Press.

Ginwright, Shawn A. 2002. "Classed Out: The Challenges of Social Class in Black Community Change." *Social Problems* 49 (4): 544–62.

Gomolla, Mechthild, and Frank-Olaf Radtke. 2009. *Institutionelle Diskriminierung: Die Herstellung ethnischer Differenz in der Schule.* Wiesbaden: VS Verlag für Sozialwissenschaften.

Gooden, Susan Tinsley. 1998. "All Things Not Being Equal: Differences in Caseworker Support toward Black and White Welfare Clients." *Harvard Journal of African-American Public Policy* 4:23–33.

Goodin, Robert E., Bruce Heady, Ruud Muffels, and Henk-Jan Dirven. 1999. *The Real Worlds of Welfare Capitalism.* New York: Cambridge University Press.

Goodin, Robert E. 2001. "Work and Welfare: Towards a Post-productivist Welfare Regime." *British Journal of Political Science* 31 (1): 13–39.

Gottfried, Heidi, and Jacqueline O'Reilly. 2002. "Der Geschlechtervertrag in Deutschland und Japan: Die Schwäche eines starken Ernährermodells." In *Zukunft der Arbeit und Geschlecht: Diskurse, Entwicklungspfade und Reformoptionen im internationalen Vergleich,* edited by Karin Gottschall and Birgit Pfau-Effinger, 29–58. Opladen: Leske & Budrich.

Greenberg, David, and Andreas Cebulla. 2008. "The Cost-Effectiveness of Welfare-to-Work Programs: A Meta-anaylsis." *Public Budgeting and Finance* 10 (2): 112–45.

Greenberg, David, Andreas Cebulla, and Stacey Bouchet. 2005. "Report on a Meta-analysis of Welfare-to-Work Programs." Discussion Paper 1312–05, Institute for Research on Poverty, University of Wisconsin.

Gregg, Paul. 2008. *Realising Potential: A Vision for Personalised Conditionality and Support.* London: Stationery Office. www.dwp.gov.uk/docs/realisingpotential .pdf.

Griffin, Cary, and Beth Keeton. 2009. *Customized Employment: A Curriculum for Creating Community Careers.* Langley, BC: Langley Association for Community Living / Griffin-Hammis Associates.

Grogger, Jeffery, and Lynn A. Karoly. 2005. *Welfare Reform: Effects of a Decade of Change.* Cambridge, MA: Harvard University Press.

Grover, Chris. 2005. "Advertising Social Security Fraud." *Benefits* 13 (3): 199–205.

Gruber, Jon, and Emmanuel Saez. 2002. "The Elasticity of Taxable Income: Evidence and Implications." *Journal of Public Economics* 84 (1): 1–32.

Grundig, Beate, and Carsten Pohl. 2006. *Qualifikationsspezifische Arbeitslosigkeit: Gibt es Unterschiede zwischen Deutschen und Immigranten?* www.cesifo-group.de/link/ifodb_2006_4_33–36.pdf.

Gueron, Judith M. 1987. *Reforming Welfare with Work.* New York: Ford Foundation.

Hacker, Jacob. 2002. *The Divided Welfare State: The Battle over Public and Private Social Benefits in the United States.* New York: Cambridge University Press.

———. 2006. *The Great Risk Shift: The New Economic Insecurity and the Decline of the American Dream.* New York: Oxford University Press.

Haley-Lock, Anna, and Stephanie Ewert. 2011. "Waiting for the Minimum: U.S. State Wage Laws, Firm Strategy and Chain Restaurant Job Quality." *Journal of Industrial Relations* 53 (1): 31–48.

Halstead, Ted, and Michael Lind. 2001. *The Radical Center: The Future of American Politics.* New York: Doubleday.

Hancock, Linda. 2006. "Bringing in the Community Sector: Partnerships and Advocacy." In *Beyond the Policy Cycle: The Policy Process in Australia,* edited by Hal K. Colebatch. Crows Nest, NSW: Allen & Unwin.

Handler, Joel, and Amanda Sheely Babcock. 2006. "The Failure of Workfare: Another Reason for a Basic Income Guarantee." *Basic Income Studies* 1 (1).

Handler, Joel, and Yeheskel Hasenfeld. 1991. *The Moral Construction of Poverty: Welfare Reform in America.* Newbury Park, CA: Sage.

———. 2007. *Blame Welfare: Ignore Poverty and Inequality.* Cambridge: Cambridge University Press.

Handler, Joel F., and Ellen Jane Hollingsworth. 1970. "Reforming Welfare: The Constraints of the Bureaucracy and the Clients." *University of Pennsylvania Law Review* 118 (8): 1167–87.

———. 1971. *The "Deserving Poor": A Study of Welfare Administration.* Chicago: Markham.

Harrington, Michael. 1962. *The Other America.* New York: Macmillan.

Hartz Commission. 2002. *Modern Services on the Labour Market: Report of the Commission.* Berlin: Department for Economy and Employment.

Hasenfeld, Yeheskel. 1972. "People Processing Organizations: An Exchange Approach." *American Sociological Review* 37 (3): 256–63.

———. 1983. *Human Service Organizations.* Englewood Cliffs, NJ: Prentice Hall.

———. 2000. "Organizational Forms as Moral Practices: The Case of Welfare Departments." *Social Service Review* 74 (3): 329–51.

Haskins, Ron. 2002. "Ending Entitlements Works for the Poor." *Philanthropy* 16 (1): 15–19.

Hays, Sharon. 2003. *Flat Broke with Children: Women in the Age of Welfare Reform.* New York: Oxford University Press.

Heckman, James, Carolyn Heinrich, and James Smith. 1997. "Assessing the Performance of Performance Standards in Public Bureaucracies." *American Economic Review* 87 (2): 389–95.

Hefetz, Amir, and Mildred Warner. 2004. "Privatization and Its Reverse: Explaining the Dynamics of the Government Contracting Process." *Journal of Public Administration Research and Theory* 14 (2): 171–90.

Hendra, Richard, Keri-Nicole Dillman, Gayle Hamilton, Erika Lundquist, Karin Martinson, and Melissa Wavele. 2010. *How Effective Are Different Approaches Aiming to Increase Employment Retention and Advancement? Final Impacts for Twelve Models.* New York: MDRC.

REFERENCES

Henley, John. 2013. "Victory of the Unsung Hero in the Workfare Battle," *Guardian*, February 13, 2013.

Henly, Julia R., and Susan J. Lambert. 2005. "Nonstandard Work and Child Care Needs of Low-Income Parents." In *Work, Family, Health, and Well-being*, edited by Suzanne M. Bianchi, Lynne M. Casper, and Rosalind Berkowitz King. Mahwah, NJ: Lawrence Erlbaum.

Henson, Eric C., Jonathan B. Taylor, Catherine E. A. Curtis, Stephen Cornell, Kenneth W. Grant, Miriam R. Jorgensen, Joseph P. Kalt, Andrew J. Lee, and Harvard Project on American Indian Economic Development. 2008. *The State of the Native Nations: Conditions under U.S. Policies of Self-Determination.* New York: Oxford University Press.

Herd, Dean, and Ernest Lightman. 2005. "Rituals of Degradation: Administration as Policy in the Ontario Works Programme." *Social Policy and Administration* 39 (1): 65–79.

Hetzler, Antoinette. 2009. "Labour Market Activation Policies for the Long-Term Ill—A Sick Idea." *European Journal of Social Security* 11 (4): 369–401.

Hielscher, Volker, and Peter Ochs. 2009. *Arbeitslose als Kunden?* Vol. 32 of *Modernisierung des öffentlichen Sektors.* Berlin: Edition Sigma.

Hill, Carolyn J. 2006. "Casework Job Design and Client Outcomes in Welfare-to-Work Offices." *Journal of Public Administration Research and Theory* 16 (2): 263–88.

Hilton, Timothy, and Susan J. Lambert. 2012. "Employers' Use of Labor Market Intermediaries in Filling Low-Level Jobs: Sorting Disadvantaged Job Seekers and Employment Opportunities." Paper presented at the annual meeting of the Society for Social Work and Research

Hindera, John. 1993a. "Representation Bureaucracy: Further Evidence of Active Representation in the EEOC District Offices." *Journal of Public Administration Research and Theory* 3 (4): 415–29.

———. 1993b. "Representative Bureaucracy: Imprimis Evidence of Active Representation in the EEOC District Offices." *Social Science Quarterly* 74 (1): 95–108.

Hoekstra, E. Josette, Karin Sanders, Willem-Jan van den Heuvel, Dann Post, and Jaap W. Groothoff. 2004. "Supported Employment in the Netherlands for People with an Intellectual Disability, a Psychiatric Disability and a Chronic Disease: A Comparative Study." *Journal of Vocational Rehabilitation* 21 (1): 39–48.

Holzer, Harry. 1996. *What Employers Want: Job Prospects for Less-Educated Workers.* New York: Russell Sage Foundation.

Holzer, Harry, and Robert LaLonde. 2000. "Job Change and Job Stability among Less Skilled Young Workers." In *Finding Jobs: Work and Welfare Reform*, edited by David Card and Rebecca Blank, 125–59. New York: Russell Sage Foundation.

House of Commons Work and Pensions Committee. 2010. *Decision Making and Appeals in the Benefits System.*

Howard, Christopher. 2003. "Is the American Welfare State Unusually Small?" *PS: Political Science and Politics* 36 (3): 411–16.

Hupe, Peter, and Michael Hill. 2007. "Street-Level Bureaucracy and Public Accountability." *Public Administration* 85 (2): 279–99.

Jacobs, Lawrence. 2007. "The Implementation and Evolution of Medicare: The Distributional Effects of 'Positive' Policy Feedbacks." In *Remaking America: Democracy and Public Policy in the Age of Incrementalism*, edited by Joe Soss, Jacob Hacker, and Suzanne Metler, 77–98. New York: Russell Sage Foundation.

Jayasuri, Kanishka. 2001. "Autonomy, Liberalism and the New Contractualism." *Law in Context* 18 (2): 57–78.

Jessup, Bob. 1993. "Towards a Schumpeterian Workfare State? Preliminary Remarks on Post-Fordist Political Economy." *Studies in Political Economy* 40:7–40.

Jewell, Christopher. 2007. *Agents of the Welfare State: How Caseworkers Respond to Need in the United States, Germany, and Sweden.* New York: Palgrave MacMillan.

Jolly, Deb. 2003. "The Government of Disability: Economics and Power in Welfare and Work." *Disability and Society* 18 (4): 509–22.

Jones-Correa, Michael, and David Leal. 1996. "Becoming 'Hispanic': Secondary Panethnic Identification among Latin American–Origin Populations in the United States." *Hispanic Journal of Behavioral Sciences* 18 (2): 214–54.

Jordan, Laura. 2011. "Avoiding the 'Trap': Discursive Framing as a Means of Coping with Working Poverty." In *Retail Work*, edited by Irena Grugulis and Ödül Bozkurt, 149–71. Hampshire, UK: Palgrave.

Jørgensen, Henning. 2002. *Consensus, Cooperation and Conflict—the Policy Making Process in Denmark.* Cheltenham: Edward Elgar.

Jørgensen, Henning, Kelvin Baadsgaard, Iben Nørup, and Søren Peter Olesen. 2012. *Jobcentre og klemte kvalifikationer: Hvorfor og hvordan studere faglig praksis og kvalificering til arbejdet i beskæftigelsessystemet med kontanthjælpsmodtagere og sygemeldte.* Aalborg: Center for Arbejdsmarkedsforskning, Aalborg Universitet.

Jørgensen, Henning, Iben Nørup, and Kelvin Baadsgaard. 2010. "De-professionalization in Danish Labour Market Policy Implementation?" Paper presented at the IIRA European Regional Conference, Copenhagen.

Kalleberg, Arne L. 2009. "Precarious Work, Insecure Workers: Employment Relations in Transition." *American Sociological Review* 74:1–22. doi:10.1177/000312240907400101.

———. 2011. *Good Jobs, Bad Jobs: The Rise of Polarized and Precarious Employment Systems in the United States, 1970s to 2000s.* New York: Russell Sage Foundation.

Kaltenborn, Bruno, and Nina Wielage. 2010. "Konsequenzen der Leistungsreform für Hilfebedürftige mit Migrationshintergrund." In *Arbeitsmarktintegration und Integrationspolitik—zur notwendigen Verknüpfung zweier Politikfelder: Eine Untersuchung über SGB II-Leistungsbeziehende mit Migrationshintergrund*, edited by Matthias Knuth, 81–92. Baden-Baden: Nomos Verlagsgesellschaft.

Katz, Michael. 2001. *The Price of Citizenship.* New York: Henry Holt.

Katznelson, Ira. 1996. *Liberalism's Crooked Circle: Letters to Adam Michnik.* Princeton, NJ: Princeton University Press.

Kaufman, Herbert. 1960. *The Forest Ranger: A Study in Administrative Behavior.* Baltimore: Johns Hopkins Press.

Keane, Michael, and Robert Moffitt. 1998. "A Structural Model of Multiple Welfare Program Participation and Labor Supply." *International Economic Review* 39 (3): 553–89.

Kelman, Steven. 1988. "Why Public Ideas Matter." In R. Reich, ed., *The Power of Public Ideas*, 31–53. Cambridge, MA: Ballinger.

Kemp, Peter A., and Jacqueline Davidson. 2010. "Employability Trajectories among New Claimants of Incapacity Benefit." *Policy Studies* 31 (2): 203–21.

Ketscher, Kirsten. 2007. "Contrasting Legal Concepts of Active Citizenship: Europe and Nordic Countries." In *Citizenship in Nordic Welfare States—Dynamics of Choice, Duties and Participation in a Changing Europe*, edited by Bjørn Hvinden and Håkan Johannson. London: Routledge.

Kettl, Donald F. 1998. *Reinventing Government: A Fifth-Year Report Card.* Washington, DC: Brookings Institution Press.

———. 2005. *The Global Public Management Revolution: A Report on the Transformation of Governance.* Washington, DC: Brookings Institution Press.

Kildal, Nana. 2001. *Workfare Tendencies in Scandinavian Welfare Policies.* Geneva: International Labour Organization.

Kingsley, J. Donald. 1944. *Representative Bureaucracy: An Interpretation of the British Civil Service.* Yellow Springs, OH: Antioch.

Klitgaard, Michael Baggesen, and Asbjørn Sonne Nørgaard. 2010. "Afmagtens mekanismer: Den danske fagbevægelse og arbejdsmarkedspolitikken siden 1960'erne." *Politica* 42 (1): 5–26.

Knijn, Trudie, Claude Martin, and Jane Millar. 2007. "Activation as a Common Framework for Social Policies towards Lone Parents." *Social Policy and Administration* 41 (6): 638–52.

Knuth, Matthias. 2009. "Path Shifting and Path Dependence: Labour Market Policy Reforms under German Federalism." *International Journal of Public Administration* 32 (12): 1048–69.

Knuth, Matthias, and Flemming Larsen. 2009. "Municipalisation in the German and the Danish Public Employment Service." Paper presented at the 7th ESPAnet Conference, Urbino, Italy.

Kogan, Irena. 2012. "Potenziale nutzen! Determinanten und Konsequenzen der Anerkennung von Bildungsabschlüssen bei Zuwanderern aus der ehemaligen Sowjetunion in Deutschland." *Kölner Zeitschrift für Soziologie und Sozialpsychologie* 64 (1): 67–89.

Kok, Lucy, Inge Groot, and Derya Güler. 2007. *Kwantitatief effect WWB.* Amsterdam: SEO.

Konsortium Bildungsberichterstattung. 2006. *Bildung in Deutschland: Ein indikatorengestützter Bericht mit einer Analyse zu Bildung und Migration.* Bielefeld: Bertelsmann.

Kooiman, Jan, and Maarten Bavinck. 2005. "The Governance Perspective." In *Fish for Life: Interactive Governance for Fisheries*, edited by Jan Kooiman, Maarten Bavinck, Svein Jentoft, and Roger Pullin, 11–25. Amsterdam: Amsterdam University Press.

Korteweg, Anna. 2003. "Welfare Reform and the Subject of the Working Mother: 'Get a Job, a Better Job, Then a Career.'" *Theory and Society* 32 (4): 445–80.

———. 2006. "The Construction of Gendered Citizenship at the Welfare Office: An Ethnographic Comparison of Welfare-to-Work Workshops in the United States and the Netherlands." *Social Politics: International Studies in Gender, State and Society* 13 (3): 313–40.

Kritzer, Herbert M., and Susan Silbey. 2003. *In Litigation: Do the "Have's" Still Come Out Ahead?* Stanford, CA: Stanford University Press.

Kuttner, Robert. 1996. *Everything for Sale: The Virtues and Limits of Markets*. New York: Alfred Knopf.

Lambert, Susan J. 2008. "Passing the Buck: Labour Flexibility Practices That Transfer Risk onto Hourly Workers." *Human Relations* 61 (9): 1203–27.

Lambert, Susan J., Anna Haley-Lock, and Julia R. Henly. 2012. "Schedule Flexibility in Hourly Jobs: Unanticipated Consequences and Promising Directions." *Community, Work and Family* 15 (3): 293–315.

Lambert, Susan J., and Julia R. Henly. 2010. *Retail Managers' Strategies for Balancing Business Requirements with Employee Needs: Manager Survey Results*. Chicago: University of Chicago Work Scheduling Study.

———. 2012. "Frontline Managers Matter: Labour Flexibility Practices and Sustained Employment in Hourly Retail Jobs in the U.S." In *Are Bad Jobs Inevitable? Trends, Determinants and Responses to Job Quality in the Twenty-First Century*, edited by Chris Warhurst, Francoise Carré, Patricia Findlay, and Chris Tilly. London: Palgrave Macmillan.

Lambert, Susan J., Julia R. Henly, and Eric Hedberg. 2011. "Precarious Work Schedules in Hourly Jobs: Implications for Employment Stability and Work-Life Interferences." Paper presented at the Stress & Health Conference of the American Psychological Association, Orlando, FL.

Lambert, Susan J., and Elaine Waxman. 2005. "Organizational Stratification: Distributing Opportunities for Work-Life Balance." In *Work and Life Integration: Organizational, Cultural, and Individual Perspective*, edited by Ellen Ernst Kossek and Susan J. Lambert, 99–122. Mahwah, NJ: Lawrence Erlbaum.

Landry, Bart. 1988. *The New Black Middle Class*. Berkeley: University of California Press.

Lane, Julia. 2000. "The Role of Job Turnover in the Low-Wage Labor Market." In *The Low-Wage Labor Market: Challenges and Opportunities for Economic Self-Sufficiency*, edited by Kelleen Kaye and Demetra Smith Nightingale, 185–98. Washington, DC: US Department of Health and Human Services.

Lane, Julia, and David Stevens. 1997. "Welfare-to-Work Policy: Employer Hiring and Retention of Former Welfare Recipients." Working Paper 3, Northwestern / University of Chicago Joint Center for Poverty Research, Chicago.

Larsen, Flemming. 2002. "Labor Market Policies." In *Consensus, Cooperation and Conflict—The Policy Making Process in Denmark*, edited by Henning Jørgensen. Cheltenham: Edward Elgar.

———. 2004. "The Importance of Institutional Regimes for Active Labor Market Policies—the Case of Denmark." *European Journal of Social Security* 6 (2): 137–55.

———. 2009. *Kommunal beskæftigelsespolitik—Jobcentrenes implementering af beskæftigelsesindsatsen i krydsfeltet mellem statslig styring og kommunal autonomi* [Municipal employment policies—the job centers' implementation of employment services at the intersection of state steering and municipal autonomy]. Frederiksberg: Frydenlund Academic.

Larsen, Flemming, Nicolai Abildgaard, Thomas Bredgaard, and Lene Dalsgaard. 2001. *Kommunal aktivering—mellem disciplinering og integration*. Aalborg: Aalborg Universitetsforlag.

Larsen, Flemming, and Rik Van Berkel. 2009a. "Introduction." In *New Governance and Implementation*, edited by Flemming Larsen and Rik Van Berkel.

———, eds. 2009b. *The New Governance and Implementation of Labour-Market Policies*. Copenhagen: DJØF.

Lasswell, Harold D. 1936. *Politics: Who Gets What, When, How*. New York: McGraw-Hill.

Lawson, Leslie, and Christopher King. 1997. *The Reality of Welfare-to-Work: Employment Opportunities for Women Affected by Welfare Time Limits in Texas*. Austin: Center for the Study of Human Resources, University of Texas at Austin.

Lawton, Alan, David McKevitt, and Michelle Millar. 2000. "Coping with Ambiguity: Reconciling External Legitimacy and Organizational Implementation in Performance Measurement." *Public Money and Management* 20 (3): 13–19.

Lens, Vicki. 2006. "Examining the Administration of Work Sanctions on the Front Lines of the Welfare System." *Social Science Quarterly* 87 (3): 573–90.

———. 2008. "Welfare and Work Sanctions: Examining Discretion on the Front Lines." *Social Service Review* 82 (2): 197–222.

Leschke, Janine. 2011. "Transition from Unemployment to Work and the Role of Active Labour Market Policies during the Lisbon Strategy Period and the Economic Crisis." *German Policy Studies* 7 (1): 135–70.

Levine, Judith. 2013. *Ain't No Trust: How Bosses, Boyfriends, and Bureaucrats Fail Low-Income Mothers and Why It Matters*. Berkeley: University of California Press.

Lewis, Gail. 2000. *"Race," Gender, Social Welfare: Encounters in a Postcolonial Society*. Cambridge: Polity.

Lieberman, Robert. 2001. *Shifting the Color Line: Race and the American Welfare State*. Cambridge, MA: Harvard University Press.

Light, Paul. 2002. *Government's Greatest Achievements: From Civil Rights to Homeland Security*. Washington, DC: Brookings Institution Press.

Lin, Ann Chih. 2002. *Reform in the Making: The Implementation of Social Policy in Prison*. Princeton, NJ: Princeton University Press.

Lindblom, Charles E. 1979. "Still Muddling, Not Yet Through." *Public Administration Review* 39 (6): 517–26.

Lipsky, Michael. 1980a. "Standing the Study of Public Policy Implementation on Its Head." In *American Politics and Public Policy*, edited by Walter Dean Burnham and Martha W. Weinberg. Boston: MIT Press.

———. 1980b. *Street-Level Bureaucracy: Dilemmas of the Individual in Public Services*. New York: Russell Sage Foundation.

———. 2008. "Revenues and Access to Public Benefits." In *The State of Access*, edited by Jorrit de Jong and Gowher Rizvi, 137–47. Washington, DC: Brookings Institution Press.

Lipsky, Michael, Dianne Stewart, Patrick Bresette, Marcia Kinsey, Clarissa Martinez DeCastro, and Mark Schmitt. 2005. *Defending the Public Sector: An Assessment, Survey and Recommendations*. New York: Demos.

Lister, Ruth. 2001. "'Work for Those Who Can, Security for Those Who Cannot': A Third Way in Social Security Reform or Fractured Social Citizenship?" In *Risk and Citizenship: Key Issues in Welfare*, edited by Rosalind Edwards and Judith Glover. London: Routledge.

Lødemel, Ivar, and Heather Trickey, eds. 2001. *An Offer You Can't Refuse: Workfare in International Perspective*. Bristol: Policy Press.

Loeb, Susanna, and Mary Corcoran. 2001. "Welfare, Work Experience, and Economic Self-Sufficiency." *Journal of Policy Analysis and Management* 20 (1): 1–20.

Looney, Adam, and Day Manoli. 2012. *Are There Returns to Experience at Low-Skill Jobs? Evidence from Single Mothers in the United States over the 1990s*. Washington, DC: Brookings Institution Press.

Lower-Basch, Elizabeth. "Cash Assistance Since Welfare Reform." TANF Policy Brief, CLASP, Washington, DC. www.clasp.org/admin/site/publications/files/CashAssistance.pdf.

Lowi, Theodore J. 1979. *The End of Liberalism: The Second Republic of the United States*. 2nd ed. New York: W. W. Norton.

Loyens, Kim, and Jeroen Maesschalck. 2010. "Toward a Theoretical Framework for Ethical Decision Making of Street-level Bureaucracy: Existing Models Reconsidered." *Administration and Society* 42 (1): 66–101.

Lukes, Steven. 1974. *Power: A Radical View*. London: Macmillan.

Lurie, Irene. 2006. *At the Front Lines of the Welfare System: A Perspective on the Decline in Welfare Caseloads*. Albany, NY: Rockefeller Institute Press.

Macali, Lucy. 2006. "Contemporary Disability Employment Policy in Australia: How Can It Best Support Transitions from Welfare to Work?" *Australian Bulletin of Labour* 32 (3): 227–39.

Madsen, Per Kongshøj. 1999. *Denmark: Flexibility, Security and Labour Market Success.* Geneva: International Labour Office.

———. 2008a. "The Danish Road to 'Flexicurity': Where Are We Compared to Others? And How Did We Get There?" In *Flexibility and Employment Security in Europe: Labor Markets in Transition*, edited by Ruud Muffels, 341–62. Cheltenham: Edward Elgar.

———. 2008b. "Flexicurity in Denmark: A Model for Labor Market Reforms in the EU?" In *Growth versus Security: Old and New EU Members Quest for a New Economic and Social Model*, edited by Wojciech Bienkowski, Josef C. Brada, and Mariusz-Jan Radlo, 33–53. Basingstoke: Palgrave Macmillan.

Maloney, Carolyn B., and Charles E. Schumer. 2010. *Expanding Access to Paid Sick Leave: The Impact of the Healthy Families Act on America's Workers.* Washington, DC: US Congress Joint Economic Committee.

Marshall, Will, and Martin Schram, eds. 1993. *Mandate for Change.* New York: Berkley Books.

Marston, Gregory, and Catherine McDonald. 2006. "The Political Tensions and Street-Level Dimensions of Employment Services in Australia." In *Road to Where? The Politics and Practice of Welfare to Work; Refereed Proceedings of the 2006 National Conference*, edited by Gregory Marston, Paul Henman, and Catherine McDonald. Brisbane: Social Policy Unit, School of Social Work and Applied Human Sciences, University of Queensland. www.uq.edu.au/swahs/welfareto work/Final/paperMarstonandMcDonald.pdf.

Mashaw, Jerry. 1974. "The Management Side of Due Process: Some Theoretical and Litigation Notes on the Assurance of Accuracy, Fairness and Timeliness in the Adjudication of Social Welfare Claims." *Cornell Law Review*, no. 59 (1973–74): 772–824.

Mashaw, Jerry L. 1983. *Bureaucratic Justice: Managing Social Security.* New Haven, CT: Yale University Press.

Mason, Geoff, and Wiemer Salverda. 2009. "Low Pay, Working Conditions, and Living Standards." In *Low Wage Work in the Wealthy World*, edited by Jerome Gautie and John Schmitt, 35–90. New York: Russell Sage Foundation.

Masuoka, Natalie. 2006. "Together They Become One: Examining the Predictors of Panethnic Group Consciousness among Asian Americans and Latinos." *Social Science Quarterly* 87 (5): 993–1011.

Matland, Richard. 1995. "Synthesizing the Implementation Literature: The Ambiguity-Conflict Model of Policy Implementation." *Journal of Public Administration Research and Theory* 5 (2): 145–74.

Mau, Steffen, and Christoph Burkhardt. 2009. "Migration and Welfare State Solidarity in Western Europe." *Journal of European Social Policy* 19 (3): 213–29.

Maynard-Moody, Steven, and Michael Musheno. 2000. "State Agent or Citizen Agent: Two Narratives of Discretion." *Journal of Public Administration and Theory* 10 (2): 329–58.

———. 2003. *Cops, Teachers, Counselors: Stories from the Front Lines of Public Service.* Ann Arbor: University of Michigan Press.

McBeath, Grahame, and Stephen Webb. 2002. "Virtue Ethics and Social Work: Being Lucky, Realistic, and Not Doing One's Duty." *British Journal of Social Work* 32 (8) 1015–36.

McCleary, Richard. 1978. "On Becoming a Client." *Journal of Social Issues* 34 (4): 57–75.

McGuire, Linda. 2004. "Counting Quality or Qualities That Count? An Inquiry into Performance Reporting for Public Services in Australia." Monash University.

Mead, Lawrence M. 2001. *Beyond Entitlement: The Social Obligations of Citizenship.* New York: Free Press.

———. 2004. *Government Matters: Welfare Reform in Wisconsin.* Princeton, NJ: Princeton University Press.

Meekosha, Helen, and Leanne Dowse. 2007. "Integrating Critical Disability Studies into Social Work Education and Practice: An Australian Perspective." *Practice* 19 (3): 169–83.

Meidner, Rudolf. 1997. "The Swedish Model in an Era of Mass Unemployment." *Economic and Industrial Democracy* 18 (1): 87–97.

Meier, Kenneth J. 1993. "Latinos and Representative Bureaucracy: Testing the Thompson and Henderson Hypotheses." *Journal of Public Administration Research and Theory* 3 (4): 393–414.

Meier, Kenneth J., and Daniel P. Hawes. 2009. "Ethnic Conflict in France: A Case for Representative Bureaucracy?" *American Review of Public Administration* 39 (3): 269–85.

Meier, Kenneth J., and Tabitha Morton. 2010. *Representative Bureaucracy in a Cross-national Context: Politics, Identity, Structure and Discretion.* Paper presented at the Towards a Representative Bureaucracy? Multicultural Europe and Diversity in the Public Sector Workforce, Zeppelin University, Friedrichshafen, Lake Constnce, Germany.

Meier, Kenneth J., and Lawrence J. O'Toole. 2006. "Political Control versus Bureaucratic Values: Reframing the Debate." *Public Administration Review* 66 (2): 177–92.

Meier, Kenneth J., and Joseph Stewart Jr. 1992. "Active Representation in Educational Bureaucracies: Policy Impacts." *American Review of Public Administration* 22:157–72.

Meyer, Bruce D. 2002. "Labor Supply at the Extensive and Intensive Margins: The EITC, Welfare, and Hours Worked." *American Economic Review* 92 (2): 373–79.

Meyer, John W., and Brian Rowan. 1977. "Institutional Organizations: Formal Structure as Myth and Ceremony." *American Journal of Sociology* 83 (2): 340–63.

Meyers, Marcia K., Bonnie Glaser, and Karin MacDonald. 1998. "On the Front Lines of Welfare Delivery: Are Workers Implementing Policy Reforms?" *Journal of Policy Analysis and Management* 17 (1): 1–22.

Meyers, Marcia, Shannon Harper, Marieka Klawitter, and Taryn Lindhorst. 2006. *Review of Research on TANF Sanctions: Report to Washington State WorkFirst Sub-Cabinet.* Seattle: University of Washington.

Millar, Jane. 2003a. "From Wage Replacement to Wage Supplement: Benefits and Tax Credits." In *Understanding Social Security*, edited by Jane Millar.

————, ed. 2003b. *Understanding Social Security.* Bristol: Policy Press.

Miller, Gale. 1983. "Holding Clients Accountable: The Micro-politics of Trouble in a Work Incentive Program." *Social Problems* 31 (2): 139–51.

Mills, C. Wright. 1956. *The Power Elite.* New York: Oxford University Press.

Mintzberg. Henry. 1983. *Structure in Fives: Designing Effective Organizations.* Englewood Cliffs, NJ: Prentice Hall.

Morgen, Sandra. 2001. "The Agency of Welfare Workers: Negotiating Devolution, Privatization, and the Meaning of Self-Sufficiency." *American Anthropologist* 103 (3): 747–61.

Moynihan, Donald P. 2008. *The Dynamics of Performance Management: Constructing Information and Reform.* Washington, DC: Georgetown University Press.

Moynihan, Donald P., and Pamela Herd. 2010. "Red Tape and Democracy: How Rules Affect Citizenship Rights." *American Review of Public Administration* 40 (6): 654–70.

Nadesen, Premilla. 2005. *Welfare Warriors: The Welfare Rights Movement in the United States.* New York: Routledge.

Naff, Katherine C. 2001. *To Look Like America: Dismantling Barriers for Women and Minorities in Government.* Boulder, CO: Westview.

National Audit Office. 2006. *Jobcentre Plus: Delivering Effective Services through Personal Advisers.* London: Stationery Office.

Nelson, Barbara. 1984. *Making an Issue of Child Abuse: Political Agenda Setting for Social Problems.* Chicago: University of Chicago Press.

Neubeck, Kenneth J., and Noel A. Cazenave. 2001. *Welfare Racism: Playing the Race Card against America's Poor.* New York: Routledge.

O'Connor, Alice. 2001. *Poverty Knowledge: Social Science, Social Policy, and the Poor in Twentieth-Century U.S. History.* Princeton, NJ: Princeton University Press.

OECD (Organisation for Economic Co-operation and Development). 1994. *The OECD Jobs Study: Facts, Analysis, Strategies.* Paris: OECD.

Oliver, Melvin, and Thomas Shapiro. 1997. *White Wealth/Black Wealth.* New York: Routledge.

Oliver, Michael. 1990. *The Politics of Disablement.* Basingstoke: Macmillan.

Oliver, Michael, and Colin Barnes. 1998. *Disabled People and Social Policy: From Exclusion to Inclusion.* London: Longman.

Oorschot, Wim Van. 2006. "The Dutch Welfare State: Recent Trends and Challenges in Historical Perspective." *European Journal of Social Security* 8 (1): 58–76.

Orleck, Annelise. 2005. *Storming Caesars Palace: How Black Mothers Fought Their Own War on Poverty.* Boston: Beacon Press.

Osterman, Paul, and Beth Shulman. 2011. *Good Jobs America: Making Work Better for Everyone.* New York: Russell Sage Foundation.

Page, Benjamin I., and James R. Simmons. 2000. *What Government Can Do: Dealing with Poverty and Inequality.* Chicago: University of Chicago Press.

Park, Alison, John Curtice, Elizabeth Clery, and Caroline Bryson, eds. 2011. *British Social Attitudes: The 27th Report; Exploring Labour's Legacy.* London: Sage.

Pattillo, Mary. 2007. *Black on the Block: The Politics of Race and Class in the City.* Chicago: University of Chicago Press.

Pavetti, LaDonna, Michelle Derr, Gretchen Kirby, Robert Wood, and Melissa Clark. 2004. *The Use of TANF Work-Oriented Sanctions in Illinois, New Jersey and South Carolina.* Washington, DC: Mathematica Policy Research.

Pavetti, LaDonna, Danilo Trisi, and Liz Schott. 2011. *TANF Responded Unevenly to Increase in Need during Downturn.* Washington, DC: Center on Budget and Policy Priorities.

Peck, Jamie. 2001. *Workfare States.* New York: Guilford.

Peters, Mark, and Lucy Joyce. 2006. *A Review of the JSA Sanctions Regime: Summary Research Findings.* Research Report 31. London: Department for Work and Pensions.

Pfeffer, Jeffrey. 1998. "Six Dangerous Myths about Pay." *Harvard Business Review* 76 (3): 109–19.

Pierson, Paul. 1993. "When Effect Becomes Cause: Policy Feedback and Political Change." *World Politics* 45 (4): 595–628.

———. 1994. *Dismantling the Welfare State: Reagan, Thatcher, and the Politics of Retrenchment.* New York: Cambridge University Press.

———. 2005. "The Study of Policy Development." *Journal of Policy History* 17 (1): 34–51.

———. 2007. "The Rise and Reconfiguration of Activist Government." In *The Transformation of American Politics: Activist Government and the Rise of Conservatism,* edited by Paul Pierson and Theda Skocpol, 19–38. Princeton, NJ: Princeton University Press.

Piven, Frances Fox. 2008. "Welfare Reform and the Economic and Cultural Reconstruction of Low Wage Labor Markets." *City & Society* 10 (1): 21–36.

Piven, Frances Fox, and Richard Cloward. 1971. *Regulating the Poor: The Functions of Public Welfare.* New York: Random House.

Plantinga, Mirjam, Ko de Ridder, and Alex Cora. 2011. "Choosing Whether to Buy or Make: The Contracting Out of Employment Reintegration Services by Dutch Municipalities." *Social Policy and Administration* 45 (3): 245–63.

Pollitt, Christopher, and Geert Bouckaert. 2000. *Public Management Reform: A Comparative Analysis.* Oxford: Oxford University Press.

Potts, Blyden. 2005. "Disability and Employment: Considering the Importance of Social Capital." *Journal of Rehabilitation* 71 (3): 20–25.

Presser, Harriett B., and Amy G. Cox. 1997. "The Work Schedules of Low-Educated American Women and Welfare Reform." *Monthly Labor Review* 120 (4): 25–34.

Pressman, Jeffrey, and Aaron Wildavsky. 1973. *Implementation*. Berkeley: University of California Press.

Price, David. 1978. "Policy Making in Congressional Committees: The Impact of 'Environmental' Factors." *American Political Science Review* 72 (2): 548–74.

———. 2003. "Outcome-Based Tyranny: Teaching Compliance While Testing Like a State." *Anthropological Quarterly* 76 (4): 715–30.

Radin, Beryl A. 2006. *Challenging the Performance Movement: Accountability, Complexity, and Democratic Values*. Washington, DC: Georgetown University Press.

Ramia, Gaby, and Terry Carney. 2003. "New Public Management, the Job Network and Non-Profit Strategy."*Australian Journal of Labour Economics*, 6 (2): 253–75.

Raskin, Carl. 1994. "Employment Equity for the Disabled in Canada." *International Labour Review* 133 (1): 75–88.

Razin, Assaf, and Efraim Sadka. 2004. *Welfare Migration: Is the Net Fiscal Burden a Good Measure of Its Economic Impact on the Welfare of the Native-Born Population?* Vol. 1273. Munich: Center for Economic Studies.

Reed, Adolph. 1999. *Stirrings in the Jug: Black Politics in the Post-segregation Era*. Minneapolis: University of Minnesota Press.

Reich, Robert. 1987. *Tales of a New America: The Anxious Liberal's Guide to the Future*. New York: Times Books.

Riccio, James, Daniel Friedlander, and Stephen Freedman. 1994. *GAIN: Benefits, Costs, and Three-Year Impacts of a Welfare-to-Work Program*. New York: MDRC.

Riccucci, Norma M. 2005. *How Management Matters: Street-Level Bureaucrats and Welfare Reform*. Washington, DC: Georgetown University Press.

Riccucci, Norma M., and Marcia K. Meyers. 2004. "Linking Passive and Active Representation: The Case of Frontline Workers in Welfare Agencies." *Journal of Public Administration Research and Theory* 14 (4): 585–97.

Riccucci, Norma M., Marcia Meyers, Irene Lurie, and Jun Seop Han. 2004. "The Implementation of Welfare Reform Policy: The Role of Public Managers in Front-line Practices." *Public Administration Review* 64 (4): 438–48.

Rich, Andrew. 2005. "War of Ideas: Why Mainstream and Liberal Foundations and the Think Tanks They Support Are Losing in the War of Ideas in American Politics." *Stanford Social Innovation Review* 3:18–25.

Ridzi, Frank. 2009. *Selling Welfare Reform: Work-First and the New Common Sense of Employment*. New York: New York University Press.

Romich, Jennifer. 2006. "Difficult Calculations: Low-Income Workers and Marginal Tax Rates." *Social Service Review* 80 (1): 27–66.

Rosenbloom, David H., and Howard McCurdy, eds. 2006. *Revisiting Waldo's Administrative State: Constancy and Change in Public Administration*. Washington, DC: Georgetown University Press.

Rothstein, Bo. 1996. *The Social Democratic State: The Swedish Model and the Bureaucratic Problems of Social Reforms*. Pittsburgh: University of Pittsburgh Press.

———. 1998. *Just Institutions Matter: The Moral and Political Logic of the Universal Welfare State*. Cambridge: Cambridge University Press.

Roulstone, Alan, and Jon Warren. 2006. "Applying a Barriers Approach to Monitoring Disabled People's Employment: Implications for the Disability Discrimination Act." *Disability and Society* 21 (2): 115–31.

RWI (Rheinisch-Westfälisches Institut für Wirtschaftsforschung). 2009. *Diagnose bij reïntegratie: Analyse en aanbevelingen*. The Hague: RWI.

Sainsbury, Roy. 2003. "Understanding Social Security Fraud." In *Understanding Social Security*, edited by Jane Millar.

———. 2008. "Administrative Justice, Discretion and the 'Welfare to Work' Project." *Journal of Social Welfare and Family Law* 30 (4): 323–38.

———. 2009. "Sickness, Incapacity and Disability." In *Understanding Social Security*, 2nd ed., edited by Jane Millar. Bristol: Policy Press.

Samuelson, Robert. "Europe's Predicament Is Similar to Ours." Real Clear Markets. www.realclearmarkets.com/articles/2011/12/05/europes_predicament_sililar_to_ours_99403.html (Accessed December 12, 2011).

Sanger, M. Bryna. 2003. *The Welfare Marketplace: Privatization and Welfare Reform*. Washington, DC: Brookings Institution Press.

Schattschneider, Elmer E. 1960. *The SemiSovereign People: A Realist's View of Democracy in America*. New York: Holt, Rinehart & Winston.

Schneider, Jan, Michael Fischer, and Vesela Kovacheva. 2008. *Migrants in the Job Centre: Qualitative Findings on Migrants' Experiences with Public Employment Support Services in Germany*. Hamburg: Hamburg Institute of International Economics.

Schott, Liz, and LaDonna Pavetti. 2010. *Federal TANF Funding Shrinking while Need Remains High*. Washington, DC: Center on Budget and Policy Priorities.

Schram, Sanford F., Joe Soss, Richard C. Fording, and Linda Houser. 2009. "Deciding to Discipline: Race, Choice, and Punishment at the Frontlines of Welfare Reform." *American Sociological Review* 74 (3): 398–422.

Schram, Sanford F., Joe Soss, Linda Houser, and Richard C. Fording. 2010. "The Third Level of US Welfare Reform: Governmentality under Neoliberal Paternalism." *Citizenship Studies* 14:6.

Schram, Sanford, Joe Soss, and Richard Fording, eds. 2003. *Race and the Politics of Welfare Reform*. Ann Arbor: University of Michigan Press.

Schwarzkopf, Manuela. 2009. *Doppelt gefordert, wenig gefördert: Alleinerziehende Frauen in der Grundsicherung für Arbeitsuchende*. Berlin: Edition Sigma.

Scott, Ellen, Kathryn Edin, Andrew London, and Rebecca Joyce Kissane. 2004. "Unstable Work, Unstable Income: Implications for Family Well-being in the Era of Time-Limited Welfare." *Journal of Poverty* 8 (1): 61–88.

Scott, James. 1998. *Seeing Like a State: How Certain Schemes to Improve the Human Condition Have Failed*. New Haven, CT: Yale University Press.

Scrivener, Susan, and Johanna Walter. 2001. *Evaluating Two Approaches to Case Management: Implementation, Participation Patterns, Costs and Three-Year Impact of the Columbus Welfare-to-Work Program*. New York: MDRC.

Segura, Gary M., and Helene Alves Rodrigues. 2006. "Comparative Ethnic Politics in the United States: Beyond Black." *Annual Review of Political Science* 9:375–95.

Sherradan, Michael. 1991. *Assets and the Poor*. Armonk, NY: M. E. Sharpe.

Silbey, Susan. 2005. "After Legal Consciousness." *Annual Review of Law and Social Science* 1:323–68.

Simon, William. 1983. "Legality, Bureaucracy and Class in the Welfare System." *Yale Law Journal* 92 (7): 1198–269.

Sinfield, Adrian. 2001. "Benefits and Research in the Labour Market." *European Journal of Social Security* 3 (3): 209–35.

Skocpol, Theda. 1985. "Bringing the State Back In: Strategies of Analysis in Current Research." In *Bringing the State Back In*, edited by Peter B. Evans, Dietrich Rueschmeyer, and Theda Skocpol, 3–43. Cambridge: Cambridge University Press.

———. 1992. *Protecting Soldiers and Mothers: The Political Origins of Social Policy in the United States*. Cambridge, MA: Harvard University Press.

Skrentny, John D. 2002. *The Minority Rights Revolution*. Cambridge, MA: Harvard University Press.

Smith, Brenda D., and Stella E. F. Donovan. 2003. "Child Welfare Practice in Organizational and Institutional Context." *Social Service Review* 77 (4): 541–63.

Smith, Mark A. 2007. *The Right Talk: How Conservatives Transformed the Great Society into the Economic Society*. Princeton, NJ: Princeton University Press.

Sol, Els, Julie Castonguay, Hanneke van Lindert, and Yvonne van Amstel. 2007. *Work First Werkt: Op Weg Naar Evidencebased Work First*. Utrecht: Divosa.

Sol, Els, and Mies Westerveld, eds. 2005. *Contractualism in Employment Services: A New Form of Welfare State Governance*. The Hague: Kluwer Law International.

Soss, Joe. 1999. "Welfare Application Encounters: Subordination, Satisfaction and the Puzzle of Client Expectations." *Administration and Society* 31 (1): 50–94.

———. 2000. *Unwanted Claims: The Politics of Participation in the U.S. Welfare System*. Ann Arbor: University of Michigan Press.

———. 2002. *Unwanted Claims: The Politics of Participation in the U.S. Welfare System*. Paperback ed. Ann Arbor: University of Michigan Press.

Soss, Joe, Richard C. Fording, and Sanford F. Schram. 2011. *Disciplining the Poor: Neoliberal Paternalism and the Persistent Power of Race*. Chicago: University of Chicago Press.

Stafford, Bruce. 2003. "Service Delivery and the User." In *Understanding Social Security*, edited by Jane Millar.

Stafford, Bruce, Anne Corden, Angela Meah, Roy Sainsbury, and Patricia Thornton. 2007. *New Deal for Disabled People: Third Synthesis Report—Key Findings from the Evaluation*. Vol. 430. London: Department for Work and Pensions.

Stafford, Bruce, and Karen Kellard. 2007. "Reforming the Public Sector: Personalised Activation Services in the UK." In *Making It Personal: Individualising Activation Services in the EU*, edited by Rik Van Berkel and Ben Valkenberg. Bristol: Policy Press.

Statistisches Bundesamt. 2010. *Bevölkerung und Erwerbstätigkeit: Bevölkerung mit Migrationshintergrund—Ergebnisse des Mikrozensus 2009.* Wiesbaden.

Steurle, Eugene. 1996. "Financing the American State at the Turn of the Century." In *Funding the Modern American State, 1941–1995*, edited by W. Elliott Brownlee, 409–44. Washington, DC: Woodrow Wilson Center Press/Cambridge University Press.

Stichnoth, Holger. 2010. "Does Immigration Weaken Natives' Support for the Welfare State? Evidence from Germany." SOEP Papers on Multidisciplinary Panel Data Research, German Institute for Economic Research, Berlin.

Stigaard, Mads V., Mette Fjord Sørensen, Søren C. Winter, and Nina Friisberg. 2006. *Kommunernes Beskæftigelsesindsats.* Copenhagen: Socialforskningsinsti tuttet.

Stokes, Atiya Kai. 2003. "Latino Group Consciousness and Political Participation." *American Politics Research* 31 (4): 361–78.

Stone, Bob. 2003. *Confessions of a Civil Servant: Lessons in Changing America's Government and Military.* Lanham, MD: Rowman & Littlefield.

Stone, Deborah. 1984. *The Disabled State.* Philadelphia: Temple University Press.

Struyven, Ludo. 2004. *Design Choices in Market Competition for Employment Services for the Long-Term Unemployed.* OECD Social, Employment and Migration Working Papers, Organisation for Economic Co-operation and Development, Paris.

Struyven, Ludo, and Geert Steurs. 2005. "Design and Redesign of a Quasi-Market for the Reintegration of Jobseekers: Empirical Evidence from Australia and the Netherlands." *Journal of European Social Policy* 15 (3): 211–29.

Super, David K. 2005. "Are Rights Efficient? Challenging the Managerial Critique of Individual Rights." *California Law Review* 93 (4): 1051–142.

Talbot, Colin. 2005. "Performance Management." In *The Oxford Handbook of Public Management*, edited by Ewan Ferlie, Laurence E. Lynn Jr., and Christopher Pollitt, 491–517. Oxford: Oxford University Press.

Tawney, Richard Henry. 1912. *The Agrarian Problem in the Sixteenth Century.* New York: Longmans, Green.

Taylor, Sunny. 2004. "The Right Not to Work: Power and Disability." *Monthly Review* 55 (10): 30–44.

Taylor-Gooby, Peter, Johannes Kananen, and Trine Larsen. 2004. "Paradigm Shifts and Labour Market Reform." Paper presented at the Conference on Welfare Reform and Management of Societal Change, Berlin.

Terpstra, Jan, and Tetty Havinga. 2001. "Implementation between Tradition and Management: Structuration and Styles of Implementation." *Law and Policy* 23 (1): 95–117.

Thielemann, Gregory S., and Joseph Stewart Jr. 1996. "A Demand-Side Perspective on the Importance of Representative Bureaucracy: AIDS, Ethnicity, Gender, and Sexual Orientation." *Public Administration Review* 56 (2): 168–73.

Thornton, Stephen and Gregory Marston. 2009. "Who to Serve? The Ethical Dilemma of Employment Consultants in Nonprofit Disability Employment Network Organisations." *Australian Journal of Social Issues* 44 (1): 73–89.

Thuy, Phan, Ellen Hansen, and David Price. 2001. *The Public Employment Service in a Changing Labor Market*. Geneva: International Labour Organization.

Torfing, Jacob. 1999. "Welfare with Workfare: Recent Reforms of the Danish Welfare State." *Journal of European Social Policy* 9 (1): 5–28.

———. 2004. *Det stille sporskifte i velfærdsstaten—en diskursteoretisk beslutnings procesanalyse*. Aarhus: Magtudredningen.

Trappmann, Mark, Bernhard Christoph, Juliane Achatz, and Claudia Wenzig. 2007. *'Labour Market and Social Security': A New Panel Study for Research on German Social Code II*. Nuremberg: Institute für Arbeitsmarkt- und Berufsforschung. http://doku.iab.de/veranstaltungen/2007/cape_2007_trappmann.pdf.

Tregaskis, Claire. 2002. "Social Model Theory: The Story So Far . . ." *Disability and Society* 17 (4): 457–70.

Trim, John, Jürgen Quetz, Raimund Schieß, and Günther Schenider. 2009. *Gemeinsamer Europäischer Referenzrahmen für Sprachen. Lernen, lehren, beurteilen*. [reprint]. Berlin: Langenscheidt.

Trisi, Danilo, and LaDonna Pavetti. 2012. *TANF Weakening as a Safety Net for Poor Families*. Washington, DC: Center on Budget and Policy Priorities.

UK Department for Work and Pensions. 2012. *Early Impacts of Mandatory Work Activity*.

US Bureau of Labor Statistics, US Department of Labor. 2007. *Employment and Earnings*.

———. 2011. *Union Members Survey*.

UWV (Institute for Employee Insurance). 2007. *Kroniek van de sociale verzekeringen 2007. Wetgeving en volume-ontwikkeling in historisch perspectief*. Amsterdam: UWV.

Van Berkel, Rik. 2006. "The Decentralization of Social Assistance in the Netherlands." *International Journal of Sociology and Social Policy* 26 (1/2): 20–32.

———. 2009. "Bureaucracies under Pressure? How Dutch Local Welfare Agencies Cope with Policy and Governance Reforms." In *New Governance and Implementation*, edited by Flemming Larsen and Rik Van Berkel, 115–39.

Van Berkel, Rik, and Vando Borghi. 2007. "Contextualising New Modes of Governance in Activation Policies." *International Journal of Sociology and Social Policy* 27 (9/10): 353–63.

———. 2008. "Introduction: The Governance of Activation." *Social Policy and Society* 7 (3): 331–40.

Van Berkel, Rik, Willibrord de Graaf, and Tomá Sirovátka, eds. 2011. *The Governance of Active Welfare States in Europe*. Basingstoke: Palgrave.

Van Berkel, Rik, and Ben Valkenberg, eds. *Making It Personal: Individualising Activation Services in the EU*. Bristol: Policy Press.

Van Berkel, Rik, and Paul van der Aa. 2005. "The Marketization of Activation Services: A Modern Panacea? Some Lessons from the Dutch Experience." *Journal of European Social Policy* 15 (4): 329–49.

Van Berkel, Rik, Paul van der Aa, and Nicolette Van Gestel. 2010. "Professionals without a Profession? Redesigning Case Management in Dutch Local Welfare Agencies." *European Journal of Social Work* 10 (2): 447–63.

Van Aerschot, Paul. 2011. *Activation Policies and the Protection of Individual Rights: A Critical Assessment of the Situation in Denmark, Finland and Sweden*. Farnham, VT: Ashgate.

Van der Aa, Paul. 2009. "Activation and Discretion at the Front Lines of Active Welfare States." Paper presented at the 7th ESPAnet Conference, September 17–19, Urbino, Italy.

———. 2012. "Activeringswerk in Uitvoering: Bureaucratische en Professionele Dienstverlening in Drie Sociale Diensten." Utrecht University, Ph.D. dissertation.

Van der Veen, Romke, and Willem Trommel. 1999. "Managed Liberalization of the Dutch Welfare State: A Review and Analysis of the Reform of the Dutch Social Security System, 1985–1998." *Governance* 12 (3): 289–310.

Van Gestel, Nicolette, Paul de Beer, and Marc van der Meer. 2009. *Het Hervormingsmoeras van de Verzorgingsstaat: Veranderingen in de Organisatie van de Sociale Zekerheid*. Amsterdam: Amsterdam University Press.

Van Oorschot, Wim. 2010. "Public Perceptions of the Economic, Moral, Social and Migration Consequences of the Welfare State: An Empirical Analysis of Welfare State Legitimacy." *Journal of European Social Policy* 20 (1): 19–31.

Van Slyke, David M. 2003. "The Mythology of Privatization in Contracting for Social Services." *Public Administration Review* 63 (3): 296–315.

Vis, Barbara. 2007. "States of Welfare or States of Workfare? Welfare State Restructuring in 16 Capitalist Democracies, 1985–2002." *Policy and Politics* 35 (1): 105–22.

Wacquant, Loic. 2010. "Crafting the Neoliberal State: Workfare, Prinsonfare, and Social Insecurity." *Sociological Forum* 25 (2): 197–220.

Wade, John, and William Bell. 2003. *Towards Best Practice: Report of the Open Employment Services Research Project, 2001–03*. Simpson Norris.

Watkins-Hayes, Celeste. 2009. *The New Welfare Bureaucrats: Entanglements of Race, Class, and Policy Reform*. Chicago: University of Chicago Press.

Weaver, R. Kent. 2000. *Ending Welfare as We Know It*. Washington, DC: Brookings Institution Press.

Webster, Elizabeth, and Glenys Harding. 2000. "Outsourcing Public Employment Services: The Australian Experience." *Australian Economic Review* 34:231–42.

Weill, Pierre-Eduoard. 2011. "Who Knows How to Assert the Right to Housing? Popular Appropriations of Administrative Justice." Paper presented at the International Conference in Interpretive Policy Analysis, Cardiff, Wales.

White, Lucie E. 1990. "*Goldberg v. Kelly*: On the Paradox of Lawyering for the Poor." *Brooklyn Law Review* 56:861–87.

Wichowsky, Amber, and Donald Moynihan. 2008. "Measuring How Performance Measurement Shapes Citizenship: A Policy Feedback Perspective on Performance Measurement." *Public Administration Review* 68 (5): 908–20.

Wikeley, Nicholas J. 2005. *The Law of Social Security*. 5th ed. Oxford: Oxford University Press.

Wikeley, Nicholas, with Ogus, Anthony I. 2005. *Wikeley, Ogus and Barendt's 'The Law of Social Security,'* 5th ed. Oxford: Oxford University Press.

Wright, Sharon. 2006. "The Administration of Transformation: A Case Study of Implementing Welfare Reform in the UK." In *Administering Welfare Reform: International Transformations in Welfare Governance*, edited by Paul Henman and Menno Fenger, 161–83. Bristol: Policy Press.

———. 2009. "Welfare to Work." In *Understanding Social Security*, 2nd ed., edited by Jane Millar. Bristol: Policy Press.

Wu, Chi-Fang, Maria Cancian, Daniel R. Meyer, and Geoffrey Wallace. 2006. "How Do Welfare Sanctions Work?" *Social Service Review* 30 (1): 33–51.

Yeatman, Anna. 2000. "What Can Disability Tell Us about Participation?" *Law in Context* 17 (2): 181–202.

Zatz, Noah. 2006a. "Welfare to What?" *Hastings Law Journal* 57:1131–88.

———. 2006b. "What Welfare Requires from Work." *UCLA Law Review* 54 (2): 373–464.

Zentrum für Europäische Wirtschaftsforschung Institut Arbeit und Qualifikation, Universität Magdeburg, Stiftung Zentrum für Türkeistudien, Team Dr. Kaltenborn, TNS Emnid, and Dorothee Frings. 2008. *Wirkungen des SGB II auf Personen mit Migrationshintergrund: Jahresbericht 2008; Anhang A des Abschlussberichts 2009*. Berlin: .

ABOUT THE CONTRIBUTORS

MICHAEL ADLER is emeritus professor of sociolegal studies in the School of Social and Political Science at Edinburgh University and a member of the Scottish Committee of the Administrative Justice and Tribunals Council, whose function is to review the administrative justice system and advise the government on how to make it more accessible, fair, and efficient. In recent years, Adler's research has concerned the interface between social policy and public law, in particular, disputes between the citizen and the state and the means by which they can be resolved. His most recent book is *Administrative Justice in Context* (Hart, 2010).

EVELYN Z. BRODKIN is associate professor in the School of Social Service Administration at the University of Chicago. She has published widely on street-level organizations, social policy and politics, and public management, including *The False Promise of Administrative Reform*, and, most recently, "Street-Level Organizations: New Directions for Social Policy and Management Research," a special issue of the *Journal of Public Administration Research and Theory*. Brodkin has been visiting professor in Australia, Denmark, France, and Mexico; Fellow of the Open Society Institute and the Kennedy School of Government; and recipient of the Herbert Kaufman Award from APSA and the Burchfield Award from ASPA. She holds a PhD in political science from the Massachusetts Institute of Technology.

MARTIN BRUSSIG studied sociology in Berlin and New York, and received his PhD from the Friedrich-Schiller-University in Jena. Since 2003, he has worked at the Institute for Work, Skills, and Training (IAQ) within the University of Duisburg-Essen, where he is now leading the Employment—Inclusion—Mobility research unit. His main fields of interest are labor market sociology and human resource strategies of firms. He has published widely about transitions into retirement and labor-market policy reforms in Germany.

RICHARD C. FORDING is professor of political science at the University of Alabama. His primary teaching and research interests include welfare policy, policy adoption and implementation, poverty, and race and politics. He is the author or coauthor of articles appearing in a variety of journals, including *American Political Science Review*, *American Sociological Review*, *American Journal of Political Science*, and *Journal of Politics*. He is the coauthor of *Disciplining the Poor: Neoliberal Paternalism and the Persistent Power of Race* (with Joe Soss and Sanford Schram; University of Chicago Press, 2011).

JULIA HENLY is associate professor in the School of Social Service Administration at the University of Chicago. Her research focuses on the intersection of low-wage employment, caregiving, and welfare and child care policy, with particular attention to the work-family and poverty-management strategies of low-income families. Henly's work has appeared in peer-reviewed journals such as *Journal of Urban Affairs*, *Journal of Marriage and Family*, *Social Service Review*, *Early Childhood Research Quarterly*, and *Children and Youth Services Review*, as well as several edited volumes.

MATTHIAS KNUTH, a sociologist, headed the Labour Market—Integration—Mobility research unit at the Institute for Work, Skills and Training within the University of Duisburg-Essen, where he was appointed associate professor. He continues to work as a member of the department. He is president of the German Association for Social Scientific Labour Market Research. His research fields are mobility in the labor market, labor-market policies, the international comparison of welfare state reforms, employment and retirement under conditions of demographic aging, and the integration of ethnic minorities in the labor market. He was involved in several evaluations of the German labor-market reforms.

SUSAN LAMBERT is associate professor in the School of Social Service Administration at the University of Chicago. She has conducted a series of studies on employer practices in low-level hourly jobs with the goal of identifying avenues for improving workers' economic security, health, and well-being. The sites for Lambert's research span both production and nonproduction industries and both publicly held and family-owned companies. Her research appears in leading journals, including the *Academy of Management Journal*, *Human Relations*, and *Social Service Review*, as well as in edited volumes and policy briefs.

FLEMMING LARSEN is professor in the Department of Political Science and head of the Research Center for Evaluation at Aalborg University in Denmark. Larsen has been studying labor market and social policy issues for many years.

One research topic has been labor-market models, including international comparative research applying the concepts of flexicurity and transitional labor markets. Larsen has also examined labor market and social policy reforms, studying changes (and trends) in policies (e.g., the move toward workfare and work first), as well as the motives and consequences of introducing new governance and operational reforms.

VICKI LENS is currently an associate professor at the Columbia University School of Social Work. Prior to earning her PhD in social welfare, Lens worked as a public interest lawyer, providing legal services to low-income people in the area of public benefits. Her research interests include welfare reform, administrative justice, and sociolegal studies, where she uses ethnographic and other methods to study legal settings. Her work has been published in leading scholarly journals, including *Law and Society Review, Social Service Review, Law and Social Inquiry*, and the *Journal of Public Administration Research and Theory*.

MICHAEL LIPSKY is distinguished senior fellow at Demos. He taught at the University of Wisconsin and for twenty-one years was a professor of political science at the Massachusetts Institute of Technology. Before coming to Demos in 2003, he served for twelve years as a program officer in the Ford Foundation's Peace and Social Justice Program. His publications include *Protest in City Politics* (Rand McNally, 1969); the award-winning *Street-Level Bureaucracy* (Russell Sage Foundation, 1980, 2010); and *Nonprofits for Hire: The Welfare State in the Age of Contracting* (with Steven Rathgeb Smith; Harvard University Press, 1993). He is a graduate of Oberlin College, and holds a PhD in politics from Princeton University.

GREGORY MARSTON is professor of social policy in the School of Public Health and Social Work at Queensland University of Technology and coeditor of this book. He has previously held academic positions at the University of Queensland and RMIT University and visiting appointments at Melbourne University and Lund University. Prior to entering academia Marston worked in community services at the local, state, and national level. His main research interests concern contemporary social theory and the impact of various social and economic policies on ordinary citizens. He is widely published and is at present completing a book on the tensions between occupational, fiscal, and social welfare.

SANFORD SCHRAM teaches social theory and policy at the Bryn Mawr College Graduate School of Social Work and Social Research. He has published twelve books, including *Words of Welfare: The Poverty of Social Science and the Social Science of Poverty* (University of Minnesota Press, 1995) and *Disciplining the*

Poor: Neoliberal Paternalism and the Persistent Power of Race (with Joe Soss and Richard Fording; University of Chicago Press, 2011), both of which won the Michael Harrington Award from the American Political Science Association. Schram is also the 2012 recipient of the Charles McCoy Career Achievement Award from the American Political Science Association.

Joe Soss is Cowles Chair for the Study of Public Service at the University of Minnesota, where he holds positions in the Humphrey School of Public Affairs and the departments of political science and sociology. His research and teaching explore the interplay of democratic politics, socioeconomic inequalities, and public policy. He is particularly interested in the political sources and consequences of policies that govern social marginality and shape life conditions for socially marginal groups. His most recent coauthored book, *Disciplining the Poor: Neoliberal Paternalism and the Persistent Power of Race* (with Richard Fording and Sanford Schram; University of Chicago Press, 2011), received the Michael Harrington Award and the Oliver Cromwell Cox Award.

Rik Van Berkel is associate professor at the Utrecht School of Governance of Utrecht University in the Netherlands. His research interests include welfare state transformations, new models for the provision of social services, and the implementation of social policy and governance reforms by frontline workers. His work focuses particularly on activation and welfare-to-work reforms and their implementation. He has published on these issues in, among others, *Journal of European Social Policy*, *Public Management*, *Journal of Social Policy*, and *Social Policy and Society*.

Celeste Watkins-Hayes is associate professor of sociology and African American studies at Northwestern University. In addition to her faculty appointment, Watkins-Hayes is a faculty fellow at Northwestern's Institute for Policy Research. Her research focuses on urban poverty, social policy, HIV/AIDS, nonprofit and government organizations, and race, class, and gender. Her book, *The New Welfare Bureaucrats: Entanglements of Race, Class, and Policy Reform* (University of Chicago Press, 2009), was a finalist for the 2009 C. Wright Mills Book Award from the Society for the Study of Social Problems and the 2011 Max Weber Book Award from the American Sociological Association.

INDEX

Figures, notes, and tables are indicated by "f," "n," and "t" following page numbers.

315

Jacobs, Lawrence, 46
Jayasuri, Kanishka, 215
job-club participation, 154–56, 162
job realities, 69–84; "bad jobs," 26, 81, 277;
cost-containment policies, 71–74; cost-
containment practices, 74–77, 83n2;
mismatch with workfare programs, 14,
77–80; part-time employment, increase
in, 70; preference for employees with
"open availability," 76, 77; quality of jobs
in race to the bottom, 83; real-time
adjustments to work schedules, 76;
seniority as reason to stay with employer,
79, 82; staffing strategies, 74–75; stickiness of low-wage careers, 79;
supplemental wages proposed for periods
of reduced work hours, 82; turnover rates
in certain industries, 77–78; wages of
welfare leavers, 69; waiting periods to
access employer-sponsored benefits, 79;
work-hour requirements, 70–71, 78, 79,
81; workloading, 75
Johnson, Nancy, 165n7
Jolly, Deb, 219

Katznelson, Ira, 46
Kelman, Steven, 53
Kildal, Nana, 16n5, 280n2
Knuth, Matthias, 15, 31, 32, 185, 275
Korteweg, Anna, 32

labor unions. See organized labor
Lambert, Susan, 14, 26, 69, 73, 75, 77, 278
Lane, Julia, 77
Larsen, Flemming, 14, 25, 57, 103, 273
Lasswell, Harold, 24, 26
Latinos. See race and ethnicity
Legal Services, 43
Lens, Vicki, 15, 30, 244, 248n36, 249, 276
Leschke, Janine, 63
liberal narrative: and American welfare state,
38, 42–43, 53n5; and role of government,
49–51
liberal welfare states, 9, 10, 16n8, 105, 279
Lindqvist, Linus, 16n6

Lipsky, Michael, 14, 18–19, 20, 21, 34n11,
37, 88, 138, 166n20, 169, 240, 248n32,
274, 279
list work, 98–99
Lowi, Theodore J., 21

MacDonald, Helen, 212
Majmundar, Malay, 30, 255
Major, John, 230
male-breadwinner model and migrants in
Germany, 196–97, 198t
managerial regimes. See governance and
management
Manpower Development Research Corpo-
ration, 44
marginalization: and racial differences
between providers and clients, 170; and
workfare in practice, 275
Marston, Gregory, 15, 209, 275
Mashaw, Jerry L., 251
Massachusetts Department of Transitional
Assistance (MDTA), 168, 171–72
Mathematica, 44
Maynard-Moody, Steven, 99
McBeath, Grahame, 223
McDonald, Dwight, 43
McGuire, Linda, 26
mediation role of SLOs: in policy, 17, 18,
21–23, 272; in politics, 17–18, 23–32;
and social identity, 210, 220–23
Medicaid, 45, 73
Medicare, 45, 51–52, 54n19
Meidner, Rudolf, 62, 63
Meier, Kenneth J., 183
mental health issues of clients, 157–58, 159
merits review in British New Deal, 241
migrant populations in Germany, 15, 31,
185–208, 275; and background of job-
center staff, 199; and breadwinner role
model, 196–97, 198t; characteristics of
migrants, 189–91, 190t, 206–7n1; and
credentials and assessment of human
capital, 191–95, 192t, 193f; federal
employment agency website, translation
of, 200; and German-language proficiency and labor-market opportunities,